GUERRILLA
INVESTING

GUERRILLA INVESTING

Winning Strategies for Beating the Wall Street Professionals

Revised and Expanded Edition

PETER SIRIS

LONGSTREET
Atlanta, Georgia

Published by
LONGSTREET
A subsidiary of Cox Newspapers,
A subsidiary of Cox Enterprises, Inc.
2140 Newmarket Parkway
Suite 122
Marietta, GA 30067
www.lspress.com

First edition 1998.
Second edition 2000.

Printed in the United States of America

1st printing, 2000

Library of Congress Catalog Card Number: 99-067254
ISBN: 1-56352-601-8

Jacket and book design by Jill Dible and Megan Wilson

To my mother, Elaine Winik, who taught
me how to think, and my father,
Burt Siris, who taught me how to invest.

ACKNOWLEDGMENTS

I would like to thank my grandfather, Sam Kappel, and my father, Burt Siris, who taught me about the stock market when I was a young boy. I guess the lessons must have amounted to something after all. And I would like to thank my mother who taught me the value of learning, even if I was not the easiest student. You always said if I could not find work, I could write a book. This makes two. Now you need to write one more and we will be even.

First I would like to thank my partner, Leigh Curry, who not only kept me up-to-date on research and trading, but also read the manuscript and provided me with excellent inputs. Some of the better lines in this book belong to Leigh. (Leigh's lines are easy to spot. They are the ones with the Texas drawl.) Carol Hart was a great aid in compiling the research for this book.

I would also like to acknowledge some of the people whom I have worked with on Wall Street. David Keidan and David Goldsmith of The Buckingham Research Group run one of the finest boutique brokerage firms on Wall Street. While quality work may not be the hallmark at many firms, it is at Buckingham. Mark Suvall, Andy Rodman, and Charlie

Frumberg of UBS Securities took an almost dormant brokerage firm and built it into a power, and they did it without compromising either quality or morality. Dick Keim, David Wilson, and the others at Keim-Wilson have provided strong support.

I would like to thank Linda Wachner, the chairman of both Warnaco and Authentic Fitness, for giving me the opportunity to work for her. In my years on Wall Street, I have known many of the most successful executives in American industry. Linda is, quite simply, the smartest. She also has a dedication to her work and a will to win that few have ever matched.

I would like to thank all of the partners in our Guerrilla funds as well as all of the people at ING Barings Furman Selz Prime Brokerage.

I would like to thank my agent, Carol Mann, and all of the people at Longstreet Press, especially my editors Suzanne de Galan and Sherry Wade. They worked tirelessly on my manuscript and greatly enhanced the quality of this book. Their perspective has been invaluable.

Finally, I would like to thank my loving wife, Barbara Wyckoff, and my children, Alex and Tracy, for putting up with me while I wrote this book, especially during crunch time. Having a husband or a father who is sitting up in a study typing away until the middle of the night is probably not their idea of fun. But I greatly appreciate their love and support.

Despite the advice from a wide range of friends and associates, all of the opinions in this book are mine. In writing the book, I have referred to specific companies, executives, brokerage firms, and analysts. All of the references are for illustrative purposes only. There is no intent to recommend or criticize any particular stocks, brokerage firms, or analysts. Nor should any comment, taken out of context, be used as a judgment of the overall quality of a particular individual or firm. Every analyst and brokerage firm makes mistakes. I know I certainly have. My intention is not to take a cheap shot at anyone, but rather to explain how the investing game is played. My hope is that this book will help individual investors understand more about how to win.

Peter Siris
New York, New York

TABLE OF CONTENTS

—

Introduction   xiii

PART 1   The Battle Plan   1

   CHAPTER 1: *Understand the Field of Battle*   3

   CHAPTER 2: *Know Your Enemy, Know Yourself*   25

   CHAPTER 3: *Avoid the Enemy's Strengths*   37

   CHAPTER 4: *Fight on Your Home Turf*   75

   CHAPTER 5: *Attack the Enemy's Weaknesses*   97

PART 2   The Weapons of Warfare   131

   CHAPTER 6: *Fundamental Weapons*   133

   CHAPTER 7: *Technical Weapons*   177

   CHAPTER 8: *Connect the Dots*   207

   CHAPTER 9: *The Resources of the Web*   231

   CHAPTER 10: *Chat Rooms and
                  Message Boards*   253

PART 3   Hostile Territory   285

   CHAPTER 11: *Beware False Intelligence:
                  The Analysts*   287

   CHAPTER 12: *Pitfalls (and Opportunities)*   313

   CHAPTER 13: *Trading with the Enemy:
                  Buying and Selling*   343

GUERRILLA
INVESTING

Introduction

When I was a boy, I would go to my grandparents' house. While we watched the Brooklyn Dodgers on television, my father would read the market quotes to my grandfather and they would talk about the stocks. I can still remember most of the stocks that my grandfather owned, even though many have long ceased to exist. It was the early 1950s, and most Americans were learning how to invest. Later, I took the money that I had earned delivering newspapers and bought my first stock: American Motors. (I liked the little Nash Rambler, whose horn went "beep, beep, beep.") My first investment worked out well. From then on, I have been fascinated by the market.

For many years, few shared my interest. After all, the market was lower in 1982 than it had been in 1969. Smart investors were putting their money in real estate, commodities, gold, impressionist paintings, and even baseball cards. Five cards had come with a piece of bubble gum for a nickel, but they were now worth hundreds of dollars. Why should anyone gamble in the stock market when they could invest in baseball cards? (Of course, my mother had thrown out my collection when I was away at camp. She thought they were junk. She did not realize that I was count-ing on them for my retirement. Nor could she have imagined that one day I could have taken my cards to Ebay and sold them to other collectors for millions of dollars. You can bet I will be smart enough to save all of my children's Pokemon cards.) Besides with bonds and money funds paying more than 10 percent, who needed a dead stock market?

Even after the stock market began to advance, few were interested. The increase seemed a temporary aberration. When the crash came in 1987 and the stock market dropped 500 points in one day, it confirmed what everyone already knew, investing in stocks was for fools. My friends called to console me. Some offered to lend me baseball cards, and one even offered me a job as a waiter. *"If unemployed actors can do it,"* he encour-aged me, *"so can unemployed investment managers."* (I was hoping for a job as a taxicab driver, but in New York my ability to speak English worked against me.)

Fortunately, for me, the market did shrug off the crash and begin to rally. Soon, people started to take an interest in Wall Street. Their interest may have been stimulated by the fact that real estate had collapsed or by the fact that everybody knew someone who was making serious money in the market.

As the advance continued, stocks supplanted real estate as the investment of choice and the subject of the cocktail-party conversations. People stopped asking questions and started giving advice. Everyone has hot stocks. My friends in real estate have hot stocks. So does my doctor, my lawyer, my cable TV man, my plumber, and my auto mechanic. The cable man loves media stocks, and the plumber loves biotechs. But my garage mechanic is constantly bemoaning the fact that he missed the move in auto stocks. *"I drive these American cars every day. I could see that they were getting better,"* he tells me when I come in for a repair. *"So how was I so stupid to miss it?"* Now everyone wants into the stock market. People even day trade while at work. (It only takes a few hours a day.)

DOWNSIZED TO RICHES

The reason for the resurgence of stocks is very simple. As the baby boomers approached middle age, they hit a crisis. The 20 percent salary increases and constant promotions stopped as millions clogged the few openings at the top of the pyramid. Companies started to downsize. Now it was the turn of white-collar workers to lose their jobs. The baby boomers suddenly found that they were approaching retirement with little saved for it. The clock was ticking. They had to accumulate money, and they had to do it quickly.

Ironically, the baby boomers' problems also became their solution. Corporate downsizing, a flattening of real estate, and somewhat lower spending (because the boomers had already bought everything they would ever need) led to a sharp decline in inflation. Bonds, which had once yielded over 10 percent, were now yielding 6 percent. Money market funds were now yielding 4 percent. Real estate was dead. Gold was selling for less than half of its all-time high. Even baseball cards stopped appreciating. There was no choice but to invest in stocks.

Money flowed from bonds, money funds, real estate, collectibles, and even from spending into stocks. The flow of funds pushed up prices of stocks, while the very downsizing that had jeopardized the boomers' future made companies more efficient and led to higher earnings. With lower interest rates, investors were willing to pay more for the same stream of earnings. So the combination of better earnings and higher p/e ratios propelled the stock market upward. The huge run in the market has given many of the baby boomers financial security, and it has made the game look easy.

THEN REALITY HITS

But nothing goes up forever. Just as real estate boomed in the earlier decades only to flatten in the 1980s, just as gold went from $32 to $800 an ounce only to drop to under $300, just as collectibles have had boom and bust cycles—so the market will do the same. There is no way to know when the market will flatten out and when it will decline. But this much is certain: No class of assets, not stocks, not real estate, not paintings, not even baseball cards can grow at a compounded rate of 16 percent per year forever.

When the stock market stops going up, many new investors will face a flat or even a down market for the first time. Most were not investing in 1987. To them, October 19 was just a date. They did not have to sit and watch as their net worth was slashed before their eyes. Fewer still can remember the slow death of the stock market in the 1970s, when, for 13 years, the market went sideways and valuations dropped. A flat or a down market will be a new experience for most investors and it will most likely separate the strong from the weak.

WHY YOU NEED THIS BOOK

It would be nice if individuals could choose to only invest in bull markets, but such an alternative is not possible. The only effective way to stay ahead of the game is try to outperform the averages in all markets. If an investor can make more money than the average in an up market, make some money in a flat market, and lose less money than the average in a down market, that investor will end up being very rich.

To outperform the market, you must beat the competition. If you cannot beat the average investor, you cannot win. But the average investor is not a widow in an old-age home or an orphan seeking to protect an inheritance. Instead, the average investor is usually a well-trained professional, who wants to win as much or more than you do and will use every tool at his disposal to defeat you.

The individual, however, has some weapons. The Internet is dramatically leveling the playing field by putting information at the fingertips of everyone. Now, with a click, people can monitor their portfolios, receive quotes, utilize charts, follow the earnings estimates and recommendations of leading analysts, stay abreast of the news, study financial reports from the companies themselves, and trade at costs equal to or below those available to professionals. The challenge for the individual investor is to learn how to use this new powerful resource.

To win, individual investors must find ways of getting the upper hand. For those with limited time, this may mean nothing more than buying good stocks and holding them, and thus avoiding the trading games of the professionals. But for those with more time and resources, guerrilla investing will present a number of more action-oriented strategies.

This book is written for the serious amateur investor who wants to compete against the professional in good markets and bad. This book will not provide you with ten secrets to success that guarantee a profit. Profit is never guaranteed and if there were such secrets, someone would have discovered them long ago. The market is too dynamic. In fact, change is the only certainty in the stock market. Those investors who can anticipate the changes will win, while those who cannot will lose.

This book will provide the investor with the tools to understand the dynamics of the market and anticipate the changes in it. It will also give the investor the weapons to compete with the professionals and outperform the market. **Guerrilla investing is a strategy that will allow the amateur, against all odds, to win.**

PART 1

The Battle Plan

CHAPTER ONE

Understand the Field of Battle

- Have you noticed how the professionals always seem to have news ahead of time?
- Have you watched as the professionals took every share of a hot new issue?
- Have you ever received a report from your broker and noticed that the stock had already gone up by 25 percent?

As an individual investor, you are playing a game that is rigged against you. Professionals get better information from salesmen, analysts, traders, and from the companies themselves. They have more capital and better systems. They can act quickly, completing their trades before the individual even knows what is happening. Competing against them is very difficult.

Individual investors often lose because they try to take on the professionals on their own turf. Individuals cannot trade with the professionals. They do not have the resources or the information flow. But there is a way for them to win. Think of investing as a war and the professionals as a well-trained army. The individual cannot attack them head-on. The individual does not have the weapons. But **the individual can fight them in much the same way as a guerrilla force fights a modern army:** attacking their weaknesses, avoiding their strengths, fighting on local terrain, and finding niches that they miss. We call this **Guerrilla Investing**. If individuals can think of themselves as guerrillas and plot a strategy of competing against investment professionals the way that a guerrilla force would against a well-entrenched army, they have a strong chance of winning.

INVESTING IS LIKE WAR

Investing is like war. You are trying to defeat your enemy and outperform the market, while your enemy is trying to defeat you. Each investment is like a battle, and the sum of the battles makes up the war. If you do not win most of your battles, you will never win the war. In *The Art of War*, the Chinese philosopher Sun Tzu stated his most important rule, "Know yourself, know your enemy. In one hundred battles, there will be one hundred victories." If this is the first rule of warfare, it is also the first rule of investing. **In order to win in the stock market, investors must know their strengths and weaknesses and those of their enemies.**

In investing, the enemy is anyone on the opposite side of a trade. You do not have a picture of your enemy on your wall with a bullet through his heart. In fact, it may be difficult to think of a mild-mannered portfolio manager from a bank or a charismatic CEO of a corporation as the enemy, but the fact remains that if they are selling while you are buying, they are your enemy, and only one of you will win.

When looking at a stock, an investor must ask:

> *"What does my enemy know that I do not?"*
> *"Why is my enemy selling when I am buying?"*
> *"How can I get an edge that will enable me to defeat my enemy?"*

To most people, investing does not seem like war. If you buy a stock and it goes up, you were right. If you buy a stock and it goes down, you were wrong. Most people are thrilled when the market goes up and frustrated when it goes down. Right now, most people are thrilled. But giant bull markets, like the current one, occur only once in a generation. The previous comparable market occurred in the late 1960s. Once it ended, investors had to wait thirteen years before stocks recovered. Because there is no way to predict the market, investors should train themselves to defeat their enemies and beat the averages in all markets. To achieve these ends, each investment should be looked at as a military deployment. If investors can figure out how to win most battles, they will ultimately win the war.

IN EVERY TRADE, 50 PERCENT OF INVESTORS ARE WRONG

Every time a trade is made, the buyer is saying, *"Of all the things that I could do with my money, owning this stock is the best,"* while the seller is saying, *"Of all the things that I could do with my money, owning this stock is the worst."* If the stock goes up, the buyer will have been right. If the stock goes down, the seller will have been right. It is impossible for both of them to be right at the same time.

People will say that there is more to it than this. What about those hot Internet IPOs, in which the stock is priced at $20 and the first trade is at $80? There everyone wins. At first it might look that way, but this much is certain: If the management really believed that its stock was worth $80, it would not sell for $20. Before you get set to buy at $80, just remember that management sold at $20 only a few moments before.

Every investor must understand this rule of combat: **Investing is not a win-win game. It is a win-lose game**. Everyone who plays the game is in the stock market to win. They are not in the market to make the world a better place or to help your net worth. They are in the market to make as much money as they can for themselves. If you buy a stock that a professional or a company insider is selling, only one of you will end up being right. In such a contest, the professionals and the insiders have substantial advantages. As a guerrilla investor, you must be extremely careful to not get suckered into fighting stronger enemies on their own turf.

"SMART MONEY" LOSES, TOO

Many people believe that there is "smart money" in the market and that smart money usually wins. The institutions are obviously the "smart money." Their portfolio managers and analysts are paid hundreds of thousands or millions of dollars, so they must be smart. Fidelity is obviously the smartest of the smart, because it is the biggest. When Fidelity buys or sells, the market often takes notice. I have often heard salesmen whisper, *"Fidelity is buying,"* in a voice that reverently conveyed the idea that anything Fidelity was buying must be a great stock. But if Fidelity is always right, then the person or institution on the other side of the trade must, by definition, always be wrong.

Think for a moment about the other side of the transaction. If Fidelity is buying 2,000,000 shares of a stock, who is selling? Do you think that there are 20,000 orphans, each selling 100 shares they were given at birth? How about 200 widows, each selling 10,000 shares their husbands left them? Of course not. When Fidelity buys 2,000,000 shares of a stock, the seller is probably another financial institution.

Fidelity spends millions on research, has skilled portfolio managers and traders, and receives superb inputs from the Street. But so does the financial institution on the other side of the transaction. Yet one of the institutions and its experts will be making a wrong decision.

Many will dispute this characterization. They will claim that people have different investment styles and that these styles create the trades that are mutually beneficial. A *value investor* would buy a stock that had collapsed and was selling at a discount to its enterprise value. As the stock appreciated, the value investor would sell it to a *growth investor*, who would own it from a level slightly under "fair" market value to a level somewhat above "fair" market value. The growth investor would sell it to a *momentum investor*, who buys stocks that have high earnings growth and relative strength. In these cases, one could claim that all sides were winners because each owned the stock during a period in which it conformed to their investment style.

There are obviously instances in which a stock goes up so much that everyone can feel like a winner. In January 1995, Annie Erner and I recommended CompUSA at $7. (The stock had previously declined from about $21, so the people who sold at $7 were not happy.) But at $7, CompUSA was perfect for value players, betting on a turnaround. New management had come in. The controls were improving, and insiders were buying. When the stock reached $14, value investors started to sell. Growth investors started to invest, as it became clear that the business was getting better. Management continued buying the stock. Earnings surprised on the upside. The stock reached $28. Momentum players piled in. By May 1996, CompUSA reached $45.

When a stock goes from $7 to $45 in sixteen months, it is difficult for people to think of themselves as losers, except, of course, for those who had sold it at $7. Each of the groups could be satisfied with the fact that they doubled their money in six months. The problem is that each could also second-guess themselves. The value investors who sold at $14 must have watched as the stock raced to $45 and had second thoughts about their decision to sell. The growth investors could have second-guessed themselves on both sides of the transaction. They could have bought at $10 instead of at $14, and sold at $40 instead of at $28. In doing so, they could have quadrupled, rather than doubled, their money. The momentum investors could also have moved in sooner, rather than waiting until the stock had more than tripled.

Of course, since May 1996, the price of CompUSA's stock has been crushed, dropping all the way back to $7, a complete round-trip. I don't know where the momentum investors got out, or where the "value" investors got back in, but I do know that in total, people lost as much money on the downside as they made on the upside.

Think about what happens in a less volatile case. A stock is selling for $20. Earnings are going to be reported. Someone buys it, expecting good earnings. Someone else sells it, expecting bad earnings. If earnings are above plan and the stock goes up, the buyer was right. If earnings are below plan and the stock goes down, the seller was right. If the stock is unchanged, both were wrong, because both had to pay transaction costs. The reality is simple. **This is a war. Each trade is a battle. And in each trade, only one of the sides will be right.**

STOCK PRICES: A STAND-OFF BETWEEN COMPETING FORCES

No general would ever commit troops to an attack without first surveying the battlefield and understanding the forces as they are currently arrayed. The same is true in the stock market. To defeat your enemies, you must understand the current position of the market, because it is this point around which change will occur.

Prices reflect the collective wisdom of all participants at a particular point in time. This is a simple truism, but one that is critical to investing. There is no absolute right price for a stock or for the market. The prices, at any point in time, reflect the stand-off between competing forces. Brokers are constantly calling with great pieces of advice concerning the market and individual stocks. How many times have you heard someone say,

> *"This stock is much too cheap. Buy it now!"* Or
> *"This stock is much too expensive. There is no way that it can keep going up."*

It is extremely tempting to believe that the broker actually knows something. Brokers all have opinions, but opinions are all that they have. No matter what they personally think, the reality is that at any instant, a stock is neither cheap nor expensive. It is only cheap or expensive in your broker's mind. But if your broker thinks a particular stock is "undervalued," and the stock is trading, then someone else must think that it is "overvalued." Otherwise there would never be a seller to match up with the buyer. Only when there is a balance of buyers and sellers can the stock actually trade, and when it does trade, it will trade at the price that reflects the collective wisdom of all participants at that point in time.

Each trade reflects the sum of all the opinions on a particular stock or market. There is no such thing as underpriced or overpriced. There is only one person's view relative to the rest of the world. If the Dow Jones is at 10,000, this is the level that all investors have determined is appropriate at that point in time. Some investors may believe that the Dow is overvalued. They will be sellers. But if the Dow is at 10,000, then other investors must believe that it is undervalued, and they will be buyers. Investors trade one billion shares every day. The sum of their collective wisdom is the price of the market.

The same is true of individual stocks. It is tempting to look at a stock and say that it is greatly overvalued. Well, it may be greatly overvalued in your view, but it must be undervalued in someone else's mind, or the stock would not trade. Investors have been hotly contesting the valuation of Internet stocks. eBay, AOL, Yahoo, Amazon.com, and others have been characterized as being extremely overvalued. But for every investor that has been selling one of these stocks, there is another who has been buying. For everyone who believes that the Internet is a fad, there is someone else who believes that it is the wave of the future. While half of these investors will be right, the other half will be wrong.

So it is not reasonable to say that the market or a stock is too cheap or too expensive. It is only reasonable to say that some individual has these opinions. At any point in time, the market reflects the best of everyone's expectations.

INVESTOR EXPECTATIONS CHANGE THE BATTLEFIELD BALANCE

Since the market at any point in time is selling at a level that reflects the collective expectations of all investors, **prices can only change when investors change their actions.** If a stock is trading at $30, it does so because there is a balance of buyers and sellers at that price. The price will change only when the balance is changed. If more people take action on the buy side, the price will go up. If more people take action on the sell side, the price will go down.

Changes in expectations cause people to change their behavior. The price of the stock itself can cause changes in expectations. As a stock moves up, people often believe their risk/reward ratio has changed. An investor bought IBM at $90. As IBM reached $105, that investor decided that there was now more risk and less reward and that it was time to sell. Another investor, however, may decide that if IBM reached $105, it would have broken through a "resistance" level, and it would move higher. As the stock reached $105, that investor would buy.

COMPANY ANNOUNCEMENTS CHANGE EXPECTATIONS

Changes in expectations can come from actual events, such as an earnings announcement. In July 1999, New Era Networks (NEON), which had closed at $44, announced that sales were weaker than expected. Investors were so distressed with the news that the next morning the market could only find a balance at $20 (down $24).

The announcement of a merger also involves changes in expectations. When Staples and Office Depot announced that they were going to merge, the stock of Office Depot jumped from $14 to $20, while the stock of Staples declined from $23 to $19. The reason for the change in expectations related to the terms of the merger in which the holders of Office Depot were to receive more than one share of Staples for each share of Office Depot. Since the stock price of Office Depot had been much lower than the price of Staples prior to the announcement, it went up. The stock of Staples went down because investors believed that the merger would lower its earnings. After the government rejected the merger as being anticompetitive, the stocks moved back in the opposite direction.

Changes in expectations can come from comments by analysts. As analysts follow companies, they often sense that business is better or worse than plan. Sometimes the impetus comes from their own research, while sometimes it comes from guidance from the company itself. As analysts change their earnings estimates, some investors will modify their own expectations.

ECONOMIC DATA CHANGES EXPECTATIONS

A piece of economic data can cause expectations to change. When Alan Greenspan goes to Capitol Hill, investors sit glued to their TV sets, trying to determine if the size of his briefcase will give any indication of future action by the Federal Reserve Board. On June 30, 1999, the Fed announced it was raising interest rates but also adopting a future bias towards easing. The market surged upwards. Investors had expected an increase in rates, so the increase itself did not change expectations, but they had not expected the Fed to announce that its future bias was towards easing. It was this piece of information that changed expectations and sent the market rallying.

PUBLICITY CHANGES EXPECTATIONS

Sometimes changes in expectations occur because a brokerage firm or a commentator publicizes a particular company. Other times a company may appear on television or at a conference sponsored by a brokerage house. Sometimes the company conveys a piece of hard information, but in many instances, the changes in expectations relate to the quality of the presentation. For example, if management tries to avoid answering questions, or if the key people come off looking like jerks, investors will lower their expectations, while if the management tells its story in a convincing way, investors may raise their expectations. The reason that the stock will go up or down is that investors are reevaluating their judgment of management's ability to run the company.

IT'S THE EXPECTATIONS THAT COUNT

It is critical to recognize that it is not whether the news is good or bad but whether the news is good or bad relative to expectations that impacts the prices of stocks. Virtually every investor has seen instances in which a company reported excellent earnings and the stock went down, or in which a company reported a major write-off and the stock went up. These actions seem contrary to logic. But they are not. Good earnings are never enough to push up the price of the stock. The earnings must be good relative to the expectations. Similarly, weak earnings are not enough to lower the price of the stock. They must be weak relative to expectations. If the earnings were not as weak as people expected, the stock might even go up.

In May 1997, Mecklermedia, a pioneering Internet company, announced a much better than expected quarter. But on the conference call, management cautioned that the next quarter would have a loss because of a change in timing of one of its trade shows. From management's point of view, this was a non-issue. It did not really matter whether the show was in June or in July. But investors panicked. The stock plunged by $7 within the next hour as expectations turned negative. (Mecklermedia was subsequently bought out by Penton Media, and a stub of the old company has reemerged as the highly successful Internet.com.)

When investors expect bad news, the stock sometimes goes up once the negative expectations are removed. In the early 1990s, Fruit of the Loom went on an acquisition spree, but the acquisitions were a disaster. Fruit's earnings plunged and its debt ballooned. At the end of 1995, Fruit announced that it was writing off most of the acquisitions. The stock immediately jumped. Within the next year, it almost doubled. While the write-off may have highlighted the mistakes of management, the elimination of its money-losing acquisitions allowed analysts to raise their estimates. Of course, in subsequent years, Fruit's stock plunged as investors realized write-offs or no write-offs, the management did not know how to run the business.

Many investors play stocks for "earnings surprises," buying stocks they believe will report better than expected earnings. The problem now is the definition of what constitutes a surprise. Analysts have published estimates, but in many cases, they also have "whisper" numbers. These are the expectations that are "whispered" by analysts to their best customers. *"Our official number,"* an analyst might say, *"is $0.12 but we think the company can make $0.15."* If the company reports $0.13, the stock might go down because the stock was selling based on the "whisper" number, not the published number.

At any point in time, **if more people increase their expectations, a stock or the market will go up, while if more people lower their expectations, the stock or the market will go down.** The critical variable is not whether the company reports good news or bad news, it is whether the expectations change for the positive or the negative. The problem for the investor is to figure out whether the new information raises or lowers expectations.

THE EXPERTS AS A GROUP ARE ALWAYS WRONG!

Because expectations rule the market, a funny thing happens when there is relative consensus on any issue. All the experts will be wrong. **If all the experts expect the market to go up, it will go down. If all the experts expect the market to go down, it will go up.** There is not much that is guaranteed in life. But this is.

If all the experts think that the stock market can only go up, they will all be fully invested. If every expert is fully invested, there will be no more cash to buy stocks. Without buying, the market can no longer go up. Furthermore, if everyone is already bullish, expectations can no longer change for the positive. If only a few lower their outlook, expectations will change for the negative. A negative change will create selling, which will push down the price of stocks. Thus, even if most investors are still bullish, the stock market will go down, because on balance, expectations are changing for the negative.

This pattern works equally well if all the experts are bearish. In such a situation, they will all be sitting with large amounts of cash, expecting the worst. If the news is not quite as bad as some had expected, expectations will change modestly for the positive. With large amounts of cash on hand and little appetite for more selling, stocks will begin to go up.

What works for the market also works for individual stocks. You might expect that a stock that was loved by all analysts would significantly outperform the market, while one that was hated by all analysts would significantly underperform the market. You might be wrong. If a stock is loved by everyone, valuation and the expectations will be very high, and even a small disappointment can send it plunging. If a stock is hated by everyone, the valuation and the expectations are likely to be very low, and even neutral news can push the stock up.

While consensus is often difficult to find, when it does occur, the experts will almost always be wrong and the individual can win by betting against them. In guerrilla investing, one of the best techniques is to bet against the consensus of professionals. If you know that the consensus will always be wrong, you can use the strength of the consensus to your advantage. Wait until the consensus has taken a position and then act against it. Any investor who can understand this rule has an excellent chance at outperforming the market. In chapter 5, we will show you how to win by betting against the pros.

INFORMATION IS THE CURRENCY OF WALL STREET

If changes in expectations drive changes in prices, the easiest way to defeat your enemy is to have perfect intelligence and be able to act on that intelligence before your enemy does.

- If you knew the FDA was going to approve a new wonder drug, you would buy stock in its manufacturer.
- If you knew a company was going to report disappointing earnings, you would short it.
- If you knew what stocks were going to be featured in Saturday's *Barron's*, you would buy them on Friday.

If you had perfect information about future events, you would be in a commanding position because you could act before your enemies knew what was happening. The key to investing on Wall Street is to acquire as much "inside information" as possible. If you *secretly knew* that one company was planning to make a tender offer on another, you would have a big advantage against your enemies. There is only one problem: trading on this type of inside information is highly illegal.

There is fine line between what is illegal and what is legal. The difference involves certainty. If you know that some event will definitely occur, you have inside information, but if you merely guess that the event is likely to occur, you are not in possession of inside information. A large part of the activity on Wall Street is devoted to getting as much "legal" inside information as possible.

Analysts curry favor with executives of companies so that they will get signals about earnings. *"I know I can't ask what you are going to earn,"* the analyst says, *"but I'm checking to see if my estimate of $0.26 is O.K.?"*

While companies cannot tell analysts what they are going to report, most will give some guidance.

"You won't be disappointed," the chief financial officer might respond. If the analyst trusts the CFO, the analyst will now believe that the earnings will be good and reiterate a buy on the stock. Often analysts may call other executives in the company to double-check the hints from the CFO. The analyst will pit the information from one executive against that from another, looking for an edge. Analysts will gossip and trade information, with only one goal in mind, to get guidance on the earnings that can enable them to scoop other investors.

Professional investors spend their lives trying to obtain more legal inside information than their enemy. They read financial reports. Listen to companies and competitors. Talk to analysts. Read charts. Analyze money flows. Sometimes they even resort to taking hot tips from someone they believe is well informed. With the huge sums at stake, the ability to gain small advantages in information can be substantial. Just as armies will use spies and satellites to gain an advantage over their enemies, so investors will attempt to use any type of intelligence to gain an advantage over their competitors. Information is the currency of Wall Street. **The people with the best information usually win.**

One new and intriguing area available to the individual is the online chat rooms and message boards. Much of the information in the chat rooms is junk. But increasingly, employees of corporations have taken to the chat rooms to vent their opinions, often revealing "inside" information. A corporate counsel recently lamented to me, "Every deal we have done has been talked about in our chat room before it was announced." The only problem for the individual is how to separate the wheat from the chaff. (More on chat rooms in chapter 10.)

THE PROFESSIONAL ADVANTAGE

Advantage 1: Time. If information is the currency of Wall Street, the professionals have always had a huge advantage over the amateurs. The professional devotes full time to investing. While the amateur is running his business, taking care of patients, or handling clients, the professional is usually watching a computer screen when news breaks, and is able to act before the amateur even knows that something has happened.

Information very often has a very limited shelf life. The investor has to find out the information and act on it in a very short period of time. The other day, I saw a headline that the CEO of Stride Rite had resigned. I remembered that another key executive had resigned two weeks earlier. Without hesitation, I sold the stock I owned. Twenty minutes later, when the full details crossed the tape, the stock had already declined by 15 percent.

Advantage 2: Financial resources. The professional also has financial resources that the individual cannot match. With commission dollars, the professional pays to meet with managements and analysts, purchase technical packages, and develop computer systems.

Advantage 3: "Trickle-down" information flow. With the trickle-down flow of information, the professionals usually have a head start over individuals. Financial information typically flows from companies, through professionals, to individuals in a manner that looks like an inverted funnel. When a company announces earnings, it often issues a terse press release and then gives the details to a small number of analysts and portfolio managers. The analysts tell their institutional salespeople and key clients. The institutional salespeople then call other clients. The analysts write First Call notes, which are disseminated to other institutions and to the brokers in the analysts' firm. When the brokers receive the notes, some might call a few clients, but most are too busy. After the calls and the notes are finished, the analysts will write a report, which will be mailed to more clients. If individual customers are lucky, they might receive a monthly update from their brokerage firm with a list of reports written by each analyst. If individuals see a report of interest, they can call their broker and ask to have it sent to them. By the time they receive the report, the information could be two months old, an eternity in the stock market.

Advantage 4: New technology. Over the past decade, new technologies have been created to speed the delivery of information to the professionals.

With First Call, the professional instantly receives earnings estimates, commentary, and rating changes from analysts. With conference calls, professionals can talk directly to the companies when key news is released. Bloomberg, Bridge, and other systems all provide professionals with elaborate packages of technical tools. Other proprietary systems are able to identify gaps in market valuations and generate computer-driven trading programs.

As professionals have gained more access to information, the pace of trading has changed. Turnover has increased. Professionals can respond instantly whenever they see an opportunity. For many, the long term has ceased to exist. The game is to beat your opponents by acting first. Traditionally, the individuals did not have access to these tools. They were locked into using the telephone and waiting for the newspaper, and the gap between the individuals and the professionals widened significantly.

THE NEW WALL STREET BATTLEFIELD

But now the technology changes that gave the professional a huge advantage are swinging in favor of the individual. New delivery systems are rapidly leveling the playing field. With the Internet and the financial television networks, individuals now have access to information that, while not quite on a par, is not far behind that available to the professional. Even the process of communicating information has changed. Instead of trickling down over an extended period of time, it is now instantly transmitted.

EVEN THE PROS WATCH TV

The first major change came with the creation of the financial television networks, such as CNBC, CNNfn, and Bloomberg. These networks give individuals access to a ticker tape, analysis of markets and stocks, commentary from top analysts and portfolio managers, interviews with corporate executives, and full coverage of major news stories. Key events, such as the release of government statistics, actions by the Fed, mergers and acquisitions, surprise earnings announcements, or major price swings in stocks are communicated on these networks. Reporters and industry experts are on hand to discuss the immediate impact of these events. As a result, the networks can communicate the information faster and more effectively than can most brokerage houses. In fact, traders and salespeople at most brokerage houses get fast-breaking news from television rather than from their own analysts. If you go into the trading rooms of Wall Street at 8:30 A.M., the time many government statistics are released, you will see traders and salespeople watching CNBC.

As these networks have grown, they have become the medium of choice for many companies to communicate important events, not only because they can reach a universal audience, but also because they can help companies avoid the legal risk of selective dissemination. When two companies announce a merger, both CEOs usually appear on the networks. For professionals as well as amateurs, it is much better to look the managers in the (televised) eye, see how they relate to each other, and watch how they answer questions than it is to read a selection of First Call notes. As a result, when major events occur, the professionals often sit glued to their sets watching the financial networks.

But when the professionals watch television, they have no special advantage over the amateurs. They do not have their own private network feed. The information is not coming through a narrow channel of communication. Instead it is being disseminated universally, and the professional does not learn about it any quicker than does the amateur.

Further, since professionals have much larger sums to deploy and since they also often have to deal with investment committees within their own organizations, individuals may now actually have an advantage in terms of timing. If individuals watch an interview with a manager who appears to be credible, they can move as fast or faster than the professionals.

While the development of the business news networks has partially leveled the playing field, they can only take the individual part of the way. The financial networks can discuss major stories, but they cannot focus on all stories. They can show quotes on the most volatile stocks, but they cannot show quotes on all stocks. They can offer interviews with managements, but they cannot offer interviews with all companies on demand. They can present the views of analysts and portfolio managers, but they cannot allow the individual to choose which analyst and portfolio manager.

THE INFORMATION REVOLUTION: THE INTERNET

The true challenge to the private information networks of the professional is the Internet. With the Internet, the individual now has access to services that had previously been available only to the professional. **The change in the information flow is nothing less than a revolution.** The old model of giving information to analysts and then allowing it to trickle down is being supplanted by universal dissemination. In political terms, it is a change from an oligopoly to a democracy. The individual still has to learn what to do with the information and still has to overcome the experience of the professionals, but the process of information gathering, and the balance of power, is rapidly shifting in favor of the individual. With the Internet, individuals can:

- Receive real time quotes at the same time and in the same detail as professionals;
- Utilize sophisticated portfolio management software, which allows them to monitor stocks, track their performance, and link to rapidly breaking news;
- Access the same news stories as the professionals;
- Receive notice of and participate in conference calls along with the professionals;
- Receive SEC filings, such as 10Ks and 10Qs, at the same time as the professionals;
- Gather information through the companies' own Web sites;
- Obtain online charts and other technical tools that are comparable to those that the professionals use;
- Access earnings estimates and ratings changes from the major brokerage houses within a short period of time after the changes are made;
- Obtain financial analysis and commentary from a wide

variety of sources in real time;
- Control their own trades, and often receive better execution than the professionals receive;
- Have a lower trading cost than the professionals (Professionals pay an average of $0.05 per share, while individuals can pay less than $0.01 per share.);
- Listen and watch online company conferences and roadshows.

Professionals still receive some information faster than do individuals. Changes in analysts' estimates or ratings reach professionals an hour or two before they reach the Internet. This gives the professional a substantial head start, but this is a much narrower window than the professionals have traditionally enjoyed. Professionals have hardwired systems that work very efficiently, but with faster modems, the difference is becoming less significant.

This is not to say that the advantages of the professionals have been eliminated. The professionals still have experience and knowledge. They have the time to study the market and direct access to corporate executives, analysts, technicians, strategists, and company meetings. But some advantages in terms of information gathering that had rigged the game in their favor are starting to disappear, and the tides of technological change are turning strongly in the direction of the individual investor.

A DAY ON THE WEB

I have always had an office with all of the most up-to-date professional equipment and services. I am especially partial to First Call and Bloomberg. These and other services cost thousands of dollars each month. As I became more involved in writing this book and as I traveled to see companies, I was often unable to go into the office or access the professional equipment, and instead, was forced to rely on the Internet. At first, I worried about missing key information, but to my surprise, utilizing the Internet was not as much of a detriment as I had first feared. In fact, much of the information on the

Internet was as good and as easy to access as the information on my professional equipment, and the cost was extremely modest. Almost all the services I use are free. I especially appreciate the Internet when I am on the road. I plug my computer into the phone, click on the local number for my Internet Service Provider, and all of the information that I need is at my fingertips. I rarely need to call someone in the office to ask what is going on. I can find out all of the information online.

In managing my investments, the first thing I do every day is log on to the Internet and check the list of stocks that I monitor. I keep my list on My Yahoo!, but there are many other sites on the search engines, such as Lycos and Excite; on the major service providers, such as AOL and Microsoft Network; on specialized financial services, such as pcquote.com; and on the online brokers, such as E*Trade, Datek Online, Schwab, and DLJ Direct, that provide the same information. These sites do not charge for this service.

My monitor list includes the stocks I own and those in which I have an interest. It is the same as the monitor list that I have on the professional machines in my office. When I click on My Yahoo!, I immediately see the prices of all of the stocks on my list on the left side of the screen and the recent news stories on these stocks on the right side of the screen. Before the market opens, I check the news on my stocks. This only takes a few minutes because all of the stocks on which there is news have an asterisk next to them. I page down through the list, looking at the headlines. When I see a story that interests me, I click on it. In an instant, I have the news.

Then, I go down the left side of my screen and look at the earnings surprises and the analyst's upgrades and downgrades. I check to see whether there are any other interesting stocks that have reported earnings or have new ratings.

Next, I open up my Internet mail. Every morning, I receive an e-mail from Company Sleuth.com. Company Sleuth is a neat service that scans the Web and provides me with a wealth of information on my favorite stocks. If one of my stocks is going to report earnings, I get an e-mail from Street Fusion or click over to Bestcalls, to get the information on the conference call. I check the earnings estimates on any one of a number of financial sites to see if there have been any changes. (More on these services in chapter 9.)

Each day, I pick a few stocks on my list and check out the charts. I usually do this on My Yahoo! because the charts are so easy to use. I click on the ticker symbol and then "charts." When the big charts come up, I start with a two-year time horizon, and then work down the time-frame spectrum. If I need a longer or a better chart, I might jump to one of the charting Web sites, such as BigCharts, a free service.

If there is a group of stocks in which I am especially interested, I may click over to more specialized Web sites. One of my favorites is Internet.com, which has the best analysis of Internet stocks.

Every few days, I check insider selling and buying on Yahoo!

This entire process, from the time I log onto My Yahoo! until the time that I am finished, usually takes no more than ten minutes.

Next I look through the morning newspapers. I read the *Wall Street Journal, Investors Business Daily*, and the *New York Times.* Because I have checked the prices online, I do not have to spend time paging through the financial tables. Instead, I focus on the news. If I have not been able to get a paper, I go to the online services of these periodicals. (The *Wall Street Journal* service costs $20 per year if you are already a subscriber to the newspaper.) I may also check the online brokers I have accounts with to see if they are highlighting any special news on any of my stocks. Some of the Internet brokers have excellent research, while some have none. But there is so much research information available on the Web that the broker's research services are not that critical to me. If I see an idea that requires immediate action, I research it right away. If I see an idea that has more long-term implications, I clip the article, scan it into my computer, and save it for my evening review.

During a normal day, when I am just monitoring the market, I will usually click back on My Yahoo! every few hours to see what is happening. If I see news, I will always check it out. If a stock is up or down significantly, I will click over to one of the online brokers to get a "real-time" quote. (My Yahoo! has a 20-minute delay on its quotes.) While at the broker, I will usually check out the chart. Normally, this monitoring takes only a few minutes a session.

If I see a stock that I want to buy or sell, I go to my online broker. There I check the inside prices, type the symbol of the stock, the quantity, and the nature of the trade, and click to complete it. Within a matter of seconds, the trade is done. With new systems for small orders at both the listed exchanges and at NASDAQ, I am often able to get as good or better execution online than I get through professional brokers. The cost is less than $10 per trade. Trading online is faster and easier than calling the broker, and because I can see the actual prices, I know exactly what I am paying. While I am at my online broker, I will also usually check out the value of my portfolio, which is always priced up to the minute. (If I have a very large or complex trade, I will call my traditional broker.)

At night, I usually set aside some time for serious research. I check the closing prices and trading actions of the stocks as well as the news for the day. Then I read articles from the newspapers and from the business magazines, such as *Barron's, Forbes, Fortune,* and *Business Week.* If I see a stock that interests me, I will go research it in depth. If I need specific information, I may go to the Edgar Web site and look through the company's recent filings. Most companies now file their documents online. At times, I might also click over to the company's own Web site and check out some of its newest developments.

Before going further, I will review the technicals of the company. I will usually go to BigCharts and look at a number of different technical indicators. Because stocks in an industry tend to move in tandem, I may graph the company in which I am interested against a few of its key competitors. I may also look at some of the stock screens on Morningstar.net, a free service. If I see new stocks of interest, I will go back to My Yahoo! and to Zacks.com and add them to my monitor or list.

If there is a particular question that interests me or if the stock has recently had significant volatility, I might take a look at one of the message boards to see what people are saying about it.

These are the Internet services that I use today. They are the ones that suit my investment style and with which I am the most comfortable. This is not to say that they will be right for you. Because I own a relatively small amount of high-tech stocks, I do not utilize many of the excellent Web sites that focus on the high-tech sector, such as Silicon Investor. Because I have many friends who are also professional investors, I spend relatively little time in chat rooms and do not use Street.com. Because I tend to be a long-term investor, I am less interested in some of the more active trading Web sites. With the current dramatic pace of change on the Internet, I am certain that I will be using new Web sites before this book even gets to print.

You must find the Web sites that work for you. There are a vast number of excellent sites on the Web, and new sites are being created each day. You could spend the entire day looking at information on the Web, just as you could spend your entire day reading reports from various stockbrokers. For almost everyone, this is overkill. The critical task is to find those Web sites that are easy to work with and fit your investing style and time commitments. Pick one or two to start with. Check out a new Web site each week. If you find one you like, add it to your bookmarks and remove one that you do not like as much. The trick is to get the information that you need efficiently. Once you are comfortable with the workings of the Internet, you should not have to spend very much time to stay on top of your investments.

Navigating through these tasks on the Internet is no more difficult than navigating through the same tasks on the proprietary systems that the professionals use. The task for individual investors is thus to figure out how to reduce the remaining advantages of the professional. To win, they must think like guerrillas and find areas in which they have specialized experience and contacts they can use against a stronger enemy. They must find the weaknesses in their more heavily armed opponents. **In the words of Sun Tzu, "Know yourself. Know your enemy. In one hundred battles, there will be one hundred victories."**

CHAPTER TWO

Know Your Enemy, Know Yourself

KNOW YOUR ENEMY

When you are buying a stock, someone else us selling. Otherwise, there could not be a trade. While you are betting that the best thing you can do with your money is to buy the stock, someone else is betting that the best thing that he or she can do is to sell the stock. **The person on the other side of the transaction is your enemy**. That person is betting that you are wrong. It does not matter whether that person is your neighbor, a mutual fund manager, or Warren Buffet. If you cannot defeat that person, you will lose.

If you were fighting a war, you would want to know the strength and tactics of your enemy. The same is true in investing. **Before making a trade, the first thing that you should ask is "Who is my enemy?" and "What does my enemy know that I do not?"** Is your enemy a professional or an amateur? Does your enemy have better information? Has your enemy heard the same story and is betting in the opposite direction anyway? If you cannot figure out the advantages you have over your enemy, chances are, you will lose. The only problem is that in investing, it is often difficult to pinpoint the exact identity of your enemy.

Over the years, the nature of the enemy has changed with professionals becoming far more powerful. Forty years ago, investors comforted themselves with the thought that they were competing against widows and orphans. The conventional wisdom was that the stock one was buying was being sold by Aunt Hattie, who had had it in her portfolio for 40 years, or by Grandpa Jones' estate, which was being liquidated by his grandchildren. It was easy to figure that you could defeat Aunt Hattie or Grandpa Jones' estate. After all, you had received a tip from a friend, who had a friend, who was a stockbroker.

I am not sure that investors forty years ago really did compete against Aunt Hattie or Grandpa Jones' estate, but I am sure that the competition was much less intense than it is now. The information flow was much slower and more limited. There were no conference calls and few analysts. Options and derivatives were almost nonexistent. Turnover was much lower. Mutual funds were smaller. Professionals were far less important, and many had preservation of capital, rather than capital gains, as their primary goal. And there were no day traders. The fact is that forty years ago, the game was much easier than it is now. But those days are long past.

One of the problems is that investing is one of the few games in which amateurs compete directly against professionals. In sports, people play against others at the same level. In baseball, there are the major leagues and minor leagues, and then there is the local corporate league in which you play. You can hit .300 in the Lawyers League and think you are a star. You go out after a game, have a beer, and brag to your friends about how well you played. But how would you do if you tried to bat against Randy Johnson? The chances are pretty good that you would be bailing out when a 98-mile-per-hour fastball came whizzing at your head.

In tennis, you could think of yourself as an "A" player. You might even win the local club championship. But how would you do against Pete Sampras? You would be lucky to win a point. You might suggest that this is not a fair analogy. You should not be judged by your ability to play against Sampras. You are over 40 and a cardiac surgeon. You spend your days doing bypasses, while he spends his days playing tennis. It is as ludicrous to suggest that you should compete with him on the tennis court as it would be for him to compete with you in the operating room.

Think about investing. Do you ask the same questions when you seek to compete with the top professionals in the stock market? The portfolio managers at Fidelity are professionals, as skilled in their business as Sampras is in tennis or you are in medicine. They are the best in their game, and like great athletes, they too are paid millions of dollars a year because they can consistently perform at the highest levels.

But in investing, there is only one league, and it is open to everyone. Investing does not have a club level. There is no "Doctors" league, "Lawyers" league, or Little League. **If you want to play, you have to play against the greatest investors in the world**.

Would you bet your retirement money in a tennis match against Pete Sampras or a golf match against Tiger Woods? No way! But in investing, you would think nothing of matching wits with Bob Stansky, Will Danoff, and Beth Terrana of Fidelity. You would not think anything of it, because it is the only game in town and because you do not know the exact identity of the people on the opposite side of the transaction. When you go to buy stock, your broker does not say, "Beth Terrana of Fidelity is selling the stock you are buying."

The only time when you actually know the identity of the seller is in an offering. Then your enemy is the company itself, or worse, the executives of the company, who want to diversify their holdings, build a house, or endow a foundation. Before you participate in the offering, it is useful to remember that **the seller knows a lot more about the business than you.**

Although it is almost never possible to know the exact identity of the person against whom you are competing, you can ask questions that help you understand the identity of your enemy. Your broker calls with a hot scoop about the earnings of a major company. The story sounds good. But before you buy, remember, most major companies are covered by dozens of analysts, and it is rare that one will have special information.

Even in the few instances when your broker has special information, you should question whom the broker has told before you. If your broker received some hot tip, he probably first bought the stock for himself. He can make much more in his own account than he can by getting a small commission from you. Next, he would call his best accounts. If you are not at the top of the list, the odds are against you. The questions each investor should ask are, "How many people found out the information before I did?" and "What did they do about it?"

In assessing the likelihood that a hot tip will enable you to make money, it is critical to recognize where you fit in the information flow. Let us say that a pharmaceutical company is developing a new drug to cure cancer. The first people who will know about the drug are executives within the company, who start to buy the stock. Then the directors and a few of the largest shareholders start to buy as well. The stock jumps. A few analysts discover the opportunity and issue reports. Brokers see the reports and call their best clients. Finally, after the stock has jumped $15 in three weeks, your broker calls you. *"This drug will cure cancer,"* he says. And it may. If the drug really works, the stock could go to $100. Everything tells you to buy. But before you do ask yourself who the sellers are? Are they the insiders who are unloading shares for a quick profit, or are they widows and orphans who know less than you?

There is no perfect way to answer this question. It is obviously impossible to call someone on the floor of the New York Stock Exchange and say, *"I'll buy this stock only if the person who is selling it is a widow or an orphan!"* But it is useful to stop and think about who is on the other side of the transaction.

Suppose that your enemy is the portfolio manager at Fidelity. The portfolio manager has direct access to the company, armies of analysts dissecting the data and traders who understand the flow of buying and selling. What advantages do you have? You will never be able to devise a winning battle plan if you do not first understand the identity of your enemy.

KNOW YOURSELF

Once you know your enemy, the next step is to know yourself. To succeed against a stronger enemy, the general of a guerrilla force must understand the strengths and weaknesses of his troops. If the enemy has greater strength but the guerrilla general's troops have greater quickness, he should use the quickness in planning his attack. If the enemy has more weaponry but his troops have better knowledge of the local terrain, he should attempt to lure the enemy into the jungle where their superior weapons can be neutralized and the guerrilla's knowledge of local terrain can be the key to victory. **If a general does not understand the strengths and weaknesses of his army, he will never be able to mount an effective battle plan.**

Much the same process occurs in the battlefield of the stock market. To compete against professionals, individuals must know their own skills and craft a battle plan that maximizes their strengths and minimizes their weaknesses. Individuals can make quick decisions. Others like to deliberate. Some enjoy taking risks. Others prefer a defensive posture. Some have extensive time and resources. Others do not. There will be times when the market favors one of these qualities at the expense of the others. But no matter what particular traits the market favors at any point in time, **individuals will not win unless they stick to their strengths and avoid their weaknesses.**

An individual who is comfortable in a defensive posture cannot suddenly become a risk taker as markets start to overheat. An individual who knows nothing about technology cannot suddenly jump on that group of stocks, just because it becomes hot. To avoid getting suckered into the ebbs and flows of the market, it is essential that you know yourself, and that **means knowing what you are really made of and how you compete with others.**

It is critical to understand how you compete against others. When I step on the tennis court, I would love to play like Pete Sampras, but I cannot. I am a 55-year-old with an arthritic knee, and I have to find a tennis game that works for me and play within myself.

The same is true when competing in other sports. How often have you watched a professional golfer hit a 280-yard wood over a yawning lake onto a postage-stamp-size green? The ball hits pin high and stops dead. Then you get out on the course, 280 yards from the green. Remembering the shot from the pro, you think to yourself, I can do that. Well, maybe you can, but I can't. I can't hit a 280-yard drive. I can't ignore a body of water on the golf course, and I can't stop a wood shot dead on the green, except in my fantasies. That does not mean that I cannot play golf. It only means that I cannot play golf pretending that I am a professional.

And so it is with investing. In order to win in the stock market, you have to know who you are and how you like to compete. You must be able to answer four key questions:

1. **How much money do you have to invest?**
2. **How much time do you have?**
3. **What is your tolerance for risk?**
4. **What weapons do you have that can help you in investing?**

1. HOW MUCH MONEY DO YOU HAVE TO INVEST?

The amount of money you have to invest matters for two reasons: returns and risk. If you have a small amount of capital, your returns will be limited, even if you are successful. Your payback for the time that you put in may be very small. Buying mutual funds may be a better way to go. But if you want to begin investing, a small amount of capital should not deter you. Everyone has to start somewhere.

Risk is a bigger issue. If you have a small amount of capital, it is harder to diversify. The more concentrated your portfolio, the higher your risk. The higher your risk, the more likely you will be to panic if a major holding crashes. Once you panic, the game is over. When you own many stocks, a disappointing performance from one will have a smaller impact on your portfolio and will probably not shake you up.

If you have limited capital, you have two alternatives. You can put most of your money in a mutual fund, which will minimize your risk, and use the rest to play a few stocks. Or you can buy smaller quantities of a larger number of stocks. While buying round lots (100 shares) is always a little easier, there is no reason why an investor cannot start with smaller amounts. **If you want to build a stock portfolio, try to own at least ten stocks and make a commitment to expand the portfolio to twenty when you get more capital.** In this way, your portfolio will not be overly affected if one of your stocks is trashed.

2. HOW MUCH TIME DO YOU HAVE FOR INVESTING?

Investing is a skill. Like most skills, the more you work at it, the better you will become. But **investing is much more complicated than most skills because you are not only competing against an enemy, you are also playing in an arena in which the rules are constantly changing.** Positions that worked yesterday may be outmoded today. Change is constant. Companies change. A leader like Apple Computer can suddenly start to struggle, and then just as suddenly recover. Industries change. Systems like the Internet can emerge and revolutionize people's views of communications. Commodities fluctuate. War breaks out in the Middle East and oil prices surge. Markets change. Less than two years ago, the Dow was under 4,000 and most people were bearish. As I write this, the Dow is above 11,000, and most people are bullish. Investment tools change. Program trading and index options, almost unheard of a decade ago, are now major factors in the market. It is difficult to stay on top of a world that is changing unless you are willing to devote time and energy.

Think about the time commitment that you are willing to make. Let us say that you are a doctor. You spend all day seeing patients. You perform surgery. You read medical journals. Do you have the time to read brokerage reports and pour over financial statements? Probably not. Do you have the time to watch the tape? Probably not. Do you have the time to take every call from every broker? Probably not.

THE PHYSICIAN INVESTOR

Recently, a friend who is a doctor called. He was quite upset. *"My broker called me three times about this hot stock,"* the doctor said, *"but I was in surgery. By the time I got back to him, it had gone up three points."*

"That's too bad," I replied.

"It was the nurse's fault," the surgeon said, *"I told her that she should interrupt me if the broker has a really great idea. After all, I'm just doing knees. It's not like I'm transplanting hearts or anything."* I was not sure if the surgeon was serious

or kidding, but my guess is that he was somewhat serious. A year ago, I could never have imagined a doctor being willing to be interrupted in surgery by a broker, but this is a bull market and medical cost containment is on the rise. Nonetheless, even if the doctor had been interrupted, he still could not have acted as fast as the professionals. This does not mean that individuals cannot compete, but it does mean that they will be at a disadvantage. It is crucial to recognize this limitation before you set out.

Make a realistic assessment of how much time you can spend following the stock market, and then decide what you can learn during that period of time. Pick a few areas in which you can compete and ignore the rest. Make sure that your investing strategy matches your time commitment. If you only want to spend a little time looking at stocks, a buy-and-hold strategy will suit you well. If you are willing to spend more time investing, you can utilize more of the strategies recommended in guerrilla investing. No matter how much time you have available, you should always focus on battles that you can win and avoid those that you must lose.

3. WHAT IS YOUR TOLERANCE FOR RISK?

Risk in investing is like risk in war. Some investors are daredevils. They act quickly and make big bets. Others are scared of losing money, so they make only conservative investments. **The amount of risk that individuals take should be determined by their psychological predisposition and their financial condition.** You should never bet the rent, your children's education fund, or your retirement. If you are nervous about your job, have a large mortgage, or carry a high level of debt, factor that into your investment decisions.

THE BETTING GAME

Play this simple exercise to judge your ability to take a risk. Think carefully about your answers. Pretend that the bets are real. Assume that you are risking 25 percent of your liquid net worth. If you have $400,000 in the market, assume that you are risking $100,000.

Someone offers to flip a coin. If it comes up heads, you get $200,000. If it comes up tails, you get $0. The odds are 50/50. You have an equal chance of making $100,000 or losing $100,000. Do you take the bet? Most people would not, because most people are somewhat risk averse. If you would, you are a risk taker.

Suppose the individual offers you $150,000 if it comes up heads and $0 if it comes up tails. You stand to make only $50,000, but you stand to lose $100,000. It is a sucker bet that few would take. But you would be surprised at how many people will make this type of bet in the stock market because they do not realize that the odds are against them. When amateurs buy options, these are often the real odds with which they are dealing.

Let us change the bet in your favor. Suppose you have a 50/50 chance of making $150,000 or losing $100,000. The risk/reward ratio is in your favor. Do you take the bet?

PAYOFFS ON $100,000 BET

Bet	Winning Payoff	Losing Payoff	Winning Position	Losing Position	Risk Profile
$100,000	$100,000	– $100,000	$500,000	$300,000	Coin Flip
$100,000	$50,000	– $100,000	$450,000	$300,000	Buy a Lottery Ticket
$100,000	$150,000	– $100,000	$550,000	$300,000	Good Investing Profile
$100,000	$200,000	– $100,000	$600,000	$300,000	Invest Conservatively
$100,000	$300,000	– $100,000	$700,000	$300,000	Don't Play

What if the payoff changes so that you have a 50/50 chance of making $200,000 or losing $100,000? Do you take the bet? Would you take the bet if you had a 50/50 chance of making $300,000 or losing $100,000?

The level at which you take the bet determines your level of risk aversion. If you accept the bet with a possible payoff of $150,000, you are slightly risk averse. This is probably a good position to be in if you are going to invest. If you demand a payoff of $200,000, you are moderately risk averse. At this level, you are an individual who should be diversified and invest conservatively. If you only take the bet with a possible $300,000 payoff, you are highly risk averse. If you demand a return of $3 for every $1 of risk, you are probably better off letting someone else manage your money.

You may think that this game is foolish. Investing, you may say, is a win-win game. When the stock market goes up, everyone makes money. As this book has already emphasized, the problem with this argument is that it applies only to a bull market. But if the bull market stops, what now looks like a win-win situation can become a lose-lose situation. Before you decide on your tolerance for risk, remember that the market can go down and your financial security can be jeopardized.

4. WHAT WEAPONS DO YOU HAVE?

In a war, the mechanized army has substantial advantages over a guerrilla force. The army has missiles. The guerrillas have homemade bombs. The army has tanks. The guerrillas have rifles. The army has battalions. The guerrillas have platoons. **The guerrillas possess only one real advantage. They know their home turf better than does the enemy.**

It is much the same in investing. While the professional has capital, time, training, and good sources of information, the individual does have the advantage of home turf. The challenge is to figure out what home turf is. People come into contact with public companies in their profession. They view industry trends, deal with suppliers and customers, and analyze their competitors. They also come into contact with public companies as consumers. They shop in stores, eat in restaurants, fly on airlines, stay in hotels, select long-distance carriers, and surf the Net. Finally, they come in contact with public companies in their hometowns or through friends. Because of their own perspective and knowledge of their own terrain, individuals are often able to gain insights that Wall Street misses. This knowledge of one's home turf gives the individual an edge when competing against a more experienced and well-trained enemy.

Individuals receive different types of information than do professionals. Professionals receive structured quantitative information. They read reports, listen to conference calls, talk to managements, review charts, and analyze trading patterns. Individuals receive this information too, especially through the Internet, but they also receive soft, unstructured, qualitative information that comes from their direct experience. While this information does not come neatly packaged, like an analyst report, that does not make it less valuable.

Information moves the stock market, and the professionals have an advantage in acquiring it. That is why it is so **critical for the individual investor to carefully define what he or she knows.** The task is simple. Individual investors must know themselves. They must recognize what they know from their home turf that the professionals miss, and then they must utilize that information to defeat the professionals.

CHAPTER THREE

Avoid the Enemy's Strengths

If the enemy has 100,000 troops and the guerrillas have 1,000, it would be foolhardy to mount a frontal assault. If the enemy has 200 airplanes and the guerrillas have two, it would be idiotic to engage in an air war. No matter what the guerrillas' strengths, there will be no chance for victory if they face the enemy head-on.

The same rules apply in investing. The most glaring error that individual investors commit is ignoring the enemy's strength. Although the Internet has significantly modified the balance of power, there are still areas in which the odds are set strongly in favor of the professionals. These areas include:

1. **Timing the market**
2. **Aggressive trading**
3. **Trading on earnings announcements**
4. **Actively trading big cap stocks**
5. **Trying to hit home runs with options**
6. **Mergers and acquisitions**
7. **IPOs, especially when the proceeds go to the insiders**
8. **Businesses that are too complex to understand**
9. **Emerging markets**
10. **Anything too good to be true**

1. AVOID TRYING TO TIME THE MARKET

Investors love to have opinions on the direction of the stock market. You might hear a strategist say, "My charts indicate that the market is going to go up by 1,000 points." You might read a report from a portfolio manager saying, "The market is way overextended and is going to drop by 1,500 points." Or you might talk to a friend who tells you with great certainty that the market will remain in a narrow trading range. Predictions on the stock market can be extremely seductive. People are looking for easy answers. Doing investment research is hard work. Investing on a "sure" market move is easy and much more fun.

The only problem is, **no one knows how the market will perform.** Experts conduct their analysis and make their predictions. Some are better than others. Some are even right more than they are wrong. But most experts have the same chance of being right about the market as they do of predicting whether it will be a hot summer or a snowy winter. The difference: Most people do not bet their life savings on weather predictions. From time to time, experts have emerged who many thought could predict the market. Joseph Granville was once treated as a guru because he predicted a downturn. But as the market rallied to historic heights, Granville continued to predict a crash.

Robert Prechter gained renown with his Elliot Wave Theory. In the 1980s, Prechter could move markets. But Prechter and his theory did not hold up. While a few waves hit exactly as predicted, many did not. Over time, the Elliot Wave Theory proved to be only that, a theory.

Elaine Garzarelli used technical indicators to predict the crash in 1987. Garzarelli is a good analyst, but she is not a seer. In 1996, she predicted the market would drop. Instead, it rallied to historic heights. She used the same indicators that had worked in 1987, but the market did not oblige. No one can predict the stock market because it is both extremely complex and ever-changing. A myriad of factors moves the market, including interest rates, the federal deficit, corporate profits, worldwide economic conditions, and political confidence. Understanding how these factors fit together to drive the market as a whole is a complex undertaking for even the most skilled professional. For the individual, it is almost impossible.

JUST WHEN YOU FIGURE IT OUT . . .

The market is never the same. Different factors always seem to drive stock prices.

- In the 1980s, investors waited anxiously for money supply figures to be announced. Now, no one ever talks about the money supply figures. Few even know what they are.
- Oil prices drove the market as investors looked for signs from OPEC. Now, no one seems to care what OPEC does.
- Budget deficits have driven markets, as investors worried about government debt. Now we have a surplus.
- The trade deficit and the level of the dollar have driven markets, as money flowed into and out of the United States.
- Profits have driven markets, as investors focused on earnings.
- Mergers, acquisitions, and buybacks have driven markets, as investors focused on value.
- Economic reports including consumer confidence, housing starts, leading indicators, prices, and unemployment have driven markets, as investors worried about the economy.
- Technological change, such as the Internet, has driven markets, as investors looked to a combination of higher productivity and lower interest rates.
- Political factors such as the stability of emerging countries have driven markets, as investors worried about international issues.
- The Federal Reserve Board has driven markets, as investors sat glued to their television sets, waiting to see whether Alan Greenspan was carrying a fat or a thin briefcase.

Small and Subtle Changes Can Rock the Market

Seemingly small changes in economic statistics are often sufficient to move markets.

- The government reports that new unemployment claims are 250,000 instead of a predicted 200,000. Fifty thousand more unemployed does not mean much in a country of 250 million, but the slightly higher than expected number may convince some that a slowdown is coming.
- The consumer price index comes in at +.5 percent rather than +.2 percent. The difference may be the result of higher cereal and beef prices caused by floods in the Midwest. A three-tenths-of-one-percent higher than expected increase hardly means double-digit inflation, but it can spook stock prices.
- Alan Greenspan says something about "irrational exuberance" and the market drops by 250 points.

To most individual investors, these are just minor numbers or events, but to professionals, these can be signals of future directions.

Even when individuals understand the impact of events, it often takes them longer to act, causing them to miss the window of opportunity. In the week after the election of 1996, the market staged a huge rally because voters had elected a Democratic president and a Republican Congress. Professionals had worried that the Democrats would spend too much on social programs, while the Republicans would increase the deficit by cutting taxes. They cheered the split between the White House and Congress, because they viewed gridlock as the best hope for less spending and lower deficits. When the professionals saw the results of the election, they plunged into the market. Individual investors saw the same election returns, but because they did not instantly understand the implications or act as quickly, they missed part of the move. If the individuals do not move as fast as the professionals with an event whose outcome they understand, what chance do they have when they are faced with far more complex or more distant events? **Timing the market seems like an easy**

way to invest, but the odds are so set in favor of the professional that the individual investor is almost certain to lose over an extended period of time.

While timing the market is usually a risky proposition for the individual investor, there is one significant exception to this rule. That occurs if there is a general unanimity of opinion among experts as to the direction of the market. When there is, bet against it. The propensity of the experts to be wrong will outweigh the risks to the individual in timing the market.

2. AVOID AGGRESSIVE TRADING

Aggressive trading is fun. Making quick decisions, jumping in and out of stocks, and placing big bets on short-term moves makes people feel as if they are in the middle of the action. You watch the flow of the stock, see a critical piece of news, and make your bet. In a short period of time, you have either won or lost. However, aggressive trading is a professionals' game that plays directly into their strength. This is not to say that individuals should buy and hold forever, but most should avoid getting sucked into the most aggressive trading games.

The key in aggressive trading is to be able to move instantly when a critical piece of information crosses the tape. In responding to this information, professionals have major advantages over the individual:

- Professionals are working at investing full time and see the information much sooner. In the world of active trading, "much sooner" is an eternity.
- Professionals are bombarded with inputs from analysts, traders, salespeople, and technicians.
- Professionals often receive selective dissemination of information. On June 19, 1996, the Bank of New York told 92 analysts and institutional investors on its conference call that it would set aside $350 million to cover expected losses from delinquent credit cards. The call was held at 2:00, but the news was not publicly disseminated

until 4:09. For two hours, 92 professionals knew something that the rest of the world did not. By the time that this information was disseminated, the stock had declined by $1³/₈. While losing 3 percent is not the end of the world, if you are an active trader, 3 percent moves can add up.

• Professionals talk to each other and often know what their counterparts are planning to do. If a small portfolio manager at Fidelity knows that the Magellan Fund is about to unload all auto stocks, that portfolio manager will not rush to buy Ford.

• Institutions have traditionally been able to trade after the markets have closed. Price movements in this "aftermarket" can often be dramatic if there is late breaking news. On July 16, 1996, Intel's stock closed at $70 per share. Shortly thereafter, Intel reported better than expected earnings. The stock traded up in the aftermarket. The next morning, it opened at $74. While the institutions had the ability to buy and sell between $70 and $74, the small investor did not. This is not to say that all of the institutions in the aftermarket made the right trades on Intel, but having access when others do not is always an advantage.

Now, this advantage is beginning to disappear. Online brokers are offering after hours trading until 8:30 P.M. I am sure that by the time this book is published, the hours will be further extended, both earlier and later, and one of the advantages of the professionals will have been reduced significantly.

• Professionals can more easily utilize sophisticated techniques, such as trading options, to capitalize on short-term opportunities. For example, if Intel reports bad news, the professionals may decide that the entire technology sector could come under pressure and may buy puts on an index. With computerized trading, the major institutions can play trading games that are well beyond the abilities of the individual investor.

DAY TRADERS

The one significant exception to the rule against active trading involves people who are day traders. These people are professionals, who work full-time trading stocks. Watching them in action is a fascinating experience.

Most trading floors hum with activity. Brokers are yelling orders to each other, talking on the phone with customers, and sharing inputs. Analysts come over the loudspeaker with constant updates. Jokes and stories make their way around the trading desk, and there is a strong level of camaraderie between the traders.

In the trading floors of the day traders, there is almost complete silence. Hundreds of young traders, most in their 20s, sit in compact rows, glued to their screens, oblivious of the traders to either side. There are no jokes or stories. While the market is open, they do not talk on the phone, read the newspapers, study financial reports, or listen to conference calls. Instead, they watch the signals from their sophisticated software, the most successful of which is the "Watcher," looking for instant trading opportunities. They are like kids playing video games. They are not concerned with fundamentals or earnings estimates. They may not even know the businesses of the stocks they own. They are only concerned with finding short-term gaps in the market that can give them a trading opportunity.

When a buy or sell signal is indicated, a trader who sees the opportunity and is fast enough clicks a trade. Within an instant, the trader has bought 1,000 shares. Market makers change their prices. Another signal hits the screen. The trader clicks again, selling the stock for a profit of $0.25 a share. Less than one minute has passed, and the trader has made two transactions. Other day traders may or may not have made the same trade. As in playing a video game, skills and judgment are required. There is a wide difference between the best and the worst of the day traders.

The day traders are the ultimate guerrillas. Their strategy depends on hitting weaknesses in the professionals' lines and then retreating. Like a guerrilla who stages a lightning attack and then disappears into the jungle, a good day trader may be in and out of a stock in less than one minute and may execute more than 75 trades in an average day. In fact, many of the day traders have been called SOES Bandits. SOES (Small Order Execution System) is a trading system implemented by NASDAQ for small orders. These traders have been called bandits because they have acted like guerrillas in taking profits from the professionals.

By taking profits from the professionals, the day traders have had a much more dramatic impact on the market than almost anyone will ever admit. Because the day traders pick off small price inefficiencies, through the SOES system and through ECNs, they have dramatically cut into the profits that the major firms formerly obtained from making markets in over-the-counter stocks. With their profits squeezed, the major firms sharply reduced the number of stocks and the capital employed in trading. This has made it more difficult for institutions to trade some over-the-counter stocks and has sharply increased volatility.

If you are willing to devote yourself to trading—watching the news and charts and then reacting instantly, you can often hold your own or even defeat the professional, with lightning-fast guerrilla attacks. But you should remember that these actions do not contradict the rules about active trading against professionals, because anyone who sits glued to a terminal all day long is by definition a professional.

3. AVOID TRADING ON EARNINGS ANNOUNCEMENTS

Professionals also have a big advantage in trading on earnings announcements. It is very tempting for investors to make trades based either on expected or on actual reported earnings. The stockbroker calls and tells you that XYZ Systems is going to report before the opening. He is expecting good earnings. You take a flyer and buy some stock. Ignoring the critical question of whether your broker has a clue as to what he or she is talking about, the question you should ask is, "Will you be able to evaluate the earnings when they are reported? Will you be on the conference call? Will your broker? Will you receive a fax with all of the financial data? If you do, will you know what to look for?" If you think carefully about the sequence of events, you will realize that you will be at a significant disadvantage to the professionals in acquiring and analyzing information.

Your broker calls the next morning. XYZ Systems has just reported better than expected earnings. He advises you to buy more.

"Where's the stock?" you ask.

"It's down a buck," the broker replies.

"What's going on?" you ask incredulously.

"More sellers than buyers," the broker mumbles as he scans his database for information on the earnings. *"I'm expecting a note from the analyst, but it's not on the system yet."* The stock is now down $2.00 on heavy volume. *"I'll check and call you back."*

The broker calls the analyst. *"I need to talk to her,"* your broker tells her assistant.

"She's on the Intel conference call," the assistant responds, *"and I can't interrupt her."*

"Did she say anything about XYZ Systems?" your broker asks.

"She was on the conference call," the assistant replies. *"She's working on a note."*

"What is she going to say?" the broker asks.

"We'll get back to you as soon as we can," the assistant replies politely.

The broker calls and recounts his conversation. *"Where's the stock now?"* you ask.

"It's only down $4.00 now. It was down $6.00, but it's acting better," your broker explains, certain that you will feel more comfortable.

"I guess someone did not like the earnings," you say for-lornly.

"The earnings were good," the broker responds. *"They beat our estimates."*

"Something is wrong," you say, stating the obvious.

"I'll get back to you when I know something," the broker responds and then hangs up.

At 4:10 the broker calls you back. The stock has closed down $7.00. *"I talked to the analyst,"* he says, although he probably just read the note that she wrote for the system. *"She says that while the quarter was sensational, future orders are a little soft, and next year's earnings might be flat. She also reduced the stock from a strong buy to a hold."*

"What does that mean?" you ask.

"You should dump the stock," the broker replies. You curse and hang up the phone.

Stop for a second and think about the process. When the company reported earnings, your broker called immediately, which is probably more than most brokers would do. But he only knew the earnings per share (EPS) number. He was not on the conference call. He did not know about the weakness in future orders. He did not know that his analyst would be reducing both her estimates and ratings, and he did not know that what looked to be good numbers were really a disaster. Further, he did not get an explanation until the stock had declined by $7.00 and the market had closed.

While your broker was in the dark, other people obviously knew. They were probably prepped before the announcement, having reviewed the projected earnings, sales, margins, expenses, inventories, and backlogs with the company or with an analyst.

Companies send press releases to the wire services and faxes to key investors and analysts. Although the wire services should receive and post the information first to assure universal dissemination, it does not always work this way. Sometimes the wire services have an overload of information and sometimes faxes get sent early to the professionals. A hedge fund manager I know received a fax from a retailer's PR firm indicating that comparable store sales were up 35 percent and that earnings would be above expectations. He checked his terminal. The wire services had not yet picked up the news. He bought the stock for $9.50. Twenty minutes later, the news hit the tape. One hour later, the stock was selling at $11.25. Because he received the fax before the news was broadly disseminated, he was able to make a $1.75 per share in just one hour.

Analysts are often inundated because companies in the same industry commonly report earnings on the same day. In retailing, for example, there was one day each quarter when five companies hosted hour-long conference calls on the same morning. The analysts barely had time to jump from one to the next. While analysts would like to quickly issue a note on the first company that reported, they cannot afford to miss the next call. (I have often wondered whether companies planned calls at the same time so that the analysts would not have too much time to probe.) If five companies report in a morning, a full day can pass before the analysts can write a note and disseminate it. This does not hurt the professionals, who participate in the calls, but it does hurt the individual investors, who must rely on the analysts for details.

EARNINGS REPORTS ON THE INTERNET

The Internet is rapidly eliminating many of the advantages professionals have concerning earnings reports. Internet search engines, online brokerage firms, and special online services such as Thompson, Quote.com, Zacks, Market Watch, and Briefing.com list the dates on which companies are expected to report earnings and the consensus estimates. Even if you are a long-term investor, you should check these lists each week for companies in which you are interested.

Step One. Check the earnings estimates. Watch especially for changes made close to the date of an expected earnings release.

Step Two. Click over to the company itself and look at the last time it reported earnings. See how much detail it provides online. If there is a complete breakdown of earnings and a balance sheet, you will have access to the same information as the professionals. If there are only sales and EPS, you should call the company and ask to be put on a fax list.

If you are especially interested, ask for the number of the conference call and whether there is a playback number. The Web service Street Fusion will e-mail you with the date, time, and phone number of the conference calls of the companies in which you are interested. While at the time of this writing, the playback of conference calls is a service open primarily to professionals, I am confident that it will soon be available to all investors. The Web site Bestcalls lists most of the upcoming calls.

Step Three. Check the Web early on the day that the company is to report its earnings. Most report before the market opens. Compare the reported number with the estimates. Companies "guide" analysts, so deviations from estimates will usually be upside or downside surprises. Read the company's press release. Look at the balance sheet and the income statement to see if there are any problems. Look for commentary on Web sites, such as Motley Fool. Many Web sites summarize conference calls.

Step Four. Listen to the conference calls if you have the time. Many companies are using Internet services, such as V-call, to broadcast their conference calls. When a call is broadcast on the Internet, there is true universal dissemination. This eliminates a key advantage of the professionals.

The trend of broadcasting calls on the Internet and opening calls to all investors is likely to continue to increase dramatically, because companies are concerned about **selective dissemination**. The calls on which the professionals receive selective information are not only unfair, they are in the process of becoming illegal. The SEC has recently become more aggressive in forcing companies to communicate important information universally. As a result, more companies will open their calls to all investors.

With conference calls online or open to all investors, the advantages of the professionals are clearly reduced. But professionals still do have several key advantages. They have the time to listen, which most individuals do not, and they have better inputs, so that they can understand the details of the call. Nonetheless, the trend towards universal dissemination is clearly moving in favor of the individual.

CONFERENCE CALLS

Conference calls can be a very useful tool. Listen to the tone of the management. You can often tell when management is pleased or when it is trying to hide something. The question-and-answer period is often a good indicator of how business really is. If every analyst says, "Congratulations on a great quarter," before asking a question, you can be reasonably sure that the quarter has been good. (They are probably patting themselves on the back for having recommended the stock.) If, on the other hand, the analysts sound antagonistic and keep questioning the company about inventory levels or hidden charges, you can be relatively sure that they are not pleased. You should be especially concerned when an analyst who has a buy on the stock starts to ask tough questions. Because analysts with buys want the company to look as good as possible, they frequently ask "soft" questions like "How do you keep posting such great results?" If these analysts ask tough questions, it may be a precursor to a ratings change, and you will have something to worry about. On the other hand, if bearish analysts suddenly seem to be getting more bullish and start asking about upside earnings surprises, you should consider buying, because it is a safe bet that some may raise their ratings. If the attitudes of the analysts are different from what you expected, you should act at once. Most companies replay their conference calls at later times for people who have conflicts with the live call. While the playback may not help you in terms of short-term trading, it will allow you to listen to the management at your leisure.

Step Five. Watch the initial trading pattern after the earnings have been released. This is often a critical time for a stock. Did the stock perform the way that you thought it would? If it did not, it is time to rethink your position. A stock that declines sharply on better than expected earnings is not likely to turn around quickly. On the other hand, if the company reports worse than expected earnings and the stock goes up, it may be that the reported earnings were actually better than you realized or that the stock has bottomed. Whatever the reason, the stock is likely to keep going up. These are often good opportunities for the long-term investor to reevaluate a position.

Step Six. Look for "Analyst Upgrades and Downgrades" on the Internet. Analysts frequently change their ratings when companies report, and rating changes are updated on the Internet throughout the day. Watch especially for downgrades of stocks that have performed well or upgrades of stocks that have built a strong base. Note stocks in which the analysts are either exceedingly bullish or bearish, because these stocks can have big moves if the analysts change their ratings.

Step Seven. Watch the technical pattern of the stock (the charts). Earnings announcements can be powerful catalysts in moving stocks. Good earnings can often cause a stock to break through a resistance level, while bad earnings can often cause the stock to break below a support level. If a stock breaks above or below a resistance level, it will probably keep moving in that direction. Because the next earnings announcement will not come for three months, you must respond if significant changes occur. While you may have missed the initial move, a change in a trading pattern will usually have long-term implications.

Monitoring earnings announcements and listening to conference calls can be very useful no matter what your ownership horizon. But even with the added information on the Internet, you should not assume that you now have a level playing field with the professionals. You do not. The professionals still have huge advantages. Thus, while the Internet does provide a lot of information, you should be cautious in attempting to trade against the professional on earnings announcements.

4. AVOID ACTIVELY TRADING BIG-CAP STOCKS

Don't attempt to aggressively trade the largest capitalization stocks. These are the stocks on which the professionals earn their living. They have hundreds of millions (if not billions) of dollars, as well as their reputations and careers, invested in these stocks and they will do whatever they can to win. They cover every aspect of these companies as closely as they can. If there is an easy short-term opportunity in these stocks, they are not going to miss it.

Your broker says that Intel will introduce a revolutionary new chip and that the stock should jump. It sounds like a good story. But before you buy, ask what your broker knows compared to what other professionals know. Intel is followed by 47 sell-side analysts, as well as hundreds of buy-side analysts and portfolio managers. These people have billions invested in Intel. They talk to the company, its suppliers, customers, and competitors, and often hire experts to follow the technology. If Intel is going to announce a revolutionary new chip, everyone probably knows about it and has already made his bet. It is unlikely that your broker has an inside scoop, unless his brother happens to design chips for Intel.

The next day, the broker calls and tells you to buy Philip Morris. A decision is about to be made on tobacco litigation, and the broker thinks that the tobacco companies will win. Once again, the story sounds good and you are tempted to buy Philip Morris for a short-term trade. Once again, you should resist the temptation. Philip Morris is followed by 15 sell-side analysts and hundreds of buy-side analysts and portfolio managers, who have billions of dollars invested in the company. They may even have hired lawyers to attend the trial. These lawyers have listened to the arguments, reviewed the legal issues, and watched the body language of the judge and jury. While no one can predict a jury's behavior, they are in a much better position to make a decision than you are.

On June 15, 1999, First Call listed the number of sell-side, brokerage firm analysts with earnings estimates on the following stocks:

American Online	44	Cisco	44	Yahoo	28
Merck	45	Wal-Mart	37	Sears	25
Intel	47	Microsoft	37	Bristol Myers	35

This list includes only those analysts whose firms subscribe to First Call. The total number of sell-side analysts that follow these companies is thus much larger. In addition, these companies are all closely covered by buy-side analysts and portfolio managers.

Major financial institutions have huge amounts of money invested in these stocks. In order to demonstrate the magnitude of the investments, we checked the filings of U.S. financial institutions and used the closing prices of the stocks on June 15, 1999. On that date:

- **Seventy-eight companies owned more than $300,000,000 worth of stock in Intel.** Nineteen of these owned more than $1 billion in stock, and 200 companies owned more than 1 million shares of Intel.

- **Forty-eight companies owned more than $300,000,000 worth of stock in Coca-Cola.** Thirteen of these owned more than $1 billion in stock, and 118 companies owned more than 1 million shares of Coca-Cola. The investment in Coca-Cola by Berkshire Hathaway, the company controlled by Warren Buffet, was worth $15 billion.

- **One hundred companies owned more than $300,000,000 worth of stock in General Electric.** Forty-four of these owned more than $1 billion in stock, and 280 companies owned more than 1 million shares of GE. The twenty largest holders of GE are shown in the table below.

Stop and think about the size of these investments. If you had over $1 billion invested in a stock, would you be on top of the activities of the company? You can bet on it! If one of these investors is an institution that manages some of your money, you better hope they are on top of the company news.

Few major institutions can afford to ignore companies like General Electric, Intel, Coca-Cola, IBM, and Merck. Thus, when one of these major companies reports earnings, there are often more than 500 institutional investors and analysts participating in the conference call. If you are an individual investor, it is difficult to gain an advantage against these professionals.

The same rules do not apply if you are investing for the long term. Then, the short-term movements of a stock will be much less important and the advantages of the professionals will be minimized. You may not know how the market will react to Intel's product announcement over the next week, but over the long term, you believe that Intel will outperform the market. If you think that Intel is a good company, buy it for the long term. But trying to outsmart the professionals for a short-term trade is foolhardy. Winning at investing is difficult enough without playing directly into the enemy's strengths.

5. USE OPTIONS AS A HEDGE—NOT TO HIT HOME RUNS

Options are fun! They offer the opportunity for huge profit with minimal risk. Everyone dreams of the big hit with options, and in a bull market, it often occurs.

I used to sit next to an institutional salesman. He had loaded up on options in Macy, because he thought the stock was undervalued. One morning trading in Macy was halted. News crossed the tape that there would be a leveraged buyout. The options jumped by $18 per share. In that one instant, he made a profit of $2 million on an investment of $100,000. After the shock had worn off, he turned and shook my hand. *"Good-bye,"* he said, *"I'm taking my money, and moving to Florida to play golf."* I thought he was kidding. He was only 46. He is still in Florida playing golf and has a 2 handicap.

OPTIONS EXPLAINED

An option is a leveraged way to buy or sell a specific stock. In buying an option, an individual pays an amount of money (the premium) for the right to buy (a call) or sell (a put) a particular stock at a set price (the strike price), on or before a particular date (the expiration date).

Intel, which is selling for $93, has an October $100 call option selling for $4. In this case, the expiration date is October, the strike price is $100, and the premium is $4. This means that a buyer can pay $4 for the right to buy Intel at $100 per share any time until the expiration date in October. Options are contracts for 100 shares. They are quoted on a per share basis. If the premium is $4, one option will cost you $400 ($4 per share for 100 shares).

In a call option, the investor is betting that the stock will go up. In buying a call, the investor puts up a relatively small amount of money ($4) for the right to buy the stock at a specified price ($100) at some point in the future (before October). The price of the premium will vary with both the strike price and the expiration date. The chart below shows a variety of call options for Intel.

Note how the premium varies with the stock price and the expiration date. It makes sense that you would pay more to buy the stock at $90 than you would to buy it at $100 ($8^5/_8$ vs. $4). You are paying $4^5/_8$ more for the right to buy the stock for $10 less. It also makes sense that you pay more for a longer time frame. With more time, the stock has a greater potential to move in price. You pay $4 for the right to buy the stock by October, but $10^1/_2$ for the right to buy it next April. The $6^1/_2$ difference reflects the value of this time.

The key issue with options is the leverage. An option is a leveraged play on the movement of a stock. If the stock does not reach the strike price, your options will be worthless. If the stock moves above the strike price by less than the premium, you will lose money. But if the stock moves up sharply during the option period, the payoff can be substantial.

INTEL CALL OPTIONS: EXPIRATION DATE AND PREMIUM

Option	Premium	Option	Premium	Option	Premium	Option	Premium
Oct. 80	$16	Oct. 90	$8^5/_8$	Oct. 100	$4	Oct. 105	$2^5/_8$
Jan. 80	$19	Jan. 90	$13	Jan. 100	$7^7/_8$	Jan. 105	$6^1/_4$
		April 90	$15^1/_4$	April 100	$10^1/_2$	April 105	$8^7/_8$

If you were buying 1,000 shares of Intel, you would need $93,000 but if you put the same money into Intel October $100 options, you would have the right to buy 23,250 shares. If Intel stayed the same, went down, or even went up to $100, you would lose your investment if you bought options. If it went to $102, you would lose half of your investment. (You paid $4 and it was $2 above the strike price.) If Intel went to $110, you would make $139,500 on the options and only $17,000 on the stock, but the chances of Intel going up this fast in a short period are exceedingly small.

Buying a put is the opposite of buying a call. When you buy a put, you receive the right to sell an underlying security at a specific price. For example, if you buy an Intel October $90 put option, you have the right to sell Intel at $90 before the option expires. If the stock drops below the $90 strike price, you can buy the stock at the market price, sell it at the strike price, and pocket the difference, less the cost of the option.

Options are extremely complicated. There are a huge number of options in each security. Intel currently has over 220 different call and put options (including LEAPS—two-year options). Each of these 220 options trades independently, although all trade off the price of the underlying stock. Selecting the most attractive strike price and expiration date can be a daunting task. The professionals have computer programs that track the volatility of the stock, the dividend, the cost of money, and other factors that allow them to choose the best option. With so many choices, the computer programs can often find market inefficiencies that allow professionals to trade one set of options against another, with virtually no risk.

Using options calculation tools that are available over the Internet can eliminate some of the advantages of the professionals. One of the best is on the Web site of the **Chicago Board Options Exchange** (CBOE). With these tools, the individual can calculate the optimum pricing of all options and compare this pricing with the marketplace. However, in order to do so effectively, the individual must be able to assess the volatility of the stock.

Some stocks are reasonably stable, while others are highly volatile. The higher the volatility, the greater the likelihood that the stock will move substantially, and the more expensive the option. On this date, Knight-Trimark, an over-the-counter trader tied to the Internet, and May Department Stores are both selling for about $38, but the price of $40 options, six months out, varies widely because of the different volatility of the two companies.

Name	Price	6 Month $40 Option
May Department Stores	$38	$2½
Knight-Trimark	$38	$10½

If you wanted to buy a $40 option for May, you would pay $2¹/₂, but if you wanted to buy a $40 option for Knight-Trimark, which is selling at the same price, you would pay $10^{1}/_{2}$. The difference is related solely to perceived volatility. But estimating a stock's volatility can be a complex task. If you select the wrong level, your pricing strategies will be wrong.

Buying Calls or Puts on Indexes

If the odds are against the individual in buying options on stocks, they are even more against the individual in buying options on indexes. Most of the major indexes, such as the S&P 100 & 500, the Dow Jones Industrial, the NASDAQ 100, and the Russell 2000, have options. There are also a variety of sector and international indexes. Index options can be used to make a bet for or against one of these markets. For example, if you believe that the stock market as a whole is going up, you can buy a call on a major index such as the S&P 100. If you think that small stocks will underperform, you can buy put options on the Russell 2000.

Over the past several years, buying call options has been the best of all possible investments. Because the returns on index call options have been so great, many investors believe that they are a sure path to instant wealth. The problem is that the strategy only works during a bull market. In a normal market, index options work against most individual investors. They not only require the investor to time the market, they also require the investor to time the market with leverage. In timing the market, the odds are against most individuals, and once the leverage of options is added, the odds become tougher. If you have no special ability to time the market, then timing it with leverage is a good way to lose quickly.

There is one small exception to the rule against buying index options. There may be a segment of the market, such as the Internet, which you do not fully understand but in which you want to participate. Putting a small amount of money in an Internet index, such as the ISDEX, may be a reasonable way to allow you to participate in this segment. Still you may be better off buying a specialized index fund rather than buying an option on the index.

Options are a professionals' game. They play to the professionals' greatest strengths: timing, inside information, and better systems, and against the individual's greatest weakness, greed. Options have become a core part of most professionals' investing strategies. They use options to facilitate trades, capitalize on imbalances in the market, lock in profits, and insure a portfolio against catastrophic losses. While individuals are using options to make a bet, professionals are using them to change the rules of the game.

When small investors attempt to play options, they are entering a world with its own rules and with a pace of trading that is so fast that only the most sophisticated can keep pace. It would be like entering the Indy 500 on a bicycle. As you are pedaling down the backstretch, you could get killed when cars come roaring by at 250 miles per hour.

THE EXCEPTIONS

There are, of course, some instances when an individual should consider buying options. If you have real home turf advantage and a solid piece of information that could move the stock, options are worth considering. For example, if you know that a company in your industry is about to receive a huge contract, you may want to buy calls. However, before you buy, make certain that you have the correct timing on your information. If the contract is delayed by a few weeks, you could lose your investment.

Puts may be more useful than calls because they can also be used as a substitute for shorting stocks. It is much easier to buy a stock, if you think it will go up, than it is to short a stock, if you think it will go down. In many instances, a variety of restrictions can make shorting difficult. In these cases, buying a put may be an easier way to bet against a company. But whether you are buying a call or a put, remember that the advantages of the professionals are magnified and that you should only play options if you have a real advantage in terms of home-turf information and timing.

COMPLEX OPTION STRATEGIES

While buying simple calls and puts is not a good bet for an individual, ironically some of the more complex options strategies may make sense. They can enable the individual to hedge an investment and, in so doing, manage risk and gain some peace of mind. In a complex options strategy, investors use options to limit the risk in stocks they already own. In this strategy, investors may sell a call or buy a put against an existing position. In effect, they now become long and short on the same stock. Their position is hedged.

You own a stock at $40, with a cost price of $20. You are nervous that it will drop. You can buy a **"protective put,"** for $3. This gives you the right to sell the stock at $40 before the expiration date. You have invested a little more money, but you now have an insurance policy against the stock's dropping precipitously.

On the other hand, you may think the stock will settle at this price for a while. In fact, if it got to $43, you might even sell it. Instead, you can sell a **"covered call."** In this case, you receive $3 from the buyer. If the stock remains below the strike price of $40, the $3 premium is a windfall profit. If it goes above the strike price, you will be forced to sell it. But the $3 premium will be an added profit, so you are really selling it for the $43 you wanted. For a fuller discussion of complex options, check out the Web site of the CBOE.

Investors who own a large amount of stocks in one industry and think that the market will drop can hedge their positions by buying a **put option on an index.** For example, if you own many of the major technology stocks, you can buy a put option on a technology index. If the technology stocks drop, part or all of the drop will be offset by the option. Of course, if the stocks go up, the gain will also be offset. But you will be able to hedge your bets without having to sell your stocks and pay capital gains taxes.

However, before buying a put on a sector, make sure that your portfolio is representative of the sector. If you own a collection of stocks that is not representative, the index could go up while your stocks go down, and you could lose on both sides. Exercise great caution in buying a put option on a sector. Consider this as a strategy only if you own many of the major companies in an index, have huge unrealized profits, and are searching for peace of mind.

Trading options is a complex undertaking that plays directly into the strengths of the professional and to the weaknesses of the individual. As a result, you should not buy call and put options on individual stocks, unless you have a significant home-turf advantage. But some of the complex option strategies may be of use because they can enable you to limit down-side risk, lock in gains, and gain some piece of mind. If options help you look at the market without nervously gulping antacids, they may be worth considering. The rule for options is thus: **Avoid the quick fixes of betting on pure call options for stocks or indexes, but look at strategies that can allow you to lock in your profits and minimize your risk.**

6. AVOID PLAYING MERGERS AND ACQUISITIONS

Playing mergers and acquisitions sounds like an easy way to invest. The Acquiring Company has offered to buy the Target Company at $30 a share, but the stock of the Target is still selling at $22. The deal should close within a matter of months. You think that this looks like an easy way to make a quick $8 a share. You are wrong. If a big return is to be made in a relatively short period of time in an already announced deal, some-thing is wrong. In a second deal, the stock jumps quickly to $32 when the offer is at $30. You decide to sell. After all, you are getting $2 more than the stock is worth. Once again, you are likely to be wrong.

No area on Wall Street is more dominated by professionals than the risk arbitrage. When a deal is announced, the arbitrageurs immedi-ately spring into action. They talk to the company, its competitors and suppliers, as well as to analysts, lawyers, and even government officials. They cover deals so extensively that most professional investors will not even compete with them. This certainly is not a place for individuals.

In order to value the deal, the arbitrageurs must assess the likelihood of the deal being completed and the risk to the target company if it falls apart. This can be more complicated than it might seem. In some cases, a failed merger can mortally wound a target company. It shares its secrets with a competitor, many of its managers leave, and it loses momentum.

I learned this lesson a decade ago, when Businessland made an offer for MBI Business Systems. Based on the price of the offer, MBI should have been selling at $18, but it remained at $12. I bought MBI, in expectation of the deal being completed. Unfortunately, when Businessland did its audit, it found that MBI had substantial amounts of missing inventory. (It seems that the employees had cannibalized some of the computers.) The deal was called off. MBI sank to $2 and never recovered. This is a lesson I will never forget.

In addition to looking at the risk, arbitrageurs must consider the possibility that someone else will enter the bidding. If a second or a third buyer emerges, a bidding war can take the stock well above the original offer. Several years ago, Viacom made a friendly bid for Paramount. Then QVC entered the bidding. By the time the game was finished, the offer for Paramount was raised many times. Anyone who sold the first time that Paramount reached a premium to the offer price missed out on most of the move. If the stock trades at a premium to the original offer, it is a sign that the arbitrageurs expect another higher offer.

If the deal is not friendly, the game becomes far more complex. Arbitrageurs must assess the ends to which management is likely to go to protect its independence. Managements have sold off assets, created expensive golden parachutes, made acquisitions of their own, or even turned around and tried to buy the Acquiring Company (Pac Man Defense) in order to avoid being taken over. Sometimes their actions push the stock up. Other times, they drive it down.

When the deal is for stock, the arbitrageurs will trade the two stocks against each other, buying one and shorting the other, and often using options. These games are so sophisticated and played with such speed that it is almost impossible for individual investors to keep pace.

Yet even the best arbitrageurs can end up being wrong. In 1997, British Telecom agreed to buy MCI. Most arbitrageurs assumed the deal would go through, because British Telecom already owned 20 percent of MCI and the deal had received government approval. But then MCI reported weak earnings, and the terms of the deal were changed. MCI, which one month earlier had sold at $42, dropped to $28. Because most arbitrageurs were long MCI and short British Telecom, what had appeared to be a riskless investment became a nightmare, with many of the world's top investors losing billions. Six weeks later, Worldcom bought MCI and the price surged back to over $40, but by then, most of the arbitrageurs had already lost.

The message is simple—**if the arbitrageurs, who have studied every** aspect of a deal, are losing billions, what chance does the individual investor have? The best advice for an investor is avoid playing takeover games. If you own a stock that is the subject of a takeover, you should recognize that once the takeover game begins, you are at a severe disadvantage. The longer and more complex the takeover battle, the weaker will be your relative position.

At all costs, do not try to outsmart the arbitrageurs. They will sometimes be wrong, as they were in the case of MCI/British Telecom. However, if they keep the Target stock at a big discount, they are saying that the deal may be in trouble. You might consider selling, even if it means walking away from what looks like a solid return. If they take the stock to a premium, you might hang on for a while to see if another bid materializes. But do not overstay your welcome. This is an extremely hard game to win.

7. AVOID IPOS, ESPECIALLY WHEN THE INSIDERS ARE SELLING

Ask about the best way to make money and people will invariably tell you about Initial Public Offerings (IPOs). IPOs give investors a chance to get in on the ground floor of the next great growth stock. The record of IPOs has been outstanding. Many have opened at twice their offering price, creating instant profits. But when individuals look at the record of IPOs, they are being misled. The charts that track the performance of IPOs may not really be applicable to the individual investor. Much of the return from IPOs comes from a few hot deals that double or triple on the opening. These profits may be tantalizing, but like having a date with a movie star, you can dream about it all you want, but it is not going to happen to you.

The way you can tell if an IPO is hot is simple. **An IPO is hot if your broker laughs at you when you ask for stock.** The way you can tell if an IPO is cold is also simple. **An IPO is cold if your broker tells you that the deal is hot, but there is still stock available for *you*.**

There are only three exceptions to this rule. First, if you happen to have a special relationship with the company that is going public, you can always call the CEO and ask to be included in the "friends and family" allotment. All underwriters set aside stock for friends of the company. But bear in mind that you will have to open a new account with the underwriter, and if the deal is hot, you will probably not get much stock, even if you are a good "friend."

If your brokerage firm is the lead manager (the name on the far left of the prospectus), and if your broker has clout, you can sometimes get a small allocation on a good deal. But before you buy, ask your broker why there is stock available for you. Do not place an order unless you get a good answer. Finally, online brokerage firms are starting to get some allocations for their individual customers. If you have an online account, you may actually get some stock.

Be especially wary of offerings from third-tier brokerage firms. When companies decide to go public, they shop for an investment banker. Generally they start with the best underwriters in their industry and work their way down. Most prefer the major international investment banks or national brokerage firms that are specialists in their industries. Some smaller companies may go with regional brokerage firms that understand their particular markets, but if a company cannot find a major national or even regional brokerage firm to do its IPO, there is likely to be something wrong. Avoid any offering in which a third-tier brokerage firm promises you a profit. If someone promises a profit, the market may be rigged, and you could get killed.

Be cautious of offerings in which all the proceeds go to selling shareholders (such as company management) and not to the company. Managements sell stock because they want to cash out. They know when their business has peaked and rarely sell when they believe that the stock will shoot up or the company will suddenly be taken over. If you see a case in which management is selling most or all of its stock, avoid it at all costs.

Thus, **for individuals, offerings are not as attractive as they may appear.** If the deal is hot, you will probably get little or no stock. If the deal is cold, you do not want it. You should always check the underwriter. If the underwriter is not a major name or if it does not have a strong record in the industry in question, avoid the deal. Finally, look at the use of proceeds. If most are going directly into the pockets of the management, walk away. Management knows more about the business than you do. If it is selling, you should not be buying.

8. AVOID STOCKS THAT YOU CAN'T UNDERSTAND

If information moves the stock market and if the people with the best information win, then it goes without saying that individual investors should avoid stocks that are too complex for them to understand. This may sound like an obvious comment, but you would be surprised at how many people buy stock in companies where the business is a complete mystery to them.

Investors love to play technology stocks. They offer the greatest opportunities for growth. But the problem is that the areas that are the fastest growing are also often the most difficult to understand. In these areas, individuals are at the greatest disadvantage against the professionals, who are experts in their own industries. If you cannot understand what the company does, how can you judge its prospects? And if you cannot understand the critical pathways in its development, how can you judge whether it is on the right or the wrong track?

How can you decide if the company is too complex for you to understand? The easiest way is to look at the company's mission statement or the description in an analyst's report. Below are mission statements from companies or descriptions from analyst reports for three high-tech firms.

LARSCOM (Source: Prospectus)

"Larscom develops, manufactures, and markets a broad range of high speed global internetworking solutions for network service providers ("NSPs") and corporate users. Larscom's products provide access to fractional T1, E1, T1/E1, frame relay, fractional T3/E3, channelized T3 services and Clear Channel ATM ("CCA") inverse multiplexing, with clear channel T3, ISDN, IMA, and ATM under development. . . ."

SUGEN Inc. (C. Anthony Butler, Ph.D., Lehman Brothers, 1/13/97)
"SUGEN . . . is a biopharmaceutical company focused on the discovery and development of small molecule drugs which target specific signal transduction pathways. Signal transduction is simply the process by which messages from the cell surface to the cell nucleus either activate or suppress genes. . . . SUGEN's expertise is specific to signaling pathways regulated by the receptors in families tyrosine kinases (TKs), tyrosine phosphatases (TPs) and serine-threonine kinases (STKs).

LANDEC Corp. (Jonathan H. Cohen, Smith Barney, 1/28/97)
Landec designs and manufactures temperature-activated polymer products using a proprietary side-chain crystallizable polymer technology. The company's proprietary Interlimer@ material exhibits novel properties with a wide range of commercial applications. Unlike other polymers, The Interlimer@ polymer can be engineered to change its physical characteristics sharply when heated or cooled through a pre-set temperature switch.

If you do not understand the mission of the company, you will never be able to track its progress or analyze its investment opportunities. Even if you can understand its business, you may not be able to understand critical changes when they occur. If McDonald's introduces a new burger, you can decide whether it tastes good as easily as a professional can. But if a biotechnology firm announces that it is in the first stage of clinical trials for a recombinant hemoglobin, you may not understand what recombinant hemoglobin is or how it can be used commercially. In addition, you may not understand the process of clinical trials.

While Coca-Cola sells the same product year after year, technology companies are constantly creating radically new products. An individual does not have to lose sleep wondering whether someone will invent a product that makes Coke obsolete, but the same may not be the case for a company in a high-tech field. Does anyone remember Visicalc, the company that invented the first spreadsheet? Everyone uses spreadsheets, but Visicalc is history.

This does not imply that individuals should never invest in high-tech stocks. Some individuals have specialized knowledge. Computer professionals may know about software or networking companies. Doctors may know about medical services companies. Many of the investors who made the most money in Internet stocks were early participants on the Web. Similarly, many investors in biotech stocks were people who had come into contact with the drugs through the illness of someone that they knew.

If you want to invest in high-tech stocks, you have three good alternatives. You can buy a specialized fund and let someone else pick the stocks. You can find an area of technology in which you have home turf and focus on what you already know. Or you can educate yourself about a particular niche and invest in stocks in that niche. But if you do not understand the business of these companies, you should avoid them.

UNDERSTANDING THE INTRICACIES OF EACH BUSINESS

Understanding a business involves more than just grasping its mission. You must also be able to understand the economic intricacies that determine its success or failure. Real estate companies seem easy to understand. They own buildings. Buildings are tangible. You live, work, or shop in them. But many real estate companies have extremely complex financial structures, and dissecting these structures to get at the company's true value can be a daunting task even for professionals.

I have always had a tough time evaluating oil companies. I understand their basic mission: to drill for or refine petroleum. I also understand the supply and demand factors that determine pricing. But I do not understand how to evaluate the reserves that each company possesses or the costs to commercially develop those reserves. This can be a critical factor in valuing these companies. One may be depleting its reserves by selling twice as much oil as it discovers, while another may be increasing its reserves by selling only half as much oil as it discovers. The company that is selling more may have higher earnings, but the company that is building reserves will be worth more over the long term.

Because oil stocks are so complex, I never invest in them unless I can find an expert who can explain these issues to me. Fortunately, my business partner, Leigh, is from Texas, so he is plugged into the oil community. Leigh has a friend named Rod Mitchell, who runs an investment company called The Mitchell Group. Rod lives in Houston and invests only in oil stocks. I once asked Rod the secret to understanding oil companies. He said, *"You have to know which people are lying to you the most. There is a big difference between chicken salad and chicken. . . ."* If after analyzing these companies, you cannot tell the difference, you should not invest in them.

9. AVOID EMERGING MARKETS

Foreign stocks are extremely tempting for most individual investors because they offer potentially strong growth and diversification from the U.S. market. Throughout the world, new economies are emerging. Older economies are restructuring. Former communist nations are turning towards capitalism, and nations are privatizing former government-owned businesses. Investment opportunities have never been more numerous or more exciting.

Despite the great opportunities, individual Americans are at a very significant disadvantage in attempting to buy foreign stocks because most have no "home turf." A broker may call and tell you an exciting story about a retailer in China or Chile. You are tempted to buy. But stop. Would you think of buying a retail stock in this country without first checking out the stores? The same rules should apply to retailers in China or Chile. You can count on the fact that the locals who are trading the stocks are visiting the stores.

Home turf is even more of an advantage in foreign markets than it is in the United States. In the United States, solid information is relatively easy to obtain. American companies report every quarter and have relatively full disclosure. Most participate in public forums and communicate with investors. Trading is also open to all investors. In many foreign markets, especially those that are emerging, the same rules do not apply. Companies report much less frequently and in much less detail, and they usually report only in their native language. Most do not actively communicate with investors. As a result, investors have to rely much more on gossip and friendships that give them insight into the operations of the companies. In such markets, individuals with connections to the companies can have a vast advantage.

Investing in foreign markets is made more complicated because **companies in foreign markets operate with their own unique sets of rules.** If everyone used the same accounting systems it would be easy to make adjustments, but there are many differences, which can lead to significant distortions. European drug companies may look like they are selling for lower multiples than their American counterparts. But when their earnings are adjusted to conform to American practices, it becomes clear that their multiples are actually much higher.

Japanese banks may look like they have attractive Price/Book ratios, but these banks rarely write-down bad loans and carry investments in other stocks at the prices at which they were bought. Since banks have many bad loans, and since the Japanese market is now selling at half of its previous level, the book values of these banks are all greatly overstated.

Companies in emerging nations often look as if they have low Price/Book ratios because they use "inflation accounting." In this practice, companies write-up their assets to their current market value to offset the impact of inflation. While this may be appropriate for the local market, it greatly distorts comparisons with American companies.

Trading can also be very different. In some countries, registration is not automatic. Companies often register shares selectively. If they do not want you as a shareholder, they may refuse to register your stock. Large numbers of trades are often turned back because companies do not like the buyers. Local tax issues can also present complicated problems.

Emerging markets also tend to have high volatility. In 1997, the market in Portugal increased by 51 percent while the market in Thailand declined by 77 percent, and this occurred while Europe had high unemployment and Thailand was developing as a major power. Would you have bet on Portugal being the winner and Thailand being the loser?

The volatility is compounded by extremely high stock turnover. Many markets have turnover four to five times higher than in the United States. In Turkey, for example, 70 to 80 percent of stocks are held for one day or less. (Talk about active trading!) Think about what it must be like to play in a market in which most investors turn over their portfolios every day. Do you think that you could beat the Turks at this game?

International economic factors can often play havoc with foreign stocks. If there is a significant change in the local currency, the value of the investments and state of the economy can change overnight. Mexico's devaluation of the peso in 1994 wiped out five years of profits in the Mexican market.

In 1997, the disasters included some of the markets that most individuals would have considered to be the most promising. In the twelve months ending December 14, 1997, world markets increased in U.S. dollars by 18.5 percent but many emerging Asian nations were bombed. The Thai market declined by a shocking 77 percent in U.S. dollars. One thousand dollars invested in Thailand on January 1 would have been worth less than $235 by December. But Thailand was not alone. The Philippine market dropped by 57 percent. The Malaysian market dropped by 70 percent. The Indonesian market dropped by 73 percent, and the South Korean market dropped by 72 percent. These markets, which had been the strongest in the world for most of the decade, lost more than two-thirds of their value in U.S. dollars in less than one year. Other Asian markets were also decimated. The Singapore market dropped by 36 percent, Hong Kong by 22 percent, and the once mighty Japan by 28 percent. Would you have known enough to walk away from Thailand and other markets before the bottom dropped out?

Would you have also pulled out of Brazil? It would appear that Brazil and Thailand have little to do with each other. Yet after the Thai market collapsed in July, Brazilian stocks dropped 23 percent in eight days. You may not have seen the connections, but someone else did.

Even the time changes can offer professionals a great advantage. European markets open about six hours before U.S. markets, while in Asia, the entire trading day occurs while you are asleep. Were you up watching at 2 A.M. when the Hong Kong market crashed?

Political instability may also play havoc with foreign markets. When Boris Yeltsin had a heart attack, the Russian market dropped by 25 percent. When he was re-elected, it doubled.

Political factors can be magnified, because many politicians have their hands directly in businesses. Government officials, or their families, often own huge stakes in major industries. In investing in these industries, it is critical to know whether they are correctly aligned politically and whether the government is secure. If you own stock in a company that is controlled by a dictator's son, that company may thrive so long as the son retains good relations with his father and the father remains in power. But if there is a coup, your company is in serious trouble. (Much of the current mess in Indonesia has been caused by the fact that former President Suharto's family owned major stakes in many of the largest industries. Note the Bre-X story that follows.)

Most significantly, you may never have a clue when a disaster is about to strike. In 1990, I was sitting in a friend's office at a Swiss bank. *"Something is strange,"* he said to me. *"Billions of dollars are pouring from the Gulf into Switzerland. I don't know what's going on, but a lot of people are in a big hurry to get their money out of the Mideast."* Two weeks later, Saddam Hussein invaded Kuwait. The United States government was shocked. Our allies were shocked. In fact, everyone was shocked, except for those people who had previously moved tens of billions of dollars to Switzerland. The people in the Gulf knew that a war was about to erupt, even if no one else did. If your opponent knows that a war is about to erupt and you do not, you are at a serious disadvantage. The problem is that in emerging markets, wars, coups, and other upheavals can occur with some regularity. As a result, **the individual should never underestimate the value of local intelligence.**

HOW TO INVEST SUCCESSFULLY IN INTERNATIONAL MARKETS

While the odds are dramatically against an individual investor, this does not mean that you should avoid all international markets. The challenge is to minimize the advantages of the professionals and the locals. There are a number of ways to accomplish this end.

Individual investors can purchase diversified international mutual funds run by professionals who understand the local markets. Individual investors, however, should resist the temptation to make short-term bets on specific country funds unless they have a real edge. If you would not have bet for Taiwan and against Thailand in 1977, stay away from making short-term bets on specific countries.

In some cases, individuals may actually have some home-turf advantage in other countries. When this occurs, they should capitalize on it. You may be in an international business and travel frequently to another country. You may have a supplier or a customer in another country. You may deal with a company that has opened branches in the United States, or you may buy products produced by foreign companies. Many Americans purchased stock in Nokia and Erickson when they bought cellular phones made by those companies.

Some of the problems of owning foreign stocks can be minimized if investors buy American Depository Receipts (ADRs). ADRs represent shares in foreign companies, but they trade in the United States. The Internet has excellent research on companies that have ADRs. You can get earnings estimates, upgrades and downgrades, read analyst reports, and visit Web sites—a huge plus because of much less rigorous reporting requirements in other countries. If you look at these investments as long-term, buying a group of ADRs will probably pay off.

The critical issue is to avoid aggressive trading in foreign markets unless you really have some special home-turf advantage. Because foreign markets are much more volatile, have different economic systems, and far less available information, the odds are set heavily against the individual American investor.

10. AVOID THE HYPE

It is always tempting for individual investors to chase gold mines, whether real or imagined. People want to believe that there is some easy way to get rich. In most cases, the biggest schemes are the most exotic. The reason is simple. The further investors go from their home turf, the less they know and the easier it is to pull the wool over their eyes. It is difficult to convince people that a fruit-flavored beer will put Budweiser out of business, because they can taste the beer, but it is not difficult to convince people that a biotech company has discovered a new gene that can stop aging, because people know little about genetics. The more removed a story is from an investor's own experience, the harder it is to separate myth from reality.

Hyped stories tend to involve dramatic new technologies, ventures in emerging markets, or both. The problem is that most of the time the hyped stories prove to be only hype and investors lose all of their capital. If a story seems too good to be true and if it is too far removed from your home turf for you to be able to understand what is going on, walk away from it, no matter how tempting it seems.

EVERY STOCK IS NOT A GOLD MINE—EVEN IF IT IS ONE

No company in recent memory holds more cautionary tales for the individual investor than that of Bre-X, the Canadian gold-mining company. Bre-X was founded in 1988 by David Walsh, the son and grandson of Canadian stockbrokers, who had spent most of his career vainly trying to push oil and mining investments. Bre-X struggled for many years. In the 1991 annual report Walsh even wrote, "Yes, we are still in business." Hardly a bullish statement.

By 1993, Bre-X had five employees. Walsh had been convicted for mishandling a stock transaction, and he and his wife had filed for personal bankruptcy because they had credit card debts of $59,500. Yet three years later, the man who went bankrupt because he could not pay off his credit cards controlled a company with a market capitalization of $6 billion! How could a penny stock in Calgary have become one of the most valuable mining companies in the world in such a short period of time? The answer tells a lot about greed and the investors' desire to strike it rich.

The story begins with John Felderhof, a geologist who thirty years ago helped discover one of the largest gold and copper deposits in the world, at Ok Tedi in the remote highlands of Papua New Guinea. Felderhof believed that similar deposits could be found in neighboring Indonesia at Busang Creek. Although the Australian company that had been backing him decided against developing the claim, Felderhof was undeterred. He convinced David Walsh to back him. Although Walsh had recently been bankrupt, he sold options in Bre-X, bought 90 percent of the Busang claim for $180,000, and hired another geologist named Michael de Guzman.

Walsh and the two geologists started to promote their opportunity. Even though no exploration had yet taken place, the price of Bre-X's stock shot up tenfold. Others obviously wanted to believe that Busang might become another Ok Tedi.

In early 1994, de Guzman found gold near Busang Creek. The stock price increased more than forty-fold. With more tests, estimates of the find were raised again, to 30 million ounces. The stock price tripled again. In three years, it had gone up 150,000 percent: $1,000 invested in 1993 was now worth $1.5 million. Yet no outside observer had actually checked the claim. No one seemed to care. Investors had caught the gold bug.

In April 1996, Bre-X moved to the respected Toronto Stock Exchange. In May, the stock price reached a high of $25. In June, it hired J. P. Morgan, a true white-shoe firm, as its investment banker, and increased its estimates of the find to more than 50 million ounces. This made Busang potentially the largest gold mine in the world.

The Indonesians began to maneuver for a stake of their own. Bre-X agreed to pay President Suharto's son $40 million to arrange the permits. A competing company, Barrick Gold, offered to buy Bre-X for $5 billion, and agreed to give Suharto's daughter 10 percent if she could force Bre-X to sell. Another company upped the offer to $5.5 billion. But Bre-X cut a deal of its own. To get capital, it sold a 15 percent stake to Freeport MacMoRan. To get the support of the Indonesian government, it gave a 10 percent stake to the government itself and sold 30 percent to a company controlled by President Suharto, his eldest son, and his closest advisor. With capital and with the government as a partner, Bre-X seemed like a can't-miss proposition. Estimates of the gold were increased again to 200 million ounces, making it by far the largest find ever.

Still, there were a number of very troubling signs that any investor should have noticed. During 1996, there was a large amount of insider selling in Bre-X. Walsh, his wife, Felderhof, the CFO, two other officers and a director sold at least $50.5 million in stock. If the find was so valuable, why were the executives selling?

In January 1997, a fire destroyed all of Bre-X's gold-deposit test results. There were no duplicates. Investors should be concerned when all of a company's records disappear, but few investors took much notice. After all, Bre-X owned the biggest gold mine in history.

In March, Michael de Guzman, the geologist who was responsible for the test results, jumped from a helicopter and committed suicide. He wrote a note claiming that he had malaria and hepatitis. De Guzman had become hugely rich. He had four wives who undoubtedly loved him, and he was about to be lionized as the man who found the largest gold mine in history. Yet few investors seemed troubled that he jumped to his death. Greed and ignorance can be a powerful combination.

On March 26, Freeport issued a statement that its independent tests revealed that there was only a limited amount of gold in Busang and it might not be profitable to mine it. On March 27, the price of Bre-X's stock dropped 83 percent. Trading was stopped for three days. When trading opened again on April 1, the volume was so great that it actually broke the computer at the Toronto Stock Exchange. A mineral services firm was hired to do an independent analysis. Three weeks later, it came back and said that there was little gold in Busang and that what gold there was could not be profitably mined. On May 3, Bre-X filed for bankruptcy. In four months, $6 billion of market value evaporated.

Bre-X did not sucker just individuals. Some of the top analysts had been pushing the stock, and some of the most respected investment advisors owned large amounts. But many individuals did fall for Bre-X. They wanted to believe that the largest gold mine in the world lay buried in the jungles of Indonesia. They were convinced by all of the action surrounding the stock, and they never asked why no one had verified the find, why there were no records, why the insiders were selling, and why the chief geologist committed suicide. Few understood anything about Indonesia or gold mines, they just wanted to believe that there was a pot (or in this case a mine) of gold at the end of the rainbow. What they found was that easy money is not always as easy as it seems. In investing in Bre-X, these individuals were as far from their home turf as is possible, at least on earth.

The smartest thing that an individual investor can do is to respect the strength of the enemy and avoid making a frontal assault in areas in which the enemy is well entrenched. For the most part, it means that the individual should avoid predicting the market, trading aggressively, trading on earnings announcements, actively trading big-cap stocks, trying to hit home runs with options, playing mergers and acquisitions, buying into IPOs, investing in businesses that are too complex to understand, investing directly in emerging markets, and chasing stories that are too good to be true.

The professional obviously has huge advantages over the individual, just as the modern army has huge advantages over the guerrilla. To defeat the professional, individuals must find their own strengths and the professionals' weaknesses and look for ways of changing the field of battle to their advantage. If individuals take the opportunities that the market offers without trying to overpower the more well-trained opponent, victory is not only possible, it is likely.

CHAPTER FOUR

Fight on Your Home Turf

In fighting a war against a stronger enemy, the most critical task for the guerrilla is to set the time and place for a battle in a manner that provides maximum advantage. The guerrilla should seek to engage the enemy along mountain passes or in jungles, where the army cannot use its planes, ships, or tanks. It should seek to fight house-to-house in cities, where it can blend in with the rest of the population. It should use every element of local knowledge to stage surprise attacks and then quickly disappear. This is its home turf. It is the terrain on which its strength can be used to the greatest advantage.

The same rules apply in investing. To offset the advantages of the professionals, the guerrilla investor must set the terms of battle to maximize the advantages of home turf. This means investing in companies you have firsthand experience with. Each investor has home turf. People come into contact with public companies in their profession, as consumers, and in their local communities. Because of their knowledge of their own terrain, individuals are often able to gain insights that Wall Street misses. This home-turf information does not come neatly packaged, like an analyst's report. But that does not make it less valuable. The task for individuals is to figure out how to use what they see around them.

HOME TURF IN YOUR PROFESSION

The most obvious home turf for an investor is the individual's own profession. People know the customers, suppliers, and competitors in their
own industry in a way that the analysts on Wall Street do not.

USE YOUR SPECIALIZED KNOWLEDGE OF TECHNOLOGY

You are a doctor. A company has come out with a new cardiology
stent that does not work properly. You know that the stent, which is
important to the company, will have to be recalled. You can sell or even
short the stock before the analysts realize that there is a problem.

A money manager friend of mine, Mike Hyman, dropped by my office
with his father, Stanley, a retired doctor. Dr. Hyman asked me if I had
ever looked at Virophama, a biotech company that was developing a cure
for viruses, including the common cold. He had read a story about the
company in one of his medical journals and had seen an interview with
the management on V-Call's Web site. He was convinced that Virophama
was on to something important. Two weeks later, Virophama made a
series of announcements and the stock more than doubled. Dr. Hyman
used his knowledge as a doctor to make a huge profit in a very short time.

You work on the Help Desk for a manufacturer of personal computers. A software company has introduced a hot new title. In the first week
after its release, you are inundated with calls from irate customers
screaming that the software does not work. You check with a competitor.
Its customers are having the same problem. The software has a major
glitch, and no one on Wall Street has yet picked it up. If the software is
an important product, the chances are good that the company producing
it will have problems. By the time that the analysts figure it out, the stock
could be down sharply.

PROFIT FROM THE RESTRUCTURING OF YOUR INDUSTRY

You are a banker. You see medium-sized banks in your market being
bought up by the large super-regionals. A gigantic consolidation is occurring.

You have an opinion as to which banks, including your own, would make attractive takeover targets. While people on Wall Street also evaluate potential mergers, you are in a better position to make investments because you know the players.

You are an independent pharmacist. You see the chains buying the independents, merging with each other, and then making deals to handle all the prescription business of large companies. They are getting stronger while you are being squeezed. It may be difficult to buy stock in someone who is trying to put you out of business, but no one understands the economics better than you.

You work for a telephone company. For years, you have watched new companies enter the long distance, cellular, local access, and paging businesses because of deregulation. You have often thought to yourself that you could now be rich if you had put in your own application for a cellular phone license. But if you can think strategically, you can still spot ways of profiting from the deregulation of your industry.

CAPITALIZE ON INDUSTRY TRENDS

The issues that you live with every day should enable you to find investment opportunities if you look at the broader implications.

You are in the oil business. You hear a rumor that someone has made a huge strike in the North Sea. If it is true, companies that are involved will be big winners, while oil prices as a whole will decline.

You manage an HMO. The government is discussing a new bill that will increase cost containment. You have attended three seminars on this bill. You know far more about the potential impact than do the analysts on Wall Street. It may be their profession, but it is your life. While you may be primarily concerned about your own company, you will find a variety of investment opportunities if you stop and look at the big picture.

You import products from Asia. The decline in Asian currencies has enabled you to obtain great bargains. Most of your prices have dropped by 20 percent, while your competitors, who produce in the United States, Europe, or Latin America, have the same costs. You know that other importers are in the same position. See if you can identify which importers will benefit and which domestic manufacturers will be hurt. They do not have to be your direct competitors. They just have to be impacted by the same industry conditions.

You are a banker. You see credit card delinquencies increasing rapidly. The chances are good that other banks have the same problems. You know which have the largest exposure. These stocks will not fare well if credit quality continues to deteriorate. Neither will the stocks of some major retailers that receive a large percentage of their earnings from credit cards.

FIND INVESTMENT OPPORTUNITIES FROM COMPETITORS

You know your competitors better than do the professionals on Wall Street. You deal with them in industry meetings and have the same customers, suppliers, and union. You have friends who work in each company. If you focus on what you know, you will find significant investment opportunities in your own industry.

You are in the clothing business. When you walk through the stores, you see a new brand that appears to be getting more shelf space. You talk to the retailers. They tell you that this brand is the hottest line in the country. You look at the merchandise. You know a winner when you see it. The analysts must wait until the company tells them about the sell-throughs, but you can act now, because you know that the goods are selling.

I have gotten many of my best investment ideas from my wife, Barbara Wyckoff. After more than twenty-five years in the retail and apparel business with such companies as Macy's, Dayton Hudson, Saks, and Liz Claiborne, Barbara has recently become an analyst for Buckingham Research. But she still spends time every week walking through the stores, talking to customers and employees. I'll keep listening to her.

You own a restaurant. One of the new theme restaurants, like Planet Hollywood, has opened down the street. You see the crowds and go in to see what the fuss is all about. You ask yourself whether these restaurants are the wave of the future or merely a fad, because you must find a competitive response. But the questions that you ask are the same that investors ask, except that your perspective is probably better. (If you had bet against the theme restaurants, you would have done quite well.)

You work for a timber company that has just sold a piece of land in California for a huge profit. You know that two competitors own much larger pieces of neighboring land. You do not know if these companies will sell, but if the price is high enough, they eventually will not be able to resist. If you buy the stocks now, you will be well ahead of most other investors.

BET ON THE PEOPLE YOU KNOW

Most people inside an industry have a better feel for the strengths and weaknesses of managers than do people on Wall Street. They see managers in the real world, rather than through spin control. They also see the changes that the managements are implementing faster than do investors. Betting on someone you know in an industry that you understand is probably the best way to invest.

You are a systems engineer. Your mentor has been hired as the president of a software firm that develops applications for electronic commerce. He wants you to join him. *"This is a chance of a lifetime,"* your mentor tells you. *"This company has an unbelievable technology."* You know his track record and see the opportunity, but you cannot relocate. That still should not stop you from buying the stock. No one knows your mentor better than you.

You read your trade press regularly. You see that a key executive has left one of your competitors. You call your stockbroker and ask how the stock has reacted. The broker tells you that there has been no announcement of the resignation. Because companies often delay reporting bad news, you have an edge on Wall Street. This is your equivalent of inside information. People in the industry know about the resignation, but professionals on Wall Street do not. Trust your instincts about executives you know. Companies are run by people, and good people run companies much better than mediocre people. When good senior managers leave one company and join another, there is usually an investment opportunity.

BEAT THE STREET WITH KNOWLEDGE OF YOUR SUPPLIERS

You work for an automobile manufacturer. The company has decided to expand its outsourcing in order to cut costs. It should be relatively easy for you to identify those products that will be outsourced and those companies that will pick up the contracts.

You are a lawyer in a small office. Do you remember when your secretary first asked you to let her open an account at one of the office supply superstores, such as Staples? She told you that its prices and assortments were much better than those of the distributor with whom you had been dealing. You started to buy from the superstores. The distributor called and complained. You guessed that you were not the only account that he was losing. You talked to a few other lawyers. Their secretaries were also using the superstores. When you stopped writing checks to the distributor and started writing checks to Staples, you could have realized that these superstores represented an exciting new investment opportunity.

You are a data processing manager responsible for handling the Year 2000 changeover for your company. You interviewed twenty companies, but found only three that appeared to have a solution to the problem. You recognize the magnitude of the Year 2000 issue and the opportunities for those few companies that are specializing in solving it. Buying stock in all of these companies will probably stand you in good stead.

PICK UP GOOD INVESTMENT IDEAS FROM YOUR CUSTOMERS

You sell diapers. One of your largest customers starts delaying your orders. You visit the stores. All the assortments are broken. There are no twelve- to twenty-four-pound diapers. You get a call from an associate in accounts receivable, who tells you that the retailer is ninety days late in payment. You feel a gnawing in the pit of your stomach. You have lived through this before. You guess that this retailer is going to go bankrupt. Analysts and investors do not have the same gnawing in their stomachs.

You sell real estate. An aggressive Real Estate Investment Trust has begun to buy up many of the mid-size real estate companies in your market at excellent prices, and is rapidly upgrading the properties. You have sold two pieces of property to the CEO of this REIT. He is the toughest negotiator that you have ever dealt with. Although dealing with him was no picnic, buying his stock will probably be a smart move.

You work for a travel agency. The new casinos in Las Vegas suddenly start offering incredible bargains. Rooms that had cost $200 are now going for $29.95. If this is a short-term price war, the stocks of the casino companies can continue to go up, but if Las Vegas now has too much capacity, they will go down. On the other hand, the airfares are sky-high. Sky-high airfares should be good for airline profits.

TRUST YOUR INSTINCTS

A friend of mine called to complain about a stock that she had purchased named North Face. My friend was in the apparel business. *"Why did you buy the stock?"* I asked.

"The broker said that the analyst had a good record and the stock was likely to go up," my friend said. *"But when I looked, I saw that the stores were packed with goods and that they were all marked down. I knew the goods weren't selling, but I still bought the stock. I could kick myself."* My friend could have saved herself a lot of money if she had trusted her instincts. She knew the business and had checked out the merchandise. The analysts may not have done the same. People in an industry often have excellent knowledge and should not be nervous about using it in making investment decisions.

HOME TURF AS A CONSUMER

People shop in stores, stay in hotels, fly on airplanes, buy cars, surf the Net, buy computer software, and select long-distance phone companies. They watch TV with their children and visit the mall. Changes that occur first on Main Street often take a long time to be recognized on Wall Street. If you can figure out what you know about your home turf as a consumer, you will have a big advantage over the professional investor.

THE PROS DON'T SHOP AT WAL-MART

Just remember, many of the professional investors live in New York City. They do not shop at Wal-Mart. There is no Wal-Mart in New York City. Besides, even if there were, how many Wall Street professionals would outfit their kids there? The professionals in New York do not see things that are happening in small-town America. They vacation in the South of France or in Vail, not in the Florida Panhandle or in the Ozarks. They may not even know where the Ozarks are. How many do you think have ever been to Branson, Missouri, or Pigeon Forge, Tennessee, two of the five most popular tourist destinations in the United States?

Wall Street professionals may invest in companies that manufacture RVs, but they do not travel in them. They do not stay at Motel 6 on business trips or buy time-share condos. They eat at Lutece and the Four Seasons, not at Denny's or Pizza Hut. They go to the theater, not to the multiplex at the mall. Many have never owned an American car, except for four-wheel drives. They shop in boutiques, not at Sears or JC Penney. They buy food in gourmet stores, not in Safeway. While the professionals know a lot about the companies they follow, they know less about average life than most Americans.

Because individuals tend to know a lot more about life in mainstream America than do most professionals on Wall Street, they have an advantage in making investments in businesses that they patronize on a regular basis. Individual investors can perceive small changes at stores as they shop, at restaurants where they eat, and in the services they purchase. These small changes are critical, because they often lead to the changes in sales and earnings on which Wall Street depends.

You are a housewife with three children. You buy clothes at T.J. Maxx. You are struck by the fact that the bargains are much better than they were at this time last year. You bought twice as much this year at T.J. Maxx. So did your friends. As a customer, you can recognize that T.J. Maxx must be receiving better bargains. This is good for T.J. Maxx and bad for the companies that produced the clothes. It will take weeks for TJX, the parent of T.J. Maxx, and the apparel companies that supply it to report sales and earnings, but your eyes can tell you when the stores have good inventory and when they do not. You can see which of the apparel companies are giving the biggest discounts. (If apparel companies are selling large amounts of merchandise to stores at big discounts, they are in trouble.) Because you shop in T.J. Maxx often, there is an excellent chance that you are seeing a trend first. Just remember, most investors and analysts do not shop at T.J. Maxx.

THE "KIM INDICATOR"

A smart portfolio manager told me that he had an almost perfect method for trading TJX. He called it the "Kim Indicator." I had never heard of the "Kim Indicator," so I asked him how it worked. He pushed his intercom and yelled, *"Kim."* A young woman, about 23 years old, came into the room. She had big, bleached-blonde hair and more than ample makeup. *"Did you go to T.J. Maxx this weekend?"* the portfolio manager asked.

"Of caws," Kim replied in a thick New Jersey accent. *"They had great rags on the new racks. I bought a dress from Jones and an outfit from Liz Claiborne. That makes three weeks in a row that I've found stuff I like."*

The portfolio manager picked up the phone. *"Buy 25,000 shares of TJX."* Then he turned to me. *"Investing in this company is simple,"* he said. *"Kim is their customer. She shops there every week. If she buys something three weeks in a row, I know that the merchandise is hot and the sales will be good. So I buy the stock. If she buys nothing for three weeks in a row, I know that the merchandise is cold and the sales will be bad, so I sell the stock. Kim is my perfect indicator. She is never wrong."*

As hokey as this story may seem, it gave this portfolio manager a perfect tool for deciding when to buy and sell the stock. He understood that a retailer is only as good as its merchandise. He lived in a penthouse on Fifth Avenue, so he had no clue as to the merchandise. But he knew that Kim was T.J. Maxx's ideal customer. In six years, the "Kim Indicator" was right far more than it was wrong, and it had a much better batting average than any of the high-priced analysts on Wall Street. Anyone who is a regular customer of a store can judge the merchandise as easily as the combination of the portfolio manager and Kim. The business is not complicated. If you are buying a lot more than you did last year, business is probably good and earnings should follow suit. If you are buying a lot less, the business is probably weak and earnings should be disappointing. Every store has its equivalent of Kim. These are the target customers the store depends on for the bulk of its business. If you are one of the target customers, you can easily judge the nature of the business. If the company starts to change its merchandising and you stop buying, don't wait to see what the analysts are going to say. When a retailer changes its focus, it usually turns off its core customer well before it attracts new customers. This almost always results in lower sales and earnings.

Even if you are not a store's core customer, find your own "Kim Indicator." There is a portfolio manager at Seligman named Marion Schultheis. Marion had once been the retail analyst at American Express. When I would talk to her about certain fashion stocks, Marion would say, *"I'll have to check with Lisa."* Lisa was not another analyst. Lisa was Marion's teenage daughter. Marion did not rely on Lisa to pick stocks, but she did rely on Lisa's opinion as a customer. One day, she told me that Lisa and her friends had stopped shopping in a particular chain because the merchandise had turned stodgy. Marion convinced American Express to sell its stock. Within six months, the price had dropped in half. Marion had inputs from every analyst on Wall Street, but she understood that it was more important to get the opinion of a customer.

GOOD SERVICE EQUALS GOOD INVESTMENTS: CONSIDER HOME DEPOT

Many years ago, when I was in Arizona, I went into a Home Depot. An associate came up to me immediately and asked if I needed help. I said I wanted to put in some outside lighting. The associate told me what to buy and how to install it. Home Depot was running an advertising campaign, "Friendship Not Membership," because its competitor, Home Club, was a membership club. Then, I went to Home Club. It took about ten minutes to find a clerk, who promptly told me that I had to become a member before he could help me. I mentioned Home Depot's advertising and asked what Home Club had to offer. "We offer membership, not friendship!" the clerk replied condescendingly. Guess where I decided to shop? It did not take a professional analyst to realize which of these companies was going to win.

I have a friend named Howard Perksy, who is the president of a very successful computer consulting company. Howard loves to putter. He can spend hours in Home Depot on Saturday discussing home improvement projects with other putterers. His wife, Wilma, always used to grumble about the amount of time he spent there while she cooled her heels outside. But then suddenly she stopped complaining and actually seemed happy to wait for him. One day I asked her about the change of heart. *"I bought a lot of Home Depot stock,"* Wilma replied. *"I figured if it could keep Howard entertained for an entire day, it must be some fantastic store. Now the stock is worth ten times what I paid for it, so Home Depot is paying for my new kitchen, bathroom, and swimming pool."* Like Wilma, anyone who bought the stock the first time she, or her husband, spent the day hanging out in the store would now be rich. It is much easier for a customer who is actually seeking help to understand and appreciate the level of service in a store than it is for an analyst who is reading financial statements.

CHECK THE LABEL FOR INVESTMENT IDEAS

Individuals can find good investment ideas from the products they purchase. You are a female baby boomer. When you started working twenty years ago, all your clothes had the same label, "Liz Claiborne." When you bought the clothes or read stories about the company's great success, you may have often thought to yourself, *"I should have bought the stock."* If you had, your profits could have paid for all of your clothes.

I remember when Snapple was first introduced. People cut back on sodas and coffees and started drinking Snapple. If I had put my money where my mouth was, I would have made lots of money when Snapple was taken over by Quaker Oats. Then the copycats started. While the financial analysts were raising earnings estimates, anyone who stood in the checkout line could have seen that people were buying less Snapple. The Snapple business turned into a black hole. Quaker Oats lost hundreds of millions of dollars and the price of its stock was driven down. Most consumers did not need an analyst's degree to realize what was happening. They only had to look at their own shopping carts.

While everybody eats, the supermarket may yield fewer opportunities than one would imagine. Because most of the consumer goods companies are multinational, it is often very difficult to correlate things that you see on the supermarket shelf with changes in earnings or stock prices. With Coke and Pepsi, the critical battlefields are now Beijing, Bombay, and Brussels, not Boston, Buffalo, and Baltimore. Nonetheless, you can still find clear investment opportunities at the supermarket. Two years ago, a price war broke out among producers of cereal. Profits and stock prices went down. When the war ended, profits and stock prices went up. Anyone who bought cereal knew what was happening.

FIND INVESTMENT OPPORTUNITIES WHEN YOU EAT OUT

A restaurant chain is no better or worse than the quality of food and service in each of its units. Restaurant chains are often difficult for analysts to follow because quality can change rapidly and because, with low barriers to entry, there are always a large number of publicly owned companies. Bloomberg lists over 160 public companies that are wholly or significantly in the restaurant business. Excluding those that are selling for $3 or less, these include:

PUBLICLY OWNED RESTAURANTS

APPLE SOUTH	CHEESECAKE FACTORY	EL CHICO
APPLEBEE'S INTERNATIONAL	CKE (Carl's Jr.)	ELEPHANT & CASTLE
ARK RESTAURANTS	CLUCKCORP.	ELMER'S RESTAURANTS
ARTHUR TREACHER'S	CONSOLIDATED PRODUCTS (Steak & Shake)	ELXSI
AU BON PAIN		FAMOUS DAVE'S
BACK BAY	COOKER RESTAURANTS	FOODMAKER (Jack in the Box)
BENIHANA	CRACKER BARREL	FRESH CHOICE
BERTUCCI'S	DARDEN (Red Lobster, Olive Garden, Bahama Breeze)	FRIENDLY ICE CREAM
BIG BUCK BREWERY	DAVCO	FRISCH'S
BLIMPIE INTERNATIONAL	DAVE & BUSTER'S	GB FOODS (Green Burrito)
BOB EVANS FARMS	EATERIES (Garfield's)	HOST MARRIOTT
BOSTON CHICKEN	EINSTEIN/NOAH BAGEL	IHOP

PUBLICLY OWNED RESTAURANTS (continued)

IL FORNAIO	PJ AMERICA	SIZZLER INTERNATIONAL
INTL DAIRY QUEEN	PLANET HOLLYWOOD	SKYLINE CHILI
J. ALEXANDERS	QUALITY DINING	SONIC CORP.
LANDRY'S SEAFOOD	QUIZNO'S	SPAGHETTI WAREHOUSE
LOGAN'S ROADHOUSE	RAINFOREST CAFE	STAR BUFFET
LONE STAR STEAKHOUSE	RALLY'S HAMBURGERS	STARBUCKS
LUBY'S CAFETERIAS	RARE HOSPITALITY	TACO CABANA
MAX & ERMA'S	ROADHOUSE GRILL	TCBY
MCDONALD'S	ROCK BOTTOM RESTAURANTS	TIMBER LODGE
MIKE'S ORIGINAL	RUBY TUESDAY	TOTAL ENTERTAINMENT
MORRISON'S FRESH	RUDY'S	TRICON GLOBAL (Pizza Hut, Taco Bell, KFC)
MORTON'S	RYAN'S FAMILY STEAK	UNIQUE CASUAL RESTAURANTS
NATHAN'S FAMOUS	SAGEBRUSH	UNO RESTAURANTS
NPC INTERNATIONAL	SBARRO	VICORP
OUTBACK STEAKHOUSE	SCHLOTZSKY'S	WALL STREET DELI
PAPA JOHN'S	SHELLS SEAFOOD	WENDY'S INTERNATIONAL
PERKINS FAMILY RESTAURANT	SHONEY'S	WSMP
PICADILLY CAFETERIAS	SHOWBIZ PIZZA TIME (Chuck E. Cheese)	
PIZZA INN		

You probably eat in some of these restaurants. If you like one, ask the manager to have the company send you financial information. The last two times I asked, the manager not only had it sent to me, but he also enclosed coupons for free dinners. If you like what you see after you get the financial information, eat in a few other branches of the chain. You want to make sure that the restaurant you eat in regularly is the rule, not the exception. Because you eat in these restaurants, you will be able to judge whether the service levels stay strong or deteriorate, which will give you a great advantage over most of the analysts.

INVEST IN THE SERVICES YOU USE

Individuals can find good investment ideas from the services that they use. Think about changes in telephone service. When cellular first started in the early 1980s, many of my friends bought cellular phones. One friend who was a doctor thought the cellular phone was the greatest invention of all time because it allowed him to play golf and still deal with his patients.

He was so infatuated with cellular that he bought shares of every company in the industry. As cellular thrived and many of these companies were bought out, my friend made huge gains.

Look around your home. How many telephone lines do you have? How many did you have three years ago? Did you count your cellular phone and beeper? Think about the companies that are making the equipment and providing the services. Their names are on the products or the bills. Rates may have come down, but you are probably spending more for phone service than you did before.

IF YOUR KIDS LOVE IT, SO SHOULD YOU

Your children can be an excellent source of investment ideas. If you watch the fads they jump on, you should be able to make a substantial amount of money. I know many parents who bought stock in Disney a decade ago, because their homes were filled with Disney movies and toys and because they made annual pilgrimages to Disney World and Disney Land. These parents may not have known Disney's p/e ratio, but they knew their kids loved the Disney characters. Few investments have ever worked out as well.

When my son was three, he and his friends became addicted to the Mutant Ninja Turtles. Every parent knew that Ninja Turtles were hot and that any company making Ninja Turtle merchandise would do well. Yet while Wall Street was still focusing on the Ninja Turtles, my son and his friends suddenly changed their allegiance to the Mighty Morphin Power Rangers, relegating the Turtles to the closet. As fast as analysts may be to jump on a new fad, they are no match for a four-year-old.

Now my kids are into Pokemon. Not surprisingly, the stock of the company that licenses Pokemon has increased 800 percent in the last year. When you went from store to store trying to buy Pokemon cards for your kids, did you ask who made them? My friend Wilma did.

Parents can beat Wall Street professionals on both the upside and the downside by listening to their small children. When Discovery Zone opened, every child had to have his birthday party there, and the stock of Discovery Zone soared. Parents had a big advantage over the professionals on Wall

Street because initially there were no Discovery Zones in New York. A year later, Discovery Zone started to fade. Any parent who took kids there realized that many of the centers were poorly run. Competing fun centers started to open, and restaurants like McDonald's opened play areas. Discovery Zone went bankrupt. Almost any parent should have seen it coming. Many professional investors did not.

As your children get older, the things they buy and use can often lead you to excellent investment ideas, especially if they are into technology and you are not. Ten years ago, your children may have been the ones who convinced you to buy an Apple computer (as well as Apple stock). Four years ago, they switched to Windows. (Of course, you sold your Apple stock and bought Microsoft and Intel.) Your children also convinced you to order a computer from Dell over the phone, something you never would have done on your own. (Of course, you bought Dell stock as well.) It was your children who brought educational software into the house and told you about the Internet, and it was your children who made you sign up with AOL (and buy its stock) instead of Prodigy.

Listen to what your children have to say about technology, and see if there are investment implications. When they talked about search engines, did you think they were babbling about missing trains, or did you stop and look at the new technology? Your children can often be your technology analysts. If you had followed most of the trends they suggested, you would have made huge sums in the market, and would now probably be out spending it on them.

Children are on the cutting edge of most trends. Think about sports. You ski, but they snowboard. You jog, but they blade. They want a fat-tire mountain bike so that they can ride off-road. Most of the time when there is a new trend, there is a company that profits from it. Watch how your children spend your money and look for investment implications. They often can enable you to be well ahead of most professional investors.

You have two teenage sons. They know what they want. The older one will only wear Tommy Hilfiger, Abercrombie, and clothes from American Eagle. The younger one, who is partial to the surfer look, will only wear Quicksilver, Vans, and clothes from Pacific Sunwear. Try taking them to Sears or Penney. They will come out empty-handed. You take them to school. Everyone is wearing the same clothes. It may be a trend or only a fad, but so long as your kids want these clothes, the companies that make and sell them will probably be hot.

Listen to their fashion judgments. They are the customers. After the terrible shootings in Colorado, I decided that Hot Topic would be vulnerable, because it sold the types of clothes that the "trench coat mafia" might wear. To my surprise, its business stayed strong. The lesson was simple. Kids who think of themselves as rebels are not going to be swayed by my view of the world. I guess I forgot what I was like when I was a kid.

WHY INDIVIDUALS BEAT THE PROFESSIONALS IN INTERNET STOCKS

In the past few years, many individuals have made substantial sums buying Internet stocks. While there is no exact measurement, I believe that individuals have well outperformed professionals in this niche. Some professionals would have you believe that individuals have done better because they did not understand that the Internet stocks were hugely overvalued. They bought the stock anyway. But I believe that this is not the answer. I believe that individuals outperformed the professionals because they were the ones who really used the Internet.

When I started writing the hardcover edition of this book, I talked to many of my friends who ran brokerage houses. Most of them had never invested online and never used the Internet for investment research. They did not need to. They had their own proprietary systems that cost them thousands of dollars a month. They did not care about Yahoo! finance, E-Trade, Ameritrade, or any of the other financial services on the Web, because they were professionals.

Individuals, however, understood the revolution because they were part of it. They opened online accounts, traded for $0.01 a share, got their research online, and posted on the message boards. For them, online investing was home turf. For the professionals, it was irrelevant.

The same is true with other Internet services.

- Many professionals did not open AOL accounts. They got their e-mail at work.
- Professionals did not need to save a few dollars by shopping for travel through Priceline.com, Travelocity, or Preview Travel. They had their own corporate travel departments.
- Professionals did not buy inexpensive computers through Onsale, Cyberian Outpost, or Value America. They had corporate purchasing departments.
- Professionals did not enter the various Web communities, because they had their own investment communities.
- Professionals did not subscribe to The Street.com, Marketwatch.com, or other investment services, because they had Bloomberg and First Call.
- Professionals did not trade Beanie Babies on Ebay. They were trading stocks.

In short, the individuals scooped the professionals on the Internet because it was their own home turf. They used the Web to make investments, buy computers, purchase tickets, join communities, and trade products with each other. For the professional, the Web was an intriguing concept. For many individuals, it was a way of life. Because individuals used the Internet much more than the professionals did, they were able to gain home-turf advantage that enabled them to well outperform the professionals in these stocks.

IF YOU NEED IT, SO DOES YOUR PORTFOLIO

Individuals can find good investment ideas as they reach middle age and start to plan for their retirement. You are 50. Your kids are in college. Your primary concerns are to build equity for your retirement and secure enough insurance so that you do not have to worry about catastrophic problems. Every baby boomer you know is in the same position. If you believe baby boomers are going to keep saving for retirement, then buy stock in the mutual fund companies that are managing your money and in the brokerage firms that handle your accounts. And if you believe that baby boomers are going to keep buying insurance, then buy stock in the insurance company you use. Because you are older, you look at life differently than does a young analyst, but because many people are getting older, your view of what's hot may turn out to be correct.

IF RETIREES WANT IT, INVEST IN IT

In many ways, retirees are more on the cutting edge of future trends than younger people. The population is aging. No segment is growing as fast as retired people. The trend will only accelerate. Within fifteen years, masses of baby boomers will retire. You can use the experiences of people who are retiring now to discover some of the best investment opportunities for the next several decades.

Your parents have just retired. They no longer buy work clothes or commute. They have more leisure time. Your father takes up golf. He buys Big Bertha woods, special irons, and new golf clothes. Your mother takes up gardening, crafts, and reading. Companies produce and sell these products. Your parents spend their winters in Florida or Arizona. You think about what these markets will be like when tens of millions of baby boomers begin to retire. Local home builders, land developers, real estate investment trusts, banks, hospitals, service providers, and other companies in these markets will benefit from the influx of retirees.

You watch health issues begin to crop up for your parents and their friends. They are taking more drugs, perhaps including some of the new biotech medicines. While analysts know a lot about a company, no one should know more about an experimental drug than patients or their immediate families. The analysts are earning a living, but for the families it may be a question of life or death. If a new drug begins to work, look at the stock of the company that produces it. You can see the success of the product firsthand.

Older people also visit the hospital and the doctor more often. You might be impressed with the hospital, HMO, or nursing home they use. You might find one with a strategy you believe is unique. If you are dealing with it on a daily basis, you will have a reasonably good perspective on the quality of its management. Many companies in these industries are public, and many are growing rapidly. Some, however, are having problems with reimbursing patients and doctors. If your HMO is not paying you on time, it is in trouble.

Illness can lead to other investment opportunities. When my father became ill, he had to be confined to a wheelchair. I investigated the market and found that one company, Invacare, made the best products. I had remembered wheelchairs as old, clunky products, but new state-of-the-art materials had made them much lighter and more mobile. As I watched Invacare making moves to dominate the market, I decided to buy the stock. I was sure that wheelchairs would be a growth industry for an aging population.

Individuals should use their experience as consumers to find investment ideas, but they should make sure that the information is significant to the company's fortunes. You should not sell stock in an oil company because the attendant in your service station did not wash your windows. Nor should you sell stock in Tribune Corp. because the Cubs missed the playoffs. (By that logic, no one would ever own stock in Tribune, a great company, which owns the Cubs, not a great team.) Nonetheless, the information the consumer obtains is critical to understanding a company and its products. If you can utilize your home-turf information, you have a chance against the professionals.

HOME TURF FROM YOUR COMMUNITY

A person's community can often yield tidbits of information that provide a significant edge in investing against Wall Street professionals. A community is the town in which someone lives, but it's also the collection of social circles in which the individual interacts. As people read the local newspaper, attend parties with their friends, or chat with former schoolmates, they constantly come in contact with information about public companies. Most of the time, people ignore this information as being of little value, but this is a mistake.

The most obvious source of information in your community can come from a direct personal relationship with a senior executive of a public company. CEOs, CFOs, and other senior executives belong to clubs and civic organizations, participate in sports, have children, and are often extremely visible in a community. If you are friendly with a senior executive of a company, you have an advantage that most analysts would kill for. Don't be shy about utilizing it. The analysts would utilize it if they had the contacts.

You are in a bridge game with the president of a small chain of funeral homes. He misses the game two weeks in a row. You call his office to see if he is all right. His secretary tells you that he is away on business in a particular city. You know that the largest national funeral home operator is in that city and that it has been buying up regional chains. Is an acquisition of your friend's company in the works? Perhaps. When he comes back, you ask him, but he tells you that he cannot comment on it. This is your friend. You have played bridge with him for ten years. If nothing was going on, he would have told you. You think that his chain could be an acquisition target. You will never get perfect inside information. That would be illegal. But you can make a guess. If your guess is that there will be a deal, take a chance and buy the stock. In the same position, almost every professional on Wall Street would. The only difference is that most professionals do not play bridge with your friend.

Many people live in small cities that are home to a few prominent public companies. The "feel" that individuals have for local public companies often gives them an edge over the professionals on Wall Street, especially if the company is in a small or medium-sized city that is somewhat distant from the major financial centers. In fact, the farther your city is from the major financial centers, the greater the likelihood that you can find an edge in picking good local companies.

People in these communities tend to see emerging companies first. They often know the management, either directly or by reputation. They learn about the strategy of the company from stories in the local media, and they hear the "buzz" about the company from friends who work there. Most analysts and investors, without direct contact, want to wait until the sales and earnings come through, but people with local knowledge can often make a bet based on their direct perspective of the company and its management.

Arkansas. The people in Arkansas discovered Wal-Mart well before analysts on Wall Street. Not only did they shop in the stores, they also knew that Sam Walton was a genius, and that should have been enough for any investor.

Seattle. The people in Seattle discovered Microsoft before the rest of the country. A decade ago, everyone I knew from Seattle talked with reverence about Bill Gates and his company. They all also owned stock.

Omaha. The same may be said for the people of Omaha and Warren Buffett. Before Buffett became a major international investment seer, he was a local businessman, but the people in Omaha knew he was something special, and they invested in Berkshire Hathaway.

Oregon. The entire state of Oregon is a paradise for runners. Fifteen years ago, my nephew, Sam Helphand, who was then a boy, told me that he wanted to buy stock in Nike. To me, Nike was just another sneaker, but to Sam, it was a local religion. Sam may have been just a kid, but living in Oregon, he knew a great company when he saw one.

Silicon Valley. I have a good friend from the Bay Area. He is a professor of economics and one of the least computer-literate people I know. Yet in the past decade, he has built a great investment record in technology stocks. His philosophy is simple. When he socializes with people in technology, he listens to all of the gossip. When someone talks about a new IPO, he always asks, *"How smart is the management?"* If his techie friends tell him that the management is the smartest in its niche, he buys the stock. Sometimes he calls and asks me what the company does. But when I read him the excerpts from analysts' reports, his interest level fades quickly. He is not trying to analyze the technology himself. Instead, he is betting on the advice of his colleagues, who do know technology.

The professor is lucky to live in Silicon Valley, because this area has been the spawning ground for many successful technology companies. But every region has been the spawning ground for some type of industry. There are clusters of technology companies around Seattle, Salt Lake City, Boston, Austin, and the Research Triangle of North Carolina. There are entertainment companies in Los Angeles, furniture companies in

North Carolina, automobile companies in Michigan, petroleum companies in Texas and Oklahoma, agricultural companies in the farm belt, and government contractors near Washington, D.C. People in these regions often learn about the companies before most professional investors. The trick is to recognize the value of the information that they receive from the people in their local communities.

THE INTERNET COMPLETES THE HOME-TURF ADVANTAGE

Many individuals think that the information they obtain on their home turf is not as valuable as that obtained by professional investors. Professionals obtain hard inputs, such as earnings announcements, annual and quarterly reports, earnings estimates and First Call notes from analysts, and charts from technicians. Individual investors receive soft inputs, such as gossip at a trade show or the experience of eating in a restaurant. Of the two, the hard inputs would appear to be the more valuable and difficult to duplicate. But this may not be the case.

With the emergence of the Internet, business television, and other forms of communications, individual investors can receive much of the hard data available to the professionals on a relatively timely basis. On the other hand, the professionals cannot receive the firsthand experience of the individual, unless they actually live it. **The Internet can provide the individual with the earnings statement from Wal-Mart, but it cannot provide the professional with the experience of actually shopping in the stores.** Thus, the Internet gives the individual the hard data on which the professional has depended without giving the professional the soft data that the individual can use. This makes the soft data increasingly valuable. The task for the individual is to combine the soft inputs from home turf with the hard data on the Internet to gain a more complete financial picture of the company in question.

Chapter Five

Attack the Enemy's Weaknesses

Any enemy, no matter how strong, has a weakness. In fact, size itself can be a disadvantage. Like a modern army, Wall Street professionals can bring a huge number of weapons to bear against an individual. If power is matched directly against power, the individual has no chance. But the very size of the professionals can be a liability because it is difficult for them to change directions quickly or disguise their actions. Just as the guerrilla can capitalize on the lack of mobility of a mechanized army by attacking quickly and then retreating into the jungle, so the guerrilla investor can capitalize on the lack of mobility of the professional by finding those areas in which the professionals' size and strength actually work against them. There are five strategies that the individual investor should consider:

1. Buy smaller capitalization and under-followed stocks.
2. Buy and hold.
3. Act before the professionals can change direction.
4. Capitalize on the professionals' need for short-term performance.
5. Allow the professionals to overextend themselves, and then counterattack.

BUY SMALLER AND UNDER-FOLLOWED STOCKS

If institutions have a big advantage in buying and trading bigger stocks, they often have a corresponding disadvantage in buying and trading smaller stocks. This disadvantage works to the benefit of the individual.

TOO SMALL FOR THE BIG GUYS

Despite the excellent potential of many small stocks, most institutions cannot be bothered with them. A money manager can only buy 4.9 percent of a company's stock before having to file documents with the Securities and Exchange Commission. If the holdings go over 10 percent, there are restrictions on the manager's ability to trade. So, as a rule, managers very rarely buy more than 10 percent of a company.

Last year, Philip Sawyer, the chairman of a company named Fusion Medical, came to my office to visit. Philip was very excited about the prospects for his company, but he was frustrated that analysts and institutional investors seemed to be ignoring Fusion Medical. The reason was simple. Fusion had a market capitalization of only about $12 million and a float (number of shares available for trading) of less than $2 million. If a money manager bought 5 percent of Fusion, that investment would be only $600,000. While this might seem like a lot of money to you, it is nothing to a professional. Further, even 5 percent might be difficult to buy, because this would represent 20 percent of the float.

Investment advisors own varying numbers of stocks, but an advisor managing a $5 billion fund ($\frac{1}{20}$ the size of Fidelity Magellan) would rarely own more than 200 different stocks. With 200 stocks in a fund of $5 billion, the average position would be $25 million. If this advisor bought 5 percent of Fusion, **the $600,000 would represent about one-hundredth of 1 percent of the portfolio**. The advisor would have to own 8,333 stocks of similar size to fill a portfolio of $5 billion.

Because it is impossible for any portfolio manager to keep track of 8,333 stocks, many of the larger funds avoid smaller stocks. Some have minimum cap sizes as high as $2 billion. Others have minimums of $1 billion. For companies with a market capitalization of $200 million, the number of institutions that can invest in it is limited. At \$200 million, a 5 percent position is only \$10 million. For the Magellan Fund, this represents $1/_{10,000}$ of the portfolio. Even for someone managing \$5 billion, it only represents $1/_{500}$ of the portfolio.

If a stock with a \$200 million market capitalization is too small, how do you think most money managers will react when an analyst calls about a stock with a \$12 million market cap? They may laugh, hang up, or yell at the analyst for wasting their time with a stock that is too small to own. No matter what the promise, most managers will never buy a stock this small. (Unless it was a really great idea. Then they might buy it for their own personal portfolio.)

Even if a portfolio manager could invest in smaller stocks, it is extremely difficult to trade them. A professional cannot quickly move large sums in or out of a small, illiquid stock. Smaller companies also tend to be less well followed, so institutions lose some of their advantages in terms of information.

Two final factors also benefit the individual investor in small-cap stocks. If the company does not have listed options, professional investors cannot utilize some of the sophisticated options games that give them an advantage over the individual. In addition, if the stock is not in a major index, many investors cannot buy it. Some institutions have a charter that requires them to buy only stocks that are in a particular index, such as the Dow Jones or the S&P 100. If institutions are blocked from buying a stock, either by choice or by charter, the competition for that stock is much less, and the opportunities for the individual investor are much greater.

THIS REQUIRES PATIENCE

While individual investors should trade smaller capitalization stocks, these stocks do have one significant problem. Because they are small, they often trade schizophrenically. A stock may sit there for months, without moving, because it has been ignored by institutions and analysts. The fundamentals and the earnings may be there, but no one may care.

Then suddenly something will happen. The company may have a major announcement. The CEO may appear on television. The stock may get picked up by analysts at a major brokerage firm. An institution may decide to build a position, or groups of individual investors may pick up on it. Suddenly, the stock that had languished in boredom becomes the focus of attention. With a small float, the stock can often double or quadruple in a very short period of time.

Fusion Medical was such a stock. It had traded at about $3 for a long period, on almost no volume. Then Fusion gained key approvals for its main product and made presentations to the investment community. In a matter of weeks, the stock more than tripled.

When this occurs, the individual can often go along for an extended ride. If professionals decide to pick up a stock, the long-term upside can be substantial. The individual simply needs to remember why he or she bought the stock and be willing to sell it when the reasons for owning it are no longer valid.

In late 1998, I bought a major position in Intertan, the operator of Radio Shack stores in Canada and Australia. The stock was selling at $4, down from an all-time high of more than $60. Trading volume was very light and no one seemed to care about the company. After doing my research, I bought some stock and waited for it to move, but it barely budged. I listened to the conference calls, but there were few participants. I even tried to talk it up to my friends, but most were unimpressed. Each day I looked at it and growled impatiently. I was sick of watching the stock.

However, in early 1999, the pieces started to fall into place. Intertan brought in a very bright and aggressive new CEO, Brian Levy, who seemed to love the business. The company sold its money-losing business in England and resolved a major tax liability in Canada. Sales started to soar, and earnings followed suit. Suddenly three analysts picked up coverage, and investors began to talk about Intertan as a growth company. By mid-July 1999, the stock was over $20. The ride was fun, but waiting for it to move was torture.

BOOKS-A-MILLION—FROM DOG TO INTERNET DARLING

Perhaps my favorite example of an ignored stock is Books-A-Million, the third-largest book retailer in the United States. When I first noticed

Books-A-Million, the stock was selling for 7x earnings, 20 percent of sales (a very low ratio), and at a substantial discount to its book value. At the time, Books-A-Million was being battered by competition from Barnes & Noble and Borders, but it still had a strong position in the South and good distribution. It was my hope that someday the competition might abate and the price of Books-A-Million's stock might rise.

For more than one year, I watched the stock sit there. It barely budged, in either direction. Volume remained extremely light. Each day I wanted to sell it, but I resisted the temptation in the hope that it might get discovered and move up to $7 or $8.

Then, on the Wednesday before Thanksgiving 1998, the company announced it was opening an "enhanced" Web site. The initial introduction of its Web site had gone unnoticed. This was not a new business. It was just an enhancement of an old business. But with all of the excitement surrounding the Internet, investors suddenly became excited about Books-A-Million.

The stock had closed below $5 the night before. But by noon, it had surged to over $16. I sold a little stock, and congratulated myself as I watched it close at $12. My congratulations were a little premature. Two trading days later, the stock was selling for $44. The third-place book retailer had now become an "Internet" play, with millions of shares being traded each day.

As analysts and day traders picked up the stock, I realized that the game in Books-A-Million had changed. This was no longer the ignored stock, selling at a huge discount to its real valuation. This was now a hot growth stock.

I decided to sell the rest of my Books-A-Million. I had bought an ignored retailer, and I now owned an Internet stock. I had waited one year for it to move, and in three days, it had gone up almost 1,000 percent. Yet it was still essentially the same company that no one had wanted only a few days before.

The moral of these stories is simple. Small stocks may sit for months or even years before being discovered. If you own them, they will try your patience. Waiting for someone to discover them can be the most frustrating part of investing. Each day you will look at these "dogs" and want to dump them. When the game changes, it can change suddenly. With a small float and little previous coverage, these stocks can soar as they get discovered. Now, the hardest decision for all investors is to decide when to sell. The patience, which had been a virtue, may be a liability as the stock gets sucked into a more volatile arena.

WHY THE PROS IGNORED BURLINGTON COAT

Burlington Coat Factory, an operator of off-price stores, is not a small company. In fiscal 1996, BCF had sales of over $1.6 billion and a net worth of $413 million. It also had almost 50 million shares outstanding. But at the end of 1996, there were no major analysts following Burlington. When no analysts follow a company, there are no earnings estimates or guidelines that investors can use to judge whether the company is doing better or worse than expected. There is also no one promoting the stock. Institutional investors are extremely busy keeping abreast of the stocks they own and listening to analysts and salespersons. If no one is posting First Call notes on a company, many institutional investors forget that it exists.

Why did a company like Burlington Coat Factory have no analyst coverage? There were four key reasons:

1. Burlington did not have investment-banking business. The company had very strong cash flow, so it did not need to do offerings, which require investment bankers. Nor did it need investment bankers for acquisitions. Without investment-banking revenues, brokerage firms had no major incentive for following it.

2. Burlington had low trading volume. Burlington is very closely held, with 56 percent of the shares owned by officers and directors. As a result, it does not trade very much. For all of 1995, Burlington Coat traded 23.4 million shares for a total of $192 million. In one year, Burlington Coat had a dollar trading volume equal to what General Electric did in an average day. At these levels, the brokerage commissions are not sufficient to support the cost of analyst coverage.

3. Burlington had disappointed investors in the previous two years. Analysts hate to follow small companies that have disappointed them, so several dropped coverage.

4. Burlington had never done a good job communicating with investors and analysts. It rarely had conference calls, did not report monthly sales, and did not provide analysts with a wealth of data. Analysts like to be spoon-fed and do not like companies where getting information is like pulling teeth.

Low trading volume not only discourages analysts from covering the company, it also makes it much more difficult for the institutions to trade the stock. With Burlington's small float, it could take a major institution months to establish a 2 million share position, and when that position was finally acquired, it would still represent only $18 million, based on the price at the end of 1996. Many institutions need to put five to ten times that much money to work in each stock that they buy.

As difficult as it is to build such a position, liquidating it can be even harder. Suppose you owned 2 million shares of Burlington Coat and decided to sell. If the stock only traded 95,000 shares a day, and you accounted for all of the volume, it would still take you a month to liquidate the position, and during that month, the constant selling would probably push down the price. In such a situation, the best hope for the manager is to find another institution that wants to build a position in Burlington Coat. But without analyst sponsorship, it is difficult to interest another institution in buying.

If the company reported unexpected bad news, your only choices would be to dump the stock for an extremely low price and thank God that you only own a few illiquid stocks or to sit tight and hope that business would eventually get better. Because of size, the institutional investor is often locked in while the individual investor is not. An individual can almost always find another individual to buy 1,000 shares of stock, but the institution may have to wait months for another institution to step up and buy. **In a stock with a limited float, the small**

trading volume almost always benefits the small investor at the expense of the large institution.

The small float and lack of analyst coverage combined to put Burlington Coat below the radar screen for institutions, but they should not have been negatives for individual investors.

- While bankers like companies that want to raise money, individuals should like companies with low levels of debt and high free cash flow.
- High levels of insider ownership should be a strong positive for individual investors. If insiders own 56 percent of the shares, you can be certain that they are keenly interested in maximizing shareholder value. Their ownership perspective may be much more long term than that of most professionals, but this should be a positive, not a negative, for the individual investor.
- The small float, which discourages institutions, creates opportunities for individuals, who now actually gain an advantage in trading.
- When analysts walk away from stocks, individuals are better off because they can study these companies without being concerned about analysts suddenly changing their estimates.
- When companies do a poor job of communicating, it is the professionals, not the individuals, who are disadvantaged. Individuals do not usually keep track of monthly sales or get on conference calls. They can continue to obtain home-turf inputs while the institutions are shut out. **Never confuse the analysts' frustrated desire for information with the health of the company, especially if management is the largest shareholder.**

After the original edition of this book was published, things began to change for Burlington Coat. Sales and earnings improved. The company increased its expansion rate. New merchandising initiatives began to pay off, and the company hired an experienced investor relations executive. Not surprisingly, the price of the stock went from $8 to $24.

Then an interesting thing happened. While Burlington Coat was still closely held and did not have investment-banking business, its growth was too much for analysts to resist. At least four big-name analysts initiated coverage with "buy" ratings. Burlington Coat, which had been ignored for so long, suddenly became a "growth" retailer.

Needless to say, the winter of 1998–99 was unusually warm. There was no snow in New York. People were in shirtsleeves in January. While the rest of Burlington's business remained solid, coats died. Burlington reported weak comparable store sales and weaker earnings. The "growth" retailer was abandoned by the analysts, who decided that its business was too dependent on the weather. The stock dropped back to $11.

The moral of Burlington is simple. Stocks that are ignored often offer unusual potential for individual investors. But when these stocks are discovered, the rules of the game change.

OTHER STOCKS PROFESSIONALS IGNORE

You should not jump on a stock merely because no analyst covers it. However, just as individuals have a clear advantage in smaller stocks, they also have an advantage in larger companies that are under-followed. The fewer analysts that follow a company, the lower the flow of information to the institutions. Some companies may not be well followed because they have a limited float, no investment-banking business, have disappointed the Street, or do not like to communicate with analysts. **But some are not well covered merely because they do not fit into neat industry groups.**

Most analysts cover specific industries. Software analysts cover software companies. Oil analysts cover oil companies. Analysts are rated against their peers in an industry. Substantial dollars are involved for those elected to the *Institutional Investor* All-American Team. So analysts want to focus all their energy on one narrow segment. Few want to waste their time following a company that is outside their industry. To do so would hurt their compensation. As a result, most companies in well-followed industries have ample analyst coverage. (Burlington Coat

Factory, for the reasons cited above, is an exception.) But many companies that are not in major industries fall through the cracks.

Harman International is a world-class maker of loudspeakers and sound systems (JBL, Infinity, and Harman Kardon, among others). Because there are no other major publicly owned consumer electronics companies in the United States, Harman had almost no coverage for many years. The same situation applies to Valmont Industries, one of the two world leaders in the irrigation business and one of the top manufacturers of street lamps and towers used for wireless communications.

Larger companies can have limited coverage if they bridge industries in a manner that makes it difficult for analysts to follow them. USA Networks is now covered by many media analysts. But when it was Home Shopping Network, it was covered by very few. Its problem was that it was part retailer and part broadcaster. Retail analysts did not want to cover it because it was a broadcaster, and media analysts did not want to cover it because it was a retailer.

Much the same happens with conglomerates. When Sears owned Allstate, Dean Witter, Discover Card, Prodigy, and Homart, it was undercovered, even through it was a Dow component. In order to follow Sears, an analyst had to understand the retailing, insurance, stock brokerage, credit card, real estate, and online industries. Now that these businesses have all been sold or spun-off, Sears is better covered, and so are Allstate and Dean Witter (now Morgan Stanley Dean Witter).

No matter what the reason, companies that are poorly followed often offer good opportunities for individuals. With a lack of analyst coverage, the professional no longer has substantial advantages in terms of information, and the individual has a much better chance of winning.

There are many ways to find out how many analysts cover a company. Most of the financial sites will give you a list of the number of analysts following a particular stock and the analysts' current ratings. Some, such as Zacks.com, will allow you to screen for various categories, such as high or low following. But you should not be on a treasure hunt for the world's most hidden companies. Instead, you should focus on companies that you find on your home turf. If one of these companies has limited analyst coverage, consider it an advantage.

BUY AND HOLD

If the professionals have an advantage in trading, the individual may actually have an advantage in not trading. This does not mean that all individuals should hold stocks forever, but it does mean that individuals should resist the temptation to over-trade.

Professionals feel great pressure to trade stocks. Salespersons and analysts are paid to make trades, not to hold hands. They do not get paid more if the stocks go up and less if they go down. Their only interest is to make the customer take some action. How often has a broker called to say, "I love your portfolio. Don't do anything!"

Institutional investors are bombarded with calls from analysts and salespeople. Salespeople are usually pretty good at persuading. That is why they are salespeople. Companies also give impressive presentations. It is hard to have lunch with the CEO of a successful corporation and not be tempted to buy the stock. The individual faces little of this. A broker may push trades, but if the investor does not respond, the broker will stop calling, and online brokers do not call. Since the individual has no great advantage in terms of trading, getting no calls or lunch meetings may be a hidden benefit. While standing pat is not as much fun as making trades, it can be more profitable.

TRADING STOCKS CAN HURT PERFORMANCE

The pressure to trade stocks does not necessarily improve performance. Think about a trade. There is a buyer and a seller, but only one will be right. Most trades involve institutional investors. When a 100,000-share block trades, both the buyer and the seller are probably large institutions, staffed by highly paid and respected professionals. But once the cost of trading is taken into account, the net impact is that the two institutions, in sum, will end up behind. It is difficult to tell a portfolio manager who is struggling to overtake a competitor that trading will reduce his overall return.

Sometimes, portfolio managers buy and sell stocks because their view of the market changes. One portfolio manager buys drugs and sells technology, while the other fund manager buys technology and sells drugs. Sometimes professionals buy and sell stocks because they think that one will give them a better return than the other. One buys General Motors and sells Ford, while another buys Ford and sells General Motors. (Although they both probably drive Mercedes.) One may be right and the other wrong, but the market as a whole will not change.

If both stocks move by the same amount, both managers will have been wrong. The only institution that will have profited was the brokerage firm that handled the trade. There is a cost to trading. For the institution, it may not be significant. Institutions pay only about $0.05 per share in fees when they trade. If they bought and sold Ford and General Motors every year for ten years, the total cost for both stocks would be $1.00 per share. At an average price of $40 per share, this is only $2^{1}/_{2}$ percent. While this is not enough to discourage a manager from making a trade, it still could end up being the difference between outperforming or underperforming the market.

For the individual, the economics of buying and holding can be more compelling. If the individual trades on the Internet, the costs are lower than those of the professional. But if the individual trades through a traditional brokerage firm, the commissions will be much higher. At $0.25 per share, the cost of trading Ford and General Motors each year for ten years will be $12^{1}/_{2}$ percent of the stock price. More significantly, individuals must also pay capital gains taxes if they have a profit. With the difference between the short- and long-term capital gains rates, there can be a substantial tax penalty for making a trade. Had the individual stood pat, he would have had no transaction costs or tax liabilities, and he probably would have come out ahead.

WHAT'S YOUR TRADING RECORD?

Make a list of the last thirty trades you have made. In a bull market, most of the stocks you bought probably went up, but what about the stocks you sold? Compare the returns of the stocks you bought with those you sold. Did the stocks you bought do better? In many cases, the answer for the individual, as for the professional, is no.

Now assume that you had not made any of the trades and had, as a result, not paid any taxes. Would you be better off if you had stood pat? Don't be distressed if the answer is yes. With taxes and trading costs, **most investors would have been better off not making trades.** This is not to say that you should buy stocks and hold them forever, but it is to say that most investors hurt themselves by over-trading. If you would have been better off standing pat, think carefully before swapping one stock for another in the future.

Thus, the individual can compete on a level playing field against the professional by buying good companies at attractive prices and then holding them. While it is difficult to sit there and watch stocks go up and down without doing anything, you should remember that as the stocks trade, half of the professionals are wrong. **Because you do not face the same short-term performance pressure as the professional, buy and hold is a strategy that can and will work.**

ACT BEFORE PROFESSIONALS CAN CHANGE DIRECTION

Professional investors, like mechanized armies, may have the advantage of size. But size can often become a liability when it is time to change directions. It is difficult for professionals to wind or unwind a position without being noticed. Here the individual's smaller size can become an asset. While individuals should adopt a "buy and hold" strategy, they must also be ready to act when professionals telegraph major changes in direction.

If a stock has been moving up with heavy volume, it will usually continue to move up. The buying might get weaker or stronger, but the direction will not change. Because major institutions do not usually go from aggressive buyers to aggressive sellers, there are very often clear signs when a stock is getting ready to change directions.

Many people think that stocks change directions when major events are announced, but most events are foreshadowed in the action of the stocks. Look at stocks that get clobbered on a particular day. Most had already been heading down. In the three months before it announced its disaster, Oxford Health Plans had already declined from $89 to $68³/₄. The market had foreshadowed that something bad was going to happen.

Look at stocks that suddenly jump up. Most had already been moving to new highs. Once again, the market had foreshadowed the move. The reason that the market foreshadows the future direction of individual stocks is that the very size of the professionals makes it difficult for them to change directions quickly. **Because the professionals have to move cautiously, tops and bottoms of markets and stocks are usually well defined.**

Institutions have to act carefully when they move in or out of a stock. Think about the portfolio managers who own more than 10 million shares of General Electric. Even though GE has great liquidity, it is difficult to sell this large a block without disrupting the market. The portfolio manager has two choices: Dump the stock at a discount or parcel it out carefully so as not to disrupt the market. Most will choose the latter alternative to avoid a big loss.

When a portfolio manager starts to sell a major block of a stock that has been going up, most investors can easily spot the trading. Volume will increase as the stock plateaus and begins to drop. If the institution owns more than 5 percent of a company, it will have to file a record of its sale. This filing may trigger other selling, since most investors will believe that the institution will further reduce its holdings. The institution, however, must sell carefully because it needs an orderly market in order to unwind its position (in other words, it does not want to trigger widespread selling). If individual investors see selling pressure accelerate, they can often move faster than institutions in selling their stock.

WHEN BUFFETT MOVES . . .

The problem becomes more complex if the institution owns a huge stake and is a famous investor. At the time of the last filing, Warren Buffett owned 200 million shares of Coca-Cola. When investors saw Buffett building a position, they bid up the price of Coke, under the assumption that Buffett was usually right. But if Buffett's buying caused the price of Coke to go up, his selling would cause the price of the stock to go down. You cannot move 200 million shares without attracting notice, and in Buffett's case, without scaring some investors.

This is exactly what happened on August 21, 1997, with another of Buffett's holdings, Wells Fargo. On that day, the price of the bank closed down $7.50 on fears that Buffett had reduced his holdings. In fact, Buffett had not reduced his holdings. Instead, he had received permission to have "partial" confidentiality, which meant that he could keep some holdings from public view for up to fifteen months. When investors looked at his filings and saw no mention of Wells Fargo, they panicked and shaved $1.3 billion from its market value in one hour. It was a billion-dollar misunderstanding, and Buffett had not even sold his stake.

ANALYSTS TELEGRAPH THEIR ACTIONS

Like portfolio managers, analysts also have to move carefully. Even if analysts discover new information that radically alters their view of a company, they usually cannot change from buy to sell overnight. Analysts do not want to alienate the companies, who may be valuable investment-banking clients, and they do not want to alienate their customers, who may have built major positions in a company on their recommendation.

Imagine you were a money manager who had just bought 1 million shares of a stock at $31 based on an analyst's recommendation. The next day, the analyst calls and says that business is softer than plan and that you should dump the stock at $28. How would you react? You would probably slam down the phone, curse, and perhaps even instruct your trading desk to stop doing business with the analyst's firm.

Because analysts do not like to lose major accounts or make themselves look like idiots, they usually telegraph their actions so that clients do not get blind-sided. Instead of rapidly changing their views to conform to the new reality, they spoon-feed the information. When this occurs, the small investor has the advantage of speed.

The actions of the institutions in building or liquidating positions are delineated in the charts of stocks. (See chapter 7 for a discussion of using charts.) If investors utilize the charts, they will be able to see when major institutions are preparing to change direction.

The individual can thus **exploit the professionals' size by capitalizing on their inability to change directions quickly.** Watch the charts for clear signs of a bottom before buying. The professional may need to move early in order to buy a meaningful position, but the individual can wait until the stock has stopped going down and built a solid base. Watch for clear signs of a top. In most cases, stocks that have been rallying do not suddenly drop. They stop going up and strain to maintain price on higher volume. When you see a top, sell. The professional cannot unload a major position all at once, but when professionals start to lighten up on a stock, the signs of a top become unmistakably clear. Because the individual has much less capital, it is easy to spot these changes and act.

CAPITALIZE ON END-OF-QUARTER TRADING GAMES

Investment advisors feel intense pressure to show good performance before the end of the quarters, when ratings are totaled. The difference between 15 percent and 17 percent might not seem like much. On a base of $10,000, it is only $200. But to a portfolio manager whose direct competitors are all at 16 percent, it is the difference between winning and losing.

In the money management business, finishing with a winning record is not enough. As in professional sports, those who finish first can make tens of millions of dollars, while journeymen who finish in the middle of the pack are often cut from the team. Think about publicity that you have seen. How often do you see a company spending its advertising dollars trumpeting, *"The Sixth Best Small-Cap Growth Fund"*? How often have you seen Lou Rukeyser introduce a guest on *Wall Street Week* by saying, *"Our guest's fund is in the middle of the pack"*? And how often have you seen Barron's start an interview with a money manager by saying, *"Joe has had a few bad quarters, but we still have faith in him"*? Wall Street has little patience for poor results. Yet the difference between finishing near the top and finishing in the middle may only be a few percent, just as the difference between making and missing the playoffs may only be a few games. In big-time money management, as in sports, no one cheers for the "average" player.

The pressure to be a superstar impacts the trading decisions of most portfolio managers. If the manager is in second or third place, only a percent behind the leading competitor, it is very tough to stand pat and feel confident that your particular stocks will suddenly rally and boost you into the lead. Similarly, if the portfolio manager is in first place, it is difficult to sit back and relax, because in the stock market, unlike in sports, you cannot clinch the pennant before the season ends.

There is nothing more frightening to a money manager than to approach the end of a quarter significantly behind the market or behind his peers. As the situation becomes desperate, managers erupt into a trading frenzy. I have often received calls from frantic money managers: *"Find me a great stock,"* they beg. *"I need to make the quarter."* A money manager about to get fired cannot sit quietly and hope that the portfolio will suddenly improve. Instead, such a money manager will often trade like a wild man in order to salvage his career.

Assume that you are a manager in a large mutual fund company. You have had a good career, but many younger managers are moving up quickly. As the year draws to an end, you are 3 percent behind your peers and 2 percent behind other managers in your firm. If you can suddenly raise your performance above your peers, you will receive a large bonus and your fund will be widely promoted. If you cannot, you will become a journeyman, as other fund managers eclipse you. In this situation, what would you do?

BIDDING UP STOCKS

On the last day of the quarter, there are a number of tricks that fund managers can play to improve their performance. By far the most common trick is to aggressively bid up highly volatile stocks that the fund already owns. Let us say that your fund owns one million shares of Barer.com, an Internet commerce company. Barer.com, which is thinly capitalized and highly volatile, is selling at $30. You decide to buy another 100,000 shares. Normally, when a fund buys a stock it tries to pay as little as possible. If the stock is volatile, the fund will usually give the order to one broker, with a purchase limit and instructions to work carefully so as not to disrupt the market.

But on the last day of the quarter, the game may change. To show better performance, you want to drive the price of the stock up. If you can get Barer.com to close up $6, it will add at least $6 million to the fund's performance. If the fund has assets of $600 million, this is a 1 percent improvement. With three such stocks, you can draw even to your peers in one day.

How do you get the price of the stock from $30 to $36? You do it by breaking most normal investing rules. Instead of giving the buy order to one brokerage firm, you split it among four firms, making it look like there are multiple buyers for the stock. Instead of giving it to quality brokers who will carefully work the order without disrupting the market, you give it to aggressive brokers who will disrupt the market. Instead of putting price limits on the stock, you tell the brokers to buy it at any price.

When other investors see four aggressive firms all stampeding to buy Barer.com, they pull back their sell orders. The trading action makes it appear as if something big is happening to the company. The stock breaks through all resistance. It passes $36 and closes at $38. You paid an average of $34 for your 100,000 shares and $38 for the last 10,000. You probably could have bought the same 100,000 shares over the next several days for $31. By driving the stock up, you have overpaid. Two days later, the stock will be selling at $32. But at the time of the last trade of the quarter, the day on which your performance is measured, the stock closed at $38, and your performance was enhanced by $8.4 million.

With four other such stocks, you increased your performance from 12 percent to 17 percent. You went from eighth place to first place among your peers. Two days later, as the stocks retreated, your fund would find itself 5 percent in the hole for the next quarter, but this quarter was just beginning. Besides, you could not afford another quarter of coming in at the back of the pack.

Was driving up the price of Barer.com the right thing to do? Not if you are a long-term investor. Was it in the fiduciary interest of your shareholders? Probably not. Was it smart investing? Certainly not. If you were the fund manager and your job depended on it, would you do it? Perhaps and perhaps not. Not all fund managers play these games. Many reject them as against the interests of their shareholders. Many are unwilling to sacrifice long-term performance for short-term gain. Many run funds that are too large or own stocks that are too nonvolatile. But for all of the managers who reject these games, there are a substantial number who do play.

INDEXING GAMES

You may believe that these bizarre, end-of-the-quarter trading games are limited to a few portfolio managers playing highly volatile stocks. You would be wrong. These games are more widespread than most investors believe, and they are not limited to small-cap portfolio managers. Even the seemingly risk-free index funds can, wittingly or unwittingly, play these games. Take the case of ABR Information Services, an employee-benefits management company that was part of the Russell 2,000.

An index fund is supposed to mimic a particular index of stocks. It accomplishes this by calculating the total value of all stocks in the index and then dividing by the market value of each individual stock in order to arrive at appropriate market weightings. Thus, the percentage of each stock in the index will be based on its market value. The NASDAQ 100, for example, has 100 stocks, but the percentages of each stock in an index fund can vary greatly. In fact, three stocks, Microsoft, Intel, and Cisco have recently accounted for more than 30 percent of the index. As an index fund receives more money, it will invest that money by purchasing an amount of each stock equal to its weighting in the index. Thus, if the NASDAQ 100 fund receives $1 million, it invests $300,000 in Microsoft, Intel, and Cisco, and smaller amounts in other stocks.

This is usually a relatively easy proposition. Big stocks normally have a sufficient float for the fund to purchase such a large amount, and small stocks are either excluded from the index or have such a small weighting that it is not difficult to buy the needed amount of stock.

ABR was one of the stocks in the Russell 2000. When the index was calculated, ABR had a market capitalization of about $733 million. It had 28.76 million shares outstanding and was priced around $25. But then ABR agreed to be acquired by Ceridian, another health services company, for $25.50 per share.

Ceridian conducted a tender offer. On June 7, 1999, it purchased 28,271,055 shares of ABR. This left only about 489,000 shares in the hands of investors ($12.5 million). Ceridian said that it would buy these shares on or about July 19, 1999, for $25.50.

At the time of the tender offer, the keepers of the Russell index probably should have removed ABR, but they did not. Nor did they change its weighting to reflect the new reality. Perhaps they reasoned that the company still existed and still had a market capitalization of more than $700 million. Perhaps they intended to remove it on the day of the final payment, July 19.

The problem was that ABR now had a float of only 489,000 shares, and some of these shares were probably extremely difficult to find. After all, the holders of these shares had already missed a tender offer that would have paid them in full.

Because there was such a small float, the price of ABR traded above the $25.50 tender offer. The higher price did not reflect an expectation that ABR would receive more money. Rather, it reflected the fact that demand for the shares to fill the index was higher than the supply available. By June 29, the stock had actually traded above $30.

The funds that were paying $30 were obviously going to lose. In three weeks, they were going to receive only $25.50. But these funds were not in the business of picking stocks. They were in the business of mimicking the averages, and they were required to own a certain amount of ABR. This was especially critical on the last day of a quarter.

On June 30, the last day of the second quarter, ABR had the most bizarre trading I have ever seen. The stock opened at $33, a substantial premium to the $25.50. By 2:30, it was trading at $34.50. The Fed announced a 25-basis-point increase in interest rates, but it also announced that it would have a future bias towards easing. The market, which had been down, started to rally. Investors rushed to get their portfolios set in the last 90 minutes of trading in the quarter.

In order to participate in the rally, investors bought index funds. This meant that the funds had to buy the stocks in the indexes. The people who ran the Russell 2000 funds had to buy 2000 stocks. One of those stocks was ABR.

As the funds placed orders to buy ABR, they encountered one small problem: there was almost no stock available. Ceridian owned 98.3 percent of the shares. Still, these were index funds, not fundamental investors. Their job was to own every stock in the index, not to judge whether the price of every stock was appropriate.

With demand and no supply, the funds bid up the price of ABR. It did not matter to them that ABR would never be worth more than $25.50. They probably did not even know that there was a tender offer. All they knew was that they had to buy shares in each of 2,000 stocks so that their fund would mimic the index.

The price of ABR began to rocket. The following are some of the trades that were made late in the afternoon of June 30 and early in the morning of July 1.

PRICE OF ABR 6/30/99–7/1/99								
Time (P.M.)	3:32	3:37	3:47	3:48	3:51	3:53	3:58	4:01	9:30
Price	$34.50	$37	$52	$55	$58	$71	$75	$90	$27

In twenty-nine minutes, the price of the stock increased by more than $55.50 per share. A stock which was worth no more than $25.50 was now trading for $90^{1}/$_{8}$ per share. The volume was reasonably substantial. About 100,000 shares traded around the $90 level. In other words, someone invested $9 million in a stock that could never be worth more than $2.5 million. Of course, someone else reaped a windfall by selling a stock for $90^{1}/$_{8}$ that should never have been worth more than $25.50.

The next morning, July 1, the beginning of the third quarter, reality hit. Investors realized that the stock was only worth $25.50 and decided to sell. The first trade was at $27, down $63^{1}/$_{8}$. Because the stock remained in the index, it continued to trade above the $25.50 price, but by the end of the day, it closed at $29^{1}/$_{16}$, down $61^{1}/$_{16}$.

What makes this story so fascinating is that no one really did anything wrong. The people running the index funds were copying the index. They could not look at each of the 2,000 stocks. When new money came in, they started a buying program. One could argue that the keepers of the index should have removed ABR, but they didn't.

Before you decide that this is just an isolated case, you should know that ABR was not the only company in the Russell 2000 to have such a bizarre pattern. Two other stocks, Pitt–Des Moines and Chaparral Resources had similar patterns.

On June 30, some investors decided that Pitt would probably be included in Russell's third-quarter list. To get a jump on the Russell, they bid the stock up from $32\frac{1}{2}$ to $62\frac{1}{2}$. On July 1, when Pitt–Des Moines was not on the list, the stock plunged $28\frac{7}{8}$ to $33\frac{5}{8}$.

On June 30, Chaparral Resources opened at $22\frac{1}{2}$. At 1:30, it was selling at $23. In the next hour, it jumped to $35, and closed at $39\frac{1}{2}$. The next morning it opening at $31. Chaparral's jump was based on an incorrect calculation involving the company's announcement of a reverse 1-for-60 stock split. Some investors used the old share count to calculate market value, and thus, incorrectly, assumed that it would be included in the new index.

Prices	Opening June 30	Closing June 30	Opening July 1
ABR	$33	$90	$27
Pitt–Des Moines	32\frac{1}{2}$	62\frac{1}{2}$	33\frac{5}{8}$
Chaparral Resources	22\frac{1}{2}$	39\frac{1}{2}$	$31

Thus, in ninety minutes, three companies had huge price gains because of end-of-the-quarter trading games in index funds. By the opening the next morning, these gains had all but disappeared. The individual investor who had understood these games and watched these stocks could have made significant profits.

DUMPING POOR PERFORMERS

Another game that many managers play does not improve their performance, but it does improve their image. Before the end of the quarter, they dump stocks that have performed poorly or have been tainted with scandal. They do this because the fund company does not want to publish a prospectus showing the tainted stocks, and the fund manager does not want to go on interviews and explain why he owns the "bomb of the year." Even when performance isn't an issue, investors often react very negatively when they see a stock in a fund's portfolio that has been a bomb. Their first thought often is, *"This manager must be an idiot for getting suckered into this stock."* You would be surprised how often potential investors are turned off by one particular investment more than by the performance of the entire portfolio. To avoid this type of reaction, money managers routinely dump their losers at the end of a quarter so that they do not have to show up on the fund's record.

Individuals can capitalize on the end-of-the-quarter trading games by turning the professionals' need to perform against them: Buy the stocks they are selling and sell the stocks they are buying. If the professionals are driving up the price of some stocks, such as Barer.com, in order to improve their performance, individuals can sell into the spikes and often receive much higher prices than they would have thought possible. The best time for these trades is right before the closing bell on the last day of each quarter. The stocks that are the best candidates are those that are the most volatile. While it may only happen infrequently, these patterns offer an opportunity for the individual.

Stocks that money managers have dumped may not be great companies, but the prices at which they are dumped usually do not fully reflect their fundamentals. This is especially true at the end of the calendar year, when there is heavy tax-loss selling. In many cases, the stocks that perform the worst in December can often perform the best in January. If the individual watches for stocks that the institutions are throwing out, they can often find highly attractive entrance points.

At the end of the quarter, the professionals are operating with one eye on their day-to-day performance and one eye on their long-term image. Their trading may actually be against their long-term interests, but the short-term pressure to perform is powerful.

ALLOW THE PROFESSIONALS TO OVEREXTEND THEMSELVES, THEN COUNTERATTACK

The final way to capitalize on the size of the professionals is to allow them to overextend themselves and then counterattack. Professional investors often overextend themselves. The individual can almost always win by choosing a course counter to their actions. A truism in investing is that the professionals as a group are always wrong.

Whenever a majority of the professionals agree on something, they will always be wrong. This at first might seem highly contradictory. But it is almost infallible. If the amateur can understand and act on it, this rule offers substantial opportunities to defeat the professional.

Your broker calls and says his firm believes that the market will go up by 1,000 points in the next six months. Then you turn on *Wall Street Week*, and everyone is predicting the same 1,000-point increase. Finally you read *Forbes, Fortune,* and *Business Week.* Once again, there is unanimity of opinion; every seer says that the market is going to go up by 1,000 points in the next six months. You rush to place an order. But wait! Have you noticed that you always seem to get these bullish calls just as the market has reached an all-time high, and, in retrospect, just before it started a decline? It is not an accident that the market seems to behave in a way that is contrary to what just about every expert says.

Think about what the professionals were saying in 1996, before the current leg rallied the bull market to historic proportions. Most were extremely cautious. Most held large amounts of cash, and most talked about a major correction. You probably received few calls from brokers telling you to buy. Most of the calls probably told you to sell. Then, of course, the market did the opposite of what most people thought; it staged one of the greatest rallies in history. This is not happenstance.

In 1982, before the start of the greatest bull market in history, one of the business magazines ran a cover with the title "The Death of Equities." No one quarreled with this view. Everyone thought that the stock market was finished. Of course, it was just beginning.

The reality is that no one actually knows how the stock market is going to perform. The strategists, portfolio managers, and brokers all have ideas, but they do not actually know. If they did, they would not waste their time writing market letters or calling you to share their opinions. They would be playing the options market and living on a yacht in the South Pacific. Your broker might be a very nice person. But if he had perfect insight into the market, he would probably lose your phone number in an instant. Still, in those instances in which the professionals do agree on the direction of the market, they will invariably be wrong.

Why does the market always behave contrary to what most experts believe? The reason is simple and logical and relates to changes in expectations. If everyone believed that the market was going to go up by 1,000 points in the next six months, everyone would already be extremely bullish. If everyone was already bullish, there would be no one left to turn bullish. Those who have been bullish can remain bullish, but that will not push the market higher. For the market to go higher, expectations must change in a positive direction, but with everyone already bullish, expectations cannot get much more positive. Unless a new class of investors suddenly entered the market, there would be no one left to push it up any higher. On the other hand, with sentiment so bullish, there would be many people who could turn more bearish. If people turn bearish without people turning bullish, the market will go down. So when everyone says that the market is heading up, it will head down.

The exact same pattern exists at the other end of the spectrum. Whenever a large number of investors and strategists start talking about a crash, the market is usually much closer to its low than to its high. If most investment advisors are bearish, they will have already sold stocks and be sitting with a large cash position. For professionals, sitting on cash can be difficult. When they are sitting on cash, they are not investing. Further, many fund managers have limits to the amount of cash that they can hold. With lots of cash, they are not in a position to sell. If business gets worse, they won't sell, because their cash position is already large, but if business gets better, they will increase their expectations and buy. Thus:

- **If every expert believes that the stock market can only go up, every expert will be fully invested.**
- **If every expert is fully invested, there is no more cash to buy any stocks.**
- **Without buying, the stock market cannot go up.**

- **If everyone is bullish, expectations can only get more bearish, even if only a few investors change.**
- **A negative direction of change will create selling.**
- **Since there is no more money to buy, selling will push down the price of the market.**
- **Thus, even if most experts are still bullish, the market will go down because the direction of expectations will turn negative.**

It is obvious that there will never be a complete consensus. You can never get thousands of experts all to agree on everything. But you do not need absolutely every expert to get this system to work. All you need is the consensus of a strong majority of professionals.

A friend, named Steve Solomon, devised the "East Hampton *Barron's* Indicator" to tell if sentiment was bullish or bearish. He would go to the local newsstand in East Hampton at 12:30 on Saturday. If *Barron's* was sold out, it meant that there was too much interest in the stock market, and investors were too bullish. If there was a big stack of *Barron's*, it meant that there was little interest in the stock market and investors were too bearish. I'm not sure that was an entirely scientific indicator. Still, the point is that when everyone is interested in the market, bullishness may be getting extreme, while when no one is interested in the market, bearishness may be getting extreme.

THE SENTIMENT INDICATOR

The cumulative opinion of all of the professional investors is called the Sentiment Indicator. The indicator, which is listed every day in *Investors Business Daily*, is one of the most watched on Wall Street. According to *Investors Business Daily*, a bearish, or negative, signal is indicated when over 55 percent of the investment advisors are bullish or less than 20 percent are bearish. A bullish, or positive, signal is indicated when less than 35 percent are bullish or more than 50 percent are bearish. For the market to change directions, it is usually necessary to have both, i.e., too much bullishness and too little bearishness for the market to go down or too little bullishness and too much bearishness for the market to go up.

On July 11, 1994, with the Dow at 3,700, the level of bullishness reached a low of 23.3 percent. Because there had not been a corresponding increase in bearishness, the Dow continued to trade within a narrow range. However, on December 12, 1994, the level of bearishness reached a high of 59.1 percent. On that day, the Dow was at 3,682. With few people bullish and with most people bearish, cash positions were high, expectations were low, and the Dow was obviously poised for a sharp increase. Over the next seven months, the Dow jumped to 4,752, an increase of 29 percent. Over the 30 months following December 12, 1994, the Dow Jones Industrial Average jumped a staggering 122 percent.

On the other hand, during the past five years, only one time was there a high degree of bullishness and a low degree of bearishness at the same time. This bearish signal occurred on January 21, 1992. In the twelve months prior to January 21, 1992, the Dow had increased by more than 25 percent. But from the time of the bearish signal, the increase stopped. Over the next seven months, the Dow declined.

This sentiment indicator is rarely wrong over an extended period of time. Institutional investors almost always go to extremes of bullishness and bearishness. When these extremes occur, the individual investor often has a great opportunity to act contrary to the consensus. Before you invest, take a look at what the professionals are doing. You will rarely lose by betting against them if there is a high degree of consensus.

There is, however, one caveat for this indicator. The market will tend to keep going in the same direction until either the level of bullishness or the level of bearishness gets out of line. If the market is going up and the level of bullishness increases, the market will probably continue to go up until the level of bullishness exceeds 55 percent and remains there for a few weeks. Similarly, if the level of bearishness decreases, the market will probably continue to go up unless the level of bearishness drops under 20 percent. During the recent run up, there have been weeks of moderate bullishness and limited bearishness, but the percentages have never reached the levels of excess needed for a turn. While it is always good to bet against the experts, it is not good to anticipate the direction of sentiment. **Wait until the sentiment indicators show a change in direction and then act**.

THE FATE OF THE UNIVERSALLY LOVED (OR HATED) STOCK

Much the same situation applies with specific industries or stocks. When an analyst comes out with a Buy recommendation, the salespeople for the analyst's firm call their customers and push the story. If the story is a good one, the salespeople will find buyers and the stock will go up. The stock may continue to go up if a second, third, or fourth analyst recommends it. But what happens when there are twenty analysts following the stock and all have aggressive buys? Most people would guess that any stock that was loved by all of the analysts would outperform the market and be hitting new highs every day. Wrong again.

When many analysts are recommending a stock, their salespeople have already made their phone calls. Every portfolio manager, broker, and casual investor has heard the story. Anyone who liked the story has already bought the stock. Further, if every analyst rated the stock an aggressive buy, there would be no more analysts left to raise the ratings. Now the only action that an analyst could take would be to lower the rating. When an analyst lowers the rating on a stock that had previously only had aggressive buys, the downgrade often sets off selling. Of course, a company could always surprise by reporting better than expected earnings. But when analysts have aggressive buys on a stock, they also often have aggressive earnings estimates, so it is difficult for a company with a bullish following to continually surprise the Street on the upside. This is not to say that people should avoid strong industries or popular stocks. It is to say that when everybody is convinced that the market or a particular stock can only go up, it will almost surely go down. As with the market as a whole, too much bullishness can be bad for the price of a stock.

To test this theory, I took a random sample of stocks that had been rated 1.0 or 1.1 on First Call by the analysts in early 1996. A 1.0 is a perfect rating. It means that every analyst who follows the stock has given it the highest rating possible. A 1.1 is an almost perfect rating. It means that at least seven analysts follow the stock and six have given it the highest rating and one has given it the second highest rating. From the viewpoint of the analysts, the 1.0- and the 1.1-rated stocks are the crème de la crème. At any one time, of the thousands of stocks that are followed by analysts, only about twenty merit a 1.0 or a 1.1 rating.

How did the stocks in my sample perform?* From the time of the upgrade until August 20, 1996, the stocks rated 1.0 advanced an average of only 9.2 percent, below the average of the market. Further, over the next seventeen months, two-thirds of these stocks declined below their price at the time of the upgrade. During a market that increased by more than 30 percent, two-thirds of the highest-rated stocks showed declines.

Not surprisingly, these stocks had increased in price a startling 59 percent during the previous year. But during the previous year, most of these stocks had not yet received the analysts' highest ratings. They only received the highest rating *after* having performed the best. Thus, stocks tend to receive universal acclaim from the analysts after they have performed spectacularly, but once these stocks were upgraded to the highest rating, most of them (there are some exceptions) did not perform as well as the market.

The performance of the stocks that were rated 1.1 should also have been outstanding, but it was horrible. During one of the greatest bull markets in history, the stocks rated 1.1 showed an average decline of 14.6 percent. Of the fifteen stocks, only five showed increases, and only one measurably outperformed the market. More significant were the disasters. Daka International and Intervoice both lost about half of their value in less than five months. Quicksilver lost almost half of its value in four months. U.S. Robotics lost more than one-third of its value in four months. Electronic Information lost more than one-quarter of its value in two months. Inphynet Medical lost more than one-quarter of its value in less than five months, while American Oncology lost 60 percent of its value in slightly more than two months. During the next seventeen months, most of these stocks continued to underperform the market.

* To eliminate distractions caused by investment banking and allow for a sufficient time frame after an upgrade, I excluded from the sample companies that had been upgraded after June 22 and companies that were new issues.

Thus, the highest-rated stocks—those with 1.0 and 1.1 ratings— declined during the period in which they had these ratings. Despite the fact

PERFORMANCE OF HIGHEST RATED STOCKS FROM 6/98–6/99

STOCKS RATED 1.0	CHANGE	STOCKS RATED 1.1	CHANGE
Advanced Paradigm	55.1%	Monarch Dental	-76.96%
Applied Graphics	-70.3%	Morton's Restaurants	-21.35%
Amresco Capital	-23.0%	Saks Fifth Avenue	-31.73%
Central Garden	-64.7%	Pride Int'l	-37.92%
Community First	-9.8%	Landry's Seafood	-60.65%
Chattem	28.2%	Post Properties	3.15%
Cellstar	-41.5%	BE Aerospace	-36.98%
Comverse Tech.	122.1%	Healthcare Fin'l	-37.98%
Consolidated Pro	4.9%	Prentiss Properties	1.06%
Correctional Pro	-21.4%	Developers Diversified	-12.56%
Diagnostic Health	-90.8%	Saville PLC	-64.04%
Delia*s	-18.2%	Suiza Foods	-36.33%
Eastern Environ.	1.1%	Midway Games	-4.74%
Geltex Pharm.	0.0%	North Fork Bank	-16.50%
Hibbet Sports	-33.8%	Metamor Worldwide	-28.93%
Healthsouth	64.5%	Signature Resorts	-27.14%
Neomagic	-39.4%	Unibanco	-18.85%
Insight Ent.	46.4%	Cemex-Cementos	-2.60%
Personnel Group	-49.5%	Millennium Pharma	151.26%
Pomeroy Computer	-40.3%	JDA Software	-65.73%
PMT Services	-9.8%	Henry Schein	-22.98%
Pediatric Svs of Amer	-90.2%	Anixter Int'l	6.09%
PowerWave	91.4%	Legato Systems	68.82%
Regal-Beloit	-20.1%	Boston Properties	6.93%
Renters Choice	-19.1%	US Restaurants	-27.22%
Remedy Temp	-50.2%	Computer Mgmt.	14.29%
Sheridan Health	-19.6%	Computer Horizons	-53.44%
Snyder Comm.	-30.6%	Genesco	-14.12%
Sportsline USA	-3.2%	Quadramed	0.00%
Service Experts	-42.0%	Pathogenesis	-49.32%
Transkaryotic	28.2%	Dave & Busters	7.50%
Thermo Electron	-40.9%	Staffmark	-72.28%
TMP Worldwise	83.8%	Citrix Systems	72.54%
World Acess	-56.7%		
Wackenhut Corr.	-20.1%		
US Express	-40.3%		
Young & Rubicam	33.8%		
AVERAGE	**-9.6%**		**-20.32%**

that the stock market was constantly making new highs, these stocks as a group not only underperformed, they actually lost money for investors.

The level of underperformance of these top-rated stocks was so great that I decided to take another sample in 1999. I compared the prices of the stocks on June 18, 1998, and June 18, 1999. During this period, the market had advanced sharply.

The results were, to say the least, interesting. The first thing I noticed was that the list had gotten much larger. On June 18, 1998, there were 33 stocks rated 1.0 and 37 rated 1.1, about twice the number that had received the same ratings two years earlier. Another example of ratings inflation.

Next, I noticed that the top-rated stocks in 1998 had done even worse than the top-rated stocks in 1996, and the market had done better. During this period:

- **Twenty-four of the thirty-three stocks rated 1.0 declined.**
- **Eighteen declined by more than 20 percent.**
- **Eight declined by more than 49 percent.**
- **Five declined by more than 60 percent.**
- **Only two had increases of more than 15 percent.**
- **In total, the 1.0 rated stocks declined by more than 20 percent during a bull market.**

Monarch Dental dropped from $14 to $3. Staffmark plunged from $36 to $10. Saville dropped from $44 to $16. Landry's dropped from $21 to $8, and JDA dropped from $31 to $10.

The stocks rated 1.1 also lost money and well underperformed the market.

- **Twenty-five of the thirty-seven stocks rated 1.1 declined, while only eleven advanced. (One was unchanged.)**
- **Nineteen declined by more than 20 percent.**
- **Thirteen declined by more than 40 percent.**
- **Four declined by more than 60 percent.**
- **Two declined by more than 90 percent.**
- **Nine had increases of more than 15 percent.**

- **In total, the stocks rated 1.1 showed a decline of 10 percent.**

Applied Graphics dropped from $44 to $13. Central Garden dropped from $30 to $11. Diagnostic Health plunged from $9 to less than $1, while Pediatric Services sunk from $15 to $1½. These was a pretty sorry performance for a number of highly rated stocks.

Interestingly, two of the stocks that showed sharp declines, Pediatric Services and Healthsouth, made both the 1996 and the 1998–99 list of highly favored stocks, and declined both times.

Why is it that the stocks most loved by the analysts should have performed so poorly? The explanation is simple. By the time these stocks achieved their lofty ratings, there were huge expectations built into them. Every analyst was bullish. Every portfolio manager had heard the bullish story many times. The good news was in the price of the stocks. Once reality set in, many of the stocks underperformed and many others dropped precipitously.

This is not to suggest that investors should short every stock that the analysts love. But if a stock has only strong buy recommendations, the individual should watch for a sign of a top. When stocks that are universally loved top out, the next move is often sharply down. **Never underestimate the ability of the consensus to be wrong.**

The same is true with stocks on the downside. When stocks disappoint or make the pros look stupid, the analysts often walk away muttering, *"I don't care how cheap the stock is, I hate the company."* Analysts can develop blind spots more easily than can individuals. This is not to say that individuals should buy shares in bad companies. Nor should they rush in right after a company has disappointed investors. Investors have long memories and stocks do not usually rebound quickly. But many decent companies professionals have hated because of previous disappointments offer the individual excellent opportunities. When investors see stocks that are universally hated form a base and begin to move up, they usually have a good buying opportunity.

Analyst ratings are covered on many sites throughout the Internet, and most of the Internet services that provide quotes have links to one or more sites with analyst ratings. Investors should check the ratings of analysts on the stocks that they own or are interested in owning. Watch especially for extremes of bullishness or bearishness, and then look at the charts. Tops and bottoms are usually very easy to spot, and most investors will do well if they act when they see these formations. Watch especially for extremely bullish ratings on weak charts, which could portend a disaster, or extremely bearish ratings on strong charts, which could portend a great buying opportunity. Thus, while betting against individual professionals can be risky for the individual, betting against the strong consensus of professionals usually guarantees victory. If individuals can remember that the consensus is almost always wrong and have the fortitude to bet against it, they have an excellent chance of winning.

REMEMBER SUN TZU

The key to investing is simple. Individuals compete against better-trained and better-equipped professionals who have a huge advantage. Individuals must avoid attacking the professionals' strength. Instead, they must turn their strength against them. Like a well-trained guerrilla force against a mechanized army, the individual can defeat the professional so long as he or she remembers the dictum: **"Know yourself. Know your enemy. In one hundred battles, there will be one hundred victories."**

PART 2

The Weapons of Warfare

CHAPTER SIX

Fundamental Weapons

Although guerrillas may be able to avoid the enemy's strengths, identify its weaknesses, and find advantages on home turf, they still need weapons to fight the enemy. The weapons of the guerrillas must be simple and suited to the terrain on which the war will be fought. The same types of conditions apply on Wall Street. The professionals have unlimited research, direct inputs from companies, and sophisticated trading systems. The individual cannot match them in terms of resources. But individuals can still find weapons of their own.

In the stock market, there are two principal types of weapons: fundamental information and technical analysis. Fundamental information concerns the underlying business of a company, sales and earnings, the quality of management, products, competition, etc. With good fundamental information, the investor can analyze the business and make a judgment as to its earnings potential. Technical analysis concerns the trading patterns of the stock. These patterns enable the investor to observe the movements of the market and have an early warning system when professionals change direction. To win consistently, the individual should use both of these tools. The next two chapters will explain these two important weapons of warfare.

LET THE ANALYSTS DO THE WORK

Fundamental analysis is critical to understanding a company. To win, individuals must understand the company's earnings potential, as well as where the professionals are likely to be wrong and where they can gain an edge. Analyzing a company is a complex undertaking. Analysts are trained in financial analysis and accounting and spend years learning about companies. They meet with management, study financial statements, build an earnings model and make earnings estimates. It is very difficult for individuals to duplicate their work.

Analysts also specialize in one industry. They can spend a lifetime looking at no more than twenty companies. They talk to them every week, talk to competitors, customers, and suppliers, read trade publications, attend conferences, and study the financial systems that are unique to each industry.

Oil analysts study all of the factors that impact petroleum prices. Biotechnology analysts study medical journals and monitor trials of new drugs. Real estate analysts analyze the occupancy and rental rates by market. Semiconductor analysts study new technological developments. The differences between industries are so great that experienced analysts almost never switch coverage areas.

With their in-depth industry knowledge, the analysts are experts on their companies. They know when to use earnings per share and when to use cash flow. They understand which companies are growth stocks and which are value stocks, and they know how to analyze balance sheets and income statements. This is not to say that they are always right. They are not. But they are operating with a level of knowledge that the individual can never match.

If the analysts have such a huge advantage, how can the individual ever compete? The answer is easy. **Individuals do not have to do the work, because the analysts do it for them**. The analysts build models, write reports, and tell the company's story. These reports serve as a reference point around which a good deal of the information flow on Wall Street is based. If individuals use the work of the analysts as a base, they do not need to do the work themselves. They only have to decide when the analysts are too optimistic or too pessimistic.

Get ten reports on any well-followed company, especially one that has just done an offering and paid a lot of firms on Wall Street. You will notice that most of the analysts present the story in the same way and have similar models, valuations, and ratings. A few reports will differ from the norm, but these will be the exceptions. This is not to say that the analysts are correct. In fact, they are often wrong and certainly have a bullish bias, but the virtue of their work lies not in their being right or wrong, but rather in their ability to present a unified picture that investors can use as a guideline.

FIND THE CONSENSUS

If eight of ten analysts say that a company is going to grow by 18 percent a year, that becomes the consensus around its results are judged. If eight of ten analysts say that the stock will earn $2, those are the earnings that investors will expect. If the company earns $2.20, those earnings will be an upside surprise, even if two analysts had thought that it would earn $2.25.

While absolute results are important, it is the consensus that influences the stock price. How often have you seen a stock surge on what looked like mediocre earnings, because it beat "consensus"? And how often have you seen a stock plunge on what looked like great earnings because it missed "consensus"? It is fine for a company to earn $1.00 compared to $0.50 in the previous year, but if investors had been expecting earnings of $1.50, the stock will almost certainly plunge. Because the consensus is so important, companies practice spin control and work hard to ensure that analysts have the "right" numbers. In fact, some companies try to ensure that the analysts are always a little conservative in their estimates, so that they can "surprise" the Street on the upside.

Here is a neat trick that a company I know once pulled. There were five analysts covering it. Two had estimates of $0.20 and three had estimates of $0.21. The average was $0.206, which rounded up to $0.21. The company knew that it was going to report $0.20, but it still wanted to find a way to beat consensus, because it knew that stocks that beat consensus usually went up, while those that missed consensus usually went down. The CFO found a young analyst, who was looking to hustle investment-banking business and who had a very small following on Wall Street. He convinced the analyst to begin covering the company and to use $0.13 as an earnings estimate. No one took much notice of the estimate, but when the new analyst's $0.13 was added to the others, the average dropped from $0.21 to $0.19. This made the company's $0.20 announcement an upside rather than a downside surprise. When the company reported $0.20, the analysts indicated that the earnings beat consensus and the stock jumped $2.

These games notwithstanding, the existence of a consensus makes life much easier for an investor. Stocks will only move when people change their buying and selling behavior. If everyone agrees with the consensus, the stock is unlikely to move very much. But if investors believe that the consensus is too conservative, they will buy and push the stock up, while if investors feel the consensus is too aggressive, they will sell and push the price of the stock down. Thus, **the consensus forms the yardstick around which investors make their bets.**

To win, the investor has only to pick correctly whether the consensus is too high or too low. While this sounds difficult, it is not. Because the consensus has outlined the key issues, the investor merely has to draw on home-turf advantages to find a few companies in which the consensus is wrong. The first step, however, is to understand the consensus.

Find the name and phone number of the director of investor relations. If you cannot find the name in the annual report, look at the company's profile on any of the financial Web sites. When you call investor relations, ask for a complete investor's package including an annual report, a 10K, the most recent 10Qs, and some analysts' reports. (These reports are available on the Web at Edgar.com, but it is still worthwhile calling the company.) Some investor relations departments may ask if you are an individual or a professional money manager. I know some people who answer that they are a "small institution" in the belief that it will get them better service from the company. They give a name and address that makes them sound like a money management firm. They say, send it to John Doe at Doe & Buffett Capital Management in Omaha, Nebraska. No one knows the name of every small institution, and no one will ask if Buffett is Warren or

Jimmy. So making up a name probably wouldn't hurt.

Some investor relations departments are not friendly to individual share-holders, and instead focus on the larger money managers that own the bulk of their stock. There is nothing you can do about this. If the company will not answer your questions, you might be better off finding another company. If a company does not want you, why should you want it?

Some companies will send you analysts' reports as a matter of course. Others will send them only if you ask. Some will refer you to the brokerage houses. In most cases, if you beg politely, the company will send you some reports, especially if the reports say nice things about it. Do not expect the company to send you reports with sell or hold ratings, unless the stock has already soared and the writers of the reports look like complete idiots. Not having these negative reports is not as much of a drawback as it might appear. Few reports have negative ratings, and the primary reason for getting the reports is to understand the consensus. In most cases, negative reports will fall outside of the consensus.

FIGURE OUT THE INVESTMENT THESIS

When you get the reports, try to figure out the investment thesis. The investment thesis is the paragraph at the top of most reports that tells you the analysts' opinion, which is not critical, and the core issues surrounding the stock, which are. While some analysts will go their own way, most will coalesce around a particular thesis that will form the basis of the stock's valuation. Some investment theses will be straightforward and relate to earnings growth. This is especially common for complex companies that have multiple drivers to earnings:

> *"We believe that IBM can grow its earnings by 16 percent per year. Selling at 13x projected earnings, the stock is undervalued relative to its growth rate."*

This thesis says that the key items on which to focus are the earnings growth (the rate at which earnings per share will grow over time) and the p/e ratio (the stock price divided by the earnings per share). In this case, the p/e ratio is inexpensive relative to the estimated growth rate.

Some investment theses will be more complex, spelling out the specifics of the earnings argument. An analyst wrote about Tiffany:

"We are forecasting 20 to 25 percent average annual EPS growth over the next several years, assuming 10 percent to 12 percent unit growth budgeted by the company, 8 to 9 percent same-store sales growth in both the U.S. and Japan, and continued margin expansion from improving operating efficiencies. At 19.7x our fiscal 1998 EPS, TIF is selling at a 21 percent discount to its long-term growth."

A thesis like the one above makes it easy for any investor to understand how the world looks at a company. If earnings growth (20 to 25 percent) remains higher than the p/e multiple (19.7), the stock will probably go up. As a potential investor, you should focus on the two key issues for earnings growth: Can the company find good sites for its new stores? Will same-store sales remain strong both in the United States and in Japan? Given this investment thesis, it is not surprising that the stock of Tiffany declined by 25 percent when the Japanese stock market dropped in October 1997. But if you, like the analyst, had bet that Tiffany would continue to grow its comparable store sales in the United States and Japan, you would have held onto your stock and eventually beaten the market.

Some investment theses are relative, looking at the valuation of a particular company compared to other companies. An analyst wrote about PETCO Animal Supplies:

"Our simple investment thesis is that PETCO is about as strong a performer as the larger player, PETsMart, but PETCO trades at a substantial discount to PETsMart, and trades in line with other growth retailers."

Because this analyst is focusing on relative values, the investor needs to look at the fundamentals and the p/e multiples of both PETCO and PETsMart, as well as the p/e multiples of other growth retailers. During the first nine months of 1997, PETCO had superb results. Its earnings ranked in the 95th percentile of all stocks. However, its stock performance was slightly below average. The reason was simple. PETsMart's earnings fell apart and its stock dropped from $29 to $7. If the thesis was that PETCO's valuation was tied to that of PETsMart, then once PETsMart blew up, it was difficult for PETCO to advance. Any investor who ignored what happened to PETsMart lost.

Some investment theses deal with issues other than earnings, such as takeover value:

> *"Cullen Frost has a dominant position in the San Antonio banking market and could become a likely takeover target. While the stock is currently selling for $32, we believe that its takeover value is $55."*

In this thesis, the analyst is projecting the takeover value of the company at $55. There is little discussion of earnings growth. Instead, the value of the company is in its franchise. If the thesis is that a takeover is likely, then the investor should focus on other takeover action in the industry in general and in the Southwest niche in particular.

The investment thesis may or may not be correct. Just because an analyst indicates that a company will grow by 22 percent does not mean that the results will follow suit. In fact, it is almost certain that the results will in some way be different. When Rational Software Corp. was selling for $38, an analyst wrote:

> *"Rational [is] . . . the market leader in an industry segment which we expect to see a 55 percent CAGR through the year 2000. Rational clearly values revenue predictability. The company has established conservative accounting practices and . . . does an excellent job of managing its quarter-to-quarter business."*

Nine months later, the price of Rational's stock had dropped from $38 to $10. The revenues had significantly fallen short of plan. But that did not make the investment thesis less valuable. In fact, it enabled investors to focus on the key issues. When the *revenue predictability* failed to materialize, they trashed the stock. (Rational Software was one of the top-rated stocks in 1996.)

For better or worse, the issues on which analysts focus are normally the issues on which investors focus. If the fate of these issues vary substantially from the analysts' stated opinion, the company will likely perform much better or worse than expected. An analyst wrote the following on Just For Feet:

> *"Given the unique superstore format and a differentiated*

merchandising strategy, FEET is well-positioned to gain market share."

When Just For Feet made an acquisition of a chain of stores with a smaller format, investors sold, and the stock plunged from a high of $33 to a low of $11 in just nine months. The reason was simple. Just For Feet did not have a p/e ratio of 40 because it had the best earnings record. It had this lofty multiple because investors believed that its large stores made it unique. When Just For Feet bought smaller stores, it was saying to investors that it did not think its large stores were so special after all, and investors, as a result, decided that there was no reason to give it a 40x multiple.

Also, the smaller stores changed Just For Feet's business model. Now it had to run two different types of business. Those who bet that it was not up to the challenge were right. Less than two years later, inventories had ballooned out of control. (The company, in the fast-changing fashion business, had almost one year's extra inventory.) Profits had plunged. The founder had resigned as CEO and the stock was selling for less than $4.00 (one-eighth of its previous high). The message was simple. When the company diversified away from its seemingly successful superstore concept, investors should have diversified away from the company.

The investment thesis gives investors a road map for looking at a company. It details the issues that should drive earnings and valuation. **The first step is to decide if you can understand the thesis. If you cannot, drop the stock.** There are many other companies to consider. If you can understand the thesis, you have four choices. You can decide that the thesis is right and go along with the masses. You can decide that it is too optimistic, in which case you should be selling. You can decide that it is too pessimistic, in which case you should be buying. Or you can decide that it is the wrong thesis, in which case there should be a great opportunity on either the short or the long side.

THE STREAM OF EARNINGS

If you look at the investment theses cited above, you will notice that most of the valuations are based on some assessment of the long-term earnings growth rate of the company. **This is because when investors buy stock, they are purchasing a share of that company's stream of earnings.** A share of stock does not entitle investors to assets or even products. Compaq does not send its shareholders a computer at the end of each quarter. (Although some companies, like Tandy, do send their shareholders discount coupons.) A share of stock does not entitle investors to a guaranteed dividend. Nor does it offer investors any return of capital, unless the company is sold or liquidated. All that a share of stock offers an investor is a participation in the earnings stream of that company.

Therefore, the price an investor will pay will be determined by the amount and the timing of that stream. If you think the stream will increase, you will be willing to pay more. If you think it will decrease, you will want to pay less. When investors talk about management's ability to "grow" earnings, they are focusing on the long-term composition of the earnings stream.

Take a hypothetical company that earns $1.00 per share in 1999. If the earnings remain flat at $1.00 each year, the company will earn $15.00 over a fifteen-year period. If the earnings decline by 10 percent, the company will earn $7.94. If the earnings grow by 10 percent, the company will earn $31.77. If they grow by 20 percent, the company will earn $72.04, and if they grow by 30 percent, the company will earn $167.29. Over a fifteen-year period, a 30 percent growth rate will generate more than twice the income of a 20 percent growth rate and more than 15 times the income of a flat growth rate. The power of compounding is the reason analysts are so concerned with a company's long-term growth rate.

15-Year Earnings Growth					
Annual Earnings Change	-10 percent	0 percent	10 percent	20 percent	30 percent
Year 1	$1.00	$1.00	$1.00	$1.00	$1.00
Year 15	$0.23	$1.00	$3.98	$12.84	$39.37
15 Year Total	**$7.94**	**$15.00**	**$31.77**	**$72.04**	**$167.29**

The hypothetical case cited above has one major problem. It gives no more weighting to real earnings this year than it does to potential earnings in year fifteen. One dollar of earnings this year is clearly more valuable than the potential of $1 of earnings in year fifteen. This year's earnings are real. Year fifteen (or even year two) earnings are just estimates. In addition, this year's earnings can be reinvested at some rate to bring returns in subsequent years.

The only way to compare the different flows is to discount them back to the present using a formula that takes into account the cost of money and risk. Let us take the same hypothetical company cited above and discount the earnings by 10 percent. The flat earnings that were worth $15 are worth only $7.94 when discounted. The 20 percent growth that was worth $72.04 is worth only $27.15 when discounted, while the 30 percent growth that was worth $167.29 is worth only $56.11 when discounted. This discounted stream of earnings often reflects roughly what most investors would pay for a stock.

15-Year Earnings Growth					
Annual Earnings Change	-10 percent	0 percent	10 percent	20 percent	30 percent
Year 1	$1.00	$1.00	$1.00	$1.00	$1.00
Year 15	$0.05	$0.23	$0.87	$2.94	$9.01
15 Year Total	$5.04	$7.94	$13.99	$27.15	$56.11
P/E Ratio	5.0x	7.9x	14x	27.2x	56.1x

CHANGING THE DISCOUNT RATE: WHY INTEREST RATES IMPACT STOCK PRICES

A key question is what is the appropriate discount rate? Two factors impact the rate: interest rates and risk. As interest rates go up, future earnings are worth less because you can earn more with your current dollars. Which would you rather have: $10 now or $15 in five years? The answer depends on the return you could get for the money if you had it now. With a 5 percent return, the $10 would be worth $12.76 in five years. But with a 10 percent return, it would be worth $16.10. So increasing interest rates dictate increasing discount rates.

How often have you seen stocks crushed when interest rates rise and stocks rally when interest rates fall? You look at the small changes in rates and wonder why they have such a major impact on valuations. It is easy to understand why a leveraged manufacturing company, a bank, or a real estate investment trust with high levels of floating rate debt could be hurt if interest rates go up. Not only will higher rates increase interest costs, they will also slow down the economy. For a leveraged manufacturing company with high fixed costs, this is a double whammy that will seriously impact earnings. It is harder to understand why an Internet company, with cash and no debt, should be hurt even more by changes in rates.

The answer has to do with the discount rate. Changing the discount rate can have a dramatic impact on all valuations, but especially on the valuations for rapidly growing companies. The table on the next page shows the impact of changing the discount rate from 10 percent to 15 percent for companies with 0 percent and 30 percent annual growth. In the company with no growth, a change in the discount rate from 10 percent to 15 percent would lower the valuation from $7.94 to $6.08, a decline of $1.86 (23 percent). But look what happens to the valuation of the 30 percent grower. With a 10 percent discount rate, the company was worth $56.11. With a 15 percent discount rate, its value would drop to $33.06, a decline of $22.05 (41 percent).

DISCOUNT RATE		
Growth Rate	10 percent	15 percent
0 percent	$7.94	$6.08
30 percent	$56.11	$33.06

THE CHALLENGE OF THE UNKNOWN

Risk must also be factored into the discount rate. If the long-term earnings growth of a company were guaranteed, it would be easy to figure out the discount rate. But the long-term future is never guaranteed. Competition, changing market conditions, new technologies, acquisitions, new management, and other factors can significantly alter expectations. Because seemingly small increments in future growth can bring huge differences in valuations, investors must carefully assess the likelihood that the company will do better or worse than plan and incorporate some factor for risk.

If a blue-chip company projects 12 percent annual growth, you can be relatively confident that it will come to pass. But if a biotech company projects losses for five years and 30 percent compounded growth, you might be more skeptical. You are willing to accept the growth projections provided that the company's products are approved and no one comes out with any competing products. But you believe there are risks on both fronts. To value a company like this, you would want to take a higher discount rate, because there is a high degree of risk in the projections and because the company is currently losing money.

Analysts who follow biotech or Internet companies often use discount rates of 25 percent or more to incorporate the potential risk. With a discount rate of 25 percent, a company must have annual earnings growth of more than 25 percent to increase its value.

The impact of risk on the discount rate means that **companies with long-term earnings visibility will usually sell for higher multiples than companies with the same earnings growth whose future is much less certain.** Companies like Coca-Cola, Wal-Mart, Microsoft, and others that have proven they can grow consistently and have dominant market positions which should ensure continued growth, normally maintain higher multiples than companies with more uncertain futures. If you decided that Coca-Cola or Wal-Mart could grow earnings by 17 percent per year, you would probably be comfortable taking these earnings out ten or even fifteen years.

Yet even here, the distant future can be difficult to project, especially as companies begin to saturate their markets. It is easy to look back at the history of Microsoft, Intel, Wal-Mart, or other great companies and see the power of compounding, but for every company that has sustained fantastic growth, there are hundreds of wannabes that stubbed their toes. At one point in time, Wang, Polaroid, and Kmart were growth stocks whose prospects looked as exciting to investors then as those of Microsoft, Intel, and Wal-Mart do today. Yet these companies ran into trouble as competition changed and management slipped.

If assessing long-term growth is a difficult task with strong and consistent companies, it is much harder with small, rapidly growing companies. In the previous edition of this book, we looked at two very high multiple stocks, Netscape and Iomega (the manufacturer of the zip drive), and asked whether they would turn out to be great growth companies or flashes in the pan. Interestingly, in the last eighteen months, Netscape was hurt by competition from Microsoft and sold out to AOL, while Iomega stumbled. (The zip drive continues to sell, but profits have been disappointing.) In both of these cases, the estimates of growth did not pan out. In others, such as AOL or Cisco, they did.

What about today's great growth stocks? Where will they be in five years? Will Amazon still be worth more than Sears and Kmart combined? Will AOL maintain its market share? Will Yahoo! be the dominant portal? What about some of the smaller Internet stocks? It is almost impossible to accurately project long-term earnings for companies in industries that are changing by the day. But to make an investment, the investor must make projections of future earnings and then discount them back to the present.

The same techniques apply to cyclical stocks. Cyclical companies by definition have cyclical earnings. During boom periods, earnings can be very high, while during bust periods, the company may even lose money. But there is no difference in the analysis. The investor is still buying a long-term stream of earnings. It is just that the growth rate is not consistent over time. The multiple that an investor is willing to pay is based on the sum of the earnings, discounted back to the present by some reasonable amount.

It's Always Earnings

There are cases in which analysts focus on measures other than earnings, but even in these cases, the investor is purchasing an earnings stream. Analysts may base their valuations on price-to-book or break-up value. These types of valuations usually occur with companies that currently have weak earnings. But the analyst's justification for the valuation is that, in the future, the company, or whoever buys it, will be able to generate a higher earnings stream from these assets.

Since the price of the stock equates to the stream of earnings projected by the analysts, it should be relatively easy for investors to pick the winners and losers. Because analysts clearly spell out their assumptions, the individual investor merely has to study the assumptions of the analysts and decide whether they are too bullish or too bearish. If the analysts have not fully taken into account the risks, the stock will eventually go down. If they have not fully factored in the opportunities, the stock will eventually go up.

So the trick for investors is to find some piece of information that will let them decide if the growth rate selected by analysts is too high or too low. Just because an analyst says that a company will continue to grow at 25 percent a year does not make it happen. Many companies exceed analysts' targets, while others fall short. **If the investor can gain some insight into the company's ability to surprise analysts on the upside or the downside, that investor can move before the professionals have time to react.**

You should, however, be cautious when short-term results play havoc with long-term valuations. Analysts use short-term earnings to make long-term projections. If a company growing at 15 percent has a strong quarter, with sales and earnings up 30 percent, analysts will reflect this improvement by raising their long-term growth rate. You may not think that a few good months should dramatically change the long-term growth rate of the company. You may be right, over the long term. But because many investors focus on short-term momentum, stocks often respond dramatically to these changes in valuation. If growth rates are being raised, do not rush to sell. On the other hand, when companies report a weak quarter, analysts will suddenly revise their growth estimates downward. Even if you think that the change is inappropriate, don't immediately rush to buy the stock. You can be overwhelmed by momentum. Let the short-term players make their move first, then reassess the growth rate.

WHEN THE MARKET AND THE ANALYSTS DISAGREE

Sometimes there will be a vast gap between the analysts' valuation and the market price. The analysts may all say that the stock should sell for

$50, but the market price will remain stuck at $30. When this occurs either the market or the analysts are wrong.

If the company is small and is only covered by one or two analysts, the chances are reasonably good that the stock should be worth $50, and that it is selling at $30 because it has fallen below the radar screen of most professionals. This can often be an excellent buying opportunity.

If the company is large and is well-covered by many analysts, the chances are reasonably good that the stock should be worth $30, and that the analysts are wearing rose-colored glasses and have missed a critical risk factor. **If you see a group of analysts all contending that** *"the stock is highly undervalued relative to its growth rate,"* **what the analysts are really saying is,** *"No one believes our projections."* If the market does not accept the analysts' projections on a well-followed stock, neither should you.

Thus, the task for the individual investor is easier than it seems. At any point in time, the price of a stock reflects the collective wisdom of all buyers and sellers. If the stock is well followed, it should efficiently reflect the current consensus. It will move down when the consensus changes for the negative. The analysts' earnings projections and valuation parameters usually form the basis of the consensus. To win, the individual investor does not have to build an earnings model, analyze the balance sheet, or study valuation techniques. The individual merely has to find a hole in the projections and/or the valuations and act upon it. It is far easier to allow the analysts to do the work and then react off them than it is to duplicate their work from scratch.

DO A REALITY CHECK

Before you begin looking for holes in the numbers, do a reality check. Decide if the company's strategy makes sense and if the analysts' estimates appear to be reasonable.

You must decide if the market exists and if the company has the ability to capitalize on it. A company announces that it plans to launch satellites to mine minerals on asteroids. The analyst thinks that the asteroids have unlimited resources and that the company can strike it rich. **Does the market exist?** Perhaps, but there is no way of knowing if it is feasible. You are taking a shot in the dark, unless you are an astronomer or a physicist. If you cannot evaluate the consensus, you should not play the stock.

Another company announces that it intends to launch a fleet of satellites that will allow people around the world to talk seamlessly on cellular phones. Does the market exist? You believe it does. **Can the company capture it?** That depends on the costs and the competition. You may have an opinion, but you probably have no real edge.

Cott, a maker of private-label sodas, was once a high-flyer. The analysts said that Cott could undercut Coke and Pepsi and take 20 percent of the market. **Does this concept make sense to you?** It did to many investors. But betting that companies like Coke and Pepsi will willingly give up major chunks of their markets is not usually a good way to win. At the beginning of 1994, Cott was selling for $30. Two years later, it was selling for $5.

Then, another hot private-label company, USA Detergents, hit Wall Street. The analysts said that it could capture 20 percent of the detergent market from Procter & Gamble and other major manufacturers. Investors jumped at the stock, giving it a huge multiple. But again, the reality was different from the hype. At the beginning of 1997, USA Detergents was selling for $46. By the end of the year, it was selling for $8. Companies like Procter & Gamble don't get where they are by allowing small competitors to take 20 percent of their markets. This is the type of reality check that you should easily be able to make.

Reality checks are not difficult. Listen to the concept. See if it makes sense. At times a company makes a claim that is so outlandish that no one should believe it, and yet both professionals and individuals often do. One of my favorites was Value Merchants, a retailer that operated $1 stores. In 1991, management announced that it intended to corner the market on $1 stores. It talked about cornering the market on $1 items the way that someone would talk about cornering the market on gold or silver. The concept seemed truly bizarre, but investors loved it. The stock surged from $256 to $1,358 and sported a 26x multiple.

Value Merchants opened stores everywhere, even in the Galleria in

Dallas. The idea must have been that after shopping in Neiman Marcus for a designer original, women would buy their kids a present for $1. Meanwhile the company was burning cash, laying out tens of millions of dollars to corner the market on junk. The junk did not sell as well as expected. Value Merchants started to lose money. The price of the stock plunged from $1,358 to $0.50 (cheap enough to be sold in the company's $1 stores). The lesson of Value Merchants was simple. The concept of cornering the market on $1 stores was idiotic. But because investors often like to buy into exciting-sounding concepts, few did a reality check until it was too late. Remember, junk is not a growth industry.

PRICE OF VALUE MERCHANTS' STOCK						
Date	10/90	10/91	10/92	10/93	10/94	10/95
Price	$275	$1,358	$460	$95	$28.50	$0.50

Wall Street is littered with companies that should never have passed anyone's reality check. Do you remember Silk Greenhouse, the company that ran artificial-flower superstores? It was a ridiculous concept, but it was also a high-flying stock. Many professionals, who were inundated with pitches from analysts, salespersons, and from the company itself, never did a reality check until Silk Greenhouse self-destructed. They could not see the forest for the (artificial) trees. Here the individual may actually have an advantage. Anyone who walked into one of these cavernous stores would have realized that this was a concept which could never work.

In doing a reality check, you often must go beyond the basic concept and look at the valuations. Many concepts sound good and even work, but they may not be worth the multiple at which the stock is selling.

It is often far more important to look at the risks before the opportunities. Analysts and companies want to tell the positive side of the story. Few companies will say that Wal-Mart is eating their lunch, and few analysts will issue reports contending that the management has no clue how to control costs. Instead, most accentuate the positives. Thus, spend more time looking at the potential negatives than at the potential positives.

REALITY CHECKS BEGIN AT HOME

When doing your reality check, draw on your direct experience. Review the process outlined in chapter 4 and see if you have any home-turf advantage. Do you have any specialized knowledge about the basic business? Do you use the company's products? Do you know anyone who works for the company, or for its competitors, customers, and suppliers? You see things every day that you can use in making investment decisions. You just have to be able to appreciate the value of those things and dig for information. If you have no home-turf advantage, look for another company to invest in.

If you read a report about a fast-growing retailer catering to teenagers, visit the stores. Are they crowded or empty? Does the merchandise look new or old? Is everything at full price, or is it on sale? Are the customers buying one item or many? Talk to the teenagers. Ask how they like the store and where else they shop. If they tell you that they would never shop anywhere else, you may have a winner. If they tell you that they are getting bored with the store, you may have a loser.

Watch the people who work in the stores. Are they helping the customers or sitting in the back chatting? A store with helpful personnel is often a well-managed company. When the store has quieted down, go talk to the employees. Tell them that you own the stock. Ask how they like the company and how business is. Don't be shy. Most people like to talk and will tell you interesting things about their company. You are not looking for inside information. You are only looking for a flavor of how the business is running.

Little things may tell you a lot. Have you ever wondered why the greeter in front of the Wal-Mart store always seems to smile while the Kmart greeter does not? One day I asked. The Kmart greeter growled:

"The Wal-Mart greeter has worked there for twenty years. He has so many stock options that he bought a second home. I live in a trailer. On weekends, I mow his lawn while he goes to the beach. When Kmart's stock is at $60 and Wal-Mart's stock is at $10, I'll smile for you."

For information about a manufacturer of a consumer product, follow the same pattern. If you are interested in a bicycle manufacturer, hang out in a bike shop. If you are interested in a maker of computer peripherals, go to a CompUSA store. If you are interested in Mattel and Hasbro, go to Toys R Us. Talk to the customers. Ask the salespeople if the products are selling, if there are delivery problems, and if the quality is up to par. If everyone tells you that a business is hot, it probably is.

The same process applies to other businesses, like restaurants. Look at what the analysts are saying is the key to success and see if you can see it for yourself. Are the parking lots full? Does the restaurant turn its tables? Ask to speak to the manager. Tell the manager that you own stock in the company and ask about the key issues in running the business. Managers will spend time with you if they are not too busy. They may even buy you a drink. After all, they do not know whether you own 100 or 100,000 shares.

The Web is particularly well suited to reality checks. Most people have computers and are currently online. (If you are not online, you should never invest in Internet stocks on your own.) If you hear of a hot Internet stock, check out the Web site yourself. Sign up for the product or service. See if it is as good as advertised.

If you are interested in a company that you buy from, ask your sales representatives for information. See if you can get them to explain how the company works. If the analysts are focusing on a particular point of competitive advantage, ask about it. Most salespeople will give you a straight answer. After all, they want to keep your business. If you buy the stock and it goes down, you will lose money, and they could lose the account.

If you are interested in one of your customers, talk to the person who is buying your products. If analysts are talking about new growth plans, ask about them. Besides impacting the stock, they may also impact your business. Most customers will be pleased to see that you are taking an interest in their business and will get you the answers.

If the company is in your hometown, look at stories in the local newspaper. Talk to your friends who work there. Tell them what the analysts have to say and ask their opinion. Ask if they are buying the stock of their company. You only need a small edge to win.

Try to zero in on the key issues. If you work for an advertising agency and are placing online ads with one of the search-engine companies, ask about the economics of the business. Perhaps the search-engine company will say, *"We are planning to move beyond advertising and start taking a fee for every product sold on our search engine."* Go back to the analyst reports. No one has calculated any direct product sales in their models, but you think this could be a huge business for the search-engine company. You now have a information that will put you ahead of the analysts.

When you talk to someone who works for a company, try to gain insights that other investors do not have. Ask a person about his or her own job, the management, and the corporate culture. Ask the type of questions that you would want to know if you were going to work for a company. Employees usually have a good feel for the people who run the business. If the company has a key executive who has gotten a lot of press, ask for an opinion on that person.

Your objective is very simple: **to uncover information that will lead you to a different view of the company than other investors have.** Don't waste your time asking questions that the person cannot answer. Don't ask a salesperson about earnings estimates. Salespeople usually do not know, and you can easily find the answers online. Ask about the things that will give you a special insight.

TALK TO INVESTOR RELATIONS

Once you have found a key issue that you can use to differentiate yourself from the consensus, your next step should be to talk to the company. Call back investor relations. (The first time you called, you simply asked for an information package.) The key in talking to investor relations is to get a handle on some facet of the business that will enable you to decide if the consensus is wrong.

Don't be afraid to ask questions. The professionals aren't. Don't worry if your questions are not perfect. This is not an exam. It is a learning process. The worst that can happen is that investor relations will hang up on you. Don't worry about asking stupid questions. If this were a crime, half of Wall Street would now be in jail. I remember going to a lunch with the chairman of an athletic-shoe company. During the presentation, he passed around his company's most high-tech basketball shoe. *"This shoe,"* the chairman said, *"is state of the art for only $105."*

A portfolio manager who ran a $400 million fund looked up. *"Each?"* she asked.

"We sell them by the pair," the chairman said, trying to avoid a smirk.

It is unlikely that you can ask a more foolish question than if sneakers are priced by the piece. Investor relations departments are used to foolish questions from even the largest investors, so don't feel self-conscious if you do not understand everything. But do your homework in advance. Companies will spend more time with you if they think you know what you are talking about.

What to Ask

- **Ask about specific things that you do not understand.** This is especially true if the business has a complex technology. Don't be embarrassed if you do not know what an EEPROM is. Many professionals don't either. Explaining these issues is the job of investor relations. If after the explanation, you still don't understand, drop the company. You will never win if you cannot understand its business.

- **Ask about the economics of the business.** You are not expected to know the intricacies of each industry, but you should be able to understand the issues that drive the valuation. It is perfectly acceptable to ask, "How do I understand the economics of your company?" If investor relations talks about cash flow, go to the cash flow page in the annual report and have them walk you through the numbers.

- **Ask about anything in an analyst's report that seems controversial or at odds with the company's stated objectives.** Companies will go to great lengths to explain why they think an analyst has gotten a story wrong. If an analyst says that the break-up value of a company is twice the stock price, ask investor relations why the company does not break itself up. The answer may be very interesting.

• **Ask why an analyst has just changed earnings estimates or ratings** (if one has). The company may merely say, "that is one analyst's opinion," but it is a question worth asking.

• **Ask about your direct experience with key issues.** An auto company talks about its cost-cutting measures. You have received four recall notices for your own car in six months. Ask whether the lower costs have resulted in quality problems. A discount store chain talks about its rapid new store opening programs. You could not find bicycles or gas grills in three of the branches at the start of the spring selling season. Ask whether the growth plans have exceeded the logistics capabilities of the company. An online service touts its growth, but you can never get connected. Ask whether the company has capacity constraints and how it intends to resolve them. Direct experience can lead you into an interesting dialog with a company. But make sure your questions are corporate ones and not minor customer service issues that apply primarily to you. Do not tell investor relations that you could not find the car color you wanted or you had to wait in a long line, unless you believe that these are companywide problems. If you can get in a dialog with the IR person, you can often get a solid piece of information that can help you make your investment decision.

WHAT *NOT* TO ASK

• **Don't ask what the company is going to earn.** Companies do not usually give projections. Check on the Web for the analysts' estimates. Then ask if the company is comfortable with the range. If the company is comfortable at the low end of the range, analysts may lower estimates and the stock may come under pressure. If it is comfortable at the high end, analysts may raise estimates and the stock may go up.

• **Don't ask if the stock is going to go up or down.** These people don't know, and if they did, they would not tell you. Ask about the price action of the stock only when there are major increases in volume and volatility and you have first checked the news, analysts' ratings, and earnings estimates.

• **Don't ask if you should buy or sell.** That is your decision, not theirs. This question will always give you away as an amateur. Your focus should not be on getting investment advise, but rather on finding out when the consensus is right or wrong.

You can also call the investor relations departments of customers, suppliers, and competitors. Some of the best information comes from firms that deal directly with the company in which you are interested. Customers and suppliers know which products are selling well, but they must be careful in commenting about the companies they deal with. If you want to get information from them, you have to be a little cagey. Instead of asking point blank how a supplier is doing, start asking questions about the customer's own business, and then segue into questions about the companies in which you are interested. For example, if you want to know about branded jeans, call investor relations of a department store chain. When investor relations talks about men's clothing, you might comment, *"I heard that Tommy, Calvin, and Guess are doing well, but that Mossimo and Lee are doing lousy."* You may often get no reaction, but sometimes the customer will give inputs that can be invaluable.

Talking to competitors can also be very valuable, even though they obviously have an ax to grind. They are, after all, competitors. Competitors will always give you a different point of view. They will usually tell you why they are better than the company in which you are interested. Comparing one view with the other may be extremely useful. But in talking to competitors, you should have done your homework. You cannot call up Compaq just to ask about Dell. If you call Compaq, you should first ask about its business, and then ask how it compares with Dell. Further, you must be sure that the two companies really are competitors. Coke and Pepsi are competitors, but Coke and Budweiser are not. Unless the competition is direct or intense, one company will probably not give you good feedback on the other. A small, regional discount store may consider Wal-Mart to be its competitor, but the reverse may not be true. It never hurts to ask the questions. Some investor relations departments have people who know a lot about their industry and are willing to share information.

LOOK FOR HOLES IN THE NUMBERS

Once you have a basic view of the company, the next step in fundamental analysis is to look for holes in the numbers. All that you are trying to do is to identify where the consensus is wrong. You do not need to figure out what numbers are the most important. Most reports will highlight the critical issues. Nor do you need to build an earnings or valuation model or calculate the ratios. The analysts have already done this. Your job is to look at the numbers and spot the holes.

Don't bury yourself in details. Find the page in the annual report that gives you the five- or ten-year summary. The summary page often combines numbers from the income statement, balance sheet, and cash flow statement, as well as other numbers that the company considers to be critical. A retailer might show the number of stores and the sales per square foot. A cable television company might show the number of households in its market, the percentage with cable, and the average revenue per household. The biggest advantage to the summary page is that it has only the most important numbers and presents them with a long-term, historic view. While you may miss out on some of the details, the advantages of having a good overview may more than compensate. In talking to companies for the first time, I have often pulled out the summary page and reviewed it line by line.

When you look at the summary page, see if you can spot any patterns. What does sales growth look like historically? Has it been consistent or erratic? Have margins been getting better or worse? How have expenses compared to sales? What has been the trend in earnings per share? How has return on equity (ROE) varied over time? How has the debt-to-equity ratio changed? What are the industry-specific issues on which the company has chosen to focus? We will be looking at each of these issues in detail.

Unless there have been many acquisitions or divestitures, most companies will show clear patterns. Make a mental picture of the patterns. Then look at the analysts' projections. Are any of their numbers inconsistent with the historical trends? If so, these numbers may be the key to the story. Don't worry about the numbers that are consistent. **Focus on the areas in which you see significant changes.** This will usually lead you to the issues that are at the heart of the company's success or failure.

This is not to say that change cannot occur. It can. But change is less common than constancy. Think about people. People can change. Overweight people can lose forty pounds and middle-aged couch potatoes can run a marathon. But most of the time, overweight people will stay overweight, and couch potatoes will choose to watch the marathon. It is the same with companies. Most will continue to follow the same pattern they have followed for years. So if someone is suggesting that the company is about to be transformed from a middle-aged couch potato into a marathon runner, the investor needs to focus on whether that's possible and why.

WATCH THE CHANGES IN SALES AND MARGINS

After looking at the summary page, look at the income statement. The company's income statement has the historical numbers, while the analysts' models also have their projections. The critical task is once again to look for changes. If sales, margins, expenses, and EPS have historically grown 10 percent every year, and if analysts are carrying a projected 10 percent growth rate, there is not much to the story. If analysts say a company that has been growing by 10 percent is now going to grow by 20 percent, you have a key issue on which to focus.

For many companies, the sales figures are the most important item. Look at the long-term historical record. Some companies grow consistently, while some have records that are much more cyclical. Look at the more recent record. Is growth accelerating or declining? See what the analysts expect. You could win or lose right here.

This may be a good time for another reality check. You can usually form your own opinion about sales growth. A company has grown from 5 percent to 35 percent of a market by buying up small competitors. The analysts say that they believe it can capture 55 percent, but as you look at the competition you believe that growth may become more difficult. Ask investor relations where the company thinks it can gain market share. Ask the competitors the same question, or go back to your home turf and see if you can find any inputs on your own.

QUESTIONS TO ASK FOR SALES-GROWTH REALITY CHECK

1. Ask about the overall growth of the market. Think about whether it is sustainable. People in a company are often more optimistic than people outside of it.

2. Ask about industry-specific issues. Is technology changing? What are the competitors doing? Some companies have a narrow view of their environment and can get blind-sided.

3. Ask about any projection by the analysts that you have difficulty accepting. If the analyst says that same-store gains, which have been averaging 2 percent, will jump to 10 percent, ask why? When the company explains the answer, see if you believe it. This could be the heart of your investment decision.

4. Ask what external factors most worry the company. Don't settle for pie-in-the-sky answers, like *the stock market could crash.* These types of comments are useless. Keep asking until you get specific answers, such as, *"We are terrified that Microsoft will turn out a product that competes directly against ours."*

5. If you see a product line that you believe is starting to sell very well, ask about it versus the analysts' expectations. Venture a concrete opinion and force investor relations to give you an answer. *"I think that your new products are selling better than the analysts think and that sales will*

surprise on the upside. " If you are right, investor relations may confirm your view or at least say that the company is optimistic. Concrete questions often bring concrete answers.

Next, look at the gross margins as a percent of sales. Gross margins are the profits that a company makes on its sales. Margins should show a relatively consistent historical pattern. They may be flat, or they may be going up or down slightly, but there is often a discernible trend. One again, the key is not the trend itself, but rather the changes. If margins start dropping sharply, it could mean that competition is getting more difficult. If margins start increasing sharply, it could mean that the competition is being less aggressive, which is good, or the company is getting greedy, which is bad. If margins jump to record levels, it could mean that the company has conquered its competition or is playing games with the numbers. If there are significant changes in the margins, the investor must check the cause.

This is not as difficult as it sounds because factors impacting margins should make common sense. Higher competition should lead to lower margins, as competitors squeeze each other on price. Lower competition should lead to higher margins, as competitive pressures abate. Look at the closest competitors. Are their margins moving in the same direction? If your company has higher margins while the closest competitors have much lower margins, something could be wrong. Do another reality check.

A large number of companies have recently begun to sell computers over the Internet. A few decided to cut prices and sell for cost. You can see the price changes every time you click on to their Web sites. Needless to say, their gross margins were trashed. But what about their competitors? In most cases, they should also suffer sharp declines in margins. If the analysts are not planning for these sharp declines, there could be disappointments.

COMPANIES CAN HIDE EARNINGS IN INVENTORIES AND RECEIVABLES

Turn to the balance sheet. Many investors are scared of working with balance sheets, but they are very simple. Remember, don't worry about industry standards or ratios; just look at the changes from period to period. Look first at the inventories. Inventories should grow at about the same rate as sales. If they grow faster, the company is either making too much or not selling enough.

The importance of inventories in most companies cannot be overstated. **Unlike fine wines, inventory does not improve with age.** A company that has too much inventory can be seriously overstating its earnings. Suppose that a computer manufacturer ended 1996 with sales of $100 million up from $90 million in 1995 and gross profits of $50 million up from $40 million. At first glance, it would appear that the company had a good 1996. But assume that inventories grew from $10 million to $40 million. What do you think last year's computers will be worth next year? Not much! The inventory may be sitting on the books for $40 million, but there is no way that anyone would ever pay that amount for the old computers. If you see that inventory jumped from $10 to $40 million while sales increased by only $10 million, you know the company has a major problem.

If the company had sold the extra inventory for a $20 million loss, profits would have plunged from $50 to $30 million. What looked like a good year was really a disaster. By keeping the extra inventory, the manufacturer was able to report much better profits, but it was only postponing its day of reckoning and jeopardizing its future.

Companies frequently put spin control on the level of their inventories. One of the most common sayings is, "Inventory is on plan." Don't try to ask what the plan is. You will never get a straight answer. Companies also say they are "bringing in new merchandise early" or "building inventories for better sales in the future." While there are times when these statements are appropriate, in most cases, higher inventory is a bad sign. The rule with inventories is simple: If inventory is growing faster than sales, current earnings may be overstated and future earnings could be at risk. If inventory is growing slower than sales, the current earnings could be understated and future earnings could be better than planned.

Before going back to the income statement, look at receivables. This is the money that the company is owed by customers. Receivables should be growing at the same rate as sales. If they are growing much faster, it could be a sign of trouble. It means the company is not getting paid and that it is giving special terms to customers to generate business. This can artificially inflate its sales and margins.

Consider the computer manufacturer. Instead of selling the computers at a big loss, the manufacturer might "sell" them for $50 million and make another $20 million profit. It would now appear to have record sales, record earnings, and no inventory problem. Analysts would be falling all over each other to raise estimates and pronounce the manufacturer a "growth company." However, in order to get the retailers to take the lousy merchandise, the manufacturer might have to promise that the retailer would not have to pay for two years and that any computers not sold could be returned for full credit. This, of course, is a sham. If the retailers do not have to pay and if they can return what they do not sell, then the sales are bogus and the earnings are way overstated. Unless you looked at the receivables, you would never see that there was a problem. It is fine for a company to say that it sold goods and made a nice profit, but if it never gets paid, what is the point?

These types of practices occur much more frequently than most investors believe. Even great companies sometimes have soft quarters and play subtle games to make sales and earnings look better. For years, at the end of many quarters, the major manufacturers of personal computers, such as Compaq and IBM, have offered special deals so that the computer resellers would "buy" extra computers. (In the industry, this technique is known as "stuffing the channel.") Because the resellers could return what they did not sell, many of the sales were not "real." But it was a convenient way for the manufacturers to get extra merchandise off their books and make their sales gain look better than it really was. In a world in which small changes in sales can impact the company's p/e ratio, these "deals" have had a major impact on the prices of the stocks. Of course, if the computers are sitting in warehouses waiting to be returned, the manufacturers are just postponing their day of reckoning.

The moral: **If receivables are growing much faster than sales, some serious games may be going on.** If companies are offering special deals to move merchandise, the deals will usually come back to haunt them. Analysts often do not pay enough attention to inventories and receivables, or they get suckered in to a company's spin control. As a result, inventories and receivables offer a good opportunity for individual investors to spot opportunities that the analysts miss.

A Case Study: The North Face

The North Face is a manufacturer of performance outerwear. Analysts loved the company, because it made great products and had what appeared to be an excellent growth rate. There were only two major problems. Inventories were growing much faster than sales. In a fashion business, too much inventory is especially risky. Perhaps more worrisome, receivables were growing faster than inventories. This meant that North Face was not getting paid. Since the customers were probably solvent, the logical explanation was that North Face was allowing customers to postpone payment so that they would take more merchandise. In other words, it was stuffing the stores with goods.

Eventually the game caught up with North Face. Sales and earnings started to slow. But inventories and receivables did not. The price of North Face's stock dropped. Management proposed to buy the company and take it private.

Unfortunately for management and North Face's shareholders, the auditors started checking the inventory and receivables and found a series of problems. North Face's stock plunged. The offer to buy the company was tabled. Incredibly, sometimes even managements do not realize that their inventories and receivables may be greatly exaggerating their earnings. But these are critical issues that every investor should watch.

MAKE SURE EXPENSES ARE IN LINE

Look at the relationship of expenses to sales. These lines show how the company is managing the cost side of its business. If expenses are declining very slightly as a percent of sales, it is usually a sign that management is doing a good job of running its business. If expenses are going up faster than sales, it could be a sign that the management is losing control. If the expenses are declining much faster than sales, it is usually a sign that management has taken draconian measures with regard to costs. This can be very positive, but sometimes cost-cutting can backfire.

If there is more than one category for expenses, note where the numbers are getting better or worse. When you have more detail, you can better judge whether the company is building for the future or just trying to report the best possible numbers in the present. If a company is spending more for marketing and advertising, these expenses may hurt its current year but make it stronger in the long term. If, on the other hand, the company is cutting back dramatically on these expenses, it may make more money this year, but lose in the long term. There is a fine balance between saving money now and building for the future. Every type of industry has critical issues. Research and development is a critical expense for technology and drug companies. Drilling exploratory wells is critical for an oil company. **When you look at a company, make sure that it is not cutting back on a critical category to meet its earnings estimates.** If it is, the current year may be fine, but the long-term growth rate may be at risk.

EXTRAORDINARY GOBBLEDYGOOK

Before you go any further, see if there are any special items that impact the earnings. Companies have learned how to turn a simple income statement into gobbledygook by making acquisitions and divestitures, writing off goodwill, and taking reserves for extraordinary items. **If the company has made a major acquisition or divestiture, ask yourself and investor relations departments if the analysts have correctly understood its financial implications.** If they have not, there is a problem, because the company has done a bad job of explaining the deal and the consensus is working with wrong information. If the company's explanation is too confusing, find another stock.

If you can understand the gobbledygook, the company may be worth looking at. Through the wonders of accounting, many companies have learned how to use gobbledygook to allow them to report better than expected earnings in the future. When a company makes an acquisition or a divestiture, it often takes reserves for closing facilities and discontinuing product lines. Without these reserves, these costs would impact future earnings, but now they are buried in a one-time charge that most investors ignore. If the reserves are sufficiently high, the company could be almost guaranteed of beating or at least meeting earnings estimates in the upcoming years. If you see a company that has made a simple acquisition or divestiture, ask investor relations about the amount and composition of its reserves. If you can understand how these reserves will impact future earnings, it could be worth the trouble to push through the gobbledygook.

WATCH FOR CHANGES IN INCOME

Look next at the level of pre-tax income as a percentage of sales. Is it consistent with the company's historical pattern? Some companies have very simple patterns. For the past ten years, pre-tax income might have been 8 percent of sales or it might have grown from 7 percent to 9 percent. In either case, the pattern will be very easy to see. If the projections show a sharp divergence from the historical pattern, ask what has changed in the company or the environment that will lead to this different result.

Some companies, such as steel, autos, and oils, have much more cyclical patterns. They can go from making a lot of money to losing money. With these companies, looking at a pattern becomes more difficult. Still other companies may not have income. Some, such as cable television or real estate investment trusts, may have high depreciation and amortization. Others, such as biotechs, may have high research and development expenditures. In these cases, there are obviously no pre-tax income patterns that can be of use. If pre-tax income as a percent of sales is not a good measure, ask investor relations what is.

If there is a reasonably stable pattern of pre-tax earnings as a percent of sales, look at the annual earnings progression. Many companies will have a consistent historical pattern. Growth companies, like Intel and Microsoft, will show 20 percent-plus improvement in pre-tax income. More mature growth companies, like Wal-Mart or Coke, should show 15 percent growth. Well-managed industry leaders, like May Department Stores, will grow 10 to 15 percent each year.

Some companies are very good at managing their earnings. Stable companies often take extra reserves if business is a little better than normal and fewer reserves if business is a little worse than normal so that they can show a consistent pattern. If you see a company that has reported twenty straight years of improving earnings, with each year in a relatively narrow band, you can be reasonably sure that not only is this a good business, but also that management is expert at managing its earnings.

Investors, especially professionals, almost always pay more for earnings consistency, because it is easier for them to sleep at night with companies that they know will not disappoint them. This is not to say that you should buy companies with consistent records. These companies are usually well followed and have higher p/e ratios than their less consistent counterparts. But consistent companies, for better or worse, present fewer challenges for the investor and that is why these stocks always look more expensive than comparable companies.

If the profit level changes significantly from historical levels, you should ask why. If a company has been growing by 15 percent a year and suddenly shows a year of 25 percent growth, you must ask, *"Was the increase a flash in the pan or is it sustainable?"* If the increase is sustainable, the company will gain a new p/e multiple, and the stock will soar. If the increase is not sustainable, the price of the stock may come down.

The reverse happens when companies have years that are below par. If a company that has been growing by 15 percent has a year of 5 percent growth, investors may rethink their views. If the 5 percent growth continues, the stock may be dead money or worse, but if the 15 percent growth rate returns, the stock could be very attractive. All of the analysis that has gone before should bring you to the point of evaluating the short- and long-term earnings growth rates, because it is these growth rates on which stock prices are based.

CASH FLOW: SHOW ME THE MONEY!

Next, look at the cash flow statement. Cash flow reflects all moneys flowing into and out of a company. Because cash flow focuses on money rather than on reported earnings or balance sheet items, it can often give a very different view of the company; and because cash flow is not as simple a measure as earnings, some analysts give it less attention than it deserves. **This often gives investors an opportunity that analysts have missed.**

The first part of the cash flow statement is the *Sources of Funds from Operations*. These are the funds generated by the company's business. Profits are a source of cash. (Losses are a use of cash.) Depreciation and amortization are also sources of cash. While these are charges against earnings, they have no impact on cash, and so must be added back in. Finally, there are changes in inventories, receivables, and other working capital items. The total of the earnings, depreciation, amortization, and changes in working capital comprise the sources of cash available to the company.

The next section of the cash flow statement is the *Uses of Funds in Operations*. It includes capital expenditures and acquisitions. The difference between the sources of funds and the uses of funds is the free cash flow.

Compare the level of capital expenditures and depreciation. Capital expenditures are the funds that the company is spending to build new facilities. Depreciation is used to write down the value of older assets. Theoretically, if the company is not growing, depreciation and capital expenditures should be in balance. If the company is growing, capital expenditures should be higher than depreciation.

Be cautious if capital expenditures look too low. Some companies, especially those that are highly leveraged, often spend less than they should. If an airline has capital expenditures that are half of depreciation, it is probably not replacing its old planes fast enough. Its fleet may be aging, and it might soon start to face higher breakdowns or worse. **If you see a company reduce its capital expenditures, ask what is happening. The company may be jeopardizing its future.**

Amortization is similar to depreciation except that it is usually used with intangible assets. Items that are amortized, such as goodwill, come when a company makes an acquisition. Goodwill represents the difference between what a company paid for a business and the business's real assets. Under the assumption that the value of the business will decline over time, the goodwill must be written off, or amortized.

In most cases, depreciation and amortization provide a fair view of the value of older assets, but sometimes the value of an asset declines faster or slower in the real world than it does on the books of the company. If the assets are declining in value faster than they are being depreciated, the earnings of the company will be overstated. This often happens with technology companies. If the assets are decline in value slower than they are being depreciated, the earnings will be understated. This often happens in real estate and media.

In real estate, for example, companies have to depreciate their buildings, but the value of the buildings may not be declining. It may actually be increasing. Yet each year, the company must take a charge against its earnings and reduce its book value by depreciating the property. This charge clearly understates the company's financial position. Properties that are written down to almost nothing on the books can be worth millions. For that reason, cash flow is a better measure than earnings and book value in looking at real estate companies. Cash flow is also a better measure for media companies which have to depreciate and amortize the costs of their stations, even though the stations usually increase in value.

THE IMPORTANCE OF POSITIVE CASH FLOW

Once you know the sources and uses of funds, look at free cash flow. If cash flow is positive, a company can use it to make acquisitions, buy back stock, or otherwise enhance earnings. If it is negative, the company will have to raise capital to keep growing. Everything else being equal, positive cash flow is very important.

Rapidly growing companies can be cash-flow negative because they need capital to fund their growth. There is nothing wrong with being cash-flow negative as long as the company has cash and access to the capital markets. But if something goes wrong, these companies could face a liquidity crisis. More than one fast-growing company has been forced into bankruptcy because it had too high a negative free cash flow and could not raise new capital. Thus, if a company is running a large negative cash flow, you should always check to see how much cash or lines of credit it has on hand. **If the company does not have enough credit to weather a storm, you may want to think about putting your money somewhere else.**

Think about an Internet company that is burning money in an effort to build its customer base. This game works as long as its stock price stays high, so that it can sell more equity to finance future growth. But what happens if the stock price drops and the company can no longer access the equity markets? Now the negative cash flow could jeopardize its future.

Just because a company is growing does not mean that it has to burn cash. Many of the greatest companies, like Microsoft or Wal-Mart, have been cash-flow positive or neutral during many of their fastest growth years. With the exception of a few industries that are extremely capital intensive, most great companies should be able to control their capital expenditures and their working capital in order to be cash-flow positive. If you look at two companies in the same industry with the same growth rate, the better company will usually have the higher free cash flow. Cash flow is a critical measure of a company's health and a good barometer of management's ability to run its business.

The cash flow statement ties into the level of debt and equity on the balance sheet. If the company is generating positive cash flow, the ratio of debt to equity will usually decline. If cash flow is negative, the ratio will usually increase. While most analysts pay only lip service to this ratio, it often offers investors the opportunity to find companies that will surprise on the upside or the downside.

Look at the debt/equity ratio over time. Most companies try to keep it within a narrow range. If the ratio is going up quickly, some of the company's recent earnings improvement may have come from higher leverage, and the company may have problems financing future growth. On the other hand, if the debt/equity ratio has declined below its historical norms, the company may be able to leverage its earnings by buying back stock or making acquisitions. **Analysts often ignore the opportunities in companies with low debt/equity ratios because they are difficult to quantify.** Unless a company announces a buyback, most analysts will not incorporate it into their models. But companies with low debt/equity ratios very often re-lever themselves, and in so doing, provide upside surprises in earnings.

RETURN ON EQUITY IS A USEFUL MEASURE

Before making a final valuation, take a quick look at the company's return on equity (ROE). Return on equity is a critical number because it shows the profits that a company has been able to generate with a particular level of equity. It often corresponds directly to the earnings growth rate. Generally, the higher the return on equity, the better the company.

Analysts often underrate good companies with high returns on equity, if those companies lack glamour or upside earnings surprises. They may look at a company with a 20 percent return on equity and only a 10 percent gain in sales and assume that the company no longer has growth opportunities. But companies with high returns on equity can usually show strong earnings growth by making acquisitions or by buying back their stock. **Long-term investors can often outperform the market by buying companies whose p/e ratio is well below their ROE.**

The reverse also occurs. Analysts can fall in love with companies with mediocre returns on equity, if they are in a hot industry or if they suddenly produce upside surprises in earnings. But matter how much the analysts may love a stock and no matter how much it may outperform in the short term, few companies will be able to support a lofty stock price if their ROE is much lower than their p/e ratio. Except in high-growth startups or in businesses in which "equity" may not be a fair gauge, such as media or real estate, it is always useful for investors to compare the p/e ratio with the return on equity.

LET'S MAKE A DEAL: TAKEOVER TARGETS

Finally, you may want to look at the breakup or takeover value of a company. Vast sums have been made in takeovers. In the early 1980s, the media companies were takeover targets. Then the action shifted to department-store chains, drug companies, and now to financial services and brokerage companies. Almost every industry has seen a large number of takeovers and most have been at a substantial premium to the market price.

While you should not try to compete with the risk arbitrageurs on companies that are already "in play," it is perfectly acceptable to buy companies that you believe *could* become takeover targets, and then hold them in the hope that lightning will strike. But if you intend to look at a stock as a potential takeover target, you must follow a few basic steps. See if other takeovers are occurring in the industry. If there is a stock on your monitor list that is being taken over, take a look at its closest competitors. If you see a number of takeovers in an industry, go to a Web site such as Morningstar.net and screen the names of all the public companies in the industry. Takeovers follow patterns. When one company in an industry makes an acquisition, others commonly follow.

Look at the last several acquisitions and at the analysts' comments on them. Is there a pattern to the valuations? If there is serious merger activity in an industry, most analysts will have some type of takeover valuation you can use to figure out the stock's takeover value.

Also, look at the stock's takeover premium, the difference between the current price and the price that the stock would have if there were no talk of takeovers. Now you have a very simple risk/reward analysis. Compare the takeover value to the current price. That gives you your upside. Look at the takeover premium. That gives you your downside. Look at the level of deals in an industry and make your best guess. You are interested in a large regional bank that you believe would be worth $60 in a takeover and would normally sell for $30 based on its earnings. If the stock is at $35, the takeover premium is only $5, and it is probably a good investment. But if it is selling at $55, with a $25 takeover premium, it may already be too expensive. If the takeover premium is low and merger activity is high, the stock could be worth a look. If the takeover premium is high, it may not be worth your trouble.

Playing takeovers requires patience, so that you don't give up on a stock just before the takeover comes. If you play takeovers, understand why you are buying a particular stock. Watch the action in the industry. As long as the potential acquirers still appear to have an appetite, be patient. Your day will come.

Dividends: Much Ado About Nothing

In most cases, **dividends should be irrelevant or perhaps even negative for the individual investor.** For companies and investors, dividends have unfavorable tax treatment. Companies must pay taxes on their earnings, even if they pay them out as dividends. Individuals, with taxable accounts, must also pay taxes on their dividends at ordinary income rates. This means that dividends are taxed twice at high rates. (For this reason, companies with high dividends are usually more appropriate for tax-free accounts, such as IRAs.) Most individuals with regular accounts will be better off if the companies use their profits to spur growth or take the money they would have paid out in dividends and use it to buy back stock.

Investors often see companies with high dividends and think that they are getting a bargain. In some cases, they may be. But if the company is not earning its dividend, there is a risk that it could be cut. Some stocks, such as real estate investment trusts (REITs), are considered to be dividend plays. In these stocks, investors often equate dividends with earnings. The problem is that if the fundamentals are not strong, the dividends will be slashed. Over the past few years, utility investors have learned to their dismay that "dividend plays" can spell disaster.

This said, companies with higher dividends tend to have less volatile stock prices. This is especially relevant when the market drops and investors seek some current yield. Some companies also use dividends as a way of signaling projected earnings. These are usually larger companies with a solid history of raising the dividend each year. If a company has raised its dividend between 10 percent and 15 percent every year for twenty years, and it announces that this year its dividend will increase by 15 percent, it is reasonably safe to assume that the company believes its earnings will be better than average. In companies with this pattern, investors should look at dividends if the current earnings are disappointing. If the company continues to increase its dividend, it is sending a signal to investors that it is confident about its future.

VALUING A STOCK

Now that you have looked at the earnings statement, the balance sheet, and the income statement, and made your reality checks, it is time to come up with a valuation so you can decide whether to buy or sell the stock. There are a vast number of ways to value stocks. Different investors have their own preferences and most industries have their own unique formulas. There is no way to cover all the alternatives, but **you do not need to understand all of the intricacies of valuing stocks, because you are only trying to decide when the consensus is off target.**

In most cases, the consensus of the analysts will tell you how they believe the stock should be valued. Their valuation model is usually on the top of their reports. Price/earnings ratios are the most common model. Some industries will use *price/cash flow ratios* or their equivalent. A few industries will have other formulas, such as *price/discounted future earnings*. In most cases, the consensus is useful as a starting point.

Utilizing the work that you have done, make your own decision as to the growth rate of the stock. You want to buy those stocks with an earnings stream worth more than the stock price and sell those stocks with a stream worth less. If you cannot calculate the value of the stream, look at the p/e ratio. The table below indicates the appropriate p/e ratios for stocks with consistent earnings patterns. (It is derived by taking the earnings growth and discounting it back to the present at 10 percent.) At current interest levels, a slightly lower discount rate could be used, which would justify slightly higher multiples. If interest rates were to go up sharply, the discount rate would have to be increased, which would justify lower multiples.

Earnings Growth Rate	-10%	-5%	0%	+5%	+10%	+15%	+20%	+25%	+30%
P/E Ratio	5x	6.5x	8x	10x	14x	19x	27x	39x	56x

Thus, if you think that the growth will approximate 10 percent, the stock should probably have about a 14x multiple, while if you think that the growth will approximate 20 percent, the stock should probably have a 27x multiple. This chart is obviously of little use with cyclical companies.

However, since many companies have a somewhat consistent earnings pattern, it will work in a reasonable number of cases.

Before you finish, double-check your valuation. If you are a little away from consensus, you are probably in good shape, but if you are too far away, take another look at your analysis. Focus on the issues that differentiate you from the analysts. If you believe that sales growth will be better than expected, check those numbers. If you believe that inventories will lead to lower than expected earnings, check those. If you are buying the stock based on something other than earnings growth, check the issues that are at the core of your valuation. If, for example, you are buying a company based on a takeover value, look at other deals in the industry to make sure that you are using the correct valuation techniques.

Do not spend too much time with a calculator. You are not trying to become a Certified Financial Analyst. All you have to do is look at the consensus and decide when it is right or wrong by using the tools discussed in this section. Listen to the company's strategy. Does it make sense? Are the products good? Do you like the management? Draw from your own experience. Look at the expectations. Look at the earnings. Are they clean? Look at the balance sheet. Are there items that appear to be growing too fast? Pay special attention to the inventory. Look at the cash flow. Is it positive? Look at the return on equity. Could the company be a takeover play? Look at the p/e ratio. Is it in line with the growth rate? Look back at your analysis. See if you have an edge over the analysts. There are thousands of stocks. It is best to find those in which you have an edge.

You should now be in a good position to start to make some investment decisions based on your fundamental analysis. However, before you do, it would be extremely useful to stop and look at the technical pattern of the stock. Very often technical patterns can highlight critical issues that analysts and institutional investors miss.

VALUATION MATTERS, EVEN FOR INTERNET STOCKS

Before turning to technical analysis, one last fundamental subject should be addressed. Over the last year, the market has been driven by

Internet stocks. Internet analysts say that we are at the beginning of a new industrial revolution. I agree with them. They say that many Internet companies will come to dominate their industries. I agree with them. They say that with the huge potential growth, we are in a new "paradigm" in which old valuation measures are irrelevant. They say that these stocks should not be judged by discounted sales, earnings, and cash flow. Instead they should be judged by new metrics, like "hits" or "page views." This is nonsense!

Internet analysts and investors have junked the old valuation measures and jumped on the new "paradigm" because it is the only thing they can say to justify having buy recommendations on some of the companies that comprise the major part of their investment-banking activities.

In the beginning, analysts justified the Internet stocks using traditional valuation measures. They looked at companies, like Amazon.com, the way they would look at a retailer. They estimated its share of the publishing business ten years out, made assumptions about margins and costs, and came up with a discounted cash flow analysis. Much of the work was highly hypothetical, because it is impossible to predict where a new business will be ten years from now. But it was based on sound analysis.

Yet as the stocks continued to rocket upwards, the analysts had a problem. They could no longer justify the prices using fundamental analysis. To justify Amazon, you had to assume that it could control half of the book business in the United States and make margins twice that of anyone else.

How could you justify giving Etoys a valuation double that of Toys R Us? Toys R Us has a 20 percent market share. To justify the valuations, Etoys would have to have a much higher market share and a much higher level of profitability.

What about the Internet stocks in the financial services industry? In the beginning, the analysts estimated the revenues and earnings over an extended period, discounted them back to the present, and made their valuations. The only problem was that the earnings usually did not materialize. Many leaders, like Etrade and Ameritrade, decided to step up their advertising expenses in order to gain "first mover advantages." Revenues went up, but margins went down and losses increased. It was difficult to make a case that profits and margins would improve when they were both going down.

The problems of the analysts became more complicated because barriers to starting a business on the Web became lower than people had thought. Look at all the companies selling computers and software. Most are lowering their margins to build traffic. How do you build an earnings model for a company that says it is selling products at cost and making it up on volume?

If these online retail companies were difficult to value, what could analysts do with other types of start-ups? How were they going to value all of the non-trading financial sites, such as The Street.com, Hoovers, Multex, or Market Watch.com? There was not enough advertising in the world to justify the valuations.

What about the new media businesses, such as iVillage? You could not value this company as you would a magazine. You had to assume that it would build all sorts of revenue-producing ancillary businesses. But estimating the value of these businesses was near impossible because there were none.

So the analysts were in a quandary. The valuation measures that they, and everyone else, had always used did not work, and the prices of the stocks kept going higher and higher. These analysts and their firms were making millions on the investment-banking business from the Internet companies. Investors had an unquenchable desire for these stocks, so the analysts had to find some way of justifying the prices.

The easiest way to justify valuations that are not justifiable is to say that the old methods of valuation were no longer valid. By contending that we are in a new "paradigm," analysts could dispense with the problems of making long-term earnings estimates and analyzing cash flows. They could come up with their own "metrics" that would enable them to pedal stocks at levels never before seen. Investors also bought into the concept, because they wanted to own these stocks.

This is not to say that every Internet stock is overpriced. Many are not, especially at the time that I am writing this book, because they are down dramatically from their highs. Nor is it to say that analyzing an Internet stock is easy. It is not. In fact, it is extremely difficult. Some of these stocks, which currently have no sales and earnings, are occupying turf that could allow them to develop wonderful sources of revenue and profits. Early dominant companies, like Yahoo! and AOL, are generating revenues from companies that want to have prime positions on their sites. It is easy to make the case that these companies will eventually take a fee for every transaction that occurs on their sites and will become immensely profitable. This is also not to say that investors should not own some of these stocks. I own some Internet stocks in my fund. And it's fun to trade them.

The problem with a new "paradigm" is that it permits sloppy thinking. It allows analysts to come up with valuations that can never be justified and will never have any basis in reality. In the end, the valuation for the Internet stocks must be comparable to the valuations of stocks in other industries. They may be growing faster. They may have huge potential, but they will still have to generate profits, or at least cash flow. There is nothing wrong with looking at the "metrics" of the Internet. Perhaps "click-throughs" and "hits" are the only good way to judge the progress of many new businesses. But as they mature, investors will have to take a more rigorous look at their economics. When they do, they will find that valuations do matter.

CHAPTER SEVEN

Technical Weapons

In war, guerrillas must develop better sources of intelligence than their more powerful enemy. This may seem like an impossible task, but guerrillas have an ironic advantage. An army's size makes it easy to track, while the guerrillas' lack of size often enables them to avoid a direct assault and gives them opportunities to counterattack.

The situation in investing is similar. Professionals obtain the best intelligence that money can buy by hiring analysts to predict earnings, technicians to chart stocks, and strategists to predict the market. Individuals cannot match these resources. The task for the individual may sound daunting, but it is actually much easier than it would appear, because the professionals present a huge target that is easy to track. Professionals on Wall Street, like armies, move en masse. Their investments often form clear patterns that individuals can easily follow. If an investor can gain a good overview of the professionals' movements, that individual can take measures to avoid the professionals' strengths and can counterattack to expose their weaknesses. **Charts are the technical weapons that the individual can use to follow the actions of the professionals and anticipate critical changes in direction**.

CHARTS: THE EARLY WARNING SYSTEM

Charts in investing are the equivalent of the satellite photographs in war. They present a picture of all of the trading in a particular stock, index, or market. The chart shows how prices and volumes are moving. Since the professionals make up most of the trading, and since they move in much more dramatic ways than do individuals, their actions make up the preponderance of the information on the charts. As a result, just as satellite photographs are especially effective in showing the movement of the army, so charts are especially effective in showing the actions of professionals.

A chart shows a historical picture of how a stock has performed, but many charts also seem to be able to predict the future action of a stock. A chart often shows when a stock is about to break out and begin a long run on the upside as well as when it is about to break down and begin a long move on the downside.

Most fundamental investors reject the notion that chart patterns can foreshadow the future. They look at technical analysis as akin to voodoo. While many portfolio managers use charts religiously, few institutional salespersons and even fewer analysts use them. When I was an analyst, my partner, Leigh Curry, was an institutional salesman. Every time an analyst talked about a new idea, Leigh checked the technical pattern of the stock. In most cases, the analysts would have done well to listen to what Leigh had to say, because he often saw signs on the charts that the analysts had missed. The reality is that technical analysis is much more predictive than most fundamental investors would admit.

There are three key reasons that charts can often predict the future price behavior of stocks:

1. Because professionals cannot change directions quickly, their future actions are often foreshadowed on the charts. The charts do not actually predict the future. Rather they show signs of a move before it has become apparent to most investors. When you look at a chart, you can often see signs of a major change. You can see when a stock enters an up trend, when it starts to plateau out, when it begins a decline, and when it bottoms. While small movements may be hard to track, major changes are usually well defined.

2. Technical patterns influence technical investors. As trading patterns of stocks change, they often become self-fulfilling prophecies, because many investors use them as their primary investment technique. Stocks that develop strong trading patterns will usually keep moving up because technical investors are buying, while stocks that develop weak trading patterns will usually keep moving down because technical investors are selling. In fact, stocks with strong or weak trading patterns can react in dramatically different ways to the same event. How often have you watched a stock that has been "acting strong" shrug off what appears to be bad news and continue moving up? Or how often have you seen a stock that has been "acting weak" get pummeled by a seemingly inconsequential piece of information? Thus, the actions of the technical investors combined with the actions of the mass of professionals will emphasize the direction of the stock, making it even easier for the individual to spot the future trends.

3. The trading pattern of a stock very often presages, not reflects, the news. Some investors will always have information sooner than others. They may be insiders, industry experts, or well-informed investors. If they act on their knowledge by buying or selling, they will create a new trading pattern. This trading pattern begins to reflect fundamentals of which the market as a whole is still ignorant. Individuals may watch a stock begin to break out and wonder what is happening. They may even call the company or the analysts and be told that there has been no change in the fundamentals. Then, several months later, when the company reports earnings that are much better than expected, it becomes clear that the trading action did mean something. Someone had known that business was going to be better than planned and had aggressively bought the stock.

How often have you seen a stock drop sharply on little or no news? Your broker tells you that an analyst reduced estimates by $0.02, the market completely overreacted, and this is a great buying opportunity. You buy the stock. Then, three weeks later, the company announces that earnings will be disappointing. The stock plunges. *"I knew something was wrong,"* you mutter as you dump your stock. In retrospect, it was clear that someone had a different view of the fundamentals, and that they had been right. When stocks get crushed on a particular day because of a disappointing announcement, look at the trading pattern in the previous weeks. In most cases, stocks will have already traded down, usually on strong volume. While the horrible news may have been a surprise to you, many investors had been expecting problems and had already been selling.

The most common error investors make is to ignore strong opposing signs on the charts. Investors often become wed to a company. When a minor event occurs, the analysts, who are also wed to the stock, rush to issue reports saying that "the market has overreacted." The investors read the reports and feel comforted. They want to believe that the analysts are right. But very often this "overreaction" turns out to be anything but that. Changing technicals often presage changing fundamentals. When the direction of a stock changes, the smart investor should always study the trading pattern and try to figure out what others see. **Fighting or ignoring the tape can be a sure-fire way for investors to lose money.**

Because the technical patterns in the charts reflect the collective wisdom of all investors, the easiest way to spot future trends is to watch for significant changes in the patterns. Even if you are a fundamental investor, you should watch the chart of a stock and look for clues to its future direction. Sometimes the tape will not tell you much, but sometimes it will form a pattern that is so dramatic that even a novice can see bullish or bearish signals. If you see these signals, use them either to confirm an existing position or rethink a particular strategy. More often than not, it will enable you to significantly improve your performance.

THE TREND IS YOUR FRIEND

The first thing to understand about technical patterns is that once stocks start to go up, they go up much further than most people think, and once they start to go down, they go down much more than most people think. This is Newton's First Law of Physics. A body in motion stays in motion until stopped by a greater force. On Wall Street, traders refer to this as the "trend." A common saying is *"The trend is your friend."* What is means is simple: **Stick with what is working. Avoid what is not working.**

This is a critical lesson for all investors, but it is especially critical for individuals. You would not think of standing on a railroad track as a freight train came speeding towards you. Nor would you think of blocking the exit as hundreds of screaming people came rushing out of a burning theater. These would be acts of total stupidity. But would you think of buying a stock that was plunging to new lows on huge volume as professional investors rushed to the exit? Few individual investors know enough about a particular company to buy when the masses of investors are selling or sell when the masses are investors are buying.

This is often a difficult issue for most investors, professionals and well as individuals, because most people do not like to admit when they are wrong. You see a stock you like and buy it. Then something happens. Investors rush to sell as the stock plunges. You review your analysis and decide that you are right and the rest of the Street is wrong. You double your holdings. After all, you have studied the company and have home-turf advantages. But what about all of the other people? What are they thinking? What do they know? This much is certain. Even if you did your homework and everyone else is simply panicked, there will be no rationality in the price or in the trading action of the stock.

Admitting a mistake is tough. It may be the most difficult lesson that I have tried to learn. But trying to stop panicked investors is tougher. When I see a stock rapidly change direction, I always review my analysis and try to figure out what others see that I do not.

Stocks are much more volatile than most investors think. Look at Oxford Health Plan, which went from $15 to $90 and back to $15 in four years; Just for Feet, which went from $12 to $36 and back to $4 in just over two years; or Rational Software, which went from $11 to $48 and back to $11 in little more than one year. Was it merely changes in fundamentals that accounted for these remarkable moves? The answer is no. These stocks had huge moves up and down because of the power of momentum.

A particular stock may have acted like a dog, by trading around the same price for months while the market rallied. Then, what seems like a small event occurs. Perhaps the growth rate is slightly higher than the analysts had expected. The buyers nudge the stock up. It breaks through a resistance level and starts to run. Analysts raise their estimates. Technicians say the stock has broken out. Momentum investors pile in. The stock doubles or even quadruples. You look at the price of the stock and think that the market is irrational. From your point of view, it may be. But you should never make the mistake of betting against it. **Momentum can take a stock up much further than anyone would ever expect**.

Momentum works on the downside as well, as the owners of Oxford Health Plans, Just For Feet, and Rational Software can testify. The stock struggles to maintain its price, usually on higher volume. Then another seemingly small event occurs. Perhaps earnings were slightly lower than investors had expected. The stock breaks through a support level and starts to drop. As it does, analysts lower their estimates, technicians say the stock has broken down, and momentum investors flee. The stock plunges. In fact, **momentum on the downside is usually faster and stronger than momentum on the upside**. Some investors buy, believing that the stock is now "cheap," but this is usually a mistake. When a momentum stock plunges, it will usually keep plunging. The first major decline is rarely the last.

You may look quizzically at stocks that surge and then fall back, wondering how the bulls could have loved them and then the bears could have hated them so much. There may be no completely logical answer as to why small changes in sales and earnings can transform a company from a dog to a growth company and back to a dog, but those who look for logic and fight the tape lose money.

It is often tempting for an investor to sell a stock that is going up strongly or buy a stock that has started to "correct." But most of the time, these decisions will be wrong. Holding your position against a powerful tape is like holding your position against a powerful army. You will be annihilated. In the long run, your judgment may be vindicated, but by then, you will have already been wiped out. If a stock has strong momentum, the wise investor should avoid fighting the tape and wait for signs of a top or a bottom before acting.

Investors often confuse betting against the trend with betting against the consensus. These are not the same. The consensus shows the views of all professionals, while the trend shows the direction of a stock or of the market as a whole. Typically, the consensus reaches extremes after the market has already had a major move. High levels of bullishness do not emerge when stocks or markets break out. Instead, they emerge when stocks or markets reach peaks. (Remember that the stocks with the highest ratings only received those ratings after they had sustained major advances.) Similarly, high levels of bearishness do not emerge when stocks start to break down. Instead, they emerge when stocks have bottomed out and the selling is over. In fact, the best times to act are when the consensus and the trend are at odds with each other. You should buy when the trend is up, but the consensus is still bearish, while you should sell when the trend is turning down, but the consensus is still bullish.

THE BREAKOUT

In order to anticipate the moves of the professionals, there are a few simple chart patterns that all investors should understand. The first is the breakout. **Every time a stock begins a major move, there is an instant in which the direction of the move becomes clear.** The instant occurs when the power balance between buyers and sellers shifts and the change in direction begins to emerge. It is typically defined not by a surge in price, but by a combination of a minor change in price and a major change in volume. While price is the factor that most investors watch, volume may be more important in determining future price movements.

A stock may have formed a solid base by trading around the same price for six months with buyers and sellers roughly in balance. The first sign that a change is about to occur is reflected in higher volume. If volume suddenly surges, it is a sign that a large number of people are making new bets. In most cases when the volume surges, the bets are being made by professionals and most are reacting to some perceived change in the company. If volume surges while the stock inches up, it is a sign that more people are making bets on the upside. If you look at the chart of a stock, you can always see when these changes are occurring.

Identifying the breakout offers a great opportunity to make money. Since the breakout occurs before the stock has had much of a move, the individual is not allowing the professionals to make most of the early profits. Because it takes the professionals a long time to complete most moves, the individual can often spot the breakout the moment it occurs, and move without much risk, since the professionals will drive the stock higher. If individuals can respond to the breakout by moving quickly, they can capitalize on the professionals' new behavior and still beat the move up.

THE TUG OF WAR

Think of the stock pattern as a tug of war between buyers and sellers. In a tug of war, there will be two teams pulling on a rope with a flag in the middle. The two teams may be fighting to a standstill, using moderate amounts of energy. But then one team begins to pull with greater power. This is the instant at which the tide has turned. The flag is still in the center. Both teams are still straining for an advantage, but you can look at the two teams and sense that the momentum has swung. The first team seems to pull with ease. The other team digs in. You can see the strain on the faces of its members. They are pulling as hard as they can. But they are not pulling to win. They are pulling to avoid losing. Both sides are now exerting more energy.

Then the first team exerts a strong, coordinated pull. The flag moves a few feet. The members of the second team scramble to regain their balance. Perhaps they even pull the flag back a foot. But then the first team exerts another coordinated pull, and the flag moves another two feet. The flag is still near the middle, but you know who is going to win. These are the "breakout" pulls that permanently set the direction of the tug of war. This is when you want to make your move. The pullers on the second team lose their footing. Their will is broken. The rout is on, as the first team now relentlessly drags the second team over the finish line.

This tug-of-war pattern is very common in the trading of stocks. The buyers and sellers may be fighting to a standstill. Then some event occurs that gives one side an advantage. As in the tug of war, there will be a small change in the price of the stock and a big increase in the trading volume. The volume is the equivalent of the energy level in the tug of war. The volume reflects the commitment of the professionals to changing the price of the stock.

When the momentum swings to the side of the buyers, the stock moves up on very high trading volume. But the sellers do not immediately capitulate. They dig in and attempt to keep the stock in the range. Now the buyers move the stock up on very high volume, while the sellers bring it down on much lower volume. The price may still not have changed much, but you can see the differences in the power of the buyers and the sellers. The tide permanently swings when there is a record increase in volume accompanied by a small increase in price that is often above the range in which the stock has been trading. This is known as the breakout. It is the instant at which the buyers have exerted their will over the sellers and the direction of the price of the stock has been set.

After the breakout, the volume declines from its peak, not because the buyers have lost their zest, but because the sellers have capitulated. As the volume settles down, the stock moves up faster. As the stock continues its advance, most of the sellers finally capitulate. Volume often drops again. Finally, the sellers are routed.

The key is to understand the timing of the struggle between the two forces. In watching the tug of war, the time to bet is when the momentum has turned, not when the losing team is lying on the ground. In picking stocks, **the time to buy or sell is when the direction becomes clear, not after the stocks have already moved.** The easiest way to do this is to watch the trading patterns and understand the signals that they convey.

Nothing demonstrates the tug of war between buyers and sellers better than Price & Volume Charts. These charts show both the price and the volume at various points in time. The price is shown as a line across the top of the chart. (Prices are on the left-hand axis.) The volume is shown in columns at the bottom of the chart. (Volume is on the right-hand axis.) When reading the chart, investors should look at both price and volume together. Investors should seek to find the point when changes in volume are about to result in changes in price. If investors can identify this point, they can move before the market does.

THE MOVE UP

The biggest opportunity to make a large profit comes in stocks that break out. These stocks tend to gain momentum and move up much further than one would ever imagine. In most cases, the pattern is easy to see. To summarize:

1. The stock builds a strong base at a price for an extended period of time.

2. It trades up on heavy volume, down on light volume, and refuses to break below the base.

3. Huge volume is traded on the upside as the stock breaks out of the range.

4. The volume drops below the breakout level as the stock continues to move up.

5. The stock maintains its move as long as upside volume is higher than downside volume.

A CASE STUDY: ROSS STORES

Ross Stores, an off-price retailer, demonstrated this breakout pattern in 1995 and 1996. The following chart shows the two major components of trading, price and volume. The price is depicted by the line in the upper section of the chart, while the volume is depicted by the columns in the lower section of the chart.

The first pattern investors should look for is a long solid base followed by strong breakout volume. In early 1995, Ross Stores formed a strong base at the $5 to $6 level. During the week of May 19, Ross traded five times its normal volume. This spike in volume was the first sign of a breakout and an unmistakable buy signal. With this breakout volume, the price moved up to $6. While the volume had broken out, the stock price was still in the trading range. In August, the volume accelerated again. This was the second buy signal. Ross broke above the critical $6 level and moved to $8, firmly breaking out of its trading range. Acting on either of these buy signals would have enabled the investor to purchase Ross Stores at the beginning of its move.

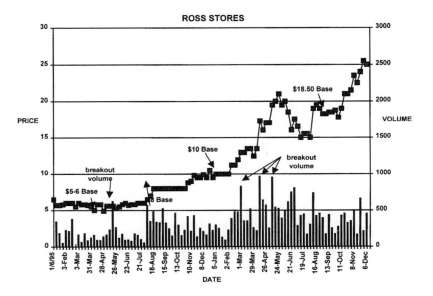

Ross remained in the $8 range for 11 weeks, another good sign. When a stock moves up, it must form a new base, otherwise it is susceptible to sharp downdrafts. Think of the move up as flights of stairs. There must be landings where stocks can rest and catch their breath. Otherwise, if they start to fall, they will drop back to where they started. A base is a place where a stock can consolidate its gains and stabilize itself. However, if the stock is to form a solid base, the volume must be moderate, indicating that many of the original investors are comfortable with their position. Moderate volume at a base is a sign of stability. Huge volume at a base is a sign of future instability.

Once a new base is formed, the stock should be able to break out again. A second stage breakout should have volume that is substantially higher than the previous base ($8 for Ross) but lower than the original breakout. In early November, Ross began its second-stage breakout. As Ross continued its upward move, it followed this pattern of forming a base on moderate volume and then breaking out on higher volume.

After trading up to $10, it formed a new base for eleven weeks. Then, in February, it broke out again, trading very heavy volume as the stock went from $10 to $13. This move was especially critical for two reasons. First, the volume was higher than that of the original breakout. Because there were long and stable bases at $8 and $10, the strong upside volume was a very bullish sign, indicating that the breakout on higher volume could be sustained. Second, $13 was an all-time high for the stock. Whenever a stock reaches an all-time high, it is usually critical that it breaks through that high on very strong volume. If it does not, it will usually drop back.

ROSS LONG TERM

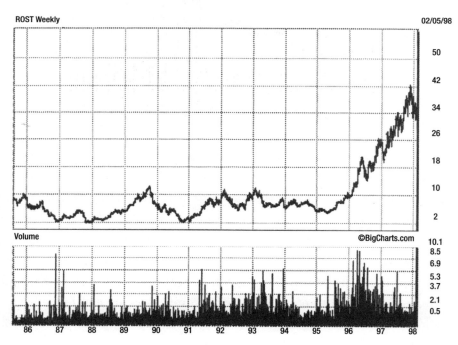

In the previous ten years, Ross had moved above $10 on three occasions, but each time, it had been unable to penetrate $12. Look at Ross's long-term chart. You will see that the stock kept bounding off $3 at the bottom and $12 at the top. While the stock moved back and forth, it was never able to break out of this range until the volume started to build in 1996.

The more times a stock tries to break through a price and fails, the stronger will be the resistance at that price. There are always investors who say, *"This stock can never get above $12,"* and sell when the stock reaches that price. Thus, **if the stock is to continue its move upward, it must break through the all-time high with sufficient volume to maintain the momentum.** Given the decade-long duration of this top, the strength of Ross' breakout was especially significant and indicated that the stock would continue to move up.

Having broken through its last resistance, Ross no longer had a "top" to penetrate. It surged upwards again. In seven weeks, it reached $21, trading 44.4 million shares. No stock goes straight up forever. In the next ten weeks, Ross dropped to $15. This could have been the sign of a top, but the down volume was lower and of less duration than the up volume. Stocks do not collapse on light volume. As per Newton's Law, they need a greater force to change their direction. In the next four weeks, Ross moved back up on high volume. As it had done at $6, $8, $10, and $13, Ross now formed another base at $18.50. After forming its new base, Ross surged upwards again and reached $25.

During 1997, with no top to hold it back and strong fundamentals, Ross Stores continued its run, reaching $40 by November. Most investors would have been pleased to participate in any major segment of the move in Ross from $5 to $40. However, anyone who took a close look at the chart could have bought Ross at the $6 level and held on to it for most of the run up. The tape was telling investors that the stock was going up. Anyone who did not listen lost out on most of the move.

THE ROUND TRIP

Professionals can take stocks a long way up, but the time always arrives when a stock runs out of steam and turns down. Identifying the "top" is the second pattern that all investors should understand. While it is critical for investors to be able to see the breakout and participate in the ride up, it is also critical for them to see the top and avoid the ride down. In many cases, **the ride down is quicker and more brutal than the ride up.** This is especially true of stocks with the sharpest moves up. Without solid intervening bases, stocks can plummet much faster and further than anyone ever believes.

In many cases, the trading pattern will give buy signals at the bottom and sell signals at the top, but investors often ignore these signals. When the stock is at the bottom, investors often wait until the breakout is already in progress before buying. When the stock reaches a top, investors are often so euphoric with the profits that they have made that they fail to notice the signal of an abrupt change in direction. Micron Technologies is an interesting example of a stock that took the round trip.

A CASE STUDY: MICRON TECHNOLOGIES

Micron Technologies is a major manufacturer of semiconductors and one of the most volatile and actively traded stocks in the market. When the stock went up, it went up like a rocket and ran to heights that even its most ardent fans could not have imagined. When it finally petered out and went down, it dropped like a stone, sinking much further and much faster than its most vociferous detractors could have imagined. Look at Micron's trading pattern and ask, when would have been the most appropriate time to buy and sell this stock?

At the start of 1993, Micron was selling for $3.78. By July 1995, it had surged to $89. In 30 months, its price had increased by 2,278 percent. However, from its peak, Micron headed straight down until it reached $19.50 in July 1996, a decline of 79 percent. In 42 months, Micron went from $4 to $89 and back to $19 without any major, long-term fundamental change in its business. It did not invent a new type of chip, put Intel out of business, or get acquired. No amount of "rational" fundamental analysis could have explained this volatility. **But the stock market is not always about "rational" analysis. It is often about momentum.** In Micron's case, the chart of the stock almost always foretold its future price direction. Those who used the chart as a tool probably made money. Those who ignored it probably were annihilated.

In the case of Micron Technologies, the word "investor" is highly inappropriate. **Most people who bought Micron's stock were trading, not investing.** Micron has about 200 million shares. In 1995 and 1996, Micron traded 2.8 billion shares. The shares turned over an average of seven times per year, making the average holding period well less than two months. In 1996, it was the most actively traded stock on the New York Stock Exchange. If the average investor owned the stock for less than two months, most were traders, playing the momentum game. A fundamental investor might look at Micron and be bewildered by its volatility. But that investor would have only two choices: respect the power of momentum or avoid the stock.

MICRON'S CHART CLEARLY POINTED THE WAY

Micron's chart pattern is extremely common, with clearly delineated buy and sell signals. From December 1992 through May 1993, Micron formed a solid base under $6. In June and July, volume increased as the price went to $8.97. This surge represented the first buy signal. Volume continued to jump, reaching 146 million shares in October. Unlike Ross, which had a surge in volume followed by a surge in price, Micron had a simultaneous price and volume breakout. This type of breakout always indicates sharp future volatility. With this type of action, investors must be cautious because a month like October 1993 can signal either a continuing breakout or a top.

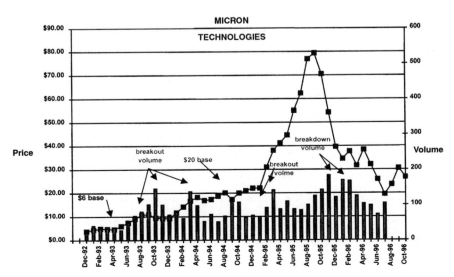

In the next several months, Micron formed a base in the $9 range and then traded up to $14 on somewhat lower volume. In some cases, lower volume on the upside would have been a negative, but in Micron's case, it was a positive because it showed that despite the 275 percent increase in price, investors were still comfortable with the stock. In March, volume increased again, as Micron surged upwards. This was the second buy signal, indicating that the upside trend was still intact. Micron moved up to $20 and consolidated its base. It remained near $20 for eleven months, trading on lower but consistent volume. This was a very positive sign. The base formed by Micron at $20 laid the foundation for the next move up.

In February and March 1995 volume picked up as the stock surged to $31. This was Micron's third buy signal. From February to August, the stock almost quadrupled on heavy volume. Many investors sold the stock during this period, but in doing so, they were making a mistake. Nothing in Micron's chart gave any indication of a change in direction. Despite the gigantic run up and the huge trading volume, the volume remained relatively consistent and never exceeded the level it reached during the breakout month. If volume is consistent, the momentum of the stock tends to continue.

During September, Micron reached a high of $90, before closing the month at $79.38. As Micron's stock continued its sharp advance to $90, it was sowing the seeds of its own decline. While the stock had formed bases at $10 and $20, there were no bases between $20 and $90. **As a stock moves up, it is critical that it forms intermediate bases so that it can consolidate its position.** If Micron could not form a base near its top, it could be vulnerable to dropping all the way to $20.

Anyone who doubts the importance of forming bases on the way up should look at the trading patterns of the Internet stocks in the summer of 1999. Many of these stocks plunged as fast as they had soared because they had no intermediate bases on which to consolidate.

As Micron moved towards its peak, volatility and volume increased, both troubling signs. In the week of September 8, Micron surged from $76 to almost $90, but in the next three weeks, it dropped to $79³/₈ on four times the volume. This downside volume was troubling, because it indicated that the professionals were rapidly switching from buyers to sellers and that they were doing so with conviction.

Just as momentum can support a stock on the upside, so it can destroy a stock on the downside. Volume is a critical component, because it reflects the movement of the army of professionals. In Micron's case, volume continued to increase as the stock moved down. Micron traded 174 million shares as it went from $55 to $90 and 352 million shares as it went from $90 to $55. (Note on the chart below how volume surged as the stock dropped.)

MICRON'S TOP

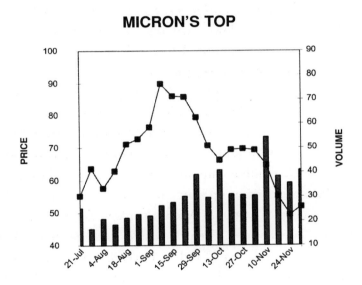

The point here is very simple, but it is one that investors continually miss:
- A stock that has been surging upward can only change direction if it meets a greater force.
- That greater force is almost always manifest in higher volume.
- If a stock declines on huge volume, don't wait to read the analysts' reports. Head for the exits.

Following sharp technical sell signals is one of the most important things any investor can learn. It is easy to dismiss a sell signal with comforting words from an analyst. After all, if you own a stock that has started to drop, you want to be reassured. But, more often than not, these signals presage a sharp price decline and often a fundamental deterioration.

Anyone who looked at the chart would have sold Micron as it started to trade down. In most cases, this sign will not occur exactly at the top. But if you had bought Micron at $10, you would have been delighted to sell at $79. Giving up $10 at the top was surely better than the alternative of hanging on. Remember, surging downside volume is a stock's way of telling you there is trouble ahead. Unless you think you have some secret inside information, it is not worth fighting the tape.

This is usually the time when the broker calls urging you to buy. *"Our analysts still love it, and it is 30 percent off the high."* But Micron had no base at which to stop a downward plunge. In the next six weeks, it dropped to $43 on heavy volume. **Downside moves can be quick and brutal if there is no base to support the stock.**

After a few quiet weeks during the Christmas season, volume exploded. In January and February, Micron traded 338 million shares. In one week, it traded 70 million shares, one-third of its stock. After the peak in February, the price and volume continued to decline. In seven weeks, volume was less than 20 million, and in three weeks, it was less than 10 million. The selling was drying up, but there was no buying. At the end of July, volume again picked up, as Micron sunk under $20. The downside momentum was now broken. The price could stabilize. While Micron rallied during 1997, it sunk back and in December was again selling just above $20. (Once stocks round-trip, they usually have to build a long base before they can move again.)

The message of Micron Technologies is simple. The stock went up far more than anyone would have expected. So long as the volume was consistent, the stock kept going up. Once the volume pattern was broken, the stock changed directions and plunged. Investors who studied the chart could have seen the breakout and taken the entire ride up. They also could have seen the top and avoided the entire ride down. Those who did not study the charts probably got whipsawed in both directions.

THE MARKET DOES NOT OVERREACT

Charts often signal when a company is going to face some unusually good or bad news—especially bad news. When stocks plunge on bad news, analysts often issue reports indicating their surprise at the news, but in many cases, the stock itself has already foreshadowed the problem. A careful look at the charts usually reveals the signs of coming difficulties.

Sometimes a minor event, such as a small reduction in earnings estimates, leads to a dramatic revaluation of a stock. An analyst may cut earnings estimates by 5 percent and the stock may drop 35 percent. When this occurs, other analysts often say, *"the market has overreacted"* and urge investors to double up their holdings. After all, a 5 percent cut in earnings should not have had such a devastating impact on the stock. Investors should be wary. The market rarely overreacts. In fact, in many cases when stocks are trashed, future events prove that the earnings reduction was just the tip of the iceberg, and that something was radically wrong with the company. Further, the first "overreaction" is rarely the last. **Collapses in a stock, like earthquakes, are usually preceded by smaller tremors and followed by aftershocks.**

If a stock behaves in a manner that most analysts consider to be irrational, the first question you should ask is, *"Why is everyone else panicking when they are not?"* When the masses run for the exits, even if you do not see a fire or smell the smoke, you would do well to listen to the screams. Professional investors do not panic over small items. If they are rushing for the exits, it is because they fear that there are greater problems ahead. If you are tempted to buy a stock that is being trashed, remember, the market rarely overreacts."

A CASE STUDY: DONNKENNY

Donnkenny produces moderately priced sportswear for women. The company went public in June 1993. In December, its president, Richard Rubin, sold 100,000 shares. In April 1994, Rubin sold 330,000 shares, and Merrill Lynch, which had backed the company, sold 1.6 million shares. In July 1995, Rubin sold 100,000 shares. In November 1995,

Rubin sold 200,000 more shares. Donnkenny announced that it would distribute Mickey Mouse clothing in China and take a fourth-quarter charge. The stock dropped from $18 to $14 on six times normal volume. Anyone looking at the chart should have been concerned. The company reported good year-end results and said that it would have a strong 1995. The stock moved up to $19. In August 1996, Rubin sold another 150,000 shares. A consistent pattern of sales by management is never a bullish sign.

In September 1996, the company announced that it was changing its fiscal year from November to December. Several analysts reaffirmed their estimates, while one, whose estimates had been the highest on the street, lowered her numbers by $0.05 to be in line with consensus. The stock reacted strongly, dropping more than 20 percent on eight times normal volume. (Note on the chart on the next page that all of the major increases in volume were accompanied by sharp declines in price.) Another analyst, whose position had been more conservative to begin with, wrote a First Call note with the headline *"Market Overreacts Again."* This analyst happens to be very intelligent, but when analysts write that the "market has overreacted," it is they, not the market, who are usually wrong.

The change in the fiscal year and the small adjustment in earnings were not significant, so why did the stock react so strongly? Perhaps someone suspected something, but whatever the reason, the huge downside volume on what appeared to be insignificant news was a decidedly negative sign. The chart was telling investors that there was something more seriously wrong with Donnkenny.

On October 28, an analyst wrote a First Call note indicating that Donnkenny would report its earnings in mid-November, instead of in late October as originally planned. Neither the analyst nor the investors took much note of this delay, but it was a significant signal. **Whenever a company delays its reporting date, it is always a sign of trouble.** If you own stock in a company that has a material delay in reporting, don't wait around to find out why.

The trouble did not take long to materialize. On November 6, the company's auditors, KPMG Peat Marwick, resigned. The company demoted its chief financial officer and appointed someone new. The company implied that KPMG had been fired. First Call carried a note from an analyst entitled *"New CFO a Positive,"* noting that the new CFO had spent five years at Ralph Lauren. Another firm also praised the appointment. Both talked about the strengthening of the management team. Neither seemed concerned about the change in auditors. But the analyst who had previously talked about the market overreacting lowered her rating because she believed that the "firing of the CFO and the auditor just before the release of earnings . . . is not positive." (A smart call, but a major understatement.)

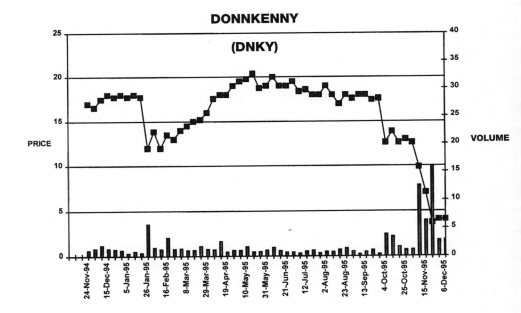

The stock, which had closed at $12^{1/2}$, would not open. By midmorning it was selling at $6^{1/2}$. Two firms downgraded the stock. Donnkenny closed at $8^{7/8}$ on 9.3 million shares. About two-thirds of the shares outstanding traded. A lot of investors were making bets.

On November 8, Prudential Securities raised its rating to buy. The First Call note was entitled *"Panic Sell-off Overdone."* This was the second time that an analyst had said that the tape was wrong. The Prudential analyst noted that investors were concerned about possible fraud, but that the new CFO and a board member had assured him everything was all right. With estimates of $1.38 for 1996 and $1.60 for 1997, Donnkenny looked like a very cheap stock. The Prudential recommendation pushed Donnkenny up to $9⁷/₈.

On November 12, Donnkenny released a statement saying that KPMG had resigned, not been fired, and that it had resigned because of poor data access. (Never a good sign. It is difficult for auditors to do a good job if you don't let them look at your books.) On November 14, the *Wall Street Journal* reported that three executives had sold $13.4 million in stock over the past eighteen months, a fact that must have inspired investors.

Finally, on November 15, Donnkenny reported that third-quarter earnings would be below analysts' estimates and that it would have to restate its earnings from the previous years. The stock dropped to 4³/₁₆. Prudential lowered its rating from buy to sell. Two other firms also reduced their ratings.

Look at the chart and the volume. All the shares were changing hands. The auditors had resigned. The earnings report was delayed. There was no way that good news could follow. In fact, there is almost never an instance in which good news follows the dismissal of the auditors in the middle of the year. One rule that every investor should remember is never buy a stock if the auditors resign in the middle of the year.

When the stock dropped from $16 to $12 in October, the market was sending a message that something was wrong. From then until the problems fully materialized, two analysts wrote notes saying that the market had overreacted, and investors traded millions of shares as the stock plunged. The lessons of Donnkenny:

- There is almost never a good reason for late reporting.
- There is *never* a good reason for changing auditors in the middle of the year.
- When a stock acts "sick," the company usually has major problems.
- The market does not overreact.
- Investors who fight the tape do so at their own peril.

In 1997, new management took over Donnkenny. Richard Rubin pleaded guilty to concocting false invoices and revenues to meet earnings goals. His sentence is still pending, but he faces a maximum of five years in jail. Stocks that have broken down and burned investors do not rapidly recover.

With Charts, the Greatest Virtue Is Simplicity

In looking at the Price & Volume Charts of Ross, Micron, and Donnkenny, it is very easy to see when the stock began a major move up and when it began a major move down. The basic Price & Volume Chart has the advantage of simplicity. An investor can look at it and see when the volume is increasing and how the price is reacting to changes in volume. A breakout volume is always extremely easy to spot. Upside versus downside volume is also extremely easy to spot. If the volume is increasing as the stock is declining, there is much more downside risk.

When stocks break out or plunge for no apparent reason, it is wise to assume that someone knows something you do not. When people who are closer to the company than you are begin to buy or sell, causing dramatic new patterns to emerge, do not wait around to learn what they know. If the charts tell you that something is wrong, sell the stock. Don't fight the tape.

The only complex issue in the Price & Volume Charts is the time frame. If you are looking at what you believe is a breakout from a base, you must go back to the formation of the base. If you take too short a time frame, a surge in volume can look like a breakout but not be of sufficient power to move away from the base. A true breakout occurs only on the highest volume. Similarly, if you are looking at a breakdown, you must look at the volume during the stock's entire move up. Most tops require volume higher than the original breakout.

Price and Volume Charts on the Web

The Internet has made Price & Volume Charts extremely easy to use. All Internet brokers have chart services, as do the search engines (such as Yahoo!) and most of the financial sites. My particular favorite is BigCharts. The online brokers tend to have better short-term charts. But for most investors, long-term charts will do. In many ways, the charts on the Internet are easier to work with than the charts that the professionals use. The major advantage of the Internet charts is the ease with which investors can switch between time frames.

Most charts have five-year, two-year, one-year, six-month, three-month, and one-month time frames. The more sophisticated sites even have one-day charts. On BigCharts, for example, you have the following choices: 5 minutes; 15 minutes; 5 days; 1, 2, 3, and 6 months, year-to-date, 1, 2, 3, 4, and 5 years; 1 decade, and all historical data.

Pick a stock in which you are interested. Click on the basic chart. You will see choices for different time frames. Start with a long one. Five years is probably sufficient to get a picture of the long-term pattern of the stock. Is it in an uptrend or a downtrend? Has it formed a solid base? Watch the battle between buyers and sellers. Look at the spikes in volume. How did the stock perform as volume increased or decreased? Look at the peaks and valleys in price. How did price and volume correlate at these points? Think of the chart as the movement of an army. You can see where it has been, but can you see where it is going?

Click on next shorter time frame, such as two years. Does the slightly shorter-term pattern look different? Continue clicking down the time-frame spectrum. Each click will take only seconds, and each chart will give you a different view. Keep focusing on the periods in which there were the most dramatic price and volume changes. If the stock has been in a long-term trend, you will need a long-term chart, but if the peaks in volume have recently changed the direction of the stock, you can use a shorter-term chart. When you get to the shortest-term chart, look at the recent trading pattern. Is there a significant change in price or volume? Does the stock seem to be diverging from its basic trend?

Many charts will be largely nondescript, but some charts will show dramatic changes in price and volume. If you see a breakout on the upside, buy or certainly continue holding the stock. Stick with it as long as the trend is in place. If you see a top accompanied by a surge in volume, don't wait around for the bad news. Sell the stock and take your profits. Just remember, the market usually knows more than you do.

INTRADAY TRADING CHARTS SHOW SHORT-TERM DETAIL

Price & Volume Charts are extremely effective in providing investors with a simple overview of the long-term movements of stocks. The tops, bottoms, breakouts, and bases are all easy to see. But while they are excellent for long-term moves, their very simplicity makes them less useful in understanding shorter-term moves. For individuals who are more trading-oriented, Intraday Trading Charts are more useful.

The difference between the Price & Volume Chart and the Intraday Trading Chart is the difference between a photograph taken from a satellite and one taken from the top of a hill. They both focus on the same battlefield, but the Price & Volume Chart shows more of an overview, and the Intraday Trading Chart shows more detail.

The two charting systems are similar, but while the Price & Volume Charts use a single point to show the prices on each day, the Intraday Trading Charts use a bar. The bar offers the opportunity to show more detail.

The short horizontal lines on the right and left sides of the bar indicate the opening and closing prices, respectively. The relationship between the opening and closing prices helps to indicate the potential trading pattern. If the closings are consistently lower than the openings, the stock will probably trade down. If the closings are consistently higher than the openings, the stock will probably trade up. The wider the range between opening and closing prices, the higher the volatility is likely to be.

The length of the bar represents the range of price swings during the day. Short bars indicate a narrow trading range, while long bars indicate a wide trading range. If the length of the bars suddenly increases, it is a sign of sharp divergences of opinion. When these divergences occur, the stock is likely to enter a period of higher volatility. As a result, these are critical changes for an investor to watch. Price reversals occur when there is a wide intraday trading range, a wide spread between opening and closing prices, and a substantial change in volume.

The Intraday Trading Charts also show the "moving average" of the stock. The moving average, which represents the historical price action of a stock over a specified period of time (10 days, 50 days, 200 days, etc.), is another key technical indicator. **Most technicians believe that a move above or below the moving average line signifies a change in direction of the stock.** When a stock breaks above the averages, it often moves higher. When it drops sharply below these averages, it often breaks down.

The easiest way to understand these averages is to think of them as a base. Consistent stocks will trade around the base. The more a stock diverges from its base, the greater the risk of volatility. Even stocks that surge up often drop back to their moving averages.

Because the Intraday Trading Charts show much more detail, they have to have a shorter time frame. It is not possible to clearly show every opening and closing price and all intraday price swings on a long-term chart. The optimum time period for an Intraday Chart is six months, and the best use of these charts is in making short-term trading decisions. The chart below presents a picture of the daily trading of IBM during a six-month period.

IBM INTRADAY

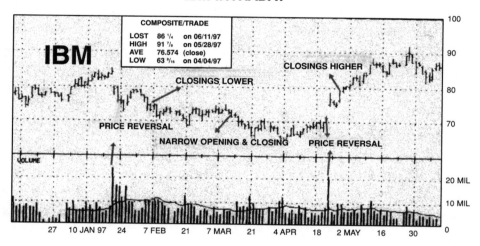

Source: Bloomberg

At the beginning of the chart, IBM was trading up in an orderly fashion, with narrow spreads between openings and closings, but with closings on balance higher. On January 23, 1997, IBM had a wide intraday range. The closing price was about $4 lower than the opening price. Volume tripled off previous levels, and the stock dropped below its moving average. The sharp price decline on heavy volume was a key signal. While bargain hunters stepped in to buy, this trading pattern indicated a price reversal from the increases of the previous weeks. **It is never wise to stand in front of a price reversal.** In six weeks, IBM dropped from $79 to $64.

In the middle of March, the price began to stabilize. The differences between the opening and closing prices narrowed, indicating a more orderly trading pattern. Then closings began to be higher than openings, indicating a trend up. In the fourth week of April, the trading range widened and the volume tripled, indicating another Price/Volume reversal. In the next month, the price of IBM jumped from $68 to $90.

In using Intraday Trading Charts, the most important thing to look for is a price and volume reversal. A price and volume reversal shows that the professionals are changing their stance on the stock. If the stock swings from down closings to up closings on higher volume, it is a sign that professionals are buying and the stock will probably move up. If it swings from up closings to down closings on higher volume, it is a sign that professionals are selling and the stock will probably move down. If these reversals cause the stock to break through the moving averages, the extent of the move is likely to be greater.

Like Price & Volume Charts, Intraday Trading Charts are easily located on the Internet. The best of the charts are available through chart services such as BigCharts.com, online brokers, or other specialized financial services. As with the Price & Volume Charts, it is useful to click on the Intraday Charts and play with different time frames. Most of the online services use Price & Volume Charts for the longest time frames and Intraday Trading Charts for the rest, so there is no need to worry about which one to pick. The service will give you the one that is best for the period in which you are interested.

The Price & Volume Charts and the Intraday Trading Charts are early warning systems for the individual investor because they reflect the past and give strong indications as to the potential future moves of a stock. For the individual, who probably knows less about the company than the professional, charts can be critical. When volume starts to increase, it is a sign the professionals are becoming more active. If volume increases and the stock moves up, it is a sign the professionals are buying. If volume increases and the stock moves down, it is a sign the professionals are selling.

By waiting for the major price and volume changes before acting, the individual will allow the professionals to set the direction. But by moving quickly once these changes appear, the individual will be able to take action before the professionals can buy or sell a full position and before critical news events dramatically change the pattern of the stock. This early warning system can neutralize many of the advantages of the professionals.

MOVING AVERAGE CONVERGENCE/DIVERGENCE INDICATOR: DIFFICULT TO UNDERSTAND, EASY TO USE

Of all of the technical indicators, the Moving Average Convergence/ Divergence Indicator (MACD) is one of the most difficult to understand and yet one of the simplest to use. The MACD tracks the changes in a stock's underlying price trend by using exponential weighting around a moving average to test whether the changes are for real or only a short-term deviation. MACD is one of a number of charts that utilize moving averages as a technical tool.

The theory of the MACD is confusing to most people and I won't explain it here, but using the MACD is extremely easy. The chart has two sections. The top section shows the stock price. The bottom section has two lines, a fast indicator and a slow indicator. A change in trend occurs when the lines in the bottom section cross at a sharp angle. When the fast line sharply crosses from below, the trend is up and you should buy the stock. When the fast line sharply crosses from above, the trend is down and you should sell the stock. If the crossing is not sharp or if the two lines continue to move together, there is no change in the trend. The divergence bars show in a magnified way the separation between the fast and the slow lines. The MACD charts are especially useful for tracking short-term moves because the weighting of the lines magnifies changes in trends. All the individual has to do is look for sharp crossing patterns and act.

Below is an MACD chart for Microsoft. Remember, the only relevant points occur when the fast line crosses the slow line at a sharp angle.

To use this chart, you only need to look for the sharp crossings. There are three during the period. The first crossing was positive, indicating a buy. It occurred at the beginning of November 1997. Microsoft was selling at about $132. In the next five weeks, it climbed to $146. The second crossing was negative, indicating a sell. It occurred in early December when Microsoft was selling at $144. The stock promptly

MICROSOFT MACD

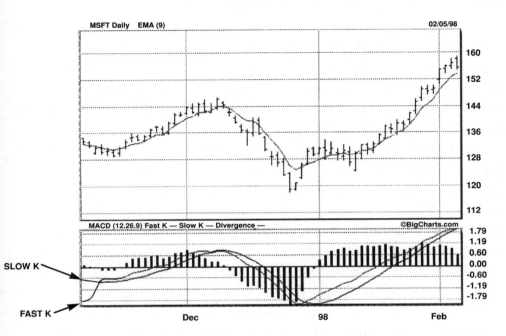

dropped to $120. The third crossing was positive, indicating a buy. It occurred at the end of December when Microsoft was selling at $120. Microsoft promptly ran to $142. In the three months of the chart, Microsoft went from $136 to $142, an increase of $6, but following the MACD signals on the upside and the downside would have enabled investors to make $60.

While the concept of MACD can be confusing, the predictive value is high, and the charts are incredibly easy to use. All you have to do is to look for the sharp crossings of the two lines and see if they indicate an advance or a decline. Go to one of the Web sites that feature MACD charts and look at the stocks in your portfolio. You will be surprised at how often the sharp crossings reflected the best buy and sell points.

As the charts in this chapter show, investors can make a lot of money if they utilize technical tools as an early warning system for the actions of the professionals. The Price & Volume and MACD charts present buy and sell points in very simple formats. But there are many other good charting systems. To see which one is right for you, go to one of the charting Web sites, such as BigCharts, and play with the alternatives. Pick a stock that you own and test the various charts. Look at different indicators, such as money flows, price channels, short interest, relative strength, and different types of moving averages. Try different chart types. See which of the technical systems presents the easiest and clearest picture for you to understand. Then try that system on a few more stocks. There is no one right technical system. You should find the one with which you are the most comfortable.

The Internet has dramatically transformed the use of charts for individual investors. Prior to the Internet, most investors could not get charts unless they subscribed to an expensive technical service, and even then the charts were often out of date. Now the charts are free and have up-to-the-minute information. They are also extremely easy to work with. Simple clicks can take you from one time frame or chart system to the other. With the Internet, individuals now have technical resources that are as good as the professionals'.

The biggest challenge lies not in understanding the charts, but in **being willing to act when the charts indicate a position that is opposed to your fundamental beliefs.** When most investors see a negative indicator in the chart of a stock they own, their first response usually is "the chart is wrong." This is both dangerous and foolish. The chart represents the collective wisdom of all buyers and sellers. The investor is almost always better off accepting what the charts have to say. This does not mean that you should buy or sell every time a minor signal occurs. Very often minor technical signals are reversed, and no change in investment status is necessary. But when a major signal occurs, do not wait around for second and third confirmations. Major signals indicate changes in trends, and for the most part investors should follow them.

CHAPTER EIGHT

Connect the Dots

External events can radically change the field of battle. The first general to see the event, understand its full implications, and make the right move usually wins. The key is to see the links between the events and your own battle position. The same rules apply to the stock market. It is critical to watch the external events that can change the balance of power in the market and to understand the links between the events and the prices of the stocks.

Nothing affects the stock market more than real events. When you turn on the news, you immediately know that some of the headlines are going to directly impact specific stocks, and you very often have a good guess as to the extent and the direction of the impact.

- If the headline says that Mexico is devaluing the peso by 50 percent, you know that the dollar value of Mexican stocks is going to plunge.
- If the headline says a regional brokerage firm is being bought by a major bank at twice its current price, you know that the firm's stock price will surge.
- If the headline says that biggest hurricane in history is devastating the coast of Florida, you know that the stocks of property insurance companies will go down.

Since you know the news, you know that there are vast sums to be made if you can get your orders executed before everyone else. The problem is that you cannot. You are not the only person who reads the newspaper or watches television. When major events occur, stocks have huge influxes of orders. The market makers or specialists immediately adjust the prices to conform to the new reality. By the time you make your trade, the stocks may have already had major moves.

- The Mexican stock that had closed at $20 is indicated at $10 because of the devaluation.
- The regional brokerage firm that had closed at $20 will open at $36 because of the takeover.
- The insurance company that had closed at $60 will now open at $55 because of the hurricane.

When important news breaks, investors rush for the entrances or the exits like a crowd of Latin American soccer fans. Even if you are going in the right direction, you can still get trampled. **The heightened volatility brought about by news events always benefits the professionals.** They are in a position to understand the news and analyze its implications faster than the average investor.

- When the peso is devalued, the professionals know which Mexican companies will be decimated (importers of luxury goods) and which may actually benefit (exporters of inexpensive goods). You may not.
- When a takeover is announced, the professionals have an educated view as to whether the deal will go through and whether the bid will be raised. You may not.
- When a hurricane hits, the professionals know which firms are the most exposed and which have laid off much of their disaster risk.

Because of the heightened volatility, making direct investments based on major news stories is often unwise. If you see a news item with black-and-white implications and you own the affected stock, wait until the volatility abates and then reevaluate your holdings. If you do not own the stock, resist the temptation to play. If volatility is high, you cannot afford to be a step behind the professionals.

THE INDIVIDUAL'S EDGE

The individual investor will be better served by looking at the more subtle connections between stocks. When an event occurs that has a major impact on one stock, it usually has a less direct impact on other stocks. While most investors jump on the stock that is the focus on the news, the best opportunities often come in stocks on which the event has a secondary or even tertiary impact. The key is to identify those companies before the rest of the market does.

- If the peso is devalued, companies that import inexpensive goods from Mexico, such as clothing, may benefit, while companies that sell products to Mexico may suffer.

- If a regional brokerage firm receives a takeover offer from a major bank, stocks of other regional brokerage firms and money management firms that might become takeover targets will surge. Stocks of other banks could go down if investors think they might be disadvantaged by not owning a brokerage firm or might overpay to make an acquisition of their own.

- When a disaster such as a hurricane hits, unfortunate as it may seem, there are winners. The insurance funds pouring into the market are a boon to home builders, building supply firms, and appliance stores. While most people do not look at disasters and say, *"What a great opportunity for Home Depot,"* the reality is that every house that is knocked down has to be rebuilt, and someone has to provide the supplies.

The stock market is a dynamic environment in which almost everything is interrelated. One of the biggest errors that investors make is to ignore the links between events, or else to be swayed into accepting a company's or analyst's spin on the situation. The reality is:

1. Events create ripples that impact a broad range of stocks.

2. Whether the impact is real, causing a change in earnings, or psychological, causing a change in investors' views, it may often be greater than most initially believe.

3. If one company shows a sharp break in its trading pattern,

investors should look at related companies. Their moves may not be far behind.

There is one major difference between positive and negative changes. When the change is positive, companies rush to trumpet the good news, but when the change is negative, they put on spin control. Few companies issue press releases stating that a new competitive threat will materially hurt their business, and few analysts, who do investment-banking business, will issue a report saying that a company is now toast. Because companies and analysts are more forthcoming about good news than they are about bad news, investors must look more diligently at negative changes in the competitive environment.

Too many investors ignore or even fight the news if it presents a picture they do not like. But fighting the news, like fighting the tape, is a recipe for disaster. If the news and the tape combine to sound a warning, the negative impact is usually dramatic.

LINKS BETWEEN COMPETITORS

Most industries are a zero-sum game. There is only so much business to go around. When a new competitor, such as Wal-Mart, enters a market, its share must come from someone's hide. Over the years, I have watched company after company offer reams of statistics to show that Wal-Mart did not really represent a competitive threat. Some even claimed Wal-Mart helped their business. One does not have to be a retail expert to understand that Wal-Mart's $100 billion in annual sales had to be taken from someone. Despite the spin control, most retailers have been hurt by Wal-Mart. If you see a new major competitive threat that could affect one of your stocks, be cautious in accepting your company's spin control.

Be especially cautious if you see a large number of new companies entering a business. A decade ago, there were a large number of fast-growing companies in the convenience-store business. At first, they did well. But as competition intensified, margins suffered. Then the oil companies turned their service stations into convenience stores. It doesn't take a Certified Financial Analyst to recognize that when tens of thousands of gas stations stopped repairing cars and started selling milk, the convenience stores would suffer. Price wars developed, and most of the publicly owned convenience-store chains went bankrupt. **No matter how good a market looks, it will never be healthy if there are too many new competitors.**

Look at the change in competition of companies selling computers on the Internet. How many companies are now online selling computers? Do you think there is room for all of them? Does each new competitor expand the market, or is there relatively finite demand? When Onsale announced that it was going to sell computers at cost, what was the response of its competitors? Since computers are a commodity item, many decided to match its price. If you think these are reasonable questions, ask yourself one more. If everyone is selling computers for cost, how is anyone going to make money?

While increased competition can hurt a market, consolidation can help it, both because the number of competitors is reduced and because the consolidating companies can leverage their overhead. Banking is currently going through a huge consolidation. When you see banks merging, closing branches, laying off employees, and reducing the number of competitors in a market, it should be easy to guess that profits should improve, not only for the banks that are merging, but for other competitors as well.

You should always be wary of industries in which the number of competitors is increasing and look for industries in which it is shrinking. There are three good ways to profit from shrinking levels of competition:

1. **Buy the attractive regionals.** Look for consolidating industries in which the largest companies are buying up strong regional companies, such as the current banking industry. When mergers start in an industry, they usually continue until all of the attractive candidates have been bought.

2. **Buy the survivors.** Look for companies that take up the slack when other companies close their facilities. After Merry-Go-Round, Edison Brothers, and others went bankrupt, teen retailers like Pacific Sunwear, American Eagle, and Abercrombie rapidly filled the void.

3. **Buy the consolidators.** Look for highly fragmented industries in which public companies are buying up small

independents. The consolidators are usually able to gain pricing and capital leverage. (There is only one caveat. Make sure the consolidators are good companies and not financial pyramid schemes. See Ha-Lo Industries in chapter 12.)

Understanding the level of competition can be a good tool in making investments. If competition is increasing either because powerful firms are moving into the market or because there are too many companies in a niche, the investor should be cautious. If competition is decreasing because of bankruptcies or because a company is consolidating the market, investors should look for opportunities.

LINKS BETWEEN CUSTOMERS AND SUPPLIERS

The fortunes of a large major company will tell you a lot about what is happening to its key suppliers. If you own stock in a manufacturer and one retailer accounts for 30 percent of its sales, it seems logical that you would listen to the reports from the retailer as a guide to how your company is doing. But you would be shocked at how many investors ignore this type of news. Even professionals sometimes miss the connections. Analysts may miss them because they are focused on one industry, while busy portfolio managers may miss them because no one helps them connect the dots.

BRIGHT SELL SIGNALS IN THE SUNGLASS BUSINESS

A perfect example of this situation can be found with Sunglass Hut (RAYS), the largest retailer of sunglasses, and Oakley, a major sunglass brand. Sunglass Hut went public in 1993 at $5. The company went on an acquisition binge and became a darling of growth investors. By March 1996, RAYS had soared more than 700 percent to almost $37 and commanded a lofty 45x p/e multiple. As it climbed from $7 to $36⁵/₁₆, Sunglass Hut had only one down month. It never stopped to form a base.

After surging above $36 in March, RAYS was unable to hold the price and started to decline. Downside volume increased. By the middle of April, RAYS was under $30 and struggling to form a base. Then in the last two weeks of June, volume suddenly surged. Many investors were betting that the key summer selling season would be weak.

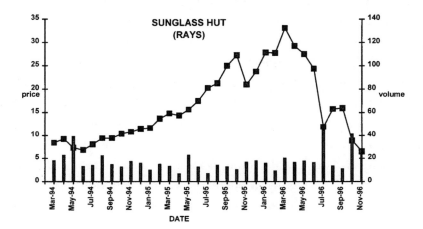

As is so often the case, the news followed the charts. On July 1, Sunglass Hut told analysts that its June comp store sales would be 1 to 3 percent below plan. Such a shortfall is not the end of the world, but because RAYS's chart was already weak, the impact was quick and brutal. In three days, RAYS dropped from $24³/₈ to $18 on 9.4 million shares. Now the stock was broken. Anyone looking for a sign to sell had one. Analysts tried to rally the stock, but the bottom fell out again. In ten days, Sunglass Hut dropped below $11 because of a minor shortfall in June sales.

Investors often ignore the warning signs of stocks. Despite the huge price drop and jump in volume, investors began to bid up the price of the stock. RAYS rallied from $12 to $18. But the upside volume was troublingly light. Sunglass Hut was sending a second invitation to sell for anyone who was interested.

Those who did not sell did not have to wait long to regret their inaction. In early October, RAYS said that September sales had been weak and that the weakness might continue into the fourth quarter. Ordinarily,

September is a meaningless month for sunglasses, but because RAYS had a vulnerable chart, the news set off a panic. In five days, the stock dropped from $16 to $9. By the end of November, RAYS had declined to $6³/₄. In three years, sales had tripled and earnings per share had more than doubled, and RAYS was selling for less than it had in its first week of trading.

Anyone who had been watching the news and the trading patterns of Sunglass Hut should have understood the warning signals. Besides sending a warning to its own shareholders, RAYS was also sending a warning to others in the sunglass industry, especially to shareholders of Oakley, one of its largest suppliers. Oakley was a hot company. It went public in August 1995 at $11½, and by June 1996 it had reached $27. At its high, Oakley was selling for 41x earnings and 9.5x sales, astoundingly high valuations.

It is interesting to compare the charts of Sunglass Hut and Oakley. While Sunglass Hut was declining from $36 to $27, Oakley was rallying from $16 to $27. It is always possible for one company to do well when its largest customer is hurting, but weak retail sales are never a good sign for major suppliers.

SUNGLASS HUT & OAKLEY

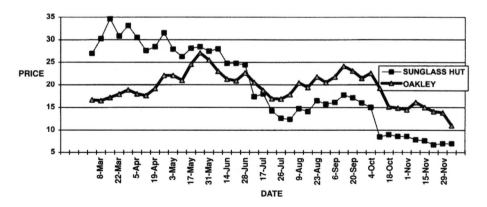

Oakley had a secondary offering on June 12. The president and the CEO sold 10 million shares at about $24. Did they know that Sunglass Hut's comp store sales were below plan and that its inventories were too high? Whatever the answer, this sale by the two top executives of Oakley at the same time as the stock of Sunglass Hut was weakening should have sent a strong message to investors.

After the secondary offering, Oakley did not hold its price. As Sunglass Hut dropped from $24 to $18, Oakley dropped from $22 to $17. But then an interesting divergence began to occur. Many of the investment bankers who had handled Oakley's offering recommended the stock. Oakley rallied to $21, while Sunglass Hut dropped to $12. In May, both had been selling at $27. Both were in the same business. The executives of Oakley had unloaded a huge block of stock, and yet by August, Sunglass Hut had declined to $12, while Oakley was selling for $21.

In the first week of October, Sunglass Hut and Bausch & Lomb, the largest manufacturer of sunglasses, both announced that business was weak and inventories were high. Oakley's investors should have listened. The stock of Oakley was in a downtrend. Its largest customer and biggest competitor had announced that business was soft. Yet Oakley rallied its the stock by telling investors that business was still good.

OAKLEY

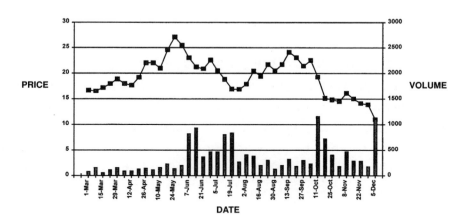

Oakley reported strong earnings and announced a 3-million-share stock buyback, but the price still dropped to $16. When a company reports good news and the stock declines, it is sending investors another message. If good news pushes the stock down, what will happen if bad news is reported? Oakley had played its card, but the market reacted negatively. This was another warning sign, but many investors still ignored the obvious.

Then the bomb dropped. On December 3, Sunglass Hut reported more weak sales. Oakley responded by saying that its earnings per share would show a decline of 30 percent. Analysts cut their earnings estimates and ratings, and the stock plunged to $11⁵/₈.

Why was anyone surprised? The chart had been warning investors. Insiders had sold. Customers and competitors had said sales were weak. One does not have to be a highly paid analyst to figure out that if retailers cannot sell sunglasses, manufacturers will eventually be hurt. Oakley may be a fine company, but if your largest customer says that business is terrible, there is no point in hoping that you will be the only supplier exempted. The surprise was not that Oakley reported weak numbers on December 3. The surprise was that with all of the signs of problems, it took investors so long to figure it out.

In 1998, the stocks of both Sunglass Hut and Oakley stagnated. Sunglass Hut cut its inventory levels in half, closed underperforming sunglass stores, and opened some watch station stores. By 1999, cost controls and diversification helped to improve its earnings, but lower inventory levels and fewer stores did not help Oakley.

DON'T SEND ROTTEN APPLES BY MAIL!

Another example of how investors can fail to read both the tape and the news is the story of Apple Computer and Micro Warehouse, a company in the mail-order computer business. On February 1996, Micro Warehouse was given a 1.0 rating by every analyst who followed it and was one of the ten highest-rated stocks. Micro Warehouse had a dynamic record, with its earnings per share surging from $0.22 in 1991 to $1.48 in 1995. With this growth rate, it was easy for analysts to value it at 30x earnings. But Micro Warehouse primarily sold Apple products. One does not have to be a computer wizard to remember that Windows 95 was introduced in the summer of 1995 and that its primary victim was Apple. The Mac, which had once been hailed as a revolutionary machine, was now an also-ran. Wintel had emerged victorious, and there were even those who questioned whether Apple could survive.

Not surprisingly, Apple's stock was hammered. On July 14, 1995,

Apple was selling for $48³/₄. One year later, it reached a low of $16⁷/₈, a decline of almost two-thirds. Apple ran a large loss. Its management was in turmoil.

Investors should have asked how could Micro Warehouse do well if its major supplier, Apple, was sucking wind? While mail order was growing rapidly, how could a company that made its living selling Macintoshes continue to thrive? Micro Warehouse took steps to diversify away from Apple, but Macintosh was its bread and butter. Despite the fact that Micro Warehouse sold mostly Apple products, its stock performed much better than that of Apple. When Windows 95 was introduced, the two stocks were at about $47. By the following March, Apple had sunk to $26 while Micro Warehouse had risen to $50.

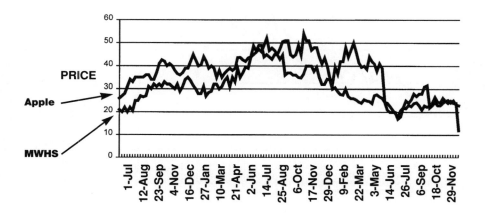

While the stock price was holding up, the technical pattern had begun to deteriorate. Volume increased, but the stock was unable to break through resistance levels. Then it began to decline. Seven insiders sold stock. On May 28, Bloomberg ran a story entitled, "Micro Warehouse Insider Selling May Mean That More Weakness Remains." Unfortunately, the analysts, who continued to give this stock the highest ranking, and the investors, who continued to buy, did not put much credence in this story. Then the first bomb dropped. On June 5, Micro Warehouse issued a press release stating that net income would be below analysts' estimates. The company attributed the expected lower net income to the continued weakness in its Apple Macintosh business. This statement came as a gigantic surprise to investors. The next day, Micro Warehouse's stock fell 11⁷/₈ to 22⁷/₈, a loss of almost one-third of its value. Most of the analysts reduced their rating on the stock. In the next month, MWHS dropped to $17.

Why were investors surprised by this announcement? Apple's business had been terrible for months. The trading pattern of MWHS had been deteriorating and insiders had been selling. Obviously, even the most sophisticated of investors often do not connect the dots.

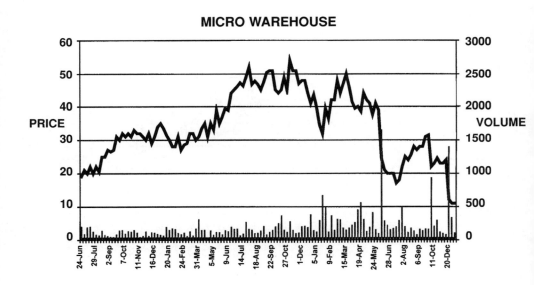

MICRO WAREHOUSE

The Micro Warehouse story should have ended here with the stock plunging immediately to new lows, but as in so many other cases, **the first major drop is rarely the last. Instead, it is an opportunity for more people who do not connect the dots to lose more money.** From July 12 to September 21, MWHS moved up from $17 to $31¹/₂, almost doubling in price. Why was the stock going up when Apple's business was clearly not getting better and the volume was light? The analysts were still bullish, and there are always "bargain hunters."

In the week of October 4, the next bomb dropped. Business continued to be weak. Micro Warehouse's stock dropped from $31½ to $22. For the next ten weeks, the stock traded in the low $20s on light volume. The final bomb dropped during the week of December 20, just in time for the end-of-the-year tax-loss selling. Micro Warehouse said that business remained weak. How could it have said anything else? Apple was still losing share. MWHS dropped to $12 on gigantic volume. Analysts cut their numbers again. The stock that had been loved by analysts at $45 was now hated by analysts at $12.

From the time that Apple started to rapidly lose share, MWHS had three bombs. In June, October, and December, the stock had declines of at least $10 each. Why in the face of Apple's problems and the chart's weakness did investors continue to jump back into Micro Warehouse? Once again, investors failed to look at the charts and connect the dots. Investing can be very simple if you don't try to fight the tape or the news.

CONNECTIONS WITHIN INDUSTRY GROUPS

Although companies within an industry compete with each other, their stocks have a surprising tendency to move in the same direction at the same time. At first this might seem illogical. It might seem as if some companies and their stocks would do well while competing companies and their stocks did poorly. But in many instances, stocks within an industry move in concert. This occurs for both fundamental and technical reasons.

Fundamentally, companies can be impacted by the same industry-wide conditions. If Microsoft introduces a new operating system or Intel develops a new chip, demand for computers will be high. If interest rates go down, financial service stocks will benefit. But there is more to the common movement than can be attributed to fundamentals alone.

Industry groups, like stocks, have technical patterns. These technical patterns contribute to what is viewed as the "fashion" of investing. An industry group can be sitting relatively unchanged, with buyers and sellers in balance. Then, what seems like a minor event happens. Suddenly, the group breaks out and starts to rally. Analysts jump on it. The biggest stocks may move first, but soon the rally takes the others along with it. It often continues longer and further than most investors would have expected. Then, at some point, the group stops moving up. A top is reached. The news is still positive, but the stocks are no longer rallying. Another seemingly minor event occurs, this one negative. A few months earlier, the market would have ignored it, but now it sends all the stocks in the group plummeting.

The explanation for the behavior of the group is the same as for individual stocks. When a group is ready to break out, investors focus on the good news. When it is ready to break down, investors focus on the bad news. In both cases, minor events can be magnified. While there may be fundamental reasons for the move, the technical patterns are often as significant.

The market runs in rhythms, and the rhythms need not have a particular fundamental rationale. The semiconductor book-to-bill ratio comes in slightly higher than plan and suddenly all of the technology stocks start to run. You wonder why such a small change should have sent the stocks up by 20 percent. Probably, the group had a technical pattern that was ready for a breakout and the small change pushed it over the top. Focusing on events that change a group's technical pattern can often give individual investors a great opportunity to make money, because many investors fail to grasp their importance. They ignore the trading action of the stock and its group, and instead listen to the spin control from the companies and look for rationality in the market.

RUNNING ON EMPTY

An interesting example of such a minor event occurred early in 1997 in the athletic footwear industry. On Thursday, April 17, a company named Footstar, a recent spin-off from Melville, reported earnings. Footstar operates Footaction athletic-shoe stores and leases footwear departments in Kmart. It is a large, but by no means dominant, company in its industry.

The day started well for Footstar. Analysts had been looking for earnings of $0.06 per share, but Footstar blew away the estimates and reported $0.16. The stock immediately traded up $2 to $28. An analyst who had recommended Footstar called: *"You better move quickly before it runs away. Footstar is at only 10x earnings. With these numbers it can double."*

The early-morning conference call started promisingly, with management detailing the strong performance. Then it started to talk about sales in the previous two weeks. It said business since Easter had been a little weak. Inventories were too high. Some goods were being returned to manufacturers, such as Nike and Fila, and earnings in the next quarter might be a little below plan. Some companies would have been more aggressive in managing their earnings. They could have reported $0.08 rather than $0.16 in the first quarter and used the hidden earnings to cushion the next several quarters. (You should never underestimate a company's ability to manage its earnings. There are vast numbers of games that a company can play to modify the earnings in a particular quarter.) But Footstar was a new public company. It had little experience with analysts, and its management may not have learned how to play earnings games.

As the conference call continued, the Footstar stock price began to drop. Investors scurried from the call to sell their stock. By 10:30, Footstar had dropped to $25. At 10:50, it was halted for a trading imbalance. One hour later, Footstar reopened at $19. (This was another good indication of the advantages of being on a conference call — you can move fast.)

Analysts talked about Footstar's problems. Some noted that Footstar was sending products back to Fila and Nike. Those stocks started to take a hit. Nike dropped almost $4. The next day, it dropped another $2. Fila dropped $3.50. The next day, it dropped another $3.25. Investors also sold shares of other athletic-shoe retailers. Finish Line, which had reported surprisingly strong earnings the week before, saw the price of its stock plunge from $16 to $12. Even Woolworth, now called Venator, dropped $2.

At the end of the day, most of the stocks in the group had been hit. A few remained unscathed. Holders of these companies must have gone to sleep feeling a sense of relief, thinking they had dodged the bombs. Perhaps they convinced themselves that their stocks had some special fundamentals. But their turn would come, and come quickly.

Reebok had closed Thursday at $45³/₄, down only $0.25. The next morning, it reported weak earnings and dropped $5⁵/₈. Converse had closed Thursday at $17⁷/₈, but Friday it sank $3¹/₈. Russell, a maker of athletic apparel, also reported weaker-than-expected earnings and plunged $8^1/_2$ to $27^1/_8$. The lesson of Reebok, Converse, and Russell was simple. **When stocks in an industry are self-destructing, few companies ever remain unscathed.** Before you go to sleep thinking that you alone have avoided getting killed, think again.

The carnage was complete. Anyone who had listened to the Footstar conference call could have made large amounts of money by selling or shorting athletic-footwear stocks. But many who listened had no interest in selling. After all, there was no disaster. Or so it seemed. Footstar had reported an excellent quarter, as had Finish Line and a number of other companies. Footstar had not said that business had died. It only said that there was a small slowdown for two weeks. So why did a two-week slowdown at one retailer cause all of the stocks in the group to get killed?

The explanation has less to do with the news conveyed by Footstar than with the technical trends in the athletic footwear and apparel industries. By the time Footstar indicated possible short-term problems, the companies were already in a weakened technical position. The stocks had already declined sharply and were heading lower. One year earlier, the market would have shaken off this announcement, but now, the stocks were ready to drop. Investors seized on a relatively minor comment to punish every stock in the group.

DID EVERYONE GROW A THIRD FOOT?

Look at the charts of the athletic-footwear stocks from the beginning of 1995 through April 1997. Most had reasonably similar patterns, moving from lows early in the period to their highs during the end of 1996 and beginning of 1997, and then dropping in April 1997. Even though some companies had greater volatility and others began their move later, the technical patterns had a lot in common.

It is easy to understand why stocks in some industries move in concert. Bank stocks may move together because of changes in interest rates. Oil stocks may move together because of changes in oil prices. Telecommunications companies may move together because of changes in the regulatory environment. But what accounts for the similar movement of the athletic-footwear stocks? No gigantic macro-economic trend suddenly changed demand. People did not grow a third foot. Nor was there any radical new technology that impacted everyone in the industry. These companies are competitors, fighting for market share. As one company does well, another should do badly. There is no fundamental reason that the stocks should exhibit similar trading patterns.

Look at the breadth of the moves, especially the moves up. These companies had an unbelievable run. From their lows to their highs, Nike went up by 335 percent, Fila by 472 percent, Finish Line by 733 percent, Just For Feet by 428 percent, Venator (Woolworth) by 155 percent, Reebok by 100 percent, and Converse by 700 percent. If you had bought each at their low and sold them at their high, you would have made more than five times your money in about two years. These are striking moves, especially for a mature industry like sneakers.

ATHLETIC FOOTWEAR STOCKS

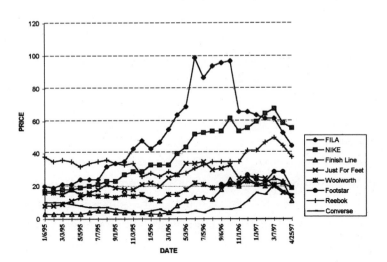

Why did the stocks of competing footwear companies have such a dramatic, unified move? The answer relates to the technical pattern of the group and power of momentum. The group had come from a low base, having been out of favor for a long time. As earnings started to improve, investors jumped on the stocks. Momentum carried them the rest of the way. Even smaller companies with marginal records obtained growth multiples.

ATHLETIC FOOTWEAR STOCKS: 1995-1997 HIGHS & LOWS			
Company	Low	High	Percent Change
Nike	$17	$74	335
Fila	$18	$103	472
Finish Line	$3	$25	733
Just For Feet	$7	$37	428
Woolworth	$9	$23	155
Reebok	$25	$50	100
Converse	$3	$24	700

Look at the history of Nike. It parlayed its start as a running shoe into a dominant position in footwear and activewear. From Michael Jordan to Tiger Woods, Nike has more great athletes than everyone else combined. When every kid in your neighborhood started to wear Nike, every picture of an athlete contained a swoosh, and everyone wanted to "be like Mike," it was probably time to buy Nike. While Nike is clearly a great company, it was also a great company in 1995. While the earnings improved significantly, was it enough to justify the jump in the price of the stock from $17 to $74? A significant portion of the advance was momentum, and while Nike soared, so did most of the other companies in the industry.

Momentum works on the downside as well. By the middle of 1996, the upside momentum for the athletic-footwear companies was coming to an end. Just For Feet was the first to crack. After surging from $4 to $37, it ran out of steam. Inventories, which investors had ignored on the way up, suddenly became critical, and its acquisition of a chain of smaller stores did not help. In July, the stock cracked down from $37 to $27 on huge volume, and its run was over.

Fila was next. Fila's pattern resembles that of many stocks that have soared without forming a base. There were the two breakouts at $20 and $30, and then an almost straight run to $103. But in October 1996, Fila had huge volume on the downside that broke the upward momentum. (It is not surprising that one year later Fila was selling near $20, the very price of its major base.)

FILA

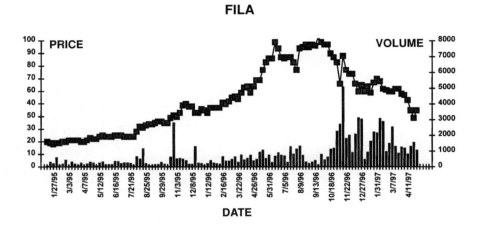

Nike's turn came in November. The stock traded 31 million shares in two weeks as it dropped from $61 to $57. In March, it dropped again on high volume. Then, on April 7, Faye Landes, a very capable analyst now at Thomas Weisel, lowered her rating. During the next week, Nike plunged $4¹/₈ on volume of 28.7 million, twice as high as its breakout volume. Despite strong earnings, this volume should have dispelled any doubt that Nike's advance was over. Nike had run from $17 to $74, but now it was on the way down.

Interestingly, the charts reveal that almost all of the stocks in the group had rolled over and were heading down before Footstar's announcement. The momentum of the athletic-footwear stocks had been broken. Footstar's announcement was only a reflection of what the charts were already saying. It was not the two weeks of softness in sales that sent the stocks dropping but rather the already-declining technical patterns, especially Nike's price decline. Look at the chart of the stocks from February to April 1997. It is easy to see the decline in the making.

And once the upside momentum was broken, the athletic-footwear stocks continued to decline. By January 1998, Nike, Fila, Reebok, and Converse were all on the new low list, while most of the other stocks were close to their lows. Momentum is always a double-edged sword. Ironically, the only stock that had started back up was Footstar, the company that seemed to have started the panic.

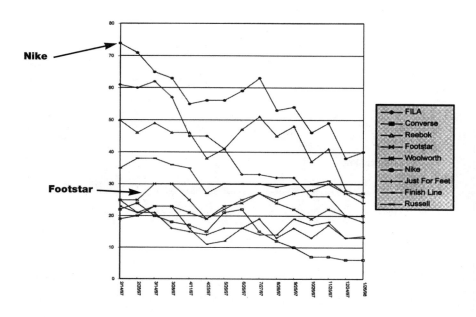

ATHLETIC FOOTWEAR STOCKS: 1997 HIGHS, APRIL 1997 & JANUARY 1998 PRICES

Company	High	4/25	1/26/98
Nike	$76	$56	$40
Fila	$74	$45	$18
Finish Line	$27	$11	$12.50
Just For Feet	$32	$14	$13.50
Woolworth	$26	$19	$20
Reebok	$53	$38	$26
Converse	$28	$15	$6

SIX WAYS TO PROFIT FROM INDUSTRY NEWS

So how can individuals use the actions of the groups to make money? Some investors play the groups themselves. They look at the charts of groups the way they would look at the charts of stocks, moving into industries that look like they are about to break out and out of industries that look like they are about to break down.

Look at the chart of America Online, compared to Lycos, Yahoo, and Amazon, in late 1998 and early 1999. (The S&P 500 is also on the chart as a frame of reference.) Despite some small intermediate peaks and valleys, the stocks all seem to have moved up and down together. If you had picked up the move in November 1998, you could have more than tripled your money by the end of April. If you had picked up the decline and shorted the stocks, you could have further doubled your money by August.

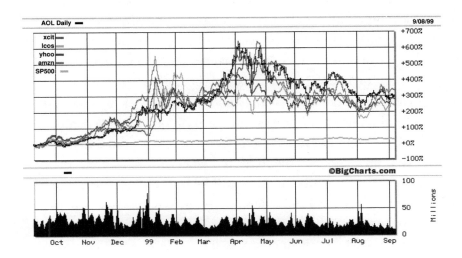

Following the technical patterns of industry groups can be an effective investment strategy, but one that requires substantial time and discipline. You have to watch events, study the charts, and be ready to move as fashion changes. If you are not on top of events, you will jump on after the group has already begun its move, and you will lose.

This does not mean you should ignore the actions of a group of stocks or wait patiently until the group in which you have your largest investments has its day in the sun. To the contrary, it is critical to watch the trading action of the competitors of your largest holdings. These competitors may tell you a lot about the stocks you own. There are six easy ways to look at stocks that compete directly with those you own:

> 1. **Look at the prices of the largest stocks in the industry to see if they are moving in the same direction as the stocks that you own.** Larger stocks will tend to move before smaller stocks. If the larger stocks in your industry move up strongly, the smaller stocks will usually follow

suit. But if the larger stocks have already had major moves upward and your stock has not budged, you may want to revisit your reason for owning it.

When the larger stocks move down, they often put a cap on the group as a whole. If AOL and Yahoo! are sinking, it is tough for smaller Internet companies to rally. These larger stocks tend to set the psychology of the group. If investors are down on great companies, they often do not want to hear about similar lesser-quality companies. In addition, the professional investors, such as the mutual fund managers, who have major positions in these companies are getting hammered. Many people invested in these mutual funds are watching the news and redeeming their shares. The fund managers will be scrambling to sell what they can to meet the redemptions and will have no appetite for buying. Thus, if the industry bellwethers are in trouble, other stocks in the industry will often have a difficult time doing well.

2. **Chart some of the competing companies against each other.** Go to your charting Web site and create a chart that includes a number of competing companies (like the athletic-footwear chart shown earlier). Look at the pattern of the group as a whole and of your stocks in particular. This can be a very interesting exercise.

3. **Look at a table that shows the price percentage leaders,** the stocks that have increased or decreased the most in price during the previous period. (It is available in every financial newspaper.) Look for stocks competing with those you own. If they have had a major move up or down, try to understand the factors behind this move and whether they will also impact your stocks.

4. **Scan a related table showing the volume percentage leaders.** These are the stocks with the biggest increase in volume. Stocks in which major events are occurring often have the highest increases in volume. (*Investors Business*

Daily has excellent tables.) If you can make the connections before the rest of the market between the stocks in these lists and the stocks in which you are interested, you can frequently win.

5. **Look at the new high and new low lists.** These lists show the stocks that are doing well or poorly. Think about where your stocks are relative to their own highs and lows. If you see a number of companies that compete with yours on the new high list while yours is mired in the middle of its range, something is wrong. If your stock is not moving up while the competitors are making new highs, how do you think it will perform when the competitors start to decline? But if your stock is holding its own while the competitors are all making new lows, you may be in a good position when the competitors turn and start to rally.

6. **Look at the relative strength of various industry groups.** The action of your stock should in some way conform to the action of the group. Pay special attention when the relative strength of the industry is increasing or decreasing significantly. Remember, momentum impacts industries as well as companies. If the relative strength of your stock is sharply different from that of its group, study the charts carefully. This could be an interesting opportunity or a significant risk.

In looking at stocks of competing companies, never underestimate the ability of seemingly minor events to have a broad impact. If you watch the news and understand the technical patterns in a particular industry, you can very often beat the professionals at their own game.

Understanding the links between news and stocks is an art, not a science. There are no exact answers as to how companies respond to a particular piece of information. If a takeover occurs, some stocks will rise because they also are considered to be takeover candidates, but others may fall because investors worry that they will become buyers or be hurt by the new competition. Sometimes stocks will move together, as was the case in the athletic-footwear and Internet industries, while sometimes they will move apart, as was the case with Apple and Microsoft.

It takes judgment to look at the fundamental news and the technical patterns and find the links that can enable you to make money. Often these links are relatively easy to see if you are looking for them. Investors could have seen the problems with Oakley and Micro Warehouse if they had simply looked at Sunglass Hut and Apple, and investors could have made money in the athletic-footwear companies on both the up and the downsides if they had simply looked for the connections between competitors. The trick is to understand the interconnections between stocks and take action when an event occurs. The ability to anticipate and act on these interconnections separates the winners from the losers.

CHAPTER NINE

The Resources of the Web

The Internet has created a revolution on Wall Street, and that revolution is still in its early stages. Online quotes, charts, trading, research, news, conference calls, chat rooms, and message boards are dramatically changing the way that people invest.

Most of these services benefit individual investors in competing against professionals. Professionals do not use these services. They have their own hardwired systems. In fact, many professionals do not even know that these services exist.

Yesterday, I sat next to one of the country's top arbitrageurs on a long train ride. We began talking about one of his deal stocks that had recently been very volatile. I told him that I had seen rumors suggesting that the deal might fall apart on the message boards. He looked at me blankly, *"What's a message board?"* As we continued to talk, I mentioned a number of other things that I had seen on the Web about this deal. Each time, his response was the same, *"Where did you find that information?"* This arbitrageur was investing more than $1 billion, but he had never looked at the resources on the Internet.

Thus, while the online services are rapidly improving, many professionals are ignoring them. This means that the benefits are accruing to individual investors. The challenge for the individual is to figure out how to utilize these new resources.

Almost every day, a new service appears on the Web, and the pace of change is accelerating. When I look back at the subjects I talked about in the hardcover edition of this book, which was published only eighteen months before this edition, I am astounded at the changes that have occurred. I am certain that in the next eighteen months, the changes will be equally dramatic.

This creates a challenge for me in writing about this subject. I know that by the time that you read this, there will be many new Web sites, and many of the services will have changed significantly. Accordingly, detailing the many current services would be of little use. Instead, my goal in approaching this chapter is to give the investor an overall view of the types of online resources that are available and to suggest directions that I expect them to take in the near future.

NEWS AND RESEARCH ONLINE

The wealth of news and research available online is unbelievable. Investors should be able to find almost anything they need on the Web. The only questions are time and cost. No one has enough time to read or listen to everything that is available, and while many services are free, some do cost money. At the moment, there are an extraordinary number of excellent free services, but some of the pay services may also be worth a look, if you are interested in their specific content.

The major newspapers and financial publications all have Web sites and almost all have some form of electronic edition (online information that is not in the publication itself). You might want to check out the Web sites of the *Wall Street Journal, Investors Business Daily, Barron's,* and the *New York Times.* (Some have fees.) If you do not have access to these papers or the time to read them in the morning, their Web sites can be useful. The major business magazines also have good Web sites. CNNfn and Bloomberg both have excellent Web sites for news.

There are many other newspapers and periodicals that could be worth looking at, especially if they have a story of interest to you. A local newspaper may be running an exposé on one of your stocks. If you want to learn more about the expose, click over to the newspaper's Web site and read all about it.

As the Internet grows, a variety of new Web sites are emerging to provide online news and research, such as CBS-Marketwatch.com. While Marketwatch and others do an excellent job covering company-specific news, I rarely go directly to these Web sites, primarily because there is too much information for me to digest. Instead, I usually end up at the site in the process of reading the news on a company that is of particular interest to me.

Other Web sites provide a good combination of news and interesting commentary. Motley Fool, Briefing.com, and The Street.com are extremely popular. (Briefing.com and The Street.com are paid services, but many of the online brokers include them as part of their package.)

There are also a number of services geared to more specific niches in the market. Silicon Investor focuses on high-tech stocks. Internet.com has an excellent Web site that features only Internet stocks.

Almost every major industry has Web sites that focus on the stocks in that industry. You will probably come across these Web sites in the course of looking at individual stocks. These Web sites are good if you are interested in a particular industry and will have in-depth and technical information on certain companies. The only problem is that many of these sites are geared to professionals within the industry, so they may not provide as much help as you might expect.

A number of the services, like Internet.com, have e-mail programs. Each day (or week), it will e-mail you information on the subjects that are of specific interest to you. These programs are easy to try. Most are free. Some have a subscription fee. Try the free service first. If you find it extremely useful, you can always opt for the pay service later. If you do not like receiving the e-mails, canceling is easy.

For the first time, research reports are also available online. Multex has a service that sells individual research reports to investors. This is a very interesting service, but you should not necessarily jump at it. It's expensive, especially if you are interested in a large number of companies. Besides, some of the companies will send you the information for free, although it may not be as timely, and some of the research reports are not worth the paper (or screen) they are written on. If the research report is written by an analyst to justify an investment-banking deal, it may not benefit you. Still, Multex is evolving, and the site might be worth looking at, especially if you have a major position in a company and there are issues that you do not understand.

Some of the online brokers also provide research. DLJ Direct, for example, provides all DLJ research to anyone with a balance over a certain level. (The last time I checked it was $100,000.) If you like doing fundamental analysis and find that the analysts at a particular firm are especially good, you might consider opening an account with an online broker that provides research from that firm. The broker's Web site will tell you what research it offers.

COMPANY-SPECIFIC INFORMATION ON THE WEB

Because I am interested in a large number of companies and have limited time, I try to focus on company-specific information. I usually get to this information from my Yahoo! monitor list. Other people I know use MoneyCentral (from Microsoft), AOL's finance channel, Lycos or Quicken as their monitor.

When I see an asterisk next to a company, indicating news, I click on the ticker symbol for the company. The Web site then takes me to the company-specific news. It may be a story from a newspaper or an online service, such as Marketwatch or Motley Fool. It may be notification of a federal filing. It may be a press release from the company or a notice of a change in ratings by analysts. If the news sounds significant, I will read it.

News can also be found on the home pages of the various companies. For me, the easiest way to find the home page is to go to the stock's page on my search engine (in this case Yahoo!). I click on "Profile" and then on "Home Page."

Most home pages are extremely rich in information. They may include complete financial information, including recent press releases and filings, as well as the latest annual report. Some companies have begun putting financial presentations on their Web sites. These talking slide shows can be fascinating. They are often equivalent to what professionals see at conferences.

Equally important, home pages usually show the companies' products and include management's discussions of current business operations and future opportunities.

Visiting a home page can be interesting. If you know nothing about a company, the page can help you to understand its business. If you know something about a company, it can help you to compare your knowledge with the company's point of view. This often gives you a good opportunity to see hype or find gaps that others miss.

ONLINE FEDERAL FILINGS

Most companies now put all their federal filings on the SEC's Edgar database of corporate information. If you are really interested in a company, it is worth looking at this information. The tables (earnings, balance sheet, cash flow, etc.) are useful, as are the footnotes, which often include very revealing information. The most interesting filings usually are:

1. Annual Report and 10K: fiscal-year reports
2. 10Q: quarterly reports
3. 8K: reports related to specific transactions, such as acquisitions, divestitures, etc.
4. 13D and F: reports about material changes in ownership by insiders or major institutions

As noted earlier in the book, I also find it useful to look at insider transactions. You can do this either on Edgar or on the financial Web site that you use. Yahoo! lists all insider purchases and sales. Following these transactions on Yahoo! is easier than following them on some of the professional systems I have in my office. For me, these transactions are a significant indicator. I do not want to own a stock that too many insiders are selling. I do want to own stocks in which insiders are increasing their positions. Insider transactions represent an extremely important clue as to how the insiders view their own company.

CUTTING THROUGH THE CLUTTER

The biggest problem in navigating the Web is cutting through the clutter. The amount of information available online is virtually unlimited. You could spend twenty-four hours a day researching subjects of interest. To limit your time online:

1. Focus on the stocks on your monitor list. You cannot chase down every story on every stock.

2. Bookmark sites that are extremely useful. This makes navigating much easier.

3. Limit the number of services you use. If you find a new one you like, eliminate one that you do not use often.

4. Don't try to learn everything about every stock you monitor. Instead, focus on the issues that will help you make buy or sell decisions.

I know that I spend too much time reading duplicate First Call notes. I do not want to miss anything. But sometimes, when I focus on learning as many details as I can, I either miss the big picture or I miss the short-term moves of a stock. Forcing yourself to cut through the clutter is not always easy, but it is always worth the effort.

COMPANY SLEUTH DOES THE WORK FOR YOU

One service that saves time and helps you focus on the stocks of most interest to you is called Company Sleuth. (Sleuth is a product of a company named Infonautics.) This service has an interesting "push" technology. When you sign up, you list ten companies that are important to you. Each day, Company Sleuth scans message boards, corporate filings, analysts' reports, and prominent business sites, such as Motley Fool. It then sends you an e-mail listing where and how your companies have been mentioned.

I like receiving this e-mail each morning. It gives me an excellent view of my most important stocks. When I get to work, the e-mail is usually waiting. I open it and check the action of the stocks on my list. On many days, I close it and go on to other things. But sometimes, something catches my eye. I click on the name of the company and Sleuth takes me to an organized page for that company.

In the center of the page is the key information on the company. On the side is a list of the sites that Sleuth scans for information (federal filings, Yahoo! message boards, Whisper Numbers, Real News, Premium Information, Motley Fool, etc.). Next to each of the sites is a number showing how many times the company was mentioned during the past day.

Sleuth tells me that the company has just filed with the SEC. I click on the filings and get the document. Sleuth also tells me that there has been some insider transactions. I click over and check out the purchases and sales.

Sleuth tells me that the company, which normally has two or three postings on the Yahoo! message board, had forty on the previous day. I click again, and I am on the message board. I take a brief look at the messages. Sometimes it is just noise, but sometimes there is an interesting debate or series of rumors that is worth following up.

Next Sleuth tells me that there are new "whisper numbers" for the company's earnings. I click on "Whisper Numbers," and compare them with the estimates I had previously expected. If the whisper numbers are lower, I might do some further checking. Finally, Sleuth tells me that the company has registered some new Uniform Resource Locators (URLs). I click over to see what these new Web sites or Internet files are. Sometimes the URLs registered by the company can give you a good feeling for its future direction.

Sleuth has a number of key advantages. It e-mails you every day (even Saturday and Sunday), so that you know exactly what is happening with your key stocks. It presents each stock in a very organized way that makes it easy to review the information. Finally, it often uncovers information that you would not have found on your own. (Maybe that is why it is called "Sleuth.")

One of the most interesting discoveries I made with Sleuth concerned Skytel, one of the leading companies in the wireless-paging industry, and MCI-Worldcom. In February 1999, Skytel was trading in the mid-teens. Then rumors start to swirl that it would be acquired by MCI-Worldcom. On May 24, Skytel closed at $18\frac{7}{8}$.

The next morning, Company Sleuth reported that MCI-Worldcom had registered the domain name "skytelworldcom.com." As subscribers read their Company Sleuth e-mail, they reached the logical conclusion that MCI-Worldcom was going to acquire Skytel. Why else would it have registered the domain name? The price of Skytel surged 16 percent to $21⅞.

MCI-Worldcom issued a press release saying that one of the top administrators of its main Internet site had acted on his own initiative and registered the name. He had read that MCI-Worldcom might acquire a paging company and was anxious to protect his company from cybersquatters. The press release said, "The action is not an indication of official company intention."

The MCI-Worldcom spokeswoman went on to say that the company would not take disciplinary action against the employee. MCI-Worldcom said that it had first asked that the name be deleted, but then decided to keep it because it jointly sold some communications services with Skytel. After the news was released, the price of Skytel's stock dropped back under $19.

Three days later, MCI-Worldcom announced that it had reached an agreement to acquire Skytel. (Surprise!) The deal was worth $21.24. Needless to say, the class-action lawyers immediately filed a suit claiming that the statements by MCI-Worldcom had deliberately misled investors and pushed down the price of Skytel's stock.

There is no way of knowing what really happened. Perhaps the employee was just trying to protect his company from "cybersquatters." Or perhaps, he knew of the acquisition and jumped the gun. Whatever the reality, Company Sleuth uncovered a critical piece of information that allowed some investors to make a quick profit.

What was most interesting is that only those people who subscribed to Company Sleuth learned about it. The information was not picked up first by analysts or professionals. It was picked up by a service that scans the Web for information. It is small pieces of information like this that can often allow individuals to use the Web to defeat the professionals. If there are a number of stocks in which you are very interested, a service like Company Sleuth can help you stay on top of the information and cut through the clutter.

CONFERENCE CALLS ON THE INTERNET

While reading information is critical, there is no substitute for seeing or listening to companies. Presentations and conference calls give an investor the opportunity to interact directly with the management and listen to questions from the professionals.

The availability of information related to conference calls as well as the calls themselves on the Internet is a significant change that benefits individual investors. Previously, conference calls were restricted to institutional investors. Often, individuals could not even find out the time or the phone number. This gave the institutions a major advantage.

In the past year, more calls have been opened to all investors. Some companies still restrict participation, but each quarter, the number is shrinking. Some companies do ask that you make a reservation, so that they can set aside enough lines. But making a reservation is simple.

Most companies now make replays available, primarily to give institutional investors who have conflicts the opportunity to participate. But replays also directly benefit the individual investor who may be working during the day. You can listen to the call at night or on weekends (when the phone rates are lower). You may miss the immediacy of the conference call, but at least you get the chance to listen directly to management. The institutions still have the advantage of having the time to listen to most of the calls live. But the availability is there, and the playing field is much more level.

There are now excellent services that list all conference calls. Mainline Internet services, like Motley Fool and MatchWatch, provide lists of conference calls, but I prefer two specialized services: Bestcalls (bestcalls.com) and StreetFusion (streetfusion.com).

The Best Calls Web site lists all upcoming conference calls. At the top is a box where you can put in a ticker symbol to ask about a particular company. Scan through the list of upcoming calls. Click on one that interests you. Best Calls has all of the information you need: the time, the call-in number, the passcode, the replay number, the time of the replay, the requirements for participation, the phone number of the company itself, and a description of the company.

Street Fusion is also an excellent service, although at the present time it is only open to institutional investors. When you subscribe to Street Fusion (there is no cost), you give it a list of the 100 companies in which you are interested. If one of these companies is having a conference call, Street Fusion will send you an e-mail reminder. This is an extremely useful service, because people tend to forget the time or the number for the calls. Street Fusion also has a significant number of conference calls available on the Internet, both live and on replay. I suspect that at some point Street Fusion will be available to a wider number of participants.

THE INTERNET BEATS THE PHONE

Companies are increasingly putting their conference calls on the Internet. The Internet provides a number of advantages over the telephone:

- It is cheaper. There are no long-distance phone calls to make. (When calls last one hour, the long-distance charges can mount up. While some companies provide 800 numbers, many do not.)
- Listening is easier. Because computers have speakers, (and often excellent sound systems) you do not have to sit with a phone scrunched against your ear or strain to make out the words on a scratchy speaker phone.
- It is multimedia. While listening to the conference call, you can click on the financials and read the press releases.
- You can listen to the call in the background while you are doing other things on the computer.
- The replays are controllable. You can stop, rewind, fast forward and listen again to subjects that interest you.
- You can listen to replays at your leisure. Most of the conference calls are archived, so you can listen to them whenever you want. The archives usually go back a reasonable period of time, so there is a wealth of information online. Before making or changing an investment, I often

find it useful to go back and listen to segments of the last conference call.

There is one negative to the online conference calls: You cannot ask a question. But this not as much of a detriment as you might expect. Even on live calls, individual investors do not usually ask questions.

The analysts ask their questions first. They want to know often-minor details for their reports (like the tax rate or the number of shares). Perhaps more critically, they want their customers as well as the company itself to know that they are on the call. Analysts do not want companies or institutional investors to think that they have missed a call. Visibility is important to their careers. So they queue up for the questions when the conference call coordinator gives the instructions at the beginning of the call, before the company has made its presentation, and before there are even any issues to ask about.

Many analysts want to be first. There are more people on the call at the beginning, and by being first, an analyst sounds more interested and aggressive than his competitors. I knew an analyst who prided himself on always being first. He usually asked about insignificant details, but he was first. He was also rated first in the *Institutional Investor* poll, although I had never once heard him say anything even remotely intelligent.

It is fun to listen to the parade of analysts, especially with a company that is doing well and has few complicated issues. The analysts will always start by saying, "Great quarter!" It never hurts to kiss up to a potential banking client. Then they will ask a self-serving question. In well-covered companies, it gets difficult for analysts who are not early in the queue. By the time they get their turn, most of the easy questions have been asked. So they say something like, "All of my questions have been answered, but I wanted to take the opportunity to congratulate you on the absolutely fantastic quarter." Of course, for the other listeners, it is extremely boring to hear this self-serving compliment for the twentieth time in half an hour.

After the analysts have their say, a number of major institutions usually want to ask questions. Institutions tend to ask more pointed questions that are quite interesting. They own, or are thinking about owning, the stock, and they do not have to kiss up to the management. If there are serious issues, they hone in on them. After all, it is their money.

Sometimes institutions that are "short" the stock ask questions. They are the polar opposite of the analysts. They want to focus on the problems, the company's greatest vulnerabilities, to make other investors nervous so the price of the stock will go down. Their accusing questions are easy to spot.

With the analysts, major institutions, and short sellers queuing up at the start of the call, most, if not all, of the question-and-answer period is accounted for. So listening online is really not a detriment. Besides, you can always speak to investor relations after the call if your question has not been answered.

Another service that provides online conference calls is Vcall (vcall.com). Vcall is open to all investors and has a clean and very easy-to-use Web site. On the home page are today's calls and upcoming calls. There is also a box where you can search for calls from the last two weeks. There is a "Company Search" box that allows you to access older calls. In addition to conference calls, Vcall has interviews with analysts, portfolio managers, market strategists, technicians, and corporate executives. It has an extremely full and interesting schedule.

Listening to calls on Vcall is a full multimedia experience, because the service provides press releases and financial statements that you can read as you listen to the call. When an analyst or a technician is being inter-viewed, Vcall often provides charts or tables to accompany the interview. The quality of the participants is quite high.

CHARTING ON THE INTERNET

As noted in chapters 7 and 8, the charting Web sites on the Internet are almost as comprehensive as the best of the services available to profession-als, and they are easier to use. I have two expensive proprietary systems on my desk, and yet, when I need a chart, I will frequently use the Internet. My favorite charting site is Bigcharts.com, but there are other excellent services. Most of the online brokers have tie-ins to good services, and even Yahoo! has decent charts.

The key to charts is to use them. This means that you should find a Web site and a group of parameters that work for you. Most people use simple Price & Volume charts, checking different time frames. Looking at a moving average is also useful, because stocks tend to trade around the moving average. When they move above it, they often continue to go up. When they drop below it, they often continue to go down.

Graphing stocks of competing companies may give you a clue to when a group is beginning or ending a move. If you see one stock acting differently from all of its competitors, it is probably worth rechecking your analysis. A company can thrive while its competitors are crashing, but this scenario is the exception, not the rule.

Many investors never become fully comfortable with charts, but the online services are so easy to use that it is worth your while to try. Save a few of your favorite charts on the charting Web sites. When you go back there, look them up. Over time, you will probably get comfortable with some form of technical analysis.

INVESTING WITH ONLINE BROKERS

One year ago, online brokers were a novelty. Now they are transforming the world of investing. Major brokerage firms, like DLJ and Morgan Stanley Dean Witter, have online services. Traditional discount brokers, like Schwab, Fidelity, and Ameritrade, have created online businesses. And new Internet start-ups, like Datek and Wit Capital, have entered the field.

Because of the rapid pace of change, it is impossible to review the specific services and make recommendations, but the following represent a list of issues that investors should consider. Each investor has different needs, and each online brokerage company offers different services. Before you select one, compare its services with your needs.

1. If you invest in **mutual funds,** make sure the service has a good fund supermarket.
2. If you play **options,** make sure it has a good options system.

3. If **research** is important to you, pick one that offers good fundamental research.

4. If you like to play **IPOs,** see which of the firms seems to have the most active calendar. You can e-mail customer support and ask about the number of IPOs, the amount of stock they offer, and how that stock is allocated. Some companies allocate their IPOs to their best customers. Others allocate the stock randomly. If you have a small account and hope to get some shares, make sure you check first with the broker about its policy.

5. If you like to **trade actively,** see which of the systems has fast execution. There are very significant differences between the online brokers. Some, such as Datek, are geared to active traders. Others are not.

6. **Ease of use** may be the most important factor. An online broker can have thousands of different services, but if it is too complicated to use, it is worthless. I have had accounts with five different online brokers. I have found the difference in ease of use to be significant. This is an issue of personal preference. You may find one broker easy to use, while a friend may find it difficult. Do not be swayed by what other people say. Find an online broker that works for you.

7. One factor that distinguishes online brokers is the amount of **human interaction** they offer. All online brokers have help desks, but some only want to talk to you if there is a problem. They do not give advice or make suggestions. Others have hybrid models: computers for trading and live people for advice. Only you can judge how much human interaction you need. But you should remember that the live "brokers" for some of the online systems are clerks, not highly paid professionals. If you really need human help, a traditional broker may be better for you.

8. The **trading costs** for the online brokers also differ substantially, although all are significantly lower than trading

costs for traditional brokers. The key question for trading costs is the amount that you will trade. If you trade once a month, the difference between $10 and $20 a trade will not amount to much. If you trade actively, it may be far more significant. Also recognize that there is a tradeoff between costs and services. If you want research, IPOs, human assistance, and other services, you should expect to pay more.

9. It always pays to check what you will be charged for **margin interest** and paid for **credit balances.** If you are borrowing a lot or leaving a lot of money in cash balances, these rates could be important (and most people forget to check them).

10. An essential for most investors is **real-time quotes.** Most of the Internet services, such as Yahoo!, provide quotes on a 20-minute delay. Some of the online brokers still do the same. Real-time quotes are important, especially with the current level of volatility. Even if you are not an active trader, you should still know the current price of a stock before you make a trading decision.

11. **Level II quotes** are another matter entirely. (They apply only to NASDAQ stocks.) While basic quotes list the bid and asked prices, the Level II quotes show the bid and asked prices by market maker. For casual investors, Level II quotes are not critical. For extremely active investors and day traders, they can be quite important. If you find yourself trading volatile NASDAQ stocks many times a day, you should use an online broker that offers Level II quotes.

In the end, there are a number of good reasons for individual investors to use an online broker. The costs are much lower. You can control your own trading decisions. You always know the status of your portfolio. You can often get services, such as research or Level II quotes, far easier than you can from your traditional broker. Finally, you can have access to your portfolio at anytime and from anyplace that has Internet access.

The choice among online brokers boils down to personal preference. Look at your own needs. If you are an active trader, costs and Level II quotes could be significant. If you like mutual funds, research, IPOs, or options, brokers providing them are optimal. If you are a neophyte investor, a hybrid model with some personal service, even at a higher cost, may be better.

You do not have to stick with the service you choose first. Over time, you may find that your needs, or the service you originally picked, change and that another broker is more appropriate. Although the brokers want to think that they are capturing your account for life, changing brokers is relatively simple. Do not agonize over your choice.

ELECTRONIC COMMERCE NETWORKS ARE HERE TO STAY

One new innovation that promises to have a far-reaching impact on investing in general and on online investing in particular are the Electronic Commerce Networks (ECNs). You may not fully understand what an ECN is. Don't feel bad. Many of the top investors on Wall Street do not either. But the ECNs are going to transform investing in the next several years far more significantly than anyone can imagine.

The New York and American Stock Exchanges trade primarily through a specialist system. When you place an order, it goes to a specialist, which puts the order in a book. The specialist then attempts to match buyers and sellers. To help facilitate the trades, the specialist will use its own money to smooth out the trades. When there is an imbalance between buyers and sellers, the specialist will halt trading until it can come up with a new price at which it can restore the balance.

When you buy or sell a stock, the specialist may be the entity on the other side of the transaction. If you are buying and the specialist is long the stock, it may sell some of its inventory to you. The specialists are highly profitable and difficult to defeat. They are experts in trading their own stocks. They know their companies, control the order book, and have some leeway over the prices. If you are trading against them, they have the advantage.

The main function of the specialists is to prevent the major imbalances that big institutions can create. To handle individual orders, the exchanges have created an electronic order book, called the DOT system. This book enables retail orders to be matched against each other. In actively traded stocks, DOT orders are executed seamlessly, which normally benefits individual investors. Nonetheless, the key pricing is set by the specialists.

In the over-the-counter market, orders go to market makers at various brokerage firms. All of the major brokerage firms make markets in over-the-counter stocks. There are also a number of firms that specialize in making markets. These firms commit sizeable amounts of capital to trading over-the-counter stocks. They expect, and usually receive, very high returns from their investments.

The market makers control the bid and asked prices. A stock may be quoted $20^1/_4$ bid, $20^3/_4$ asked. This means that you will pay $\$20^3/_4$ to buy the stock and $\$20^1/_4$ to sell it. Once again, the market makers maintain an inventory. They will buy the stock from you for $\$20^1/_4$ and then resell it to another investor for $\$20^3/_4$. The market makers earn a profit on the spread between the two prices. Because the market makers earn a fee on the trade, you are often not charged a commission on over-the-counter stocks. But you are still out the spread.

In most cases, the various market makers will have different prices. Some may have slightly higher bid prices or slightly lower asked prices. Others may be "out of the market," meaning that their bid is too low or their asked is too high. (When market makers go off the desk for a break, they normally adjust their prices so that no one will "hit" them when they are not there.)

Sometimes trades are done at prices "inside" the bid and asked. In our example, you may be able to buy at $\$20^5/_8$ and sell at $\$20^3/_8$. The Level II quotes offered by some brokers give investors the opportunity to see the bid and asked prices for each market maker and the prices at which specific trades are executed. Most professionals and day traders use Level II quotes. This gives them an advantage over other traders because they can pick and choose among market makers.

Nonetheless, the market makers have an advantage over the individual traders. They know what orders they have from the major institutions, and they adjust their bid and asked prices for their own benefit.

The ECN works differently. There are no specialists or market makers. Instead, the ECN is a pure electronic order book that matches up buyers and sellers. (The DOT system is also an electronic order book, but the pricing is still determined primarily by the specialists.)

Investors enter the prices at which they want to buy or sell, and the ECN matches them up. If a buyer and a seller are both willing to trade a stock for $21, the ECN will match them at that price. The ECN can also take orders for future trade, because the computer has a virtually unlimited memory. You may enter orders to sell the stock at $23 and buy more at $20. If the stock hits either of these two prices and the ECN finds someone who wants to take the other side, the trade will be executed.

ECNs have a number of key advantages. Because trades are done automatically, the system is extremely inexpensive. The last time I checked, Island, one of the ECNs, charged $1 per trade, a fraction of the cost anywhere else. ECNs have no highly paid traders or specialists. Equally important, no one is putting capital at risk to facilitate a trade, and there is no middleman taking a markup.

The ECN can operate twenty-four hours a day, without regard for time zones or national boundaries. The ECN does not care about the identity of the buyer or the seller. It only cares whether it can match two of them.

The ECNs currently have one major disadvantage. They are a closed system that can only match up buyers and sellers within the system. If you are on an ECN, you can only trade with someone else on the same ECN. When the market is open, this may not be a difficult problem. If the ECN does not have a trade to match up with yours, the broker can route your trade to a market maker or a specialist. The trade will take place through regular channels, outside of the ECN.

After hours, however, when the volume is much lower and there are no exchanges to turn to, the ECN could end up being extremely volatile. If you are trying to trade through an ECN after hours and there are only a few other traders on the system at the same time, it may be extremely difficult to execute your trade at a reasonable price. In this case, the ECN's low cost could be more than offset by the thin market.

In such a situation, it is very likely, even probable, that the different ECNs will have different bid and asked prices on the same stocks. This in turn could create a completely new system of arbitrage. Some enterprising trader will undoubtedly figure out how to trade one ECN against another and capitalize on the inefficiencies. If this does occur, the individual will again be at a disadvantage.

Of course, the ECNs could ultimately find a way around this problem by creating a cooperative system. The ECNs could link together to create more volume and hence more efficient prices. It is way too early in the process to predict whether this will happen, but it is clear that the Electronic Commerce Networks are here to stay.

It is also clear that ECNs will most benefit individual investors. Because ECNs must match buyers and sellers, small round lots (100, 1,000, etc.) will be the easiest for them to deal with. These are the types of trades that individuals make.

The specialists and the market makers, on the other hand, focus on the major accounts. Their most critical task is to be able to handle the major blocks that the institutions buy and sell. This means that the ECNs will provide a double benefit for the individuals. They will create a trading system primarily geared to individuals, and, because the individuals won't be available to help buy the major blocks of stock, they will make things more difficult for the trading systems geared to professionals.

AFTER-HOURS TRADING FOR INDIVIDUAL INVESTORS

Perhaps the greatest impact of the ECNs will come in after-hours trading. Until now, markets have been open during the day, when the professionals were investing and most individuals were pursuing their own careers. After the markets were seemingly closed, the professionals could trade in the aftermarket or on foreign exchanges, while the individual was shut out.

The introduction of after-hours trading will have a huge impact on the ability of the individual investor to compete against the professionals. The expansion of the hours will force professionals to work longer days. This increases the likelihood that the best of the professionals will not be trading all of the time and that individuals will sometimes compete with their less-skilled assistants. In addition, the individual will now be able to invest after the workday is over, without the distractions that a job can bring.

It may be difficult to keep exchanges open 24 hours a day. The specialists who work there do not want to staff multiple shifts. Besides the additional labor costs, operating much longer hours would mean that the specialists would have to leave their business, and hence their capital, in the hands of less experienced and probably less skilled traders.

The same situation applies to the NASDAQ. By operating significantly extended hours, the NASDAQ market makers would face a Hobson's Choice. They could keep a full complement of traders, which would entail extremely high costs for relatively little volume. Or they could let each trader handle many more stocks after hours, which would make them vulnerable to being picked off by the SOES bandits and other day traders.

The same conditions do not apply to the ECNs. Because the costs of their computer systems are largely fixed, ECNs can afford to operate significantly extended hours, even on relatively low volume. Accordingly, the ECNs should take the lead in offering after-hours trading, which will bring both opportunities and risks for individual investors.

Will the major exchanges allow the ECNs to have the after-hours trading field to themselves? If the ECNs are successful, the power of the major exchanges will be jeopardized. It is unlikely that these exchanges will want to relinquish turf to electronic upstarts. As a result, we suspect that it will only be a matter of time before the exchanges themselves start to offer expanded trading hours.

The interesting question is where will it end? If the exchanges remain open for an extra hour, will the ECNs stay open for three hours? If the exchanges stay open for three hours, will the ECNs stay open for six hours? If the exchanges stay open from 8 A.M. until 8 P.M. will the ECNs stay open twenty-four hours a day? Just remember, the ECNs have very low variable costs. As long as there are two investors who are willing to trade at a particular price, the ECNs can facilitate it. But if the ECNs stay open 24 hours a day, what will be the competitive response of the exchanges?

Logic would indicate that the time for after-hours trading will continue to increase and that the exchanges will in one way or another be involved. At some point in the not-so-distant future, twenty-four-hour-a-day trading may be a fact of life. Then, we wonder, will there be enough action at 6 P.M., not to mention 2 A.M., to make an efficient market?

These are some of the most interesting issues that the investment community will face in the next few years. The ECNs are on their way to becoming individual stock markets. If they can figure out ways of interacting with each other, they can threaten the existing markets and force them into competitive responses. Since the existing exchanges have been run for the benefit of the professionals, the competitive responses will likely benefit the individual investor.

All of these issues will emerge over the next year or two. For the moment, limited after-hours trading, especially on ECNs, will be a fact of life. While this will give the individual more time to make investments, it will also probably raise the level of volatility. **Look at after-hours trading as an opportunity for the long term, but exercise great care trading in the short term as the new systems are implemented.**

TRADING AGAINST AMATEURS

Most of this book has focused on the idea that the individual investor has to defeat the professional investor in order to win in the stock market. With the introduction of after-hours trading and the growth of ECNs, individuals may find themselves increasingly competing against other individuals, especially with highly volatile Internet stocks. When this occurs, the rules change. In some ways, the game becomes easier. In some ways, it becomes harder. But it certainly becomes more volatile.

With highly volatile stocks, many individuals have a tendency to get swept up in "stories" and "rumors." They jump on a chat-room rumor and take a stock up 200 percent or down 50 percent in a matter of minutes. This occurs because individuals have less of a grounding in the fundamentals. Unlike professionals, they often do not set buy and sell points. When they see a stock they like start to surge, they sometimes jump on it without regard to the fair value of the stock.

There is no way to set rules for dealing with this type of situation, because the behavior of a stock can vary dramatically. Take a case like

Books-A-Million. The stock went from $4 to $44 in four trading days. Then in the next two weeks, it dropped back to $12. No amount of experience could provide any investor with a guide to trading this stock.

The best advice for an individual faced with a stock that has suddenly been taken over by hordes of other individual traders is to focus on your own home turf. If you understand what is pushing the stock up and have some view as to its valuation, jump on it. If not, walk away. The problem with trading against other individuals is that the valuations and the volatility can go to extremes. This can make you a lot of money, but it can also cause you pain.

THE INTERNET REVISITED

The Internet is providing individuals with a variety of new weapons in their war against the professionals. News, federal filings, research, company-specific information, charts, and conference calls are significantly narrowing the information gap. Online trading is reducing costs to below that available to professionals. New trading systems, like ECNs, and after-hours trading will further benefit individuals. As the Internet continues to evolve, it will increasingly give the individual an edge.

CHAPTER TEN

Chat Rooms and Message Boards

One of the major advantages professionals have is their community of investors. They spend much of their day trading thoughts with each other. If professionals know each other well and have the same investing style, they will often give each other advice. But primarily, they use each other as sounding boards to test out new ideas. Some even try to find an investor with a different style to be a devil's advocate. Few professionals are secure enough in their own knowledge to go it completely alone.

With the exception of investment clubs, individuals have never had these opportunities. The fairly recent availability of chat rooms and message boards finally puts them in a community of other investors with whom they can exchange ideas. An online chat room is a live venue where investors can exchange ideas. A message board is an online location at which investors can post comments on particular stocks. If you use the Internet regularly, you've probably seen both. If you are new at the online investing game, start with the message boards: They are simpler to use because they are organized by stock.

If you do not have a favorite financial Web site, use the one offered by Yahoo!. It includes a popular message board. Click on the quote of a particular stock. After you see the stock price, you will see a list of available information about the stock, including charts, profile, news, and messages. Click on messages, and you will see a list of all of the messages posted on that stock. If you want to post a reply to any one of the messages, it merely takes a click on "Reply to Message."

Yahoo! will ask you for a screen name to use when you are posting a message. Most people do not use their own names. Instead they create monikers, like CB radio operators use. Some people use monikers like "Stud_Man" or "Stock_Genius007" that describe themselves, or at least their fantasy of themselves. When you are starting out, it is probably better to create a moniker, or screen name. You aren't stuck with your first choice. Some people create multiple monikers.

Yahoo! will ask for some personal details. Fill in those entries with which you are comfortable. Some people fill in their hometown, sex, and age. Others do not. There are no requirements. Do not give out your e-mail address, unless you want the other posters to be able to track you down.

Once you have a screen moniker, you can post a message on the board. If you are nervous about the process, post something completely innocuous just to gain experience. You would be surprised at how many people post "Test," just to see if the system works.

Asking a question is also easy. Some people start their first post with a simple question such as "When is this company going to report earnings?", "Does anyone know the phone number of the conference call?", or "Why is this stock moving up (or down)?"

Most questions on most boards will elicit a response. People who post on the boards normally like to help newcomers. If you decide that you don't like your original message, you can always change your screen name and reappear with a different identity. In making postings, you are anonymous. No one will know who you are unless you tell your real identity.

If you find the message board interesting, look at other message boards when you go to other financial sites, such as Motley Fool.

As you are navigating around the Web, you will probably bump into a live chat room. Go in and take a look at the conversation. You can register with most of these sites and participate for no cost. While message boards are best for obtaining information on particular stocks, chat rooms are best for trading stock ideas, especially with people who have a similar style, such as day traders. You may not find chat rooms useful. They take up a lot of time, and you may not find one in which you are comfortable. Don't let it worry you. Chat rooms may be fun, but they are not essential for success in the stock market.

WHERE ARE PEOPLE POSTING?

As you start checking out the message boards for individual stocks, you will immediately notice that the action varies dramatically. The table below shows the number of messages on selected stocks posted on Yahoo! as of June 24, 1999.

MESSAGES ON YAHOO					
STOCK	MESSAGES	STOCK	MESSAGES	STOCK	MESSAGES
Dell	240,888	PairGain	23,394	Pepsico	6,561
Amazon.com	121,938	Books-a-Million	20,452	Citibank	5,155
Yahoo!	112,580	IBM	19,585	Delta Air	4,814
Compaq	82,713	Coca-Cola	14,593	McDonald's	4,812
Microsoft	82,632	Hewlett Packard	13,654	CompuCom	2,585
Iomega	66,163	Wal-Mart	13,113	Bristol Myers	2,291
Ebay	46,132	VISX	12,619	AllState	2,107
Intel	45,034	Merck	10,979	J.P. Morgan	1,072
Cisco	32,483	Ford	10,285	TJX	780
Onsale	31,665	General Electric	10,094	May	270

Some companies, like Dell Computer, have very active message boards. By June 24, 1999, Dell had more than 240,000 postings on Yahoo! In the previous twelve months, this board had received more than 534 postings per day.

Other technology and Internet companies also had a large number of postings. Amazon and Yahoo! had more than 100,000, while Compaq and Microsoft had more than 80,000. Even smaller technology companies had large numbers of postings. Iomega, a $5 stock, had six times more postings than General Electric. Onsale had more than twice the postings of Coke, while Books-A-Million, a book retailer with an Internet strategy, had more postings than IBM. (Although Hewlett Packard and IBM are both technology companies, they tend to be less volatile and less oriented to day traders than some of the other companies.)

On the other hand, some major companies had very little activity on their message boards. Bristol Myers and AllState had only slightly more than 2,000 postings. J. P. Morgan, a Dow component, had barely more than 1,000, while May Department Stores, one of the largest and best-managed retailers, had only 270.

Why is there this wide range in the number of postings? Three factors impact message board use: the nature of the industry, the volatility of the stock, and the community of posters. Online investors tend to be more interested in technology stocks in general and Internet-related stocks in particular than they are in basic industries. These stocks are also much more volatile. As stocks soar up and then crash, nervous investors flock to message boards to trade advice. Finally, technology stocks tend to attract computer-literate employees and ex-employees who use the message boards as a corporate chat room.

You should not flock to companies with active boards nor avoid those with inactive boards. There is no correlation between the quality of the company and the number of postings. Books-A-Million may have had 50 percent more postings than Wal-Mart, but it is decidedly not a better company.

A CASE STUDY: RAINFOREST CAFÉ

Perhaps the easiest way of appreciating a message board is to look at the postings before and after a company has announced a major surprise. It is interesting to see whether any of the posters had advance warning and how they reacted to the issues that arose.

One of the first message boards I stopped at was that of Rainforest Café. I had eaten at Rainforest Café and enjoyed my meal, but I was skeptical of theme restaurants in general. I believed that when the novelty wore off, people went less often. Still, Rainforest Café had been a very successful stock until January 1998, when it reported weaker than expected results. The stock, which had gone from $18 to $38, dropped back to $17. I decided to go to the message board at Yahoo! and see what people were talking about.

Most of the postings related to how each investor thought that the stock would perform. Before the stock dropped, one investor ventured that

Rainforest would go to $100, while another guaranteed that it would not drop below $30. (Not!) As the stock broke down, everyone had an opinion. Some thought it would go to $10. Others thought it would bounce back up. Some told people to buy. Others told people to sell short.

Taking financial advice from someone in a chat room is dangerous. You do not know who they are. (After reading his postings, I suspected that the GeorgeSoros on the Yahoo! message board might not be the *real* George Soros.) You do not know if they have a financial ax to grind. For all you know, the person saying bad things about Rainforest Café may have just gotten fired from the company or may work for Planet Hollywood. Further, you do not know their investment style or whether they actually own (or are short) the stock. It is foolhardy to ask someone what the price of the stock is going to do. If they knew, they would not be in a chat room.

As the stock kept dropping, the messages got nastier. About one-third of the messages were attacks on each other. (GeorgeSoros seemed to be a special target.) There were even a fair number of four-letter words used, as investors took out their frustrations. Most of the messages were a waste of time. If investors are swearing at each other, it is unlikely they will be rational enough to communicate good information. (One enterprising male investor, however, was trying to make time with a female investor whose postings he found provocative.)

Nonetheless, some of the information on the message board was useful. Investors compared notes about eating in the restaurants. They informed each other about newspaper articles and the appearances of the management on CNBC. They clarified confusion about a coming stock split. They discussed the lawsuits that were brought against the company, and they presented excellent details on insider selling and management changes.

Your objective in entering a message board or chat room should not be to find some new, exotic stock idea in which you can invest, nor should it be to ask for investment advice from some anonymous "expert," even if he calls himself GeorgeSoros. Instead, your objective should be to better understand some company in which you already have a home-turf advantage. If you are interested in a bank, ask if anyone knows how banks value other banks in takeovers. If you are confused about a subject, such as a stock split or the difference between primary and fully diluted earnings, ask about it. While much of the information on the message board may be useless, you may find someone who shares your views or will help you understand a stock.

THE CHANGING ROLE OF CHAT ROOMS AND MESSAGE BOARDS

No part of investing has changed more than the role of chat rooms and message boards. Last year, chat rooms and message boards were oddities, largely the domain of novices searching for information and day traders looking for hot gossip. These rooms were filled with lots of noise, butchered grammar, and generally useless information.

Yet despite the poor quality of the information, the chat rooms and message boards started to have a significant impact on stocks. Maybe it was the day traders gossiping with each other. Maybe it was novices being suckered in. Or maybe, amidst all the chaff were kernels of valuable information. Whatever the reason, stocks started to move based on chat and messages. Day traders, stock jockeys, and even serious investors predicted on the Internet that a particular stock would double or quadruple—and it did. Others predicted that a particular stock would plunge—and it did. Many of the postings may have been nonsense. But those who were correct became instant minor celebrities on their particular message board.

Some of the posters became so good that they developed their own following. Investors would follow them from board to board and room to room. This gave them a gigantic advantage, especially in a momentum market. While professional analysts are not allowed to take a position in a stock before they make a recommendation, the amateur traders on the chat rooms and message boards have no such restrictions. An individual can buy or short a stock and then put up a bullish or bearish posting. If that person has a good following, the stock would move as predicted, and the poster's reputation, not to mention his net worth, would be further enhanced.

This movement started to drive many professionals crazy. They had done their work, met with the companies, read brokerage house research, studied the annual reports, and listened to the conference calls. They were the experts. And yet the people on the message boards were listening to anonymous, inexperienced investors, operating under fake names.

Professionals do not like to lose to amateurs. Tiger Woods would not like to lose to me in golf, and Michael Jordan would not like to lose to me in a one-on-one basketball game. Fortunately, Tiger and Michael can sleep well at night. The same, however, is not true on Wall Street. Professionals can and do lose. They lose every day, usually to each other. With the advent of chat rooms, message boards, and day traders, and with the high volatility of the Internet stocks, they have also started to lose to amateurs.

This did not set well with them, in either their egos or their wallets. Yet no matter how often they shook their heads and complained, the chat rooms and the stocks would not listen.

It reminded me of the birth of rock and roll when I was a kid in the 1950s. My parents could not believe that each week some new singer, usually still a teenager, would rocket to the top of the music charts with a classic like "Itsy Bitsy Teeny Weeny Yellow Polka Dot Bikini," while their old favorite songs were being left in the dust. So it was with professionals on Wall Street. They could no better understand how the chat rooms promoted stocks than my parents could understand how "Blue Moon" suddenly became "bop botta bop, botta bop bop bop, bop botta bop botta dang dang dang Bluuuuuue Moooon." But, like rock and roll, the chat rooms turned out to be more than a passing fad. So many professionals, opting for the precept, "if you can't beat them, join them," decided to invade the chat rooms.

THE PROFESSIONALS JOIN IN

The professionals' first temptation upon entering the chat rooms was to lay out their credentials and tell the chatters how stupid and misinformed they are. But few professionals did this. Some realized that the chatters were outperforming them. Some were concerned about being ridiculed by their peers.

Most professionals think of posting on message boards the way that college students think of writing graffiti on bathroom walls. It is really sleazy, but it is all right as long as you don't get caught. As a result, few professionals ever enter a chat room or a message board under their own name or the name of their firm. Like all other posters, they create their own unique monikers. There is, however, a significant difference between the monikers of the professionals and those of many amateurs. The amateurs often select monikers that make them sound like professionals: "George Soros," "Stockpicker," "Money Man," etc. The professionals, on the other hand, try to pick monikers that make them sound like amateurs. In their minds, they are doing something slightly naughty and definitely below their station in life. The last thing they want is for anyone to guess their real identity. **If you see a moniker "Fidelity Manager," you can bet that the person does not work for Fidelity.**

So the professionals, with their amateur names, started to make their postings. The problem for most of the professionals was that they believed they were dealing with a lower life form—the amateur, day trader, or, worst of all, their own customer. At first, many tried patiently to explain why they were right and the lower life form was wrong. The initial postings by professionals were usually easy to spot. They were the ones with a rational explanation of why a particular stock, often an Internet stock, that had surged from $10 to $50 really deserved to be selling at $10.

The postings were often intelligent, filled with interesting quotations from corporate filings or research reports or even personal experiences at corporate meetings. Of course, they were often greeted with a response such as, 'You are an idiot. This stock is going to $300,' signed GeorgeSoros."

For a while, the professionals tried to respond logically, but as the stock did go to $300, they too became increasingly irrational. To many it felt like they were being outsmarted by a five-year-old child. Worst of all, they were the ones who were losing money, or at least not making money, in these hot stocks. It was then that the professionals proved that they, like everyone else, could utilize a good four-letter word in a pinch.

THE SIX FACES OF STEIN

Some professionals, increasingly frustrated by the message boards, created new identities in the hope that they could convince all of the other investors that they were right. I know a professional investor whom we will call "Stein." That is not his real name, but it is fair to say that Stein is an exceptionally smart investor with a very successful history on Wall Street. About six months ago, Stein discovered a stock named Visx, a pioneer in laser surgery for eyes. Visx was an exciting company in a very exciting industry.

Stein believed in the industry, but there were a number of things about Visx that bothered him. He believed that the company's patent position, which allowed it to charge high per procedure fees, would be challenged. There was an FTC investigation. New and powerful competitors were entering the market, and Visx's customers hated it. Finally, Visx's CEO, Mark Logan, was continually selling stock. Stein shorted Visx.

As Stein watched Visx triple, he became increasingly frustrated. He had done the work. He thought the stock was a house of cards. Yet Visx continued to surge. One day, a friend suggested that Stein check out the Internet message boards.

After reading the postings on Yahoo!, Stein decided that Visx was up so strongly because a group of misguided investors were sharing uninformed gossip with each other. Since he was a well-informed professional, he decided to offer his knowledge to the masses on the message board.

Like other posters, Stein did not use his own name. In fact, he did not even use his own identity. He could have created a moniker that described his identity, like "Big Time Money Manager." He could also have described himself correctly as a male, in his late fifties, from New York, which was who he was. But he decided to opt for another identity.

"Stein" picked the identity of Prunelle Poontang (named after a friend's horse), a 122-year-old woman from Saint Clair, Missouri, (undoubtedly the oldest poster in any chat room). Stein's initial postings were simple and factual, stating his bearish case. But a 122-year-old woman from Missouri did not fully serve all of Stein's needs. He wanted more ammunition, so he created a second identity, named Armadillo Al. Armadillo Al was only described as a Texan.

Armadillo made a few postings, but he was one man competing against a horde of bulls. (Prunelle seemed oddly quiet. Perhaps it was old age.) So Stein created a third identity. This one was named Snake Killer 007. (The 007 is an integral part of the moniker.) Snake Killer was a 22-year-old man from Sweetwater, Texas.

After a few postings, Stein created his fourth identity. This one was named Tex Mex 007. Tex Mex 007 was another 22-year-old man from Sweetwater, Texas. (I guess that Sweetwater must be a hot bed of investing for 22-year-olds, especially those whose names end in 007.)

Now Stein had four different identities that he could use for making his postings. Most of Stein's postings were highly intelligent and meticulously researched. Some of them had headlines like:

"FTC litigation-questions answer."

"FTC Relief obtained"

"The numbers again- for confirmation."

His goal was to educate the other people on the message board so that they could begin to comprehend the truth.

Stein was extremely cooperative and quick to admit when he had made an error. Some of his other postings had headlines like:

"MABOD I owe you an apology."

"Belly Ache- I thank you for your informed..."

"Sorry Punchtheclock. I really did not intend to mislead anyone."

Yet despite his detailed postings, the stock continued to go up. Many posters ignored what Stein's four alter egos had to say. Some even ridiculed them. As the stock continued to surge, Stein became more frustrated. When no one replied to his postings, he replied to his own, using one of his other identities. He brought in reinforcements, creating two new identities: El Diablo 9, a person who would only offer "neuter" for a gender, and Horse Whisperer 011, a man from Flanders, New Jersey.

Before any of my friends attempt to guess the identity of Stein, I can say with absolute certainty that he is not my partner, Leigh Curry. Leigh is from Sweetwater, Texas, and formerly had a home in Flanders, New Jersey, so it appears that Stein decided to adopt parts of Leigh's identity.

With six identities, Stein could now reply to his own postings without arousing attention. In one posting, Snake Killer 007 writes, *"Tex Mex, Sorry, Here's the Federal Filings."* Of course, Snake Killer and Tex Mex were both Stein, so Tex Mex, by definition, already had the filings.

In another, he wrote as Armadillo Al, *"El diablo, your comment please."* Naturally, El Diablo responded.

El Diablo was very active in commenting on other postings, but he was not always friendly to Stein's other alter egos. One of his postings was entitled, *"Armadillo Al is no lawyer."* In this posting he wrote,

> *". . . Our Armadillo friend seems to have missed this entirely."*

Naturally, Armadillo Al responded,

> *"To El diablo. First, I never pretended to be a lawyer, and I doubt that anybody got the impression. Generally they have called me worse names than 'lawyer.'* [A fact that later postings would certainly prove.] *. . . I also have to admit that I did not understand what inequitable conduct was about. . . . but your comments help. . . . I thank you for your post."*

As the stock of Visx finally had a small correction, Stein decided that his dialogue and reasoned analysis was finally getting through to the message board. As the stock continued to drop, Stein became more emotional, discarding his intellectual approach. One night, at 12:09 A.M. and 12:13 A.M., Snake Killer 007 made two posts that read:

> *"Where is asshole Jack? The punk! He was singing $85 . . . $85 . . . $8.8 . . . 8 . . . 5.5. He has been very well proved. . . . Visx back in the 40s . . . 30s are not far away. ENJOY."*
>
> *"MABOD- You idiot prepare for margin call before any other damn thing!"*

Here was this middle-aged, professional portfolio manager, in the middle of the night, in New York, reverting to his identity as a 22-year-old kid from Sweetwater, Texas. I guess that message boards can reduce even the most intelligent investor to the lowest common denominator.

Unfortunately for Snake Killer, Tex Mex, Armadillo Al, El Diablo, Horse Whisperer, and the saintly but aged Prunelle Poontang, the FTC ruled in Visx's favor on June 4, 1999. The stock of Visx opened up $17 at

$69. The longs won the battle, if not the war, and the shorts were killed.

Needless to say, the longs did not delay in rubbing it into the shorts. Stein and his many identities were not spared.

Screenplay_1 wrote:

> *"Where is SNAKEKILLER now! Where are you hiding you fool! All you did is bash VISX the past couple of months, I hope you will apologize to everyone on this board."*

A true wordsmith, Gunthestops wrote:

> *"The FTC and Armadillo_al. I want to be the first to say. . . . HA HA!!! You F. . . . MORON!!!!"* [As you may be now have guessed, tempers in this chat room were running a little high.]

Adtennis decided to pile on by writing:

> *"Where's knowitall Al? Did Al jump out of a window? Or has he been drinking from Jim Jones koolaide with Anne Anderson?"* [Anne Anderson was a prominent analyst who had put a sell out on Visx.]

FiveTimesPay, who obviously watches late-night television, chimed in with an Official "Fools" List:

> *"Contestants were judged in several categories: stupidity, crassness, profanity, inaccurate information, outright lies, and of course, schizophrenic behavior.*
>
> *The top ten are (kudos to David Letterman)*
>
> *1. Scrivdog (homoerotic fantasies on a stock board?)*
>
> *2. Armadillo Al (gas station attendant/attorney poseur)*
>
> *3. TexMex (proves that everything ain't big in Texas, like brains.)*
>
> *4. joshnadler (schizo poster extraordinaire)*
>
> *5. gunsisapoopoo (same idiot as Josh, voted stupidest name also)*
>
> *6. nortonhog (misguided and confused)*
>
> *7. Snakekiller (holed up in a Sweetwater, TX hotel with a bottle of valium and a Schlitz right now.)*
>
> *8. cranksalot (champion of the grammatically incorrect post.)*

9. FredScott (very rare appearances, but really stupid)
10. cluelessyouloser (acid tongued devil that is himself clueless.)"

Stein made the list three times. Prunelle Poontang was probably spared because of her age. Horse Whisperer and El Diablo were probably spared because their postings had been more intellectual and subtle. (I am not sure if these three identities were happy or depressed to have been excluded from the list.)

By now, it should be pretty clear that these chat rooms are rough. They are not the place to venture out if you care what other people say about you or if you are squeamish about profanities. This is bare-knuckled name-calling at its best.

I have no doubt that chat rooms provide many investors with a perfect outlet for their frustrations. In a politically correct world, the chat rooms are politically incorrect. You can insult anyone you want in any way you want, and the only potential punishment is that others in the chat room may do the same to you. However, since most people are using disguised identities, the attacks are often not taken personally.

Before moving on to other chat-room subjects, I want to comment on an interesting series of postings that I saw on the Visx chat room on May 27. Someone created the moniker "Mark Logan CEO" and made a number of postings about the company. Much to the credit of the people from Yahoo! who managed the chat rooms, the postings were removed. My guess is that the company probably complained. So while you can pretend that you are George Soros and while you can use four-letter words, the chat rooms do have some limits. You cannot actually impersonate the management of the company itself.

WHO IS "FAMILY MAN"?

While it appears that no one can invade the chat rooms and the message boards using the name of the CEO, the reverse is not true. While few will admit it, many CEOs have created their own monikers and made postings on the message boards for their companies.

Go on a message board, especially one for a company that has had some problems, and read the often-devastating indictments of management. No subject, from the CEO's business performance to his sex life, is out of bounds. Now imagine that you are a CEO. Every time you look on the message board, there is some barely literate poster, accusing you of everything from gross incompetence to infidelity. As you read the postings, you become furious. So you decide to create a new identity and ride to your own rescue.

I know of one CEO who was accused of having an affair with one of his key executives. Each day, there were more lurid accusations on the message board. One day, I read a posting on the message board from someone with the moniker "Family Man." Family Man said that he knew the CEO personally. They attended the same church. Their wives were both active in the PTA, and their children were in the same grade in school. Family Man said that the CEO was a man of the highest moral caliber, a good husband, and a loyal churchgoer. He was certain that the CEO was not having an affair.

After this posting hit the message board, there were a number of similar postings from others who knew the CEO. Some claimed to be employees of the company, while others claimed to be friends from the community. All agreed the CEO was a fine and upstanding man. Within days, all of the gossip about the affair stopped.

The next week, I happened to be talking to the CEO and mentioned the postings. The CEO gave me a slightly embarrassed grin. *"Family Man was my posting,"* he confided. *"I just couldn't stand having my wife and kids read all of the ridiculous dirt that was being written about me."*

"What about the others?" I asked.

"I guess maybe I really do have some friends," the CEO responded. *"By the way, thanks for your posting."*

It was then that I realized that my moniker was not as much of a disguise as I had thought.

Other executives have taken a more proactive stance to personal libel. After a poster with the provocative screen name "I AM DIRK DIGGLER" (from the movie *Boogie Nights*) from Intercourse,

266

Pennsylvania, posted comments about the sex life of the wife of Richard Scrushy, the chairman of Healthsouth, Scrushy hired detectives. The poster, a former employee, was identified, convicted, and forced to post his affidavit on the message board.

In another case, the chairman of a large company died unexpectedly. The vice-chairman had recently retired and many investors were questioning whether the son, who had just been appointed as the successor, could run the business. One of the directors, using a pseudonym, went on the chat room, said that he had been at the annual meeting, and talked bullishly about the prospects for the company under the son's leadership. There were a number of positive replies to the posting. *"I felt better,"* the director told me. *"I like the son and I was sick and tired of seeing a few idiots questioning his ability."*

Neither of these cases dealt with inside information, but many postings on chat rooms have information that is not yet available to the public. In many cases, the postings are from executives and other employees who are privy to inside information.

THE SON ALSO POSTS

CEOs and directors are not the only people making postings to defend themselves and their firms. Sometimes people close to them, people who love them, make postings, too.

Franklin Resources (BEN), one of the largest mutual fund companies, manages the Franklin, Templeton, and Mutual Shares funds. Between 1995 and early 1998, the price of Franklin's stock surged from $11 to $54. But then, despite the bull market, the stock dropped into the $30s because many of its funds were underperforming the market.

On April 26, 1999, FlmMkr9899 made a posting defending the company:

> *". . . I also find it hard to believe that you can find fault with Charles Johnson [the chairman]—a self made billionaire elected by his peers in the industry to chairman of the NASD . . . I believe this stock will be 45 by mid July . . . I have never been disappointed investing in BEN, as I have*

done periodically over the last 20 years. I have also never been wrong on this stock."

This was pretty impressive. FlmMkr had been investing in this stock for twenty years and he had never been wrong! Now he was predicting that it would go up by 40 percent in three months. This kind of bullishness makes me want to call my broker.

FlmMkr was not finished. Over the next several weeks, he continued to make posts defending the company and its CEO. In response to other postings, he wrote:

"Attacking men like Charlie Johnson just makes you look stupid and uneducated."

"Franklin has excellent management and an amazing track record so Johnson should not and would not resign. . . . Remember he has billions invested in the stock . . . 45 is coming this week!!!!!"

FlmMkr filled his postings with elaborate details. He clearly knew what he was talking about. A few of the other posters intimated that he might be an employee. While many employees of Franklin were making postings on the Web, FlmMkr made it clear that he was only a fan of the company and its management when he posted:

"P.S. I do not work for Franklin, but I would consider it a privilege to do so."

By establishing the fact that he was not an employee, FlmMkr made himself appear to be more objective.

Nonetheless, some were suspicious about FlmMkr's identity. Most posters try to remain anonymous, but FlmMkr was different. His posting page revealed that he was a 36-year-old, divorced movie producer from Santa Monica. This, by itself, provided considerable clues as to his identity. FlmMkr, however, went further. He also talked about his movies and included his real e-mail address, *bill@demarestfilms.com.*

When I clicked over to the Web site of Demarest Films, I found a picture of a huge motor yacht at the Cannes Film Festival. There was a list of passengers. The first name was Bill Johnson, who just happens to be the youngest son of Charles Johnson, the CEO of Franklin, the brother of three other senior executives, and the nephew of a fourth.

I was, of course, not the first person to discover FlmMkr's identity. That honor belonged to someone named "lardicksen," who demanded that Bill Johnson reveal his true identity and told board members to check out his e-mail and Web site.

Outed by "lardicksen," FlmMkr decided to fess up. In a posting entitled "Goodbye Friends," FlmMkr wrote:

> *"I am the youngest son of Charlie Johnson. I am not an insider, officer, or employee of Franklin Resources. A few weeks ago a friend asked if I had ever read the BEN message board. . . . I couldn't believe the things that were being said about my father. Any one of you would have reacted the way I did. I believe my father is the greatest business man I have ever met and I respect him more than anyone else- a great sentiment to have about ones dad . . . I won't be visiting this board again because unfortunately many would attack who I am rather than debate the ideas I have expressed. . . ."*

Of course, despite the title, this was not FlmMkr's last posting. On May 6, 1999, the *Wall Street Journal* had a major story on FlmMkr entitled "Online Franklin Booster Turns Out To Be the Boss's Son." FlmMkr returned to the message board one last time to defend himself.

> *". . . I just wish I could respond in kind you see my feelings are hurt. . . . It is ridiculous because it never entered my mind that I could actually influence the market price of BEN chatting on a message board with . . . less traffic than most porno sites—its not exactly Motley Fool is it. My sole purpose for being on this board was to defend my core beliefs and my Hero—perhaps I got a little carried away in the process."*

Not surprisingly, many of the posters had comments about Bill Johnson's postings. Most defended them. After all, Johnson was just a son who was proud of his father. One investor, however, raised an interesting issue about insider trading and stockholdings. During the first five months of 1999, members of the Johnson family sold almost 370,000 shares. So while Bill Johnson was not selling shares, his father, brothers, and sister were. How would you feel if you bought stock and then learned that the person recommending it was the son of the person selling it? Even if his intentions were the highest, you might still be annoyed.

In addition, while Bill wrote that he owned 750 calls, he neglected to mention that he personally owned 300,000 shares ($11 million) and that his father was a billionaire, who owned many more shares. (Logic might indicate that Bill would get some of these shares in his father's will.)

I did respect FlmMkr for the final quote he made in the *Wall Street Journal* article. *"In a small way, I felt I did my part in defending my family name. If it looks bad, you know, my intentions were good."* I do believe that his intentions were good, but the question is whether other people, who made buy or sell decisions based on his strong defense of the management, would have done the same if they had known his real identity.

An interesting thing happened after Bill Johnson revealed his true identity. Employees of Franklin started to go on the message board debating the pros and cons of the company. One even invited all investors, employees, and friends to participate in the Franklin Employee Club online chat. Things got so bad that the vice-president and corporate secretary of the firm made the following official posting:

> *"Franklin/Templeton employees are hereby advised to consult their supervisors or the Human Resources Department before participating in public forums which purport to discuss 'private company matters.'"*

As will be seen, Franklin was not the only company in which the employees became the most active contributors on the message board.

For some companies, the message boards have become the corporate water cooler. They are the location at which workers gather to comment on business, gripe about management, and exchange gossip. The major difference is that workers can be anonymous on the message boards, so they can say things that they never would have had the courage to say in front of others.

For the investor, these message boards can be informative and fascinating. They can also be dangerous. It is very clear that there are a substantial number of insiders and employees on these boards. You can always spot them from the level of detail about the company in their postings. The problem for the investor is that employees and former employees all have an ax to grind—both positively and negatively. If you do not know the identity of the poster, it is difficult to judge the validity of his or her comments.

A CASE STUDY: THE COMPUCOM MESSAGE BOARD

One of the most interesting message boards I have visited is that of CompuCom, a computer reseller and service company. Over the past several years, the management has taken dramatic steps to reduce costs and change the company's method of doing business. The steps have included acquiring competitors, changing compensation, and closing all branch offices. Because each of these moves have had significant impacts on the employees of CompuCom, the company's message board has been unusually active. (CompuCom has more postings than Bristol Myers.)

When the message board on Yahoo! was created, CompuCom was extremely quiet. There were few postings and most of them were from people asking questions. The first change came innocently when someone named "WannaFindOut" made a posting that read, *"I am currently interviewing with this company. . . . Can anyone tell me about the corporate culture and what it is like to work at CompuCom?"*

Surprisingly, a number of people responded immediately. Typical was the response from "bspratt" entitled *"Go For It."* Bspratt was very bullish about the company.

Others responded in a similar fashion. "sysengr" replied *"Ditto on Bill's assessment. I've been with CC 2½ years and I'm proud to be an employee and a stockholder. I consider both to be a good investment."*

It is interesting that sysengr referred to bspratt as "Bill." Obviously the two people knew each other. This would not be the last time that posters on the board were coworkers who knew each other's identity.

While most people were generally positive, a few ex-workers also made comments. Many of them were bitter about the company.

At about the same time, another interesting poster, who called herself "StockGirl," showed up on the CompuCom board. She believed that the stock was going to go up. About two weeks after her first posting, StockGirl wrote that CompuCom was about to be acquired by a large retailer at a substantial premium to its current price. Few were impressed with this posting. There were only two replies, and both said that it would not happen.

StockGirl was undeterred. She told the board that they would be surprised *"this week,"* and that a major office-supply retailer would be taking over the company. Once again, there were few replies to the message. One or two posters dismissed the story, while one or two others asked where StockGirl had gotten her information. It was here that StockGirl made an interesting posting entitled *"This is not insider information."* In the posting, StockGirl claimed that she heard a rumor and did her research, just like any other good investor.

The response to her posting was best exemplified by the insider "sysengr" who posted *"Yeah Right,"* and then told StockGirl to go away.

I had noticed the posting about the takeover and dismissed it as wishful thinking. The analysts who covered the company did likewise. One evening, I mentioned the posting to Ed Anderson, the CEO of CompuCom. He laughed. Then he told me that the company in fact had been in negotiations with one of the office supply superstores for a considerable period of time, but that deal had recently fallen through.

Despite her posting to the contrary, StockGirl was clearly in possession of inside information. Who was she? She could have been an executive of CompuCom, an executive of the office-supply company, an investment banker, or a lower-level employee who somehow had been involved. (Judging by the fact that she never reappeared, the best guess is that she was employed by the potential buyer.)

Ed Anderson told me that he had no clue as to her identity. I asked what he could do to stop this type of leak. He told me that the company had few alternatives. It could have complained to Yahoo! and gotten the postings removed, but this would have given the postings even greater validity. With the openness of information on the Web, dealing with inside information and leaks has become far more complex.

The office-supply-superstore rumor was interesting for a number of reasons:

- Someone posted what appears be to inside information about a potential acquisition.

- No one believed the postings.
- No one else ever picked up the rumors, and
- In the end, the deal fell through.

But this does not change the fact that the message board had inside information that everyone else missed. If the deal had happened, StockGirl would have looked very smart, and she might have received a call from the SEC.

Several months later, rumors began that CompuCom was going to acquire Entex, a major competitor. The postings about the merger were filled with extremely detailed information, including what warehouses would be closed, which executives were to be retained, and how the combined company would be structured. From reading the postings, it was clear that most of them had come from people who were actually employees of CompuCom or Entex. In fact, many identified themselves using names like "CompuCom_engineer" "compucomrade," or "Extex_stillhere."

In January, the postings had the deal almost complete, with John McKenna of Entex having joined CompuCom in a senior management capacity. This made the deal seem more certain, but there was only one problem: There were two John McKennas, and the one from Entex was not the one now working for CompuCom. The message board had the wrong John McKenna. Anyone speculating on CMPC based on a merger with Entex would have lost.

The Entex rumors would not die, but they began to change. Instead of buying all of Entex, the rumors now had CompuCom buying only Entex's product division. On April 2, "LEOB" posted that *financial issues had caused postponement of the deal for a few weeks.* The person making this posting was clearly in possession of inside information—five weeks later, CompuCom did announce the acquisition of Entex's product business. The stock initially surged up, but then it dropped back to its previous price range.

The Entex story reflects some interesting issues about the inside information posted on the message board. From the time of the first rumors until the time of the acquisition, almost one year passed. During that year, the price of the stock actually went down. Although many people seemed to have an inside track on the acquisition, when it finally occurred the deal was for only a piece, not for the entire company, and only the most nimble of day traders would ever have made a dime trading this particular rumor. Nonetheless, it was clear that most of the people posting information came from inside the two companies. So while inside information may be quite interesting, it may not have helped the investor make money.

While CompuCom's acquisitions were obviously an issue of major importance, changes in the company and the industry were even more important to the posters on the board. CompuCom was stuck in an industry that was not doing well. To survive, quick and dramatic action was needed, and no one acted more decisively than the management of CompuCom. The company opened "co-location" facilities in the factories of the manufacturers. It slashed costs and laid off employees. Finally, it made the dramatic decision to close all its branches. Employees no longer had an office. If they were attached to a particular customer, they would work on-site. If not, they would work out of their home.

I can think of no decision that so directly impacts all employees as the act of closing offices. Needless to say, the employees of CompuCom had very mixed feelings about the changes. Since all of the employees were in the computer-services business and since most were off-site and scattered around the country, the Internet became a logical place for them to congregate. They had no offices and no union halls. For many, Yahoo! became the corporate water cooler.

One major debate concerned the closing of the two warehouses. People from Stockton, California, and Paulsboro, New Jersey, debated which warehouse had the better rating. "TXTracer" lamented, *"if that happens* [Stockton closes], *I'll just have to do like everyone else and go job-hunting again. Life sucks."*

"HappilyWorking" was a positive force:

> *"We have some of the best employees and our new Management really does have some great ideas. The only sad thing is that in order to put these great ideas to work, we have to change some things. That included letting people go."*

Even customers joined the message board. "SatisfiedUser" wrote:

> *"I have been a customer of CompuCom for the past two*

*years. Ever since we . . . obtained services from CompuCom
our customers have been much happier."*

At the end of November 1998, rumors started that Ed Anderson would resign on December 28. December 28 came and went, and Ed Anderson remained the CEO. Once again, something that looked like good inside information proved false. (Andersen did resign about six months later to form an Internet company.

There were rumors that former executives of the company were putting together an investment group to buy it out (something that might have benefited shareholders). But nothing happened.

On June 9, 1999, "dallas_stars" noted that he saw Ed Anderson sitting on the ice at the NHL playoff game against Buffalo. His conclusion was that CompuCom would fade away just like the Dallas Stars. (Of course, the Stars went on to win the Stanley Cup, but dallas_stars never did print a retraction.)

The gossiping got so bad that "eagle2000xx" had finally had enough:

"For heavens sake, GET TO WORK!!!!!
*To all CompuCom'ers on this board—What the heck are
you doing in the middle of the day sending and answering
messages to this board. You are paid to work. If you aren't
working, you are stealing from the company. . . . Do your
flipping job, or go somewhere else."*

DRIFTWOOD JACK

For all of the posters, there was none who could equal a man with the moniker of "Driftwood Jack." Driftwood appeared in September 1998. Over the next nine months, he made more than 180 postings. Counting the time that he said he was on vacation, this was almost one per day.

Driftwood's first posts concerned an SEC complaint that he claimed was filed against CompuCom "alleging fraudulent posting to their AR ledgers in an effort to pad sales revenues." He continued to attack, naming names of those he said were responsible and detailing the SEC investigation. Driftwood predicted the demise of the company: *"CompuCom associates have become mere tokens to be discarded in the game of bogus sales postings. . . . This company is going down."*

Driftwood was quiet for a while, but when he posted, he always tried to make an impact. In December, Driftwood posted, "He's back- the return of Driftwood Jack." He mentioned that he had been out of town for a few days and challenged CMPC to file a lawsuit against him. *"If CMPC wants to open its books and personnel files to my attorneys, we know where to look. And let me tell you, some of this crap borders on criminal wrongdoing."*

Posters picked up on Driftwood's SEC investigation and many focused on Tom Ducatelli, a senior executive. Some accused Ducatelli of being overpaid and padding the books. Others rushed to his defense, calling him the best salesman in the company.

Making accusations of wrongdoing and naming names presented a number of complicated problems for investors and especially for the people involved. Assume that you are one of the executives who Driftwood claims engaged in illegal activities and was the target of an SEC investigation. Every day, you would see your name dragged through the mud in the chat rooms.

But what is worse is that you would have no opportunity to confront your accuser. In fact, you would not even know the identity of your accuser. Your accuser could be a competitor, someone who wanted your job, or someone you had fired. The information might be correct or it might be a total lie. This, of course, is the downside to free speech.

The problem for the investor is equally complex. Few investors want to have anything to do with a company that is a target of an SEC investigation. The only problem is that, except for Driftwood's word, there was no evidence that there actually was an SEC investigation.

In May, Driftwood posted, *"This board is Driftwood's hobby. . . . I plan on having many more months of this stimulating skirmish."*

This was a game to Driftwood, and it was intensely personal. The problem is that it was not a game for Driftwood's targets, nor was it a game for investors who were actually seeking information about the company.

On June 3, Driftwood posted that a Mr. Neri from the SEC had e-mailed him that his office had closed the investigation of the company on

October 2, 1998. But Driftwood was still certain that the file was open, and promised to get the information for the message board.

Almost one year had passed since the first posting. The company had made an acquisition and had year-end audited financial statements. No one else had said anything about an SEC investigation, but Driftwood was keeping the dream alive and the heat on those whom he did not like.

Then only one day later, on June 4, 1999, came an extraordinary post entitled: *"The final post of Driftwood Jack."* After reading more than 180 diatribes against the company, I wondered why a man like Driftwood would suddenly walk away from his "hobby." But here it was—his final post:

> **"The Final Post of Driftwood Jack**
>
> *I have come to the realization that my aspirations have been overtaken by a turbulent insanity.*
>
> *With the appointment of Philip Wise as VP of Product Management, I am certain that the practices of the past have been laid to rest. Both Philip Wise and Jay Scott are individuals that CMPC shareholders and associates can trust with the fiduciary and humanitarian responsibilities that permit a company to pass through the gateway to greatness.*
>
> *My name is Bob McCord. My wife Kathy, who was a dedicated and loyal associate for over ten years has suffered a terrible and unjust illness brought on by the abuses of her superiors. . . .*
>
> *Because the lives of so many depend on your actions, I wish the best of luck to Mr. Anderson and Mr. Lynch. If you put your trust in those who give their all you cannot lose and neither can CompuCom.*
>
> *In closing let me say one thing to Tom Ducatelli and Chris McBride. Associates will take no more abuse from either of you. From this day on, everyone will be watching your every action."*

In reading this posting, I thought about the scene in *Tootsie* in which Dustin Hoffman reveals himself as a man. Driftwood Jack was a man, a husband, who had spent one year consumed by what he believed were injustices suffered by his wife.

What does the Driftwood Jack story teach investors? First, people posting on message boards have their own agendas. Second, these agendas often lead to views or allegations that are not true. If there ever was an SEC investigation, it does not appear to have ever gone anywhere. While Driftwood's charges of wrongdoing sounded convincing, there was never any evidence to back them up.

Finally, in reviewing these postings, I often think of Tom Ducatelli and his associates. I have never met these men, but I do feel for them. It cannot be fun to look at a message board and see someone accusing you of criminal activities, especially when they do not appear to have been true.

What makes this case interesting is not merely the extent of the postings of Driftwood Jack. It is the fact that in the end, "Driftwood" revealed his true identity and opened himself to possible legal action. On message boards and chat rooms, this rarely happens.

The example of the CompuCom board brings home a number of key lessons:

- **For many companies, the message boards have become the equivalent of the corporate water cooler.** Workers, ex-workers, relatives of workers, customers, suppliers, and competitors use the message boards for their own ends. This may involve leaking inside information, discussing corporate policies, or engaging in a vendetta against a particular executive.
- **The concept of inside information has been permanently changed by the Web.** Before message boards and chat rooms, most companies were able to control the dissemination of inside information, but now, the entire game has changed. Any corporate executive or other person in a position to know of the company's plans can get on a message board and spill the beans. I have seen a large number of message boards filled with postings that I knew fit within the legal definition of inside information.

This is creating a huge problem for corporate counsels. The corporate counsel of one of the largest aerospace companies recently told me that the SEC was hopelessly out of touch with reality with regard to inside information. "Everything we do," the counsel said, "is on the Web before we can even get out a press release. If we win a contract or have a rocket blow up, someone posts the information instantaneously. The Web allows universal dissemination of information that is too fast for the outdated rules of the SEC."

> • **The problem for most investors is to decide which of the postings are real and which are not.** If you were really an insider, or even an extremely well-informed outsider, you would be in a position to know which of the rumors were false and which were true. But for most people, there is no way to tell.

The chat rooms remind me of an old Bob Newhart comedy routine that said that if you had an infinite number of monkeys typing on an infinite number of typewriters, they would eventually write all of the great books of the English language. The only problem was that you would need an infinite number of people to read the work of the monkeys. In the routine, one of the readers shouts that he has something really exciting. "To be, or not to be," he reads the work of a monkey, "that is the gosortumplatz."

So it is with most of the information on the message boards and in the chat rooms. You often have to spend a huge amount of time to get anything that is not pure gibberish. Unless you are really interested in a company, this may be a waste of time. However, on each message board and chat room there are usually a few intelligent individuals who are engaged in serious debate. There is clearly a substantial amount of inside information. Reading a message board can often give an investor the flavor of what is going on inside of a company. The problem is that it is often difficult to tell which of the postings are real and which are nonsense. "To be or not to be" sounds reasonable. "That is the gosortumplatz" does not.

THE PAIRGAIN HOAX

Sometimes the postings on the message boards go beyond accusations and rumors and become outright hoaxes. The "PairGain Hoax" was one of the most elaborate, injuring and benefiting many investors.

PairGain Technologies is a mid-cap telecommunications company. The price of the stock had surged from $2 in 1994 to $40 in 1997, but had dropped back to the $10 range in 1998 and 1999. Like many technology stocks, PairGain had an active message board. By June 29, 1999, there were well over 23,000 messages, 20 percent more postings than IBM had at the same point in time.

On April 6, PairGain's stock had closed at $8½. Then, at 10:18 A.M., someone with the moniker "StaceyITN" made a simple posting:

> *"BUYOUT NEWS!!!!ECILF IS BUYING PAIR. Just found it*
> *on Bloomberg."*

StaceyITN also included the URL site for the news.

Others clicked over to the site. There they saw what appeared to be a Bloomberg Web page that detailed the terms of the deal. Based on the price of ECI's stock (an Israeli company), the price for PAIR would be more than $19 per share. The view of many was echoed by one who posted:

> *"Wahooooooooooooooooooooooooooooooooooooooooooooooo*
> *oooo!!!! I knew this day would come!!!!!!!!!!"*

The price of PairGain jumped to $11⅛, a gain of 32 percent. Major money managers heard about the posting and rushed to buy.

While the stock surged, not all investors were convinced. "thlanier" was disturbed by the URL address, noting that it did not seem to be a Bloomberg address.

"beauxeault" also did not believe the story. He noted that the URL was hosted by angelfire.com (part of Lycos), and that there was no information from PAIR's investor-relations department or on Bloomberg itself. Despite these warnings, many continued to cheer the buyout as the stock ran up.

As the day passed, people on the message board and investors continued to debate whether the story was real. The news and the price action both reflected a deal. But those who understood how the Internet works understood that this was a fraud.

By 1:45, the Bloomberg Feedback Team put out a notice that the story had been a fake. The stock of PairGain dropped back to 9^{3}/$_{8}$. Despite the fake, the stock closed up 7/$_{8}$ on volume of 13.7 million shares.

Logic would indicate that after the hoax was exposed, PairGain stock would drop back to its previous level and stay there, but logic does not always work in the stock market. PAIR continued to move up. On April 12, it reached $10.25, and by April 14, it reached $13, despite coming out with sub-par earnings.

Why did the stock of PairGain continue to move up if the story was a hoax? There are two possible explanations. First, some people may have continued to believe the story, on the theory that where there is smoke there is fire. In fact, the message board continued to be filled with rumors of PairGain selling out to someone. Second, many who believed that the story was a hoax shorted the stock. Buying interest then created a short squeeze.

Despite the weak earnings and the lack of a deal, during the next two months the price of PAIR reached a high of 15^{1}/$_{16}$ and never dropped below 10^{1}/$_{4}$. The false posting exactly coincided with the increase in the price of PairGain's stock.

In the end, the FBI was able to track down Gary Hoke, a mid-level engineer at PairGain. Hoke pleaded guilty to making the fraudulent posting and is likely to serve ten to sixteen months in prison. Hoke owned PairGain stock and options. He had intended to sell his stock and make money from the hoax, but he got cold feet when he saw all of the action it had attracted.

Ironically, perhaps the biggest winners may have been a group of PairGain insiders. As the price of the stock went up, five insiders unloaded 204,000 shares in the next six weeks.

PairGain offers a number of interesting lessons for investors:

1. With the right planning and a relatively sophisticated level of knowledge, it is possible to promote a successful hoax on the Web.

2. Those who understood the Web spotted the hoax, but many, including prominent investment managers and those who were looking for a fast buck, got suckered in.

3. Ironically, the hoax may have created interest in PairGain and may have also created a short squeeze. The

net impact was that the price of PAIR increased by 64 percent during the next six trading days.

Nonetheless, investors should be very cautious when they see a hot story. In this case, anyone who checked the company's own Web site or that of Bloomberg would have learned that the story was a hoax.

EIGHT RULES FOR MESSAGE BOARDS AND CHAT ROOMS

What then can the individual investor take away from this chapter?

1. **Message boards can often tell you more about a company than about its stock.** The information comes from current and former employees gathering around these sites to discuss the company and its management. What you glean is usually messy, like walking into the middle of a family fight, and often unreliable. But by listening to the debate, you can often focus in on the key internal issues and gain some valuable pieces of inside information.

2. **Message boards are a good place to get questions answered.** Many of the people on the message boards are insiders and some are experts in their companies. Almost all are willing to respond to questions. If something is happening and a stock is starting to move, someone on the message board will usually have already read the article, talked to the company, or tracked down the rumor.

3. **Watch for sharp increases in the level of postings.** One easy way to monitor the message boards is to look for sharp increases in the level of postings. If a company message board that averages three messages a day suddenly starts having forty, the chances are good that something is happening or that the stock may respond to the board itself.

4. **Message boards can be fun, if you don't take them too seriously.** Where else can you create your own identity and say anything you want to anyone you want?

5. **Message boards and chat rooms are a great place to relieve frustrations.** You buy a stock. It reports terrible earnings and gets killed. You note that management has sold large blocks of stock near the high. You are furious. You want to call up the company and leave an angry message, but you know no one will care. Go on a message board and let it all hang out. You will feel better, and someone will notice. Anyone who believes that management does not read the message boards should re-read "Who Is Family Man?" and "The Son Also Posts." Someone in management of virtually every company is reading the message board.

6. **Do not rely on message boards to pick stocks.** You never know the identity of the person posting messages. The person defending the company might be the son of the chairman. The person attacking the company might just have gotten fired or might work for a competitor. The person saying that the stock is going to get crushed might have a major short position, which he is waiting to unload. The person saying that the stock is going to go up might have a major long position, which she is waiting to sell.

With these caveats in mind, the chat rooms and message boards can be excellent sources of information and entertainment. They provide an individual with a community of other investors, who can help answer questions and flush out rumors. So long as you understand that some of the information is not reliable, using these Internet resources can be both worthwhile and fun. Perhaps most importantly, they give individual investors the type of platform that the professionals have long possessed and, in so doing, help to balance the power between the two forces.

PART 3

Hostile Territory

CHAPTER ELEVEN

Beware False Intelligence: The Analysts

Accurate intelligence is essential to a war effort. But in many cases, the intelligence-gathering arm, for political reasons, wants to portray the battle in the most favorable light. When this occurs, the information it presents is not fully accurate and works against the invading army.

Analysts are the intelligence-gathering arm of the professional investor. In theory, the analysts' job is to find good stocks for clients. But the theory is wrong. Don't get suckered into the idea that the analysts' first job is to make money for you. It is not. **The analysts' primary job is to be a supporter of their firm's investment-banking activities. Their second job is to keep institutional investors happy. Retail customers like you come in a distant third.**

Because the analysts support investment banking, they disseminate information that is often slanted. Banking revenues drive brokerage firms, and banking clients want analysts who speak favorably of their companies. When was the last time you saw a company give its banking business to an analyst who said, *"Sell the stock"*? Much of an analyst's compensation comes from investment banking, so most are going to say good things about the firm's clients. The bullishness has gotten so extreme that analysts now praise any company that could potentially be a client. With the current deal flow, most analysts now only know how to say, *"Buy!"*

Even when bad news occurs, the analyst is expected to write reports that support the client's spin. Only when they are alone with key institutional clients can their doubt, which would never find its way to paper, creep into words. Professionals understand the game. They know analysts usually maintain a more bullish pose in public. Because they have direct access, they can understand where the analysts really stand. This gives them a substantial advantage over the individual investor. If individuals are to use the work of analysts, they must learn to read between the lines and understand what the analysts are really saying. They must also find the analysts' blind side and turn it to their advantage. This is not as difficult as it might appear. In fact, **it is often easy to use the analysts' weaknesses to beat the professionals at their own game.**

MOST ANALYSTS ARE BULLISH

Have you ever noticed that the analysts at your brokerage firm are almost always bullish on most of their stocks? Most have strong buys, buys, or accumulate ratings. Very rarely do you see a sell, much less a short sell rating. Because the market has gone up so much, many believe that the analysts have been prescient and have correctly predicted the action of their stocks. The reality is: Analysts are not prescient. They are just bullish. Just as a stopped clock is right twice a day, so in a rising market the analysts often look smarter than they are.

The first reason for the bullishness is that analysts tend to cover the companies they like. Analysts can cover no more than fifteen to twenty companies, but most industries have many more. While analysts generally follow the largest firms, they have leeway in selecting others. Since covering a company represents a significant time commitment, most pick companies they like. Few would waste their time following a small company they believe has no future. If the company is not a key player, an analyst who did not like it would just ignore it.

The bullishness is enhanced because analysts like to follow winners. It is more fun to follow good firms. Investors love to receive updates on stocks that are hitting new highs and hate to talk about stocks that have been crushed. Sears was a terrible stock in the 1980s. Everyone hated the company. When I started recommending the stock, Sears had already declined sharply from its high. Although I had never before followed the stock and never lost anyone money in it, my customers still often took out their frustrations from many years of losses on me. They would say things like, *"I don't want to hear about that dog again."* In the end, Sears proved to be a huge winner, but for the first few years, following it was not fun.

Good companies are more likely to have investment-banking activities, because they are usually growing faster than are weak companies. This can be a key financial issue for analysts. Finally, investors often equate the quality of the analysts with the quality of the companies they follow. If the analyst has a list of first-rate companies, investors tend to think that the analyst is smart, while if an analyst has a list of second-rate companies, investors tend to think of the analyst as dumb. Investors have usually lost money in second-rate firms and are hostile to anyone who would follow, much less recommend, them. The quality of stocks on the list may say little about the analyst's stock-picking ability. In fact, the analyst with the list of lousy stocks may be making much more money for his customers, but investors have a tendency to think that the analyst following the winners is smarter.

Analysts usually try to keep winners and prune out losers. When a company has performed poorly, the analysts begin to mistrust everything it has to say and the investors begin to hate the analysts for putting them in a "dog." Often, when a company has a major disaster, the analysts quickly downgrade the stock to protect their record. The stock may have closed at $30, but it is clear from the news that it will open at $20. The analysts downgrade the stock before it can open. On their record, it says that they downgraded it at $30. It does not matter that their clients were not able to sell at that price. Sometimes they might even discontinue coverage, dropping the stock off their list. Thus, by keeping winners, dropping losers, and selecting the best companies to follow, analysts tend to reinforce their general bullishness.

The communication between a company and the analysts reinforces the bullishness. A company tends to be bullish about its prospects. It is difficult to spend a large amount of time talking with a management and not begin to believe the promises. This is especially true if there is a strong personal relationship between an analyst and the executives in a company. Human interaction and even friendships can have a powerful influence on analysts. Thus, a symbiotic relationship is often developed between the analyst and the company.

COMPANIES SHOW FAVORITISM TO ANALYSTS THEY LIKE

Companies have numerous ways to show favoritism to analysts they like and punish analysts they do not like. The symbiotic relationship begins with the dissemination of information. Analysts live for scooping their competition. They are the tabloid television correspondents of the investment world. If an analyst can obtain exclusive information or an interview with management, that analyst will have an edge on the competition. Companies are keenly aware of the importance of this type of information and dole out tidbits judiciously. *"Don't publish this,"* the chief financial officer might whisper to an analyst, *"but the sales of our new division are 40 percent above projection."* After the conversation is finished, the analyst will undoubtedly call many of the largest investors and share this confidential piece of information. (Sharing the news with major institutional shareholders is obviously different from "publishing" it.)

Companies may show favoritism in something as simple as returning phone calls. When a company makes a major announcement, the analysts will call immediately. Those who receive the first return calls will have a substantial advantage. Most companies will return calls selectively, talking first to the analysts who will put the most positive spin on the news. Analysts who are less positive may not receive a call for hours. By the time they do, the information will have already been disseminated, and they will have been shut out. Controlling the order of phone calls may seem like a very minor issue, but it can be extremely significant in a time-sensitive market.

Companies can also give analysts special access. They can offer private meetings with the CEO, allow analysts to sponsor a conference call with the company, and participate at a conference sponsored by the analyst's firm. There are a large number of conferences, and their success depends on the strength of the presenters. A conference with top speakers, like Bill Gates, will have a major advantage in attracting the best institutional investors. It is the responsibility of the analysts to deliver top management for their conferences. Company managements pick and choose where to speak and who to send. They naturally favor those analysts who have the most positive view of their company's future. Few will support the analyst who questions their long-term prospects. Because access to the company is important to the analyst, it is harder for the analyst to be objective.

While companies may show favoritism to analysts they like, they can also freeze out those who they do not. I once put out a sell recommendation on Sports & Recreation. Management was furious with my report. The company mobilized other analysts against me. The day after my report, there were ten First Call notes saying that I did not know what I was talking about. Then the company removed my name from its fax list and refused to talk to me. Without any access or information, it became very difficult to follow the company. (Fortunately for me, Sports & Recreation went bankrupt, so I did not miss much.)

Companies also invite analysts to special events. In 1996, many firms sponsored analyst "meetings" at the Olympics. In many cases, the analysts were flown down on private jets, lodged in deluxe hotels, and given tickets to the best events. Going to the Olympics is a special opportunity, and most analysts know that the company may exclude those who have negative ratings. **So the question that investors should ask is, can an analyst who is sitting in the front row of the basketball venue watching the Dream Team be truly impartial?**

The Olympics are not the only boondoggle offered to analysts. Cruise lines sponsor "meetings" at sea. Movie companies give analysts private screenings, and some companies even put the analysts' quotes in their annual reports. None of these actions directly compromises an analyst, but in subtle ways, they can modify the analyst's views.

So the symbiotic relationship between an analyst and the company develops on a number of levels. There is a personal relationship, friends talking to friends. There is an information relationship, giving the analyst the scoop. There is a perk relationship, allowing the analyst to sponsor meetings. Each of these factors ties the analyst and the company together and makes it more difficult for the analyst to be truly impartial.

INVESTMENT BANKING COMPROMISES ANALYSTS

While personal friendships, information flow, and perks may help develop a symbiotic relationship between analysts and companies, it is the financial relationship through investment banking that cements them together. **Investment banking, not stock trading, drives the profits of Wall Street and the compensation of analysts.**

The profit from trading stock is lower than most people think. The annual commissions from trading a stock with 100 million shares might be $5 million. If ten analysts follow the stock and if the firms for which they work trade 50 percent of all shares, these ten firms will receive an average of $250,000 each. By the time the firm pays the salesperson, the trader, the stock exchange fees, the costs of distributing the reports, and its own overhead, there is relatively little left for the analyst. In a stock with many fewer shares, the direct costs of covering the company could be more than the commissions. With these economics, it is easy to see why analysts do not follow smaller companies that do not have investment-banking business.

Compare this scenario with the economics of a company doing a stock offering. In trading stocks, the fees are about $0.05 per share on each side of the transaction. In a stock offering, the fee might average $2 per share. If the company with 100 million shares sells 10 million shares, the fees could be $20 million. If there were four lead underwriters, these firms might split 80 percent of the fees, $4 million each. This is sixteen times what they would have received from trading the stock during the year. In both cases, someone has to analyze the stock, sell it, and trade it, but in the latter case, the fee is much higher. (It is not uncommon to pay the analyst who bought the offering to the firm a bonus of 10 percent of the fees—in this case, $400,000.)

Stock underwritings are not the only ways a company can reward an investment bank. As banks and brokerage houses merge, the interaction with major corporations becomes more complex. The new financial conglomerates can assist in mergers and acquisitions, lend companies money, mortgage real estate, sell debt, offer interest-rate swaps, and provide a variety of other highly profitable services.

How do the fees from these services impact the independence of the analyst? It does not take a rocket scientist to calculate that the analyst who can snare major underwriting business is going to make much more than the analyst who concentrates on trading the stock. Many analysts see themselves as seekers of wisdom and truth, but given these economics, it is obvious why many focus on investment banking.

Think about some of the compensation packages that top analysts have recently received. There are a number with salaries in excess of $7 million a year, similar to movie stars or sports figures. These analysts receive these packages for only one reason, because they can deliver valuable investment-banking clients.

The problem for the investor is that the skills needed to be a good stock picker are often sharply at odds with the qualities that make a good investment-banking analyst. Good stockpickers should be independent. They should look at management objectively, question when its strategies seem wrong, and ferret out information that others miss. But few companies will pay large investment-banking fees to brokerage houses whose analysts probe too deeply or write too critically.

Companies want analysts who tell their story in the way they want it told. If the company wants analysts to carry earnings estimates of $1.50, that is the estimate that they should have. Independent thoughts are neither desired nor welcomed. They do not want analysts to have estimates of $1.40, because that will make the growth seem too low. Nor do they want analysts to have estimates of $1.60, because that will make it more difficult for the company to "surprise" the Street.

Analysts are punished even when they suggest a direction at odds with that of management. Suppose that an analyst wrote a report saying that a company had been mismanaged and that the stock might be worth three times the current price if it was broken up. Even if the report was responsible for the stock going up, and even if members of management were large shareholders, the analyst's firm would probably not be hired to help in the restructuring. Few managements will reward analysts who force them to restructure their company. While other investment-banking firms were receiving huge fees for selling off the pieces, the analyst who started the process would be a pariah.

On August 17, 1999, the *Wall Street Journal* ran a story about Sean Ryan, a bank analyst from Bear Stearns, and one of the companies he followed, First Union. Ryan had been critical of First Union. He thought that management was second-rate and that the only hope for shareholders was for someone to take over the bank.

Needless to say, First Union was not pleased. According to the *Journal*, it was so annoyed with Ryan that it suspended its lucrative bond-trading business with Bear Stearns, which was generating an estimated $10 million in annual revenue (many times Ryan's salary). While Bear Stearns claims that it did not muzzle Ryan, the analyst turned strangely silent on First Union. After Ryan turned silent, the bond business was reinstated. In the end, the power of the company, if utilized, may be strong enough to limit the independence of many analysts. This, of course, is a significant issue for investors, who believe that the analysts employed by their brokerage firms are objective observers whose primary goal is to make money for them.

Companies like analysts who are not controversial and who will introduce them to a large number of investors. The chairman of a large retailer once told me that he hired a firm for his offering because the analyst ran good field trips. *"He may be a dope,"* the chairman said, *"but he brings hundreds of the most important investors into my stores. I can't do that for myself."* The chairman was making a smart move, from his point of view. The question is whether the customers of this analyst realized that he was a dope and that he was making more than $1 million per year because he was a good tour guide, not because he was a good stock picker.

While analysts are supposed to follow their companies closely, it is often "advisable" not to follow them too closely. Looking closely at the numbers of a company is like looking at an eclipse of the sun. They can blind the analyst, at least as far as getting future banking business is concerned. Companies often have questionable accounting that can have a material impact on their earnings. When companies adopt these policies, they do not necessarily want to hide them. Most have to be described in the companies' financial documents, but companies do not want the analysts to look too closely. There is no reason to stir up a hornet's nest on a complicated accounting problem, especially when such a problem would negatively impact the price of the stock. Fortunately for the companies, when analysts have to follow fifteen companies, work on investment-banking projects, and travel extensively on marketing trips, they often have no time to read all of the financial documents. Analysts often rely on management to point out the issues on which they should be focusing, and management is often selective in the topics it chooses.

EXECUTIVE PAY IS OFF-LIMITS

One subject that is definitely off-limits for any analyst whose firm is looking to maintain an investment-banking relationship is executive compensation. Imagine how management would react to an analyst who wrote, "The CEO is way overpaid." Even if it were true, such a statement would not only cost the analyst banking business with that company, it would also probably scare off other companies. The CEO of a competitor might agree with the analyst's comment, but would never do business with the analyst's firm. After all, he could be the analyst's next target. As long as investment banking drives the economics of Wall Street, few analysts will question the compensation policies of the companies they follow, any more than companies will question the compensation policies of the investment banks.

Investors should be cautious about buying stocks pushed by analysts who work for the brokerage firms doing the company's

investment banking. Suppose that the analyst of a firm slated to be one of the leads in an offering thought that the business was softer than planned. What would the analyst do? You would like to think that the analyst would reduce the earnings estimates and lower the rating on the company. But if the analyst were to do this, the firm would lose the offering and the analyst would forfeit a huge bonus and potentially risk losing a job. Put yourself in the analyst's position. You have two kids in private school and a summer home in East Hampton. Besides, you are not 100 percent certain that the earnings will fall short. What would you do? Bonuses of $400,000 and jobs paying $1 million don't come along every day. Are you really willing to jeopardize all that on the chance that the earnings could fall short? In most cases, the analyst will point out the potential risks in a guarded fashion but leave the estimates and rating unchanged.

While analysts rarely lower their ratings on their investment-banking clients, they often subtly put their opinions in their reports. J.P. Morgan was one of the underwriters for Intimate Brands, the owner of Victoria Secret and Bath & Body Works. In the third quarter of 1996, Intimate indicated that earnings would be below plan. The analyst from J.P. Morgan lowered her estimates, but instead of lowering the rating, she wrote: *"We maintain our buy rating, but expect the stock to remain dead money in the near term."* With thousands of stocks available, it is difficult to understand why anyone would buy a stock that is "dead money." So while the analyst may have maintained her buy rating, anyone reading her note would have realized that she no longer thought the stock was a buy. This is the fine line that analysts have to walk in order to do their job, but as an investor, you do not have to accept what they say as gospel. (Of course, as luck would have it, Intimate Brands had excellent results in 1997 and was one of the best stocks in its group.)

While you should be cautious about buying a stock recommended by the analyst of an investment banker, you should not be cautious in selling a stock if the analyst says something negative about the company. If after an IPO, an analyst for the investment banker initiates coverage with a rating lower than strong buy or a buy it is often a sign of problems ahead. There is great pressure on an analyst to speak positively about a company that has just paid millions of dollars in fees to her firm. If an analyst selects a less positive rating, such as long-term attractive, it means that the analyst is sufficiently concerned about the prospects of the company to resist the strong pressures from her employer and company management. Since this stand will often cause the analyst considerable grief, investors should take note. This is an analyst's way of tipping off investors.

Sometimes analysts have more subtle ways of indicating their concern with investment-banking clients. Morgan Stanley was one of the lead underwriters for Designer Holdings, the manufacturer of Calvin Klein jeans. Several months after the very successful IPO, Josie Esquivel, a very capable analyst, held a seminar entitled "War for Market Share in the Jeans Business," at which she featured Designer Holdings and some of its competitors. Josie never said anything negative about Designer Holdings, but by holding the conference, she allowed investors to explore the issue of excess competition. Someone must have figured it out. Shortly before the conference, Designer Holdings was selling for $32. Two months later, it was selling for $16. (The company was later sold to Warnaco.) **If you see an analyst for an investment-banking firm say anything that could be construed as negative about a company that has recently had an offering, sell the stock.**

Little can be done to eliminate the symbiotic relationship between companies and analysts. Analysts follow companies they like, and the more they like the companies, the more information they receive. The private meetings that are offered to "friends" of the company tend to reinforce the general bullishness. Even without investment banking, the relationship between a company and its analysts would have a bullish bias. But the impact of investment banking further cements the bullishness. Most companies select investment bankers and analysts who share their views, and analysts understand that much of their compensation comes from investment banking. While they do not necessarily "shill" for the companies, they make sure that their earnings estimates and reports reflect the views that the company espouses. Like it or not, these are the rules of the game.

BEWARE OF BROKERAGE HOUSE RATINGS

The report comes from your broker. You look at the headline. The analyst has a buy on the stock. You assume that this means that the analyst wants you to buy it. Not so fast. You look at another report. It has a hold rating. You assume that the analyst wants you to hold it. Again, not so fast. Analyst ratings can be misleading. At many firms, *buy* may not mean *buy*. At most firms, *hold* certainly does not mean *hold*.

THE THREE-RATING SYSTEM

There is no consistency among brokerage house ratings. A few firms make it easy for investors. They have three ratings. *Buy* is for stocks that they want you to buy. *Hold* is for stocks that they want you to hold, and *sell* is for stocks that they want you to sell. It is, of course, reasonable to question why they need even these three ratings. Buy and sell should probably suffice. The meaning of *buy* is clear. The meaning of *sell* is also clear. The meaning of *hold* is more problematic. If a stock is no longer good enough for you to buy, why should you continue to hold it? There are probably some good reasons, such as not having to pay taxes. But in most cases, **the analyst does not really want you to hold hold-rated stocks.** The analyst normally uses a hold rating to maintain a neutral position on a stock.

The three-rating system is pretty straightforward, but most brokerage firms now have four or five ratings. The four ratings might be: 1. strong buy, 2. buy, 3. hold or market perform, and 4. unattractive or sell. The five ratings might be: 1. strong buy, 2. buy, 3. long-term attractive, 4. market perform, and 5. sell.

THE FOUR- OR FIVE-RATING SYSTEM

A strong buy in a four- or a five-rating system is like a buy in a three-rating system. It is the highest rating available to an analyst. These are the stocks that the analyst really wants you to buy. Not surprisingly, companies much prefer the analyst to have a strong buy rather than a plain buy, because it sounds more positive. When I worked for a brokerage firm with only three ratings, companies would always ask why I did not have a strong buy on their stock. I responded that the buy was my top rating. This rarely satisfied them. They liked the sound of strong buy more. Some time after I left, the brokerage firm changed to a five-rating system.

The buy rating in these systems is a place where many analysts choose to hide. When you see a stock in a five-point system rated buy, you should ask is why it isn't good enough to be a strong buy. Or to put it another way, *"Why should I purchase a stock rated buy when I could just as easily purchase rated strong buy?"* The difference between a strong buy and a buy is simple: **Strong buy means buy the stock. Buy does not.** Buy is often a rating used by analysts for investment-banking clients. It says, *"We really don't think this stock is the greatest buy in the world, but we led their last stock offering, so if we don't keep saying something positive, the management will kill us."*

The buy rating also enables analysts to avoid rocking the boat. Analysts hate to cut ratings, even if the stock has moved up sharply, because a cut in ratings could cost them investment-banking business. I knew a top-rated analyst who lowered from a strong buy to a buy a stock that had doubled. The stock dropped 20 percent on the downgrade. The CEO of the company was so infuriated that he stopped doing business with the analyst's firm, even though the firm had always been the company's investment banker. The message to competing analysts became crystal clear. The company would punish anyone who downgraded the stock. So the other analysts did the intelligent thing: They kept the company permanently at a buy. Because they never raised it to a strong buy, they never had to worry about downgrading it.

The key to understanding an analyst's buy in a five-point system is to see if the rating ever changes. If the analyst has maintained the rating for years, it's worthless. The only way to tell if the analyst actually likes the stock is to read between the lines. Analysts often find subtle ways to distinguish between *buy* and *buy*. They may use price objectives. If the stock is at $28 and it has a price objective of $30, it is not really a buy. They may also talk about the potential for upside surprises (a buy) or about downside risks (not a buy). Or, like the analyst from J.P. Morgan, they may actually tell you, *"The stock is dead money."*

The third rating in a five-point system, accumulate or long-term attractive, is the most inane. If the analyst has stocks that are buys and strong buys, why would you ever want to purchase a stock that is rated *accumulate?* Besides, what is the difference between accumulating a stock and buying it? If you accumulate, you still have to put up the same amount of money to purchase a share. So what does *accumulate* actually mean? **Accumulate is a euphemism that means this stock is not good enough to be a strong buy or a buy,** but we still want to be able to talk to management and we would like to participate in the company's next offering, so we need a rating that allows us to sound positive without being positive.

Long-term attractive is another rating that is like kissing your sister. (It is a little better than kissing your mother-in-law, but that's about it.) The first question you should ask when you see the rating long-term attractive is *"Why should I buy a stock that is not attractive short-term?"* Long-term *attractive* means, *"This stock is not cheap, and we see no reason for rating it a buy, but the company is decent and we like the management. Perhaps the stock will come down in price and we will have an opportunity to raise our rating. If you already own it, don't panic. At some point in the distant future, you may actually get your money back."* In other words, ***long-term attractive* means, *"We are sorry that you own this dog, but you'll make out in the end, if you live long enough."***

The fourth rating is hold or market perform. Both of these ratings sound pretty good. An analyst would obviously not want you to hold a stock that was going to go down, and many analysts would be happy to have you own a stock that performed as well as the market. The problem is that while the terms sound good, their meaning is not. In most cases, hold usually means, *"If you hate money, hold this stock!"* Market *perform* usually means, *"If the market performs as badly as this stock will, you are in big trouble."*

There are two exceptions to the hold rule. Sometimes analysts use a hold rating as a way of saying that they do not know much about the company. Often there are important companies in an industry that the analyst has never really followed. To comment on the company, the analyst needs an earnings estimate and a rating. The hold is the analyst's way of saying, *"I don't know much about this company."* It is relatively easy to find out if a company fits into this category. If the analyst has never published a report on the company, there is a good bet that *hold* means that the analyst really does not know much about it.

The second exception to the hold rule occurs when a group of stocks in the analyst's universe has a big move up before the analyst can initiate coverage. Last year, most of the Internet stocks started to fly before many of the software analysts even knew what *www.com* meant. Somewhere during the move, the director of research and the head of investment banking probably approached the software analyst and said something like, *"We're losing out on all this Internet banking business because you don't follow these stocks?"*

The analyst looked down at his neatly polished Gucci loafers and replied, *"I've been working on the group for three months. My report is almost ready."* Of course, the truth may be that the analyst missed the significance of the Web or was scared to jump on stocks that had already run up. But that is hardly something that you can tell your bosses. *"I want that report out next week,"* the director of research strongly suggested. *"We're making a pitch to three potential IPOs and I need to show that we cover the group."*

The analyst is in a quandary. The stocks have already quadrupled. If he initiates coverage with a buy, everyone will accuse him of having "missed the group," which in fact he has. But if he does not speak glow- ingly about the industry, his firm will never get investment-banking busi- ness. It is here that a hold rating comes in very handy. The analyst initi- ates coverage with a hold rating. This allows him to talk as an expert about the industry. He writes a report that speaks glowingly about the future, which the investment bankers can use in marketing to potential IPOs. In his report, he indicates that he is waiting for the stocks to decline by 10 to 20 percent before raising the rating to a buy. By holding out the possibility of raising his rating, the analyst can partially cover himself with the sales force that is still furious about his having missed the group. Of course, what this rating really says is, *"I screwed up and missed the stocks. I hope they go down a little, so that I can raise my rating and not look so stupid."*

This type of hold rating is always easy to identify. It is used in the initiation of coverage for a group of stocks that has had a huge upside move while the analyst sat on the sideline. It is easy to judge how much the analyst has missed the group. Look at the size of the report. The longer the report, the more the analyst believes that he has screwed up, as if length compensates for a lack of strength.

The final rating that most firms use is sell. Sell is a very simple rating. It means sell this stock. However, sell is a rating that is not often used. Investors may find the limited use of the sell rating perplexing. After all, there is a lot of selling going on. The amount of selling is equal to the amount of strong buying, buying, and accumulating combined. Since every transaction has a buyer and a seller, one would think that the analysts would spend as much time finding sells as finding buys. But the reality is: **Analysts have more than one hundred buy recommendations for every sell recommendation.**

Companies do not like analysts who have sell recommendations. Since investment banking drives the business and since companies do not give banking business to negative analysts, the analyst who wants to eat well and have a co-op on Park Avenue will probably not issue a lot of sells. Further, portfolio managers who own the stocks do not like analysts who issue sell recommendations. Since the sell rating is rare, its use often results in a stock being trashed. Even if the reasons are valid, the owners of the stock are unlikely to be pleased. So faced with a negative reaction from both companies and investors, most analysts avoid the sell rating and stick with euphemisms, like dead money or significant risk, to describe stocks they do not like.

My favorite euphemism is *source of funds*. By using the term *source of funds*, the analyst is saying, *"If there is a stock you want to buy, sell this stock and use the proceeds as a source of funds."* In other words, *source of funds* means sell.

One final investment rating, short sell, is almost never used, but is nonetheless a legitimate position for an analyst to take. In a short sell, investors "sell" a stock they do not own, betting that the stock will go down. A short sell is more than a sell. It is a bet against a company.

Some brokerage firms have created a more complicated system by using both short-term and long-term ratings for each stock. A typical rating might be 1/1, short-term buy/long-term buy, or 2/1, short-term hold/long-term buy. In theory, this is good way to look at stocks. The short-term rating reflects the analyst's view as to how the stock will perform in the immediate future. The long-term rating reflects the analyst's view of the long-term strength of the company. In practice, analysts tend to use the short-term ratings for their real views and the long-term ratings to appease banking clients. At one firm, for example, 37 percent of the stocks were rated short-term buy, but 86 percent were rated long-term buy. By carrying a short-term hold and a long-term buy, the analyst can tell the management of the company that she still rates them a buy, while telling investors that the company is a hold. The system works fine, so long as you understand the game.

ANALYSTS NEVER MEET A STOCK THEY DON'T LIKE

The biggest problem with brokerage-firm ratings is that analysts almost never meet a stock they don't like. Ratings inflation is absolutely rampant, far beyond "irrational exuberance." Many of the ratings are at best misleading and at worst meaningless.

In order to demonstrate the ratings inflation, I picked seven firms at random and used their ratings from early July 1996. Stocks with no ratings were excluded from the calculations.

> • At **Bank America-Montgomery Securities,** 368 stocks, 72 percent, had buy ratings, and only one stock had a sell rating. It is interesting to speculate what that one company must have done to the analyst to merit a sell. It is also reasonable to ask where investors would find the money to buy 368 stocks while only selling one.
> • At **BankBoston-Robertson Stevens,** 316 stocks, 79.4 percent, had bullish ratings. The remaining 20.6 percent were rated as market performers. Thus, of 398 stocks, Robertson believed that 316 would outperform the market, 82 would perform even with the market, and none would underperform the market. Since half of all stocks,

by definition, underperform, it is incredible that Robertson's analysts have the ability to completely avoid stocks that will underperform.

• **Robinson Humphrey** uses a system that has both short-term and long-term ratings. For the short term, 37 percent were rated buy, but for the long term, 86 percent were rated buy and only one stock was rated sell. (It must not have been a banking client.)

• At **Needham**, 72 percent of the stocks were rated strong buy, or buy, and 28 percent were rated hold. There were no sell-rated stocks.

• At **Gerard Klauer,** 64 percent of the stocks were rated buy, and 35 percent were rated hold. There was one sell.

• At **Wheat First,** 197 stocks had ratings of outperform or better, and only nine stocks had ratings of underperform— a pretty impressive batting average. Wheat had no sells.

• At **BT-Alex Brown,** 65 percent of the stocks had the firm's top ratings—strongest overperformance or overperformance; 35 percent of the stocks were rated market performance; and most impressively, no stock was rated either underperformance or substantial underperformance. In other words, Alex Brown had 401 stocks that it believed would outperform the market and none that it believed would underperform the market. Amazing! Of course, skeptics might ask why Alex Brown had five ratings if it only used three, but then perhaps this firm really can pick only winners.

It is pretty clear that the analysts were giving the customers little guidance. Seventy percent of the stocks were long-term buys, so it must have been difficult for the investor to select the best buys. More significantly, only three out of 1,559 stocks were rated sell, so the analysts were giving investors almost no help on what to sell. The reality is simple. Analysts' ratings are of little use in picking stocks.

RATINGS INFLATION IS RAMPANT

In writing this edition of *Guerrilla Investing*, I was curious whether there had been much of a change in ratings. I suspected that the strong market and the increase in investment-banking business had made analysts even more bullish. I called Chuck Hill, the head of Research at First Call and asked about the cumulative ratings.

On November 30, 1998, the brokerage houses that contribute to First Call had ratings on 25,795 stocks:

- 8,727 stocks (33.8 percent) were rated 1.
- 8,429 stocks (32.7 percent) were rated 2.
- 8,462 stocks (32.8 percent) were rated 3.
- 120 stocks (0.5 percent) were rated 4.
- 57 stocks (0.2 percent) were rated 5.

For most companies a 1 and a 2 are both buy ratings. In other words, 66.5 percent of the ratings were buys. For most companies a 3 rating is an accumulate or a market perform. So an additional 32.8 percent were quasi-buys. All told, more than 99 percent of the stocks had 1, 2, or 3 ratings. Only 177 of 25,795 (well less than 1 percent) had 4 or 5 ratings. In other words, the brokerage firms could find you 17,156 stocks they wanted you to buy and an additional 8,462 they wanted you to accumulate, but only 120 they wanted you to hold and 57 they wanted you to sell.

Because different firms have different rating systems and because some companies only have three or four ratings, these results are not quite as bullish as they might seem. But the fact remains that as the bull market continues, ratings inflation is becoming increasingly rampant.

TEN RULES FOR DEALING WITH ANALYSTS

The analysts do not make it easy for investors to decide what stocks to buy and sell, but they do have some tendencies that can be useful in picking stocks. Follow these ten rules for working with analysts, and you'll be ahead of the game.

1. Don't listen when analysts say that "the market has overreacted."

When a stock that an analyst is recommending plunges for no apparent reason, the analyst has two choices. He can say, "I screwed up," or he can blame it on the market. It is much easier to blame it on the market. In essence, he is saying, "I was right. Those of you who bought the stock were right. Only the market was wrong." Don't listen. As has been demonstrated repeatedly, the market does not "overreact." It is just that the analyst does not understand why he was wrong.

2. If an analyst's defense of a declining stock sounds like nonsense, it usually is. When a stock goes against an analyst, the analyst usually rushes out First Call notes and reports trying to explain the reasons for the decline. Often the explanations seem contrived. They usually are. The analyst wants the stock to go back up, but she also wants to justify herself to the sales force and customers who are giving her heat. Sell the stock before the analyst faces reality and throws in the towel.

3. Analysts who initiate coverage of a company when a stock is at a new high may just be pitching investment-banking business. You often see a strange pattern with stocks that have been ignored, then double or triple in price. Analysts suddenly discover them and initiate coverage with a buy. You wonder why the analyst ignored the stock at $10 and $20, only to recommend it at $30. The answer may be simply that the analyst is chasing banking business. As a stock moves up, there is a greater likelihood that the company or the insiders will sell, but the analyst's firm will never have a chance to participate unless the analyst is recommending the stock. The stock may continue to surge as new momentum investors pile in. But you should be careful. You have no way of knowing whether the analyst believes in the company or is just looking for a payday. (If the analyst's firm does not get the business, watch out. A drop in ratings can trash a stock.)

4. Beware of analysts lowering earnings estimates or price targets on their favorite stocks. All analysts have favorite stocks. Their reputation is often tied to these stocks, and they have probably put many of the current shareholders into them. They also undoubtedly have built strong relationships with the managements of these companies, and probably have garnered significant investment-banking business. Lowering the rating could have a huge impact on the price of the stock and could alienate investors, management, and the analyst's own sales force and investment-banking department.

As a result, analysts are leery of changing the ratings on the stocks with which they are most closely identified. I have known analysts who maintained buy recommendations on specific stocks for more than a decade. The longer the rating was maintained, the harder it became to change. Instead of changing the rating, these analysts often communicate problems by lowering the earnings estimates or the target price. When an analyst who is closely associated with a company lowers estimates or the target price, investors should start writing sell tickets. This may be the most negative the analyst will ever get.

This is especially true when the company has recently done an offering. When companies sell stock, they usually "guide" analysts to the "right" earnings estimates. Because companies and investment bankers are concerned about lawsuits, they are very careful to make sure that analysts have the right numbers. If an analyst lowers an estimate shortly after an offering, it is a sure sign of trouble, even if the analyst continues to say good things about the company.

5. Beware of analysts fine-tuning their estimates. When analysts have a buy on a stock and they decide to change the earnings estimates from $1 to $1.04, they typically say that they are "raising" the estimates. But when they change their estimates from $1.04 to $1, they typically say that they are "fine-tuning" their model. *Fine-tuning* is a euphemism that in most cases means lowering. Fine-tuning can be especially worrisome when analysts lower the current quarter but leave their annual estimates unchanged. Companies do not like to tell analysts to lower estimates unless it is absolutely necessary. The analysts often go along with the company's guidance, because they do not like to lower estimates either. So they drop this quarter by a few cents and hope that the company can pull a rabbit out of its hat before the year ends.

When analysts "fine-tune" a quarter but leave the year unchanged, they are actually raising their estimates for subsequent quarters. Given the weakness in the current quarter, this increases the likelihood that the company will disappoint investors. I have seen analysts fine-tune estimates three quarters in a row, only to find that the fourth quarter ended up a disaster. While there may be instances in which fine-tuning is appropriate, in most cases investors should recognize it for what it is—a reduction in the earnings estimate, and assume that subsequent quarters will also have to be fine-tuned, unless you hear a very convincing argument otherwise.

6. Beware of changes in the target price for no good reason. When analysts recommend a stock, they set a target price. This target price is the goal that the analyst has for the stock within a specific time frame. It is usually detailed on the cover of the research report. A funny thing often occurs when the stocks reach their target. Because analysts like to keep their winners, they merely change the target price. Changing the target price may be entirely appropriate if earnings have come in above expectations or if a long enough period of time has passed so that analysts can start looking at next year's earnings. But in many cases, the analysts are adjusting their target prices without changing either the projected earnings estimates or the projected growth rate just so they can continue their buy. When this occurs, it is a good time to start looking at the chart for a sell point. If a stock exceeds the analyst's initial projected target without any change in the estimates, do not fall for the analyst's new price target and continued buy. Ask yourself if it's time to sell.

7. Look for analysts with sell recommendations. If nothing else, analysts who issue sell recommendations are independent. By issuing sell recommendations, the analyst is making a determination that picking the right stocks is more important than generating banking fees. This is a position that analysts do not take lightly. Wall Street is not overpopulated with analysts who prefer truth to money. The seven brokerage firms cited earlier had only three long-term sells. But a few analysts do issue them. I once worked with an oil analyst named Mark Gilman who always had sells on about half of his stocks. Gilman was also one of the few analysts who would openly challenge the managements of his companies. Gilman was not always right, but he was always independent.

Sell recommendations make life easier for investors. There is no hiding behind a euphemism like *market perform.*

> • Find analysts who have sell ratings on stocks that everyone else loves. When one analyst has a sell and all the other

analysts have strong buys, that analyst usually has an opinion that, right or wrong, is worth noting.

• Find analysts with sell recommendations on companies currently doing investment-banking business. When a company does an offering, there is a payday for most of the analysts. The analyst with the sell rating is walking away from that pay. Investors would do well to listen to what that analyst has to say.

• Look at sell recommendations based on accounting issues. These are especially interesting because most analysts do not look closely at accounting issues. Analysts who have gone to the trouble of studying them may be onto something.

• Once in a very long while, an analyst may actually have a short sell recommendation. Such a recommendation is worth looking at because it is such a rare and radical step against a company. This is not to say that you should short the stock, but you should look at the argument the analyst is making.

8. Pick a few analysts and stick with them. Think of analysts the way you would think of athletes. Two people can have the same job, but there can be huge differences in their performance. Greg and Mike Maddux are brothers and major league pitchers, but their performance is hardly comparable. Greg has won four Cy Young awards, while Mike is a journeyman reliever. The performance of analysts can differ just as much. If you can pick Greg instead of Mike, you will make money. The easiest way to begin is to ask your broker which analysts are the best money makers. In every brokerage firm, there are a few great money makers, a few consistent losers, and many who are just average. Most brokers have a pretty good sense as to which are the best. Ask them which analysts they use for their own investments. Most will use only three or four. Stick with the best analysts, even if they are not in the hottest groups. The easiest way to lose money is to rely on a bad analyst in a hot group.

9. A consistent loser can be as good as a consistent winner. There is only one exception to the rule of picking good analysts. Every once in a while, you may find analysts who are always wrong. They are consistent money losers. But these analysts can be of great use because they are perfect contrary indicators.

An institutional salesman told me a story about an analyst who was always wrong. If the analyst said that a stock was going to go up, it went down, and vice versa. It was difficult trying to sell this analyst's research, but the salesman tried his best. There was, however, one portfolio manager who wanted to know everything that this analyst said. The portfolio manager told him, *"I'll pay you $100,000 per year, but I want to get the first call on anything this analyst says."* The salesman never understood why, but he was happy to make the commission, so he always promptly called the manager with any news from the analyst.

One day, the analyst recommended the stock of a large industrial company that was having financial problems. The salesman could not understand why the analyst liked the stock, and thought that the recommendation could backfire, so he did not call any clients. Within two days the stock had dropped by 50 percent. While others were fielding angry calls, he was feeling pretty smug. Then the portfolio manager called, enraged. *"Why the hell didn't you call me about the recommendation?"*

"I thought it was a dumb idea," the salesman replied. *"Besides, it dropped from $12 to $8 in two days."*

"I own the stock," the portfolio manager screamed.

"Then I saved you from buying more," the salesman replied.

"Saved me! Don't you get it?" the portfolio manager snapped, *"If I knew this idiot was recommending it, I would have sold every share. I've known this bozo for fifteen years, and he's the perfect contrary indicator! If he says, "Buy," I sell. If he says, "Sell," I buy. He is never right! Do you know how much money I can make betting against him?"*

My friend was dumbfounded. It had never occurred to him that someone would use an analyst as a contrary indicator, but analysts who are always wrong can make you as much money as analysts who are always right, as long as you remember to bet against them. So in addition to asking the broker which are the best analysts, it is also useful to ask which are the worst.

10. Try to identify what an analyst does particularly well. Some analysts are good at finding value stocks, but terrible at growth or momentum stocks. Other analysts are great with growth stocks, but terrible with value stocks. Some analysts can spot trends but cannot make earnings estimates. Some are good at a certain part of their industry, but weak in other parts. David Goldsmith, an analyst at Buckingham Research, had an uncanny ability to figure out the breakup value of media, cable, and cellular companies. During a decade in which many of these companies were taken over, Goldsmith made a huge amount of money for his clients. There have been few analysts who were ever better. However, when Goldsmith attempted to focus on more mundane issues, such as whether a movie or a TV series would be a success, he was only average. The trick was to use him for what he was great at, not to rely on him for everything. You do not need an analyst who is a jack of all trades; you need an analyst who is especially good at a few things. If you can figure out what those things are, you can use that analyst to make a lot of money.

The analysts are the intelligence-gathering arm of the brokerage houses. It is easy to read their glowing reports and rush out to buy the stocks. But before you do, remember:

- analysts are overwhelmingly bullish,
- their bullishness is augmented by the fees from investment banking, and
- brokerage house ratings are of extremely limited value.

Rather than relying on ratings, try to read between the lines of the analyst's report. If you follow these ten rules, you can use the analysts to your advantage and eliminate some of the advantages of the professionals.

CHAPTER TWELVE

Pitfalls (and Opportunities)

In addition to obtaining fundamental and technical information, learning from the news, and scooping the analysts, guerrilla investors should watch for critical pitfalls and opportunities when trading in hostile territory. These easy-to-miss situations frequently tell a lot about the future direction of a stock.

WATCH THE REVOLVING DOOR

In a seemingly strong company, too much management turnover can be a bad sign. If managers resign, they are sending a message as to their view of the future of the company's stock price. Most managers have unvested stock options that they forfeit when they leave. By leaving, the manager is walking away from what could potentially be a huge payday. Perhaps money is not important to the manager, or perhaps the manager has a different view of the future than do the analysts.

Be especially cautious when you see key managers resign from fast-growing Internet companies. With no profits and a limited history, it is often hard to find guideposts to judge a fast-growing company's potential. Analysts can make pie-in-the-sky projections as to how the business will look years into the future. But the departure of a key executive, who walks

313

away from millions of dollars of unvested options, is a tangible guidepost. The resignation may have been caused by a personality conflict, or it may have been caused by something more. It is probably not worth taking the chance. A few months ago, I saw that the COO of Efax had resigned. I did not wait to find out why. I shorted the stock and watched it fall by 50 percent in two months.

Watch which managers are leaving. If the CEO of a fast-growing company resigns "to pursue other interests," long-term fundamental problems are likely. CEOs usually don't leave businesses if everything is booming. In May 1996, the president of Aetna resigned so that he could spend more time with his family. At the time of his resignation, Aetna's stock was at about $95. In the next several months, the price increased to $120. Besides the resignation, there was also heavy insider selling. (One director dumped almost $130 million of stock.) But investors did not seem to care. Several months later, Aetna announced that it was having more problems than expected in integrating a recent acquisition. The stock tumbled to less than $70. Perhaps the news should not have been such a surprise. If everything was running smoothly, insiders would not have been dumping $130 million of stock, and the president could probably have found a way to keep his job and still spend quality time with his family.

When the chief financial officer suddenly leaves, look for potential accounting issues. CFOs often leave companies. In most cases, their departure is not a cause for concern. However, if the company has a reputation for being aggressive, the CFO could have had conflicts over accounting policy with the CEO. In almost every case, the CEO wants to report the higher numbers. A number of years ago, Garland Asher, the CFO of Intelligent Electronics (now a Wall Street analyst) resigned and refused to sign the financial statements. Because Intelligent Electronics had a reputation for aggressive accounting, the stock dropped by 50 percent and never recovered.

Look for multiple resignations, especially when they are not completely coincident. This could be a sign of internal dissension. In mid-1999, the president of the Keds division of Stride Rite resigned. Analysts wrote that she was a strong executive and would be missed. One month later, the CEO of the company resigned. Two key resignations in one month certainly sent a warning flag. While Stride Rite is an excellent company with strong brands, and while it could become a takeover target, multiple resignations are usually a sign of greater internal problems to come.

A CASE STUDY: EARTHSHELL

EarthShell is a start-up company, developing environmentally responsible disposable packaging for the food service industry. Whenever I eat in a fast-food restaurant, I look at the gigantic amount of Styrofoam and wonder where all the trash will go. A product that would "return to the earth" seemed like a winner.

I must not have been the only one who thought so. Although EarthShell had no revenues, had already lost more than $100 million, and would lose $27.4 million in fiscal 1999, it was still able to sell 13.2 million shares of stock at $21 per share, giving it a market capitalization of more than $2 billion.

Everyone was willing to give this business a shot. McDonald's gave EarthShell an order for 1.8 billion Big Mac containers over a three-year period. The Department of the Interior signed an agreement for a pilot project in its cafeteria. Domestic and international packaging companies indicated their intention to form joint ventures with EarthShell.

But even the greatest idea still has to work, and there were signs that EarthShell was having problems. On March 31, the company announced that it was delaying its first shipment to McDonald's. Simon Hodson, the vice-chairman and CEO, issued a calming press release stating, "We are very encouraged with the progress we have made toward achieving our first goal of proving that EarthShell products can be manufactured on a commercial scale. . . . We are completely confident that sufficient quantities will be supplied for McDonald's. . . ." Despite these reasonable assurances, some investors were still concerned. The price of the stock dropped $2^1/$_{16}$ to $9^3/$_4$.

The next day, Hodson announced that he was resigning and that Bill McLaughlin, the president, would become the new CEO. I was a little taken aback that the man who had reassured me the day before had suddenly decided to resign. Hodson, who was also president of

EarthShell's parent company, E. Khashoggi Industries, noted that the management change had been a part of the company's internal plan since McLaughlin was hired. Hodson had a two-year employment agreement that expired September 30. Although the plan was subject to a one-year renewal, although Hodson was president of the parent company, and although there were still four months until the end of September, Hodson decided it was time to enact the change in management. Was it merely a coincidence that the CEO resigned the day after EarthShell missed the deadline for its shipments to McDonald's? Perhaps it was, but such coincidences have to be watched.

When I read the announcement, I called a friend of mine who was EarthShell's largest shareholder. She had visited the company three days earlier and had met with Hodson. He had given her no indication that he was thinking of resigning. In fact, he had spent the entire day talking bullishly about the firm's prospects.

Over the next six weeks, the price of the stock stabilized and even went up a little. Then, on May 13, the company announced that it was ready to begin shipping to McDonald's. "This represents the realization of a dream that we have patiently awaited," said Essam Khashoggi, EarthShell's chairman of the board and largest shareholder. (Essam is the brother of Adnan, the Saudi military businessman.)

It also announced that Simon Hudson would continue his role as CEO (wait a second — didn't he resign six weeks earlier?), and that Bill McLaughlin, who had just been made CEO — or so I thought — would resign. McLaughlin cited personal reasons for leaving EarthShell. *"In consideration of my family, however, and prior to assuming the long-term obligations associated with my transition to CEO, I have made the decision to leave the company. After many years of prioritizing my career, I now wish to devote more time to family interests."* Isn't it wonderful how CEOs suddenly discover how much they love their families?

O.K., so let's understand what was going on:

1. The company missed its delivery date for McDonald's.
2. The CEO (Hodson) resigned. McLaughlin took his place.
3. The company started shipping to McDonald's.
4. The new CEO (McLaughlin) resigned to spend more time

with his family, just as the company appeared ready to revolutionize the packaging business.

5. Hodson, who six weeks previously had resigned, unresigned.

6. Not surprisingly, the stock dropped back to $8.

Will EarthShell succeed? Perhaps it will. It has a fine concept. If it can
produce products economically, it may well be a success. Perhaps
Earthshell's stock will again be worth billions, but life is too short for me
to ignore all of the red flags that this company was flying.

IF A COMPANY "FIRES" ITS EXECUTIVES, FIRE YOUR STOCK

In the world of public companies, executives are rarely "fired" publicly.
Even if the CEO walks in with a guard and says "You're outta here!" the
company will usually issue a press release saying that the executive has
resigned "to pursue other interests" (like collecting unemployment insurance). Saving face is important in the world of public companies.

If a company says that an executive has been "fired," it is usually
because he or she has done something very wrong. If more than one executive is fired, it indicates that there was serious and widespread wrongdoing. If the executives were in senior positions, the company is likely to face
serious lawsuits from shareholders and others, who were injured by the
wrongdoing. Once the lawsuits start, the business is often compromised.

Remember the 1.0-rated stocks in chapter 5? Sirena Apparel was one of
those in 1996. Several years ago, an investment group bought a control
position and brought in a new chairman and CFO. These two diversified
the company from bathing suits into intimate apparel and started online
initiatives. For a short period, Sirena again became a darling of investors.

Then the stock started to sink. There were rumors of financial irregu-
larities. One morning, Sirena issued a press release saying that the chairman and the CFO had been fired and that it might have to restate some
earnings. No one at the company was available to respond to questions.
The next day, the first class-action lawsuits were filed. A short time later,
Sirena filed Chapter 11 bankruptcy. As of today, the stock has still not
traded. The moral is simple. If a company fires its chairman and its CFO,
the problems are likely to be very serious.

THE EXCEPTIONS

While too much turnover is not positive for a successful company, it may be positive for a company that has been doing badly. The top executive who resigned could have been holding back the company or been an impediment to a proposed sale or restructuring. With the executive out of the way, the company might be in a better position to recognize value for its shareholders. This is especially critical for companies that have a strong franchise or a business that would be easy to liquidate or sell.

Sometimes, the resignation of a key executive gives others the opportunity to prove their worth. When Michael Raydon resigned as the chairman of Pacific Sunwear (he was also the largest shareholder) to run Limited Too, I thought the company was toast. I was wrong! The new CEO, Greg Weaver, re-energized the company and changed the merchandising. In two years, the stock appreciated by almost 1,000 percent. Interestingly, Raydon did a great job at Limited Too. Still, betting on new management is a hard bet to win. You should avoid doing it unless you have home-turf advantage. If the new management appears to be doing well, you can always re-place your bet.

Finally, if a new CEO is brought into a struggling company that is beginning a turnaround, you can expect, and even want, a high level of management turnover. A new CEO will want to clean house and put his own team in place. If the CEO is good and the stock is already depressed, a house-cleaning can be viewed as positive. When Barry Diller took over Home Shopping Network (now USA Networks), he brought in his own team, and the stock went up, because investors had great confidence in Diller.

Still, in most cases, too much management turnover is a bad sign. The company will always put the best spin possible on the turnover, but you should treat this spin with skepticism. Just remember, managers who resign leave lots of money on the table. Perhaps you should as well.

BEWARE OF COMPANIES THAT REPORT INFORMATION LATE

Some companies report their earnings ten days, others twenty days, and still others thirty days after the end of the quarter, but most report according to a reasonably regular schedule every year. All companies must report within forty-five days after the end of the quarter. At year-end, companies have ninety days, because they must have audited financial statements. On occasion, companies will delay their earnings report. Sometimes there is a good reason. If a company has made an acquisition or is taking a major write-off, accounting issues may require additional time. But in many cases when companies report late, they do so because they have bad news that they want to delay as long as possible. As a rule, **companies like to release good news as fast as possible and delay bad news.** They also like to release good news at a time when most investors will see it, and postpone bad news until a time when fewer investors will notice.

THE GOOD FRIDAY EARNINGS REPORT

One trick companies often use if they have bad news is to wait until Friday afternoon to report it, preferably after the market has closed and most investors have gone home. The Friday before a long holiday weekend is especially effective, since people like to leave early. One sneaky company used to report weak earnings on Good Friday, when the stock market was closed. Perhaps the hope was that no one would notice, or by the time investors returned to work, there would be other issues to worry about.

One year, I was rushing out of my office before the Jewish holiday of Yom Kippur, when a company that I followed made a very disappointing announcement. Since I was late for synagogue, I had no time to call the company. By a twist of fate, I happened to walk into synagogue with the 75-year-old chairman of the company. *"How could you have issued this disappointing news at 4:00 when many investors are leaving for the Jewish holidays?"* I asked.

"I'm sorry. The announcement was a mistake," the Chairman replied contritely. *"The news wasn't supposed to*

> *be released until 5:30.*" With many investors spending the next day atoning for their sins, they might have missed this company's disaster entirely.
>
> If you hear that a company will report after the close on a Friday (or on one of the Jewish holidays), be wary. The surprises are not likely to be on the upside.

Beware of companies that have not filed by their regulatory deadlines. When a company requests an extension, it usually signals complications with the audit. A company called Greenman (now Noodle Kidoodle) had been an extremely hot stock. An analyst who had been recommending it noticed that more than ninety days had passed since the end of the fiscal year. When he called the company, the CFO cavalierly told him that while everything was fine, the company wanted to wait a few more days before reporting. The analyst immediately reduced his rating. One week later, Greenman reported that it would have to take a major write-off. The stock fell in half. The moral is simple: **If you see a company ask for an extension, sell first, ask questions later.** Forty-five days after the end of a quarter and ninety days after the end of a year is sufficient time to report results, unless something is seriously wrong.

WATCH OUT FOR COMPANIES THAT CHANGE THEIR AUDITORS

Companies may change their auditors because the CFO and the auditors don't get along or because of a conflict with another client of the auditor. Or the company might feel that the auditors are not doing a good job. There are excellent reasons for changing auditors. But there are also not-so-excellent reasons. Often, a company changes auditors because of a disagreement over accounting policies. These differences usually concern earnings, and often the amount at issue is substantial. In a dispute between a company and its auditors, it is usually the company that wants to report the higher numbers. The executives of the company own stock and often have performance bonuses. The auditors are paid a fee and have professional reputations to protect. When in doubt, pick the side of the auditors.

If an auditor resigns during the middle of the fiscal year, don't wait around to find out why. The chances are good that something is seriously wrong. Not only will the auditors forfeit their fees, but they could also become the subject of a lawsuit from either the company or the shareholders. Mid-year resignations will occur only if the auditors and the company have reached an impasse over a very serious issue.

It would be nice if the company would explain the reason for the termination, but can you imagine a company saying, *"Our auditors quit because they thought we were cooking the books!"* Companies are never this forthright. At Donnkenny (one of the case studies in chapter 7), the most that management would admit was that the auditors complained about a lack of access to information. Of course, a few weeks later, it admitted that it would have to restate its sales and earnings. Don't be swayed if the company announces that it has immediately hired another auditor. There are always accountants willing to accept a fee, and the new auditor may not accept the company's view either. If there is a change of auditors during the year, sell your stock and let someone else worry about it.

A number of years ago, Regal Communications, a leader in infomercials, had just bought the company that ran the psychic infomercials and was about to report its year-end results. One day, the company released a short statement saying that its auditors had resigned and were immediately being replaced by another firm. On the conference call, the company assured investors that the resignation was due to a personality conflict. Shortly thereafter, the new auditors indicated that there was a problem with the financial results. In the end, the acquisition was voided. Regal Communications went bankrupt and was liquidated. (I always wondered why the management of the psychic company did not see the problems coming. Perhaps it should have called its own hot line.) The rule is simple enough: If the auditors can't stomach the numbers, neither should you.

MANAGEMENTS DON'T ALWAYS
WANT THEIR STOCKS TO GO UP

Almost every statement in this book is based on the concept that managements want the best stock price for their company. This is true 99 percent of the time, but there are a few exceptions. Sometimes management wants the price of its stock to stay low for a particular period of time. When this occurs, management may actually soft-pedal the good news, which can give investors an interesting buying opportunity.

Management will often want the price of the stock to remain low if the company is having a huge stock buyback program or if the managers themselves are buying. If management or the company is buying stock, it is obviously in its interest to pay less. This is not to say that a management will attempt to trash the price of its own stock, but it may delay or soft-pedal a bullish report until it is finished buying. If you see a company or its executives aggressively buying stock, it is a good bet that bullish pronouncements may follow the buying.

Management would also prefer a lower stock price when it receives its options. Since options are priced as of a particular day, the lower the price on that day, the more valuable the options. Most companies will not jerk around their stock price in order to get a marginally better price on a small number of options. But if the amount of the options is sufficiently large, a few companies may play some games.

A recent study by two professors has indicated that this practice is widespread. The professors found that the stock price of a large number of companies actually did decline around the time of the options grant and that many companies release bad news or delay reporting good news during these periods.

I remember going to an analyst's meeting at which the CEO stood up in front of hundreds of investors and said he was concerned about future business. In the next three days, the stock dropped $6. I happened to run into a director of the company whom I had known from school. I mentioned the meeting and the subsequent action of the stock. He smiled slyly. *"Look at the company's chart,"* he suggested. *"We always do something stupid in July. That's when we price the employee options. If we can* *get the one million options priced $6 lower, we can save $6 million in compensation. By the middle of August, the shareholders will have forgotten about it."* I looked back at the chart for twenty years, and sure enough, there was almost always a decline in the middle of July. While few companies will admit to engaging in this type of behavior: **If you see a company making a huge option grant, it is always reasonable to ask about the date on which the options are priced. This may not be a bad date on which to buy the stock.**

Another situation involving the management is easier to track—the spin-off of a subsidiary. When the company is spun off, executives are granted options. While the parent wants the highest price it can get, the executives of the subsidiary would rather see a lower price, so their options can appreciate. The executives of the subsidiary normally conduct the road show.

I remember talking to the CEO of a company that was being spun off by a large retailer. I told him that I thought that his stock could sell for $30. *"I'll be happier with $25,"* he replied. *"If the price gets too high, our options will be worthless. We've spent years building this business. My people deserve something. Besides, what's a few million dollars to . . .* [the parent company]*?"* The CEO was just being honest. He wanted the offering to go off at a slightly lower price so that his options and those of his employees would be worth something. Your strategy should be: Because companies that are being spun off often soft-pedal their prospects to get a better price for the options, consider buying spin-offs after the options are priced.

WATCH FOR INSIDER BUYING AND SELLING

Perhaps no clue is more useful to investors than signs of insider buying and selling. When insiders buy, they are making a bet for the future of their company, but when insiders sell, they are making a bet against their company. In looking at insider trading, three factors are important: the amount of stock being traded, the amount relative to insider ownership, and the people involved. If individuals are buying or selling large rather than small amounts of stock, they are making a more definitive statement. The relative quantity is also important. If executives are selling their entire position, these trades should raise more of a red flag than if they are selling only 10 percent of their stock. Finally, the number of executives and their position in the company are critical. If many key executives are buying or selling stock, they are making a broad-based statement about their company's future.

Insider buying can be a good sign that a company is turning around. When executives take their own money and buy stock in their companies, they are significantly increasing their reliance on the financial success of the company. If something goes wrong, they may not only lose their job, they may also lose the money that they have invested. Because of their focus on the fundamentals of the business and restrictions on their purchases and sales, insiders tend to be early buyers. It is very common for stocks to sit at the same price after insiders buy. But massive insider buying is a sign that the insiders regard the company more bullishly than do the analysts. The insiders may not yet have the earnings numbers, but they usually know when business is getting better or worse.

When Jim Halpin and his team joined CompUSA, the stock had been decimated. It did not take management long to realize that the underlying business was strong and that the company could be turned around. Sixteen insiders made at least one purchase of CompUSA stock, and eleven made multiple purchases. All told, these sixteen insiders invested about $4 million of their own money, a dramatic vote of confidence, which also proved to be extremely profitable when the stock soared.

If insider buying is a sign that business is improving, insider selling can be a sign that it has reached a peak or is heading down. (Remember the director of Aetna who sold $130 million of stock shortly before it plunged and Richard Rubin of Donnkenny, who also bailed out?) Investor relations usually has good explanations for each sale. "The CFO needed to pay for his kid's college. The CEO is building a new house, and the chairman is endowing a foundation." You may be pleased that these executives are all realizing the American dream, but do their sales make you eager to buy their stock? **If the stock is not good enough for its executives, why should it be good enough for you?**

In many cases, managements are lucky enough to sell shortly before a terrible announcement is made. From August 11 to August 14, 1997, Michael Cowpland, the CEO of Corel, a Canadian software company, sold $14.5 million of stock at more than $6 per share shortly before the company announced disappointing earnings and the stock declined by 33 percent. By January, the stock had dropped to less than $2, the CFO had resigned, and the company had reported an annual loss of $232 million. Cowpland claimed that he had no advance knowledge of the earnings. While that may have been true, Cowpland certainly must have had a better "feel" for the quality of the business that did other shareholders. On October 19, 1999, Cowpland was charged with three counts of violating Canadian securities law.

Insiders do not always know everything. Nor do they always sell at the top, but it is reasonable to ask whether they know more about the business of the company than you do.

WATCH FOR THE HYPE WHEN INSIDERS SELL

Be especially cautious if you see large insider selling in a company that has been hyping its stock. You can always tell the level of hype by the number of press releases and bullish analyst statements. If a company keeps issuing bullish press releases and encouraging analysts to raise earnings estimates while management bails out, you could be facing serious trouble. The question that investors should always ask is *"If business is so great, why is the management selling?"* There is rarely a good answer to this question.

A Canadian toy company named SLM International offers a good example of insider selling coupled with hype. SLM had three businesses: the CCM hockey products, Buddy L plastic toys, and above-ground swimming pools (the pool business had been purchased from Coleco in bankruptcy). SLM's financial record was modest. In November 1992, it was selling for $11. Then, in the next ten months, the stock almost tripled. One of the main drivers was a licensing agreement for a new process that SLM claimed "revived dead batteries." SLM licensed this process from a small company in Alberta, Canada, which in turn had licensed it from a company in Atlanta.

The concept of a charger that would recharge ordinary alkaline batteries is one to which everyone can relate. On the day of the announcement of this process the stocks of other battery makers were trounced. Duracell initially plunged 14 percent. Some questioned why the developer of the process was unable to market it, why it had given the license to the small company in Canada, or why this company had licensed it to SLM. But many bought into the dream that they would soon be able to recharge their batteries.

While the stock was running up, management was unloading large blocks. Look at the insider transactions that took place between July 27, 1992, and October 12, 1993, while the stock went from $12^3/_4$ to $29^1/_3$.

SLM INSIDER TRANSACTIONS

July 27, 1992	Officers and director sold 1,054,654 shares at about $12^3/_4$.
July 27, 1992	Company controlled by officers and directors sold 1,458,991 shares at about $12^3/_4$.
June 2–15, 1993	One officer and director sold 50,000 shares at about $20^5/_8$.
June 2–29, 1993	One officer and director sold 117,000 shares at about $21^1/_8$.
June 17–28, 1993	Vice president sold all of his stock at about $21.
July 12–15, 1993	One officer and director sold 83,000 shares at about $24.
Sept. 29–30, 1993	One officer and director sold 79,000 shares at about $29^1/_8$.
Oct. 7–12, 1993	One officer and director sold 21,000 shares at about $29^1/_4$.

In one year, three officers (and directors) of the company sold $40.4 million of stock. While the stock was hitting new highs, inventories were backing up. In the fourth quarter of 1992, SLM announced that sales had been much less than plan, inventories had increased sharply, and the company had lost $0.50 per share. Did the managers know when they sold their stock that revenues would be much less than plan? It is difficult to say. Perhaps they saw signs that made them nervous, or perhaps they were just lucky. The price of the stock tumbled from $29 in October 1993 to below $3 by December 1994. SLM reported a loss of $112 million for 1993 and filed for bankruptcy.

Sometimes revolutionary products work, but while people were focusing on the hype of the batteries, SLM inventories were growing out of control

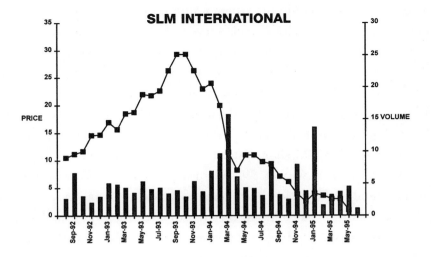

and the company was self-destructing. While the managers were, luckily, selling $40 million of stock, the investors were left in the dark (literally and figuratively, because the battery charger never really worked). Management did not try to hide their sales from investors. But investors did not have to buy the stock they were selling. Obviously, no one took the time to ask, *"If SLM is such a great company, why are all of the insiders selling?"* While there are examples to the contrary, a good rule of thumb is avoid hyped stocks with a large amount of insider selling.

SOMETIMES INVESTORS NEVER LEARN

This would have been the end of the SLM story, except SLM sold its Buddy L division (plus the pools) to Empire of Carolina, a small toy company. Empire had gotten itself the deal of the year, or so its management told investors. Acquisitions are often a good way for a company to increase its earnings. But there are two issues investors should watch. First, lousy businesses tend to remain lousy businesses, even if they are in the hands of new owners. Second, when management raves about the potential of an acquisition while simultaneously selling large amounts of stock, investors should be extremely cautious.

The businesses acquired from SLM were very large, relative to the size of Empire of Carolina, and had checkered financial histories, but Empire was confident that it could turn them around. From the time of the acquisition, the price of Empire's stock surged. Although management stated that Empire was going to have a fantastic year, it sold stock in a secondary offering, along with some of the key investors. They probably needed to diversify their holdings or build new houses.

Empire's secondary offering did not go as well as hoped. The size had to be cut back. On June 25, 1996, the company sold 1,400,000 shares and insiders sold 1,723,908 shares at $12. The stock started to drift down. Three weeks later, it was at $9. When a stock drops after an offering, investors should take notice. The company has already taken its best shot on the road show. It has told its story to any investor who would listen or wanted a free lunch. Finding new investors afterwards is difficult. Besides, many investors were now underwater. They were just hoping for a chance to get even, and with each day, were becoming increasingly nervous.

On August 7, Empire dropped a bomb. Its second-quarter loss was higher than the loss in the previous year, while its third and fourth quarters would be hurt by three problems: New blow-molding machines were not fully operational. The senior vice president of operations had cancer. And Hurricane Bertha caused the plant to be closed for several days.

EMPIRE OF CAROLINA

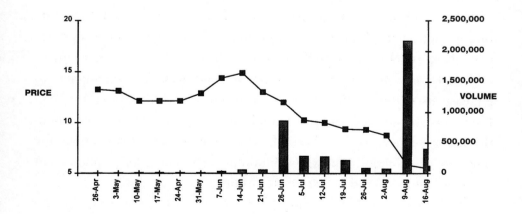

The timing of these announcements was interesting. Insiders had unloaded huge blocks of stock on June 25, so these events had to have occurred immediately afterwards or the company would have had to have informed investors on the road show. The hurricane was an act of nature, but the problem with the machines and the illness of the senior v-p must have been discovered in the days after the offering. The stock of Empire plummeted. Within the next year, it fell to less than $1.

There are a few key lessons that any investor should take from Empire:

1. Beware of a minnow trying to swallow a whale. In many cases, acquiring a larger company is much more difficult than it looks.

2. Beware of companies buying lousy businesses.

3. Watch when insiders are selling while they are hyping their stock. If they believed business was so good, why were they selling?

The management of SLM raved about the potential of Buddy L while it was selling stock, and then saw its price plummet as the business disappointed. Two years later, the management of Empire raved about the potential of Buddy L while it was selling stock, and then saw its stock price plummet. As the saying goes: Fool me once, shame on you. Fool me twice, shame on me.

AN UGLY DUCKLING CAN BECOME A SWAN OR REMAIN A DUCK

Companies can be much like people, always trying to change their image to make themselves more appealing. People go to gyms to get in shape, to the finest stores to buy new outfits, and even to plastic surgeons for an entirely new look. While the changes may have some impact, they are still the same people they always were, just in a slightly different package. Companies have their equivalents of a makeover. The stakes can be substantial. If a company can convince investors that it is a rapidly growing telecommunications company rather than a stodgy producer of frozen fish, the expansion of its p/e multiple can be substantial. But the game is tricky because, if in the end the company is really nothing but a manufacturer of frozen fish, it will smell funny to anyone who buys it on a telecommunications play.

The simplest changes are purely cosmetic: A company takes a small, rapidly growing division and asserts that the division is the key to its future and that, as a result, it deserves a growth multiple. Don't ever buy into this game. If it looks like a duck and quacks, it is a duck, even if it says it is a swan!

A slightly more substantial makeover involves a name change. Companies sometimes change their name, which is entirely appropriate if they dispose of the business that was formerly their marquee. It would be foolish for them to sport a name that now belonged to someone else. Zayre changed its name to TJX after the Zayre division was sold.

Companies can also change their name if they burn enough investors or are looking for a fresh start. When the stock of Sports & Recreation moved to the New York Stock Exchange, the management, with pure chutzpah, selected the ticker symbol WON. Unfortunately, WON lost. As the stock plunged from $25 to $1 per share, few appreciated the meaning of the ticker symbol. After the stock had collapsed, a new management changed the name of the company to Jumbo Sports and the ticker symbol to JSI. But no matter how many times the name and the ticker symbol changed, the company still went bankrupt. The stock is currently selling for two cents per share. Just because a company changes its name does not mean that all of the old problems will suddenly disappear. **This is often the corporate equivalent of the witness protection program.**

Finally, some companies create new names to reflect their new identities. As a rule, subtle changes are usually appropriate. Vanity Fair changed its name to VF Corporation after jeans became more important than intimate apparel. Dramatic changes, however, are often worrisome, especially if the company embarks on a whole new image campaign. Creating a new name and identity for a company is one of the more useless things that a company can do. It confuses employees and stockholders, costs money, and it takes management's focus away from running the business. Does anyone remember when United Airlines became Allegis? I never was able to find the Allegis terminal at the airport.

Watch for hokey names that are supposed to mean something, like Allegis or Unisys. Do you have any clue to what business the company is in? It is reasonable that Woolworth changed its name after it sold the Woolworth division, but why did it pick Venator? Does anyone know what a Venator is or what it does? Wouldn't it have been better to pick something investors could understand like "Footlocker"?

Most great companies stick to their core businesses and have simple names that employees, customers, and stockholders can understand. Think of some of the best stocks, Dell Computer, Intel, Microsoft, Wal-Mart, Costco, Coca-Cola, Citibank, J.P. Morgan. There is not a phony name in the bunch. **Obscure names are for managers who don't know what business they are in.**

Some changes are more fundamental. A company may make acquisitions in order to reposition itself. General Motors bought Hughes and EDS in order to become a technology company. Sears bought Allstate, Dean Witter, and a number of other businesses in order to become a financial services company. Kmart bought Sports Authority, Office Max, Builders Square, and PACE to become a growth specialty retailer. United Airlines bought Hertz (so did Ford) and hotel chains in order to become a travel services company. The problem is that in the end, these companies remained what they always were: a car manufacturer, a retailer, and an airline. The argument that they were being transformed into new growth companies just never held water.

Companies also make divestitures to reposition themselves. General Motors sold EDS and some of Hughes to return to its core, automobile manufacturing. Sears sold Allstate, Dean Witter, Coldwell Banker, Homart, and Prodigy to return to its core, retailing. Kmart sold Sports Authority, Office Max, Builders Square, and PACE to return to being a discount store company. Allegis sold Hertz and the hotels and became, surprise!—UAL Corp. (Now you know it's an airline.) Ford also sold Hertz to return to being a car manufacturer.

Have you noticed anything interesting about the picture? A company can make acquisitions and divestitures only to end up where it started. Along the way, the investment bankers won, because they received fees on all the transactions, but anyone who bought into the "transformation" lost, because there was no transformation. Except when divesting their core, few companies have ever been able to change their basic businesses. If you cannot decide whether the duckling is going to become a swan or remain a duck: Assume that it will remain a duck.

WATCH OUT FOR EGO TRIPS

Companies often embark on ego trips that will impress even the most casual of observers as a waste of shareholder's money. If you see such ego trips, avoid the stocks. Sports tie-ins are now extremely popular. Companies have put their names on football games (the Insight.com Copper Bowl), sports stadiums (the Delta Center), and golf tournaments (the Kmart Greater Greensboro Open). These are often intelligent marketing moves. Retailers and airlines deal with millions of consumers and probably gain good exposure. But some tie-ins seem to make less sense. 3Com Park comes to mind. (I still call it Candlestick.) Does the association with a sports stadium help the sales of 3Com's technology products, or is it more of an ego trip?

My favorite, which unfortunately ended, was the Corel Women's Tennis Tour. (I guess when you lose $232 million, something has to go.) Even if Corel had not sustained such losses, and even if its stock had not plunged from $19 to $1.71, do you think that sponsoring women's tennis tournaments could really help it to beat Microsoft? Or do you think that this type of sponsorship was really just an ego trip for the company?

Much the same applies to huge corporate headquarters that reek of an edifice complex. Sears built the tallest building in the world, and its stock sank. (It then moved out of the building, and its stock rallied.) The Pan Am building in New York survived long after the airline was history. If you see companies spending large amounts of shareholders' money for ego trips that you do not think will help its business, avoid the stocks.

PLAY BALL!

It is easy for both individuals and professionals to get suckered in by hype. By hype, I do not necessarily mean the potentially vast opportunities for companies like Amazon, Yahoo!, and Ebay. It is difficult to talk about these companies without the potential becoming blurred with the hype. Instead, I am talking about those companies with clearly "limited" potential in a relatively doggy industry, which try to convince investors that they can spin hair into gold.

One of the best examples of a company in which the hype completely overwhelmed reality was HA-LO Industries. I have never seen a company so caught up in its own hype. Of course, that may be understandable because HA-LO was one of the leading companies in the marketing services and promotion business.

I first became aware of HA-LO from "Billy," the head of sales at a brokerage firm. HA-LO had been a hot stock, having surged from $2 in November 1994 to $20 in November 1996. "Billy" told me that HA-LO was in the process of consolidating the promotional products business. Promotional products are those things that companies give away. It might be a toy at McDonald's, a tote bag at a conference, a hat with the company's name, or one of those gifts you get when you mail in four box tops. I don't know about you, but this did not seem to me to be a great business to consolidate. I did not understand why there would be great economies of scale in the promotion business.

My suspicions increased when "Billy" told me that the CEO of HA-LO always called him first to keep him up to date on what was happening. When a company calls the head of sales before it calls the analyst, you can be sure that it is in the promotion business.

I decided to research HA-LO. All the reports had exactly the same language and all the analysts had the same estimates. I called a friend who followed HA-LO. "I like the company," he told me. (He had a strong buy rating and worked for one of the investment bankers.) "But be careful. These people go ballistic if you deviate in any way from what they want you to say." This is another good sign of promotion at work. If every analyst is saying exactly the same thing and has exactly the same earnings estimate, it should be clear that someone is carefully managing the process.

I asked HA-LO to put me on the mailing list. Normally, a company is pleased to add a legitimate institutional investor to its list. But the investor relations department at HA-LO was extremely cautious. It wanted to know who told me about the company, and what my interest was. In other words, it wanted to make sure that I was not a short seller who was going to bet against the company.

In 1998, HA-LO continued to make acquisitions, using its high p/e to buy smaller companies in the promotion industry. But there was now a new spin. HA-LO told analysts that it was transforming itself into a brand-marketing company. The analysts continued to raise both their estimates and their price targets.

I started to see HA-LO signs in major league baseball parks. I thought that this was a curious way for a company like HA-LO to promote itself. After all, HA-LO was not a brand. No one knew who it was or what it did. (Some older friends thought it might be the shampoo making a comeback.) I could just see the fans rushing to the store, "Give me a Bud and a HA-LO." Perhaps ego and hype had gotten the better of this management.

On January 25, 1999, HA-LO announced a 3/2 stock split. This is usually a very bullish sign for most companies, but three days later, the analyst at Credit Suisse, one of HA-LO's investment bankers and its greatest bull, reduced his ratings and estimates. The analyst said that he had talked to management, but that they had chosen not to respond to his changes. The inference made by the other analysts was that the analyst from Credit Suisse was making the call on his own, without guidance from management.

The call panicked the market. This was a company that had always controlled its analysts. Yet the analyst who had followed it for the longest was cutting his earnings estimates and rating. Equally seriously, the management was unavailable for comment. Here were people in the promotion business who were hiding as their stock dropped. The stock of HA-LO plunged from $23\frac{5}{8}$ to $14\frac{53}{64}$ on about twenty times normal volume. The headline on one First Call note summed it up perfectly, *"HA-LO . . . Announce a stock split, get it three days later."*

Most analysts rallied around the stock using the fateful phrase, "The market has overreacted." Morgan Stanley wrote: *"We are understandably very disappointed. . . . However, we believe yesterday's sell off in the stock was overdone. . . ."*

Two weeks later, HA-LO finally did report its 1998 results. Earnings were below the new lower consensus. The stock plunged again, dropping to $9½.

One of the analysts issued a First Call note titled, *"HMK 4Q Results. Much Confusion and Consternation."* The analyst pointed out that the company compounded its problems by restricting investors on its conference call. Those who had not pre-registered were not allowed to participate. This was a very stupid move, especially for a company that is in the promotion business. Still, the analyst blamed much of the decline on short selling by "CNBC groupies."

Despite the continuing disappointments, the analysts were not ready to give up. One wrote, *"The market overreacted to the quarterly results."* (Again!) Another commented, *"Poor handling of communications* [this is a company that earns its living by communicating] *. . . has dropped the stock price to . . . a senselessly depressed level."* (Watch terms like "senselessly depressed.")

The management of HA-LO was not about to throw in the towel. It continued to make acquisitions and promote its story on Wall Street. An analyst with ABN-Amro talked about a surprise positive announcement with Discover Card, and reiterated that the "price reduction is overblown." (Don't analysts ever learn?)

Perhaps more intriguing, especially in light of future developments, was the fact that management started buying its own stock. The CEO bought 162,500 shares, while six other officers and directors bought 27,100 shares. These purchases certainly sent a bullish message to analysts.

On May 13, HA-LO held an analysts' meeting in Chicago to present its brand-marketing story. The analysts were favorably impressed with the presentation, even though not all could actually explain what a brand-marketing organization was. But six weeks later, on July 2, HA-LO warned that earnings would be below analysts' estimates for the second quarter as well as for the next two years. The company guided analysts from $0.80 down to $0.40 for 1999 and from $1.01 down to $0.55 for 2000 (a huge reduction).

As the market digested the news and analysts rushed to downgrade the stock, HA-LO dropped 44 percent to $5½. Finally, the analysts decided to throw in the towel. Morgan Stanley titled its note *"Not Again. Rating Lowered."* William Blair lowered its ratings saying that it viewed HA-LO as a "show me" stock. ABN-Amro wrote, *"Miss shakes near term confidence, downgrade to outperform."* Bear Stearns entitled its first call report, *"Another Surprise Shortfall—This time it matters."*

What happened to HA-LO? The easy explanation is that the company misled analysts and investors. But this explanation misses one critical point. Management bought large amounts of stock just before the roof fell in. Perhaps it got caught up in its own hype and never realized that its company was falling apart.

There are a number of good lessons to learn from the experience of HA-LO:

1. Beware of any company in which the management appears to be promoting itself directly to shareholders and institutional salespeople.

2. Beware of any company in which all of the analysts have exactly the same earnings estimates and write exactly the same things.

3. Beware of any company with a strategy that you cannot understand. The promotional-products business is not one begging for consolidation.

4. Beware of any company, with no brand, that splashes its name on baseball stadiums.

5. Remember that the market does not overreact.

No matter how much a company may try to hype and promote itself, it still needs to have some substance. HA-LO did not.

WALK AWAY FROM POSSIBLE SCANDALS

You will very often read stories about a dispute between a company and a government agency.

• A newspaper runs a story that a credit card company is being investigated for fraudulent practices.

- Congress takes up a bill to limit intrusions of privacy that could impact direct marketing companies.
- A hospital management company is being investigated for overcharging Medicare.

In each case, there are allegations from both sides on a highly charged issue. If the company emerges victorious, the stock will soar. If the government wins, the stock will sink. You look at the research put out by the brokerage houses. Almost all of it defends the company's viewpoint. You should not be surprised.

In a dispute between the government and a private corporation, the government does not usually put out press releases, unless it is ready to act. Government officials also do not talk to analysts, especially if there is an ongoing investigation. This would violate the law. Companies, on the other hand, have no such restrictions. At the first whiff of scandal, they spring into action, rallying the analysts to their defense, so that they can get their side of the story out into the court of public opinion.

In many cases, the companies are exonerated and the investigation goes nowhere. But it is useful to remember that only one of the sides is engaging in spin control. The other is biding its time and continuing its investigation. The analysts, who have rallied to the company, only know one side of the story. And it is the company, not the government, that is providing their firms with investment-banking fees.

Life is tough enough without trying to outguess the government. If you see a hint of scandal, it is usually better to walk away from the stock. The scandal will often blow over, but if it does not, there is always substantial downside.

BEWARE OF THE INFORMATION SHUFFLE

Be careful if you see a company start to shuffle information. Companies often change the way they report a piece of information in order to pretend that everything is still the same. If you ask about market share for the company as a whole and investor relations talks about market share for selected products, there is a problem. If you ask about backlogs and investor relations talks about the reaction of customers to the new product lines, something is wrong. The changes may be subtle, but they probably reflect a significant problem. When companies shuffle information, the chances are very good that they are trying to hide something.

A number of years ago, a few retailers such as The Limited started to build larger stores. To make their inventories seem lower, they started to give inventories per square foot rather than inventories per store. There was nothing wrong with this, except for the fact that they continued to give sales per store. Comparing inventories per square foot with sales per store was simply a way of shuffling information so that investors would not realize that the inventories were too high. By shuffling information, they fooled investors, until the day of reckoning arrived and their earnings were disappointing.

Just remember that companies give out the information that they want you to know, not the information that you should know. Their job is to market themselves to investors. They often do not want the rest of the world to know certain things, and there is no law that says they have to always be forthright. If you sense that a company is beginning to shuffle information, be extremely cautious.

DON'T BUY WHAT STOCK BROKERS ARE SELLING, BUY WHAT THEY ARE BUYING

If you are using a stockbroker, you probably assume that your broker knows something, but what your broker knows and what you think the broker knows may have little to do with each other. The broker is the financial equivalent of directory assistance. Think of all of the calls that the broker receives during the day. Someone calls about a mutual fund. Someone else calls about a tax-free bond. A third person wants a convertible debenture, while a fourth might be interested in an emerging market. Finally, you call asking about a particular stock. **It is virtually impossible for any broker to stay up to date on all information.**

Most brokerage firms receive hundreds of pages of research every day as well as prospectuses for corporate offerings. It would take the broker the entire day to read this information, and this only covers equities.

The broker must also read the reports sent out by mutual funds, fixed income analysts, and international analysts, as well as newspapers and magazines. The analyst can focus on twenty stocks, but the broker is expected to know 27,000, or rather the one of the 27,000 that you are asking about, in addition to knowing about bonds, treasuries, mutual funds, and international markets. It is obvious that no broker can know all of these things.

In most cases, the broker knows how to look things up. When you ask a question, the broker taps out the symbol and tells you what the analyst has to say. There is nothing wrong with this process, just as there is nothing wrong with calling directory assistance. In each case, the person you are asking goes to a computerized database and reads you the information. The difference is that you assume that the telephone operator is merely parroting back information, while you assume that the stockbroker is analyzing the information. In most cases: The stockbroker is no more likely to interpret the information than the directory assistance operator is likely to tell you which restaurant has the best Chinese food.

There may be better ways of getting basic information than calling a broker. The Web has up-to-date stock prices, news, and earnings estimates, while various sites, such as Motley Fool, Market Watch, or The Street.com, provide excellent commentary. Zacks, Morningstar, Big Charts, and others have good tools for screening. Mutual fund information is also more readily available online. In fact, the only proprietary information that your broker has is the work of the firm's analysts. This information can be valuable if you know how to use it. This is not to impugn your broker. Your broker is there to serve you. But there is no reason to bother the broker if you can just as easily find the information for yourself.

Directory assistance charges you for the information you receive, while the broker can only charge you if you make a transaction. The broker can talk to you five times a day, but if you do not make a trade, the broker does not get paid. It is thus in the broker's interest to get you to sell one stock and buy another. If you own one stock that has performed well and ask brokers for advice, most will suggest selling it and buying something else. This is not to suggest that brokers want to churn your account. But their interests and yours are not the same because they only get paid when you make a transaction.

The most important stocks for a broker are the firm's own under-writings. These underwritings are the most profitable business. Not only do the brokers receive a much higher fee for selling an underwrit-ing, but there is often considerable pressure on the broker to produce, especially if the underwriting is going poorly. While hot deals are easy to sell, it is the cold deals in which the retail brokers really prove their worth to the company.

This is the heart of the conflict between the broker and the client. **With the Internet and online brokerage, the traditional brokerage firm may no longer be the best vehicle for getting information or buying mutu-al funds.** One of its major advantages is its strong calendar of underwritings, which clients can purchase. But since most of the hot deals go to institutions, the calendar that is offered to individuals may not be worth the trouble. The reason that many people keep accounts at major firms is so they can partic-ipate in underwritings, most of which they should probably avoid.

Further, individuals may actually have a better chance of getting a decent allocation on hot offerings from their online brokers. These bro-kers now participate in many offerings, and their stock goes primarily to individuals, not to institutions.

This is not to say that brokers do not have good ideas. Most brokers know which of the firm's analysts are the best. Listening to the broker in this regard can be extremely useful. In many cases, it is worth having an account with a major firm if the broker can help you distinguish between the good and the mediocre analysts.

In addition, most brokers also have their own favorite stocks, often the ones that they are buying for their own account. If brokers are putting their own money in the stocks, they have done their homework. You may never find out about these stocks unless you ask directly, *"What are you buying for yourself?"* Even then, they may not tell you. Most firms do not want their brokers freelancing.

A broker from Bear Stearns called me. He ran through two of the firm's recommendations. Then I asked him what he was buying for himself. He started to tell me about some hot bank that was involved in litigation with the government. *"It's a $2 stock, but it could be worth. . . ."* He stopped in mid-sentence. *"Can't talk now,"* he said and hung up the phone. I guessed that his supervisor must have walked by while he was explaining this non-approved idea. The broker called back the next day and spun a wonderful story, which he had thoroughly researched. No analysts were following the stock, but he was on top of all of the details. *"You under-stand,"* he told me, *"this isn't the type of stock that I should be selling you. Our firm doesn't cover it and it's not a quality name, but I've bought a lot for myself."* The stock tripled in a year. If brokers are buying a stock for their personal account, at a minimum you know that they will stay on top of the information. If you decide to buy one of these stocks, remind the broker to keep you informed about the stock.

The rules with brokers are simple:

- Don't assume that brokers know more about most investments than directory assistance operators know about restaurants.
- Don't use brokers for quotes or information gathering. Use the Internet.
- Recognize that brokers get paid only when you make a transaction.
- Watch out for the "deals" that brokers push the hardest. They could be trying to salvage a poor underwriting.
- Ask brokers what they are buying for themselves. Your best shot is buying and selling along with them.
- Use brokers to guide you through the maze of the firm's own analysts.

If you assume that brokers are experts on every subject, you will lose. If you keep pestering them for information that is easier to get on your own, they may lose your phone number. But if you concentrate on what they know and what they are interested in, they can be of real use.

WOULD YOU BUY A STOCK FROM MORTIMER SNERD?

Be extremely cautious when you see "talking heads" recommending stocks on television, in periodicals, or in chat rooms on the Web. Many have excellent records and good ideas, but some are dummies. Even if you can tell the good from the bad, you still have two problems. While the talking heads may tell you when to buy, they do not come back on television to tell you when to sell. The next time you see them, they may not even mention the stock, or they may say, *"It reached my price objective, and I sold it."* That may be of little comfort if you had bought the stock and it had since declined.

Of even greater concern is that most talking heads have an ax to grind. Portfolio managers recommend stocks they already own, and they may be trying to get the price up so that they can sell. There are a number of aggressive hedge fund managers who use their appearances on television for just this purpose. The people watching television hear the exciting story and then rush to buy the stock. The fund manager then sells into the buying. This may not be the most moral thing to do, but morality has never been the long suit on Wall Street.

The rule with talking heads is simple. Don't follow their advice just because they say they like a stock. If you do, you will always be one step behind. If you hear an idea that you like, check it out yourself. Reach your own judgment, and trade it on your own terms. The fact that someone is on CNBC or in a chat room does not make him or her smart. A talking head may have good ideas, but like Mortimer Snerd, who sat on Edgar Bergen's lap, he may be a dummy. You would not buy a stock from a dummy, so don't buy one from a talking head, unless you check it out for yourself.

CHAPTER THIRTEEN

Trading with the Enemy: Buying and Selling

A strategy is a battle plan that describes how the investor intends to marshal resources and attack the enemy. Some people say that their strategy is to outperform the market. But this is a goal, not a strategy, and it is one shared by every investor. How many people want to underperform the market?

While all investment strategies have the goal of outperforming the market, most are built around buying specific investment philosophies, like the following:

- **Momentum Investing**: Buying companies with upside earnings surprises.
- **Growth Investing:** Buying fast-growth companies at moderate p/e ratios.
- **Value Investing**: Buying quality companies with low p/e and price-to-book ratios.
- **Contrarian Investing:** Betting against the consensus.
- **Day Trading:** Rapid buying and selling, based on very short-term indicators.
- **Technical Investing:** Using charts and other technical indicators to pick stocks.

Each of these strategies can work, but all have the same shortcoming: they focus on the market and are not tailored to the skills of the investor. Each may have produced great results for the professionals who follow them, but if they do not utilize *your* strengths and avoid *your* weaknesses, they will not work for you.

The strategy of guerrilla investing is different. Instead of starting with a system of investing, it starts with an understanding of the field of battle and with a specific investor. It assumes all investors have different skills, and allows them to create individualized strategies. If you are a casual investor, with limited time, you cannot utilize a strategy that works for a day trader. If you know nothing about technology and hate volatility or are uncomfortable with high multiples, you cannot utilize a momentum strategy. If you are not patient, you will never be comfortable using the takeover style. If you do not have the time to study earnings, you will never succeed with the earnings surprise style. If you are not comfortable reading charts, you will never succeed in using a technical style. **No matter how good a strategy may be for someone else, it will not work for you if it does not fit your abilities and needs.**

A professional may make billions by trading currencies and options, but that does not mean you can do the same. Following other people's guidance will work against you if you do not share their knowledge and skills. To win, you must find a strategy that works for you.

Suppose that you were the general of a guerrilla force fighting in a jungle against a modern army. Would you use the strategies that Colin Powell used in Iraq? Probably not. The Americans fought in the desert and had vast military superiority. His strategies would be of little use to an under-armed guerrilla in a jungle.

Suppose you were the coach of a small school that the football powerhouses schedule for fodder at the beginning of the year. Before the game, you look at the "West Coast" strategy of Bill Walsh. It may be a great concept, but it was not written from the perspective of a 45-point underdog. Spraying passes around the field may not be an option against a more powerful team that is blitzing on every play. The best strategy to avoid losing to the football power is: Don't schedule the game. The best strategy to avoid losing to Soros or Buffett is: Don't compete directly against them.

This may not seem like the macho thing to do. Many people have the attitude, *"Bring on the competition!"* But this is foolhardy. Most rational people would not get into a boxing ring with Mike Tyson, especially if they like having two ears. Nor would they try to stop a speeding freight train, unless they believed they were Superman. Trying to defeat a much stronger enemy head-on is suicide. If you try it in the stock market, you may not lose your life, or even your ears, but you will lose your shirt.

FIND AN INVESTMENT STYLE

Once the strategy of guerrilla investing has been adopted, you need to develop an investing style to implement it. Many of the strategies that others recommend can be used in guerrilla investing as long as they are applied in a manner that maximizes the strengths of the individual investor and minimizes the strengths of the enemy.

A strategy of buying large capitalization stocks will work within guerrilla investing if you buy and hold but not if you actively trade. A strategy of buying smaller-cap stocks can work well in guerrilla investing, because small-cap stocks are less well followed, more illiquid, and more suitable to gaining a home-turf advantage. The strategy of buying undervalued and underappreciated stocks works well for the same reasons. A strategy of following the trading patterns of insiders also fits with guerrilla investing because it minimizes the advantages of the professionals and avoids the impact of the professional's research.

Guerrilla investing can also work with more growth-oriented strategies. Momentum investing can work for individuals if they look for home-turf advantage, stay on top of the earnings, and check the charts for changes in momentum. Technical strategies can also be used within the framework of guerrilla investing, because individuals now have access to excellent charts. If they discipline themselves to check the charts on a daily basis, they can spot both breakouts and tops and use these technical patterns as an investing guide.

There are some styles that will never fit within guerrilla investing because they pit an individual's weaknesses directly against the professionals' strengths. Individuals will never win with a strategy of playing arbitrage deals, because the information is too complex; options, because the timing is too fast; and emerging markets, because the information is too far from home turf. But guerrilla investing is sufficiently broad for most other investing strategies to fit within its rules.

The effectiveness of various styles is hotly debated. But the reality is, **every investment style works some of the time, but no style works all of the time.** In strong markets, growth styles may outperform. In down markets, value styles may thrive. In fact, it is usually the success of a style that is its undoing. When a style becomes "in," investors bid up the stocks that fit its rules and dump those that do not. Soon, the valuations become too extreme. No more upside is left in the stocks that fit the style, but huge upside is in the stocks that do not. Then, investors use some seemingly minor event as an excuse to jump off one style and jump on another.

BUILD YOUR INVESTING STYLE STOCK BY STOCK

How do you find your investing style? Just like you find your clothing style. Few people start with a given clothing strategy. They rarely say, "I think I'll go for the preppy look." Instead, they go with what they need and what appeals to them. When you find an outfit you like, you try it on to see if it looks good on you and is right for your needs. The next time you go shopping, you might buy something similar or you might make small adjustments as seasons and trends dictate. Over time, your personal style will evolve. You may never articulate it, but if you look at your wardrobe, you will see that you have developed your own style.

It is much the same in investing. You should start with picking stocks you like and see if they lead you to a particular style. The following exercise should help you to understand your style:

> 1. Pick your ten favorite stocks that you have owned (if possible). These should not be the stocks that performed the best. Rather, they should be the ones you were most

comfortable owning. Write down why you bought them and why you liked them.

2. Next, pick ten current investment stories (a stock description from your broker, a newspaper, etc.) and write down why they appealed to you.

3. Pick ten stocks you did not like and write down what was wrong with them.

4. Look at your answers. See if they form patterns. Do not worry if your answers do not sound sophisticated or if more than one pattern emerges. There is nothing wrong with liking growth stocks and spin-offs.

5. Look at the stock picks or market commentary of ten professionals. The *Barron's Roundtable* is excellent because it presents many prominent investors together. *Forbes* and *Wall Street Week* also have excellent commentary. CNBC and CNNfn have good interviews. Write down your best description of each expert's style. Pick the experts with whom you are the most comfortable. Write down why you liked them.

6. Compare your reasons for liking the professionals with your reasons for liking particular stocks. There should be a consistency. If there is, you are ready to move forward. If there is not, rethink your answers. If the stocks you like are stodgy blue chips, you should not be gravitating toward a commentator who prefers technology.

7. Define your style in your own words. It does not have to sound fancy, but it has to be something you can understand. You might write, *"My style is to buy undervalued, small-cap stocks in businesses I know something about."* Or *"My style is to buy stocks that are growing by more than 20 percent per year and have p/e ratios under 20x."* There is no right style. There is only the one with which you are the most comfortable. Your style does not have to match a specific professional's any more than your clothing style has to match a particular designer's. The only critical element is that it is consistent for you.

8. Pretend you are buying a portfolio of stocks with your style. Are you satisfied with what you bought? If you are not, go back and look at how you arrived at your style. When you finish this exercise, you should have a style with which you are comfortable and a portfolio of stocks that fit the style.

STICK WITH YOUR STYLE

Many people are tempted to jump from style to style as the investing fashions dictate. When growth is in, they buy growth. When value is in, they buy value. When tech stocks are hot, they buy techs. The risk of jumping from style to style is that you have to be able to judge when styles are changing and feel comfortable using different styles. These are difficult tasks. Jumping from style to style works about as well as jumping on each new fashion craze. You will end up the investing equivalent of a "fashion victim."

Most people do better when they focus on one core investment style. Investors who stick to a particular style know how to read its signs. They know when to buy and sell, when to feel comfortable, and when to panic. Investors who jump from trend to trend may feel like they are in the middle of the action, but they are often simply chasing ghosts.

If you are a value investor, you understand what value is. When you see a cheap stock, you buy it. When it becomes fully priced, you sell it. If value stocks are out of favor and you decide to jump to a momentum style, you will lose your grounding because your head will still be stuck in a value mode. When a momentum stock disappoints, you will decide that it is a good value after all and continue to hold it. When this occurs, you are lost, because you will be trying to manage two styles at the same time.

Most successful investors usually stick to one style in all markets. They know that if they switch in midstream, they will get whipsawed. Beau Duncan of Duncan Hurst is one of the most successful momentum investors. He has a discipline of buying only stocks with high relative strength and earnings strength. Over the years, I have talked to Beau about a large number of stocks I thought were great investments. But the first question he always asks is, *"What are the earnings and relative strength ratings?"* No matter how good the story, he will not touch it if it does not meet his ratings requirements.

Other great investors are the same. Warren Buffett buys great companies at moderate price/earnings multiples. Mike Price was a brilliant value investor, buying companies with strong franchises that were out of favor. Peter Lynch was the consummate stock picker, buying thousands of companies, one stock at a time. Each of these investors built a great record because they stuck to their styles, no matter what the market was doing.

Investing styles may also relate to types of stocks and industries. Jonas Gerstl of EGS Partners is one of the best investors I know. Jonas is a value investor who specializes in buying consumer stocks. When consumer value stocks are in, no one beats Jonas. When they are out, he is an average performer. But Jonas never strays from his discipline because, over the years, it has given him one of the best records on Wall Street.

The hardest part of having a style is that it will sometimes be out of favor. If you are a value player in a bull market or a small-cap player in a big-cap market, your results will lag. It can be difficult when your style is underperforming. You look at the money other people are making and feel like an idiot. Your stocks are dogs. So you decide to jump to a new style. This will invariably be the wrong decision. Most people tend to jump just when fashions are getting ready to change. You cannot suddenly switch investment styles any more than you can make a radical change in your style of dress.

Bob Martorelli, who runs the Phoenix Fund at Merrill Lynch, is a superb investor. As the name of the fund connotes, Bob buys stocks that are down and out. Over the years, Bob has built a fine record, but, in growth markets, his stocks are often out of phase, and he can underperform. In these markets, it must be tempting for Bob to find something that is temporarily working better. But Bob hangs tough, because he knows that markets change and that, over the long term, he will outperform. In the first half of 1999, Bob had one of the top-performing funds, because he did not lose patience with his style.

If your investing style goes out of fashion, you can rethink whether it remains right for you. Styles do change, and sometimes you must change with them. If you are still waiting for your Nehru jacket to come back into fashion, you are in trouble. But most styles tend to repeat themselves, so junking one you feel comfortable with may be a mistake. If your style is out of phase, don't panic. It is fine to make subtle updates, but avoid radical makeovers. They are usually a disaster.

FIND A CORE OF STOCKS

Before you put your money to work, you must find stocks that fit your style. Create a list of stocks that you will monitor on a regular basis. It should include any stock you own, have home-turf advantage in, or have successfully traded. If you want to build a portfolio of twenty stocks, you should monitor fifty or sixty in order to find the best opportunities.

Monitoring this many stocks sounds daunting, but it is actually quite easy, especially on the Web. You merely find an online investing service, type in the ticker symbols, and the Web site creates your own custom monitor. I use My Yahoo!, a service of Yahoo!, to follow stocks. Other search engines are also excellent, as are the online brokers and many of the specialized investment services. Every time you click on to your monitor, you will see the stocks, their prices, and a list of news stories. You should be able to scan sixty stocks in less than five minutes. In fact, **it will take you far less time to screen the stocks and look at the news than it will take you just to read the prices in the newspaper.**

Click on your customized portfolio on a regular basis. Look at the news. This is easy because stocks with news are always marked with an asterisk. Watch how the stocks react to particular events. Check the earnings estimates and the analysts' ratings (the analysts' actions are always prominently shown). See how the stocks react to upgrades and downgrades in ratings. Look at stocks that have major changes in price. See if the trading volume is changing as well. Look at the charts at least once a week. Clicking through charts is easy. You do not have to study them all in detail, but you should focus on those nearing a breakout or a top. If you have a service like Company Sleuth, open your e-mail and see what is happening with your key stocks.

If you get a new stock idea that interests you, add it to your list. See if you can get a feel for it. Do not worry about missing a good chance to buy. Most stocks will usually give you more than one opportunity to buy. It is more important to get comfortable with the way a stock acts than it is to buy it the first time around.

In some cases, you will never feel comfortable with a stock. You may not like the chart. The p/e may not fit your style. You may not like the volatility or understand how it reacts to particular events. If you do not feel comfortable with a stock, drop it. You should not focus on stocks that make you feel uncomfortable, no matter how great the opportunity.

Even though I have been investing for more than forty years, there are many types of stocks that I have never been able to understand. Analysts will call with exciting stories, and I may even see the managements make presentations. But I still can never get comfortable with them. I know that I am missing opportunities, but I also know that I will never be able to win if I invest in stocks with which I am not comfortable.

If you feel comfortable with a stock, do a little more work. See if you can develop a home-turf advantage. Check out its Web site. Look at its annual report. Listen to its conference call. Get some analysts' reports. See if it fits your investing style. If it does not, drop it from the list. If you feel comfortable with it, monitor it a little more closely. Think of a stock like a blind date. **The time to get to know a stock is before you buy it, not after you are married to it.**

The more you watch a stock, the better you will understand it. You will be able to see how it trades in strong and weak markets, how it reacts to earnings and ratings changes, and how it moves compared with other stocks in its group. The more experience you have with a stock, the better will be your chances of making money on it. Don't feel under pressure to buy it immediately. You are just trying to build a base of knowledge.

Drop any stock that you have traded badly. Every investor will trade some stocks badly. I know I have. Even if it is a great stock for others, it may not be a great stock for you. While others are bragging about how much money they have made, you may find yourself buying at the high and selling at the low. Stocks are like people. You won't get along with everyone, and some won't get along with you. Unless you are very disciplined, you should bury your mistakes. Watching them will aggravate you, and it is unlikely that you will do much better the next time around. Never waste your time on a stock with which you are out of phase.

Keep on your list any stock that has ever made good money for you. The best opportunities will often come in stocks you have successfully played before. If you bought a stock three years ago and sold it after it doubled, do not forget about it. Even if it is not the greatest company in the world, it may work for you because you already understand its business and have the confidence to trade it. When you see a convergence of events that reminds you of your original purchase, you will know that it is again time to buy. But you will never notice the events unless you keep the stock on your list to monitor.

PICK A FEW INDUSTRIES

As you look at your monitor list, see if the stocks fall into industry groupings. Most people will gravitate toward industries in which they have home-turf advantage. Some stocks may relate to their professions. Others may relate to their personal interests or geographic locations.

If you are gravitating toward a few core industries, focus on them in building your knowledge base. Learn as much as you can about companies in these industries. Check the news and charts. Go to Web sites like Morningstar.net and look at comparisons between competitors. Check comparative p/e ratios, price/book, earnings growth, or any other measures that seem interesting. Your goal should be to see how similar companies compare. You should not necessarily buy the stocks that look the cheapest. There is often something wrong with stocks that look too cheap. But you should use these ratios as guidelines in evaluating companies. Click over to BigCharts.com. Look at the competing companies on the interactive charts. See how the stocks trade in relation to each other.

If you have a number of competing companies on your list, monitoring may actually become easier, because you will be able to watch more of the interactions. If you are really interested in one stock, be sure to put the names of its closest competitors on as well. They can often give you critical information about the stock in which you are the most interested.

See if you can find what makes stocks in a particular industry move. In retailing, the monthly comparable store sales are critical. In banking, interest rates and industry consolidation are key. In the petroleum industry, oil prices are vital. Try to understand how these factors impact the companies in which you are interested. If you can relate to the industry and understand what makes its stocks move, put a few more of the stocks in your list. **In investing, as in war, you need solid bases of strength. There is nothing wrong with having one or two core industries in which a substantial number of your stocks are located.** It is better to have two industries somewhat different from each other, so that they do not move in tandem. But even if the two are closely related, you are better off having a solid base than you would be if you invested all over the place.

Diversifying a portfolio is easy. You can always buy mutual funds in the areas you do not understand to limit your risk. Building a solid base of knowledge is worth the effort, even if it limits your diversification.

Once you have built a monitor list and found a few key industries on which to focus, you will have a good group of stocks from which to select. Remember, try to find stocks in which you have some home-turf advantage and which fit your style. Before plunging in, get to know them a little. The time you spend before actually investing should significantly help your performance.

PICK A FEW SOURCES OF INFORMATION

One of the toughest challenges for all investors is to limit the sources of information. There are many excellent magazines and newspapers, but you can't read them all. There are many excellent brokers, but you can't use them all. There are also hundreds of excellent Web sites. You could spend twenty-four hours a day checking out online financial information. But there is no one source that is so critical that every investor has to use it. I like to use Company Sleuth and Vcall, because I am a fundamental investor. I also use Internet.com, because I play Internet stocks. I do not actively use Silicon Investor, because I do not own other high-tech stocks. This is not to say that Silicon Investor is not an excellent site. It is. It is just not an excellent site for me because of my investing style.

Treat gathering information the way you would gathering stocks. When you start investing, pick a small number of sources. Then, slowly check out new alternatives. Experiment with them. See which is the easiest to use and understand. Don't worry about missing news. You will miss news just as you will miss stocks. The key for every investor is to find sources of information that are comfortable to use, efficient, and fit your style and time constraints. Don't overload yourself with information.

BUYING, SELLING, AND SHORTING

After articulating an investing style, building a base of stocks, and selecting your sources of information, you are ready to begin trading. Buying is easy. You call your broker or click on its Web site, and, in an instant, your money is deployed. But buying can be perilous unless you understand why you are making the purchase, how you will react to events, and when you will sell. In the stock market, as in a battle, the troops you deploy can get annihilated unless you have thought through how the enemy might respond, what countermeasures you might take, and a plan of retreat.

There are lots of good reasons to buy a stock:
- A friend told you that the company will get acquired.
- Your broker said that the company will beat the Street's earnings estimates.
- The stock has high relative strength and earnings strength.
- An analyst said that the new management would turn the business around.
- The chart shows signs of a breakout.
- You think the company's new products will be a big success.
- You believe that the company is selling for much less than its growth rate.

Each of these is a good reason to buy. No one reason is necessarily better than the others. Just make sure you know exactly why you are buying a stock, because it is the only way you'll be able to track its performance.

Even when using your own investment style, you should find a confirmation for your decision. Look at how the stock appears from the perspective of a complementary style. Confirmation can come from technical measures. If you are expecting upside surprises in earnings and the chart looks weak, it means that most investors do not share your view. This should not necessarily stop you from buying, but you should ask what you know that the rest of the Street does not.

Confirmation can also come from fundamental information. If you believe that a new product line will spur earnings, you will probably find at least one analyst who has already raised estimates. If you think that the company could be a takeover candidate, you will probably be able to find similar companies that are being taken over. If every other piece of information appears to run counter to your investment thesis, you should be wary. It is fine to bet against the Street, but you should only do so if you are relatively certain of your knowledge.

Over time, you will get to know certain companies very well and gain an appreciation for their business and trading characteristics. In these cases, you may develop a home-turf advantage significant enough to allow you to modify your style. As a value investor, you may have bought a stock because you thought it was cheap. As you study the company, you may gain more appreciation for the abilities of management and still believe that the company's opportunities have not been fully recognized, even though the stock may have tripled. You decide to keep the stock, not because you have become a momentum investor, but because you have home-turf advantage and still think that investors underrate the company. This is fine as long as you don't get suckered into thinking that the company really is a momentum play. Make sure it continues to represent a good value, or you will find yourself lost in the fast lane with the momentum investors.

While you will be better off sticking to what you know, there will be times when you buy a stock for reasons at variance with your basic style. If you take a flyer, be sure that you understand why you are going against your own style and be ready to sell at the first sign that the stock is not going to work out the way you hoped.

DON'T PLUNGE IN

When some investors see a stock they like, they often plunge in and buy all of it they want, while others sit on the sidelines, agonizing over whether they should buy. Neither of these is usually the right decision. Unless there is a very clear buy signal, the wise investor should make an initial purchase, and then build a position a little at a time.

If your goal is to own 300 shares in a company, start by buying 100. This puts less pressure on the initial purchase and gives you the opportunity to get comfortable owning the stock. If the stock shoots up, you will only make one-third as much, but at least you will be involved. Watch the stock. See how it acts. Study the news. Get comfortable with it. If it still looks attractive, buy another 100 shares. Continue the process until you have a full position.

If you start getting nervous about your holding, no matter what the reason, don't agonize over whether you should sell your entire position. This type of decision can paralyze investors. Sell 100 shares. If you have a gain, you will have locked in some of your profit. If you have a loss, you will have limited some of your risk. If the stock returns to your buy price, you can always buy the 100 shares back. If it moves to your sell price, you can always sell another 100 shares. With the current low commission rates, there is almost no penalty in buying and selling small lots.

STICK WITH STOCKS THAT WORK

If you have successfully traded a stock, you probably have some feel for the company. The more you successfully trade a stock, the better your chances of successfully trading it again. Look at the times you bought and sold the stock. See if you can find useful patterns. If you see these patterns reappear, jump on them. **Nothing will work better for you than a stock you really know.**

Most investors are always looking for new ideas, but the reality is that most do better sticking with stocks they know well and have successfully traded. If you have a choice of two stocks, one that you have never traded and one that you have traded successfully on a number of occasions, go back to the stock you know. It may be more exciting to buy a new name, but you will usually make more money in a stock that has worked for you before.

Think about how you select a restaurant when you are driving on an interstate far from home. There are four restaurants at the exit: three that you have never seen before and Denny's. As you turn into Denny's, you think to yourself, *"Known mediocrity is better than unknown mediocrity!"* You know the food is not the greatest, but you have been there before and you are comfortable with it. If you would not take a flyer with the food you eat, why should you take one with the stocks you buy? It is great to find new ideas, but before you invest, you must be comfortable with them. If you cannot thoroughly research a new idea, there is nothing wrong with returning to a stock you have played before.

Recently, I read a story about a stock I had traded successfully more than a decade ago. The stock had been in a long-term funk, trading for less than half its previous high. I had not owned the stock for years because I thought that the management was inept, but I had kept it on my monitor list because I thought it had a good franchise and would eventually be taken over. When I saw that the board of directors had thrown out the old management, I checked to see what the analysts were saying, but no one was following the company. The situation was perfect for me. The company was making needed changes and had fallen through the cracks. I did my homework and bought the stock. It may not have been a great company, but I understood what made it tick.

TRADE AROUND A CORE POSITION

When professionals find a stock they really like, they often trade around a core position. They always own a small amount in their portfolio. When the stock looks particularly attractive, they buy more. When it becomes less attractive, they pare back. You can and should do the same if you find a stock you really like.

The rationale for trading around a core position is simple: The more you trade a stock, the better you will become at it. By keeping a core position, you will be constantly looking to add to or pare back your holdings.

Since each action is incremental, it is easy to buy and sell as the stock moves up and down. If you have been successful with a stock, trading around a core position will often improve your performance.

BUY BASKETS OF STOCKS

Wall Street loves themes. Investors love to find a group of stocks that will benefit from the same condition. When airfare wars abate, most airline stocks go up. When interest rates decline, financial stocks usually rally. When markets in the Far East crashed in late 1997, investors looked for companies that would benefit from lower import prices. The connections between stocks may be based on real fundamentals, technicals, or even market fashions. Whatever the reason, stocks usually move in groups. Most investors will be well served if they can exploit these themes and connections.

As you watch a stock you like, ask yourself if other stocks in its industry will benefit from the same fundamentals:

- A chain of stores in your market that caters to teenagers is picking up share because many of its competitors have closed. Find out if other stores in other markets will benefit from the same factors.
- A bank in your market is acquired by a super-regional at a huge premium. Ask what other banks could become takeover candidates.
- Yahoo! and AOL keep surging to new highs because of the potential of Internet commerce. Ask what other companies are positioned to gain from the new technology.

Don't be worried if the connections you make between stocks are not perfect. The best investors are often those who find links that others have missed. Neal Miller, who manages the New Millennium Fund at Fidelity, is the consummate theme investor. Neal may read a small story in the newspaper that gets him thinking about a particular trend. He will start calling analysts and salesmen, but his questions will be different from those of other professionals. Many don't even understand what he is driving at. But Neal is smart. He is like a detective, trying to find the next trend and the stocks that will benefit from it before his competitors.

When most investors find a theme that connects a group of stocks, they usually try to buy the best stock in the group on the assumption that the best stock will give them the best return. But in most cases, **investors will be better served if they buy a basket of stocks that could all participate in a move.** Instead of buying 300 shares of one company, buy 100 shares of three companies in the same group.

Buying a basket of stocks limits your risk without materially jeopardizing your upside. In most cases, if the trend develops as you believe it will, all the stocks in the group will participate and you will get a good return. By diversifying your investment, you will be able to limit the risk that your favorite company will do something foolish or will have special problems that outweigh the trend.

Suppose you decide all of the regional banks in the Southwest will get acquired. You look at the companies and decide that one is the most attractive. Then, while other banks are taken over, the bank you picked makes acquisitions of its own, paying a huge premium for a brokerage firm and a money manager. You feel pretty bad because you correctly figured out the trend and then bought the one stock that did not participate in it.

Earlier this year, my partner, Leigh, and I thought that Internet commerce stocks had become extraordinarily expensive and were beginning to crack. We wanted to short these stocks, but we did not want to take too big a position in any one. We researched the entire group and then took small short positions in over twenty stocks. Almost all went down. Some went down more than others. But we were comfortable because, while we were playing a theme, we did not have too much bet on any one stock.

Dick Keim and David Wilson of Keim Wilson are among the best small-cap money managers. They too like to play themes. While they keep their portfolio diversified, about half of their stocks will fall into groups that fit specific themes. If they think oil prices are going to rise, they will buy a basket of oil and oil-service stocks. While they still have the industry risk, the basket minimizes the risk from a particular company.

Even if you have a small portfolio, you can buy a basket of stocks. You will just have to keep the quantity of each stock small. It is well worth the effort. Playing a basket of stocks will usually minimize your risk and improve your performance.

MAKE OWNERSHIP AN ACTIVE PROCESS

To win, you must make ownership an active process. Like a general with troops deployed in battle, you cannot leave your stocks in position without understanding the changes taking place on the battlefield. You must constantly reevaluate your positions and always act when the news or the charts warrant. While you do not have to take action every day, you must be in a mode in which you are ready to act.

The first step in turning ownership into an active process is to revisit your initial analysis of each stock on a periodic basis. Take a step back and start from scratch. Ignore the fact that you may have profits or losses. Look at the fundamentals, the charts, the news, and competing companies. **Would you buy this stock now? If you would not buy it now, you should sell it.** There is no reason to hold a stock that you would not buy.

If you would buy the stock, make sure that your reason for buying today is as good as your reason for your initial purchase. It should not be a rationalization to justify inaction. It is fine to say that you would buy a stock today because it is undervalued relative to its growth, but it is not fine to say that you would buy it today because it is too cheap to sell. By going back and revisiting your analysis, you should better understand when you no longer have a reason for owning a stock.

Unless you are a short-term trader, don't worry about small price movements. **The key to making money is to spot changes in the trend.** To do this, you should focus on:

- Earnings or other corporate announcements,
- Major price movements that break through resistance points,
- Unusual changes in trading volume, and
- Any unusual trading in the stocks of competing companies.

When companies report earnings, their fundamentals and the expectations of investors often change. This is a crucial time to reevaluate your reason for owning the stock. It is especially important when the stock reacts differently than you would have thought. If you thought the news was good and the stock still drops, take a fresh look at why you invested. If the stock goes down on good news, how will it react on bad news?

Major price and volume changes can set a new pattern for a stock. When there is a surge in volume, forces on the Street are changing their positions. When the stock breaks above a resistance point or below a support level, a new direction is often set. Try to understand what is behind major swings in price and/or volume. Don't be passive. Stocks can change direction rapidly.

In 1997, the stock of Paul Harris Stores plunged from $27 to $20 on huge volume because a very smart analyst named Janet Kloppenberg cut her ratings on the stock. When Paul Harris later reported good earnings, a number of investors criticized Janet for acting too quickly. But the stock continued to sink. Three weeks later, Paul Harris reported weak November sales, and the stock price dropped to $15. One month after that, it reported weak December sales, and the stock price declined below $10 as all of the analysts rushed to cut their estimates. I do not know how Janet knew that business was going to be weak, but I do know that the huge downside volume should have been a warning to all investors. **If you see a stock break down on huge volume, don't assume that the market is wrong.**

Watch especially for warning signs. Sales or earnings come in below plan. Analysts reduce their estimates. Inventories are too high. Management is dumping stock. The chart is topping out. Volume has expanded on the downside. The prices of competing stocks are dropping. These are warning signs that you should heed. Most people focus on the good news, but watching the bad news can be far more critical. Unless you incorporate the impact of these negative events into your thinking, you will lose.

Don't fall in love with your winners. Investors tend to love stocks that have performed well. If you own a big winner, you will often brag about how much money you have made, and may even feel an alliance with the company. If something goes wrong, you will try to look on the bright side. You may even create your own spin control, echoing the famous word of the analysts, *"The market has overreacted."* But it is not your company. You are just a shareholder. **The better a stock has performed, the more attached you will be to it, and the harder it will be for you to see the warning signs when business starts to change**. When a stock has performed well, keep reevaluating your reasons for owning it.

Don't panic if a stock goes down. A stock will often go down for no particularly good reason. A lower price does not necessarily mean that something is wrong. Everything else being equal, a stock at $40 should be more attractive than a stock at $50. When you go to a store, you look for bargains. If you see a $50 shirt marked down to $40, you are more likely to buy it. But in the stock market, the system often works in reverse. Most investors are more likely to buy a stock at $50 than they are to buy the same stock if it drops to $40. The reason: When the stock drops, they become worried that it is no longer exactly the same company or the same market.

At times there is something wrong, but often there is not. A minor shortfall in earnings may not be the end of the world. Momentum players should be concerned, but for most investors, it could signal a bargain. When a stock drops, reevaluate the fundamentals. Look especially at the chart. If the stock has not dropped on huge volume and broken below key support levels, the decline in price could make it more attractive.

Beware of stocks that have gotten trashed. When a stock gaps down on gigantic volume and investors run for cover, something is usually seriously wrong. Don't feel comforted when analysts write that the market has overreacted. Take a long look at your holding. Not only will more downside often come, but once the chart has been destroyed, the upside is usually a long way away. Unless you really understand the company, don't try to be a hero by holding on.

Do not worry about the amount of time that you hold a stock. Your holding period will depend on your investing style and on the action of the stock. If you are an active trader, you may turn over your position in a day. If you are a long-term investor, you may keep the stock for years. There is really only one rule that you should follow: **As long as your reason for buying a stock is still valid, keep it.**

Only one factor should influence you to keep a stock longer than usual. If you have substantial profits and are very close to the period in which the capital gain shifts from short term to long term, you should take another look at the charts and the fundamentals. If there is no compelling reason to sell immediately, you may want to hang on until your tax basis changes. But be careful. Many investors ignore clear sell signals while waiting for better tax treatment. If the stock is volatile and you are worried about the downside, don't be too greedy. Paying taxes on a gain is better than watching the gain evaporate as the stock sinks.

DON'T SELL ON EMOTIONS

Most investors have a good explanation for why they are buying, but fewer have a good explanation of why they are selling. List the reasons why you made your last ten buys. You probably have a number of well-thought-out ideas. Now list the reasons why you made your last ten sells. What do you have in the sell category?

- The stock was a dog.
- I got sick of looking at it.
- It dropped 15 percent.
- I wanted to take my tax losses.
- I made a lot of money and decided not to get greedy.
- The stock went up so fast that I got scared.

None of these "sell" reasons apply to the fundamentals and the technicals of the stock. There is no discussion of earnings, valuations, management, or technical patterns. Saying that the stock was a dog is not the same as saying that it had broken down on the charts. Saying that it went up so fast that you got scared is not the same as saying it was overpriced or topping out. Further, none of these reasons relate to your investment style. Most are emotional reactions to the performance of the stock. It is natural to get sick of stocks that have performed badly and to want to take profits in stocks that go up, but these are not good reasons for selling.

The only sure way that you can tell when it is appropriate to sell is to look back at your reason for buying. Sometimes your reason for buying does not work out. You may have bought a stock because you expected earnings to come in better than plan, and they came in below plan. You may have bought a stock because you liked a new product line, and the line bombed. You may have bought a stock because you thought it was breaking out of its technical pattern, but the stock retraced and broke down.

Sometimes your reason for buying materializes, but countervailing trends more than offset it. The earnings did surprise on the upside, but the company said it was worried about the next quarter. The new product line was a success, but there were significant weaknesses in the older product lines. The stock initially broke out, but all of the other stocks in its group got trashed. At other times, your reason for buying materializes, but, after a period of time, stops being valid. A stock that was once undervalued doubles and is no longer undervalued. A stock that broke out and ran is now forming a top and breaking down.

It does not matter if your reason for buying failed to materialize, if it materialized but was offset by other factors, or if it materialized but stopped being valid over time. If the reason for buying is no longer valid, you should sell because you will never be comfortable with the stock again.

Good reasons for selling can materialize at any time. You may have bought a stock you thought was breaking out on the charts. Three hours later, a big seller came in. The stock dropped, and the chart, which had looked positive, now looks negative. Even though you have only owned the stock for three hours, you should sell, because your reason for buying is no longer valid.

One of the biggest mistakes investors make is finding a new justification when their original reason for buying proves invalid. You bought a stock at $20 because you believed that earnings would surprise on the upside. Then earnings came in below plan and the stock dropped to $16. The temptation is to look at the stock and say, "It's too cheap to sell." This is a mistake. If you bought a stock because you expected upside earnings surprises and the earnings do not come through, sell it. The stock may be a good value at $16, but if you are not comfortable being a value investor, you will constantly be looking to sell this stock.

Think about driving on a highway. Just because other cars are ahead of you does not mean you are going in the right direction. When I was a boy, my family was driving to Florida. We were not sure which road to take. My father looked at the car in front of us, and said, *"Let's follow him. He looks like he knows where he's going."* He probably did. But the road he turned onto headed to New Orleans and we wanted to go to Miami. Ten miles later, we turned around and retraced our steps, while everyone in the car ragged my father for going the wrong way. The road may have been right for the car ahead, but it was wrong for us. In investing, as in driving, not everyone is going to the same place.

Your reason for investing, rather than the price of the stock, should be your guide. If you bought that $20 stock because you believed that the company had high intrinsic value and would be taken over, you would not be nervous when it dropped to $16. Your reason for buying the stock would still be intact, and you might even be comfortable buying more.

It might seem contradictory to suggest that one investor should sell a stock at $16 while another should buy more, but it is not. A fallen stock is fine for a value investor, who understands its intrinsic worth. The same stock is not fine for a momentum investor, who is angry at the company for disappointing. To win, investors must know why they are buying a stock and have a road map for understanding where they are trying to go. Once the stock no longer fits your road map, you will be lost. There is nothing wrong with making a mistake. But there is something wrong with holding a stock for the wrong reason.

Be willing to admit your mistakes. A stock is not like a child. It is not yours for life. A stock is a soldier in your investment army. In a war, soldiers sometimes get killed. In the market, so do stocks. If you are a general, you will be sad when one of your soldiers is killed, but you will accept it as part of the price of war. It is much the same in the stock market. You will not always be right and you cannot be wed to your stocks. If one of your stocks gets killed, bury it and go on to the next battle.

DON'T BE AFRAID TO SHORT STOCKS

Shorting is not the same as selling. It is the opposite of buying. When you short a stock, you are putting money at risk, betting that the stock will go down. That's a legitimate bet. It is just as appropriate to bet that a stock will go down as to bet that it will go up, but it is tougher to win. Because the stock market usually goes up, the odds are much worse in shorting, and because the short is open-ended, your risk is unlimited. If you buy a stock and it goes to $0, you could lose your investment, but if you short a stock and it quadruples, you could lose four times your investment. While it is much more difficult to make money on the short side than on the long side, it does not mean that you should never short.

Companies have given short sellers a bad name by claiming that they disseminate bearish information in order to push down the price of a stock. Of course, these same companies will never complain when they, or the analysts who work so hard for them, issue bullish information to push up the price of the stock. Companies spend billions of dollars to tell their stories in the way they want them told. Analysts are paid huge sums and know that part of their job is to push the stocks of their banking clients. No one is paying the short sellers. Yes, they want to see their stocks go down but the owners want equally as much to see them go up.

Nothing is wrong with believing that a stock is overvalued, the balance sheet is deteriorating, the accounting is too aggressive, or the company will not meet earnings estimates. Nor is anything wrong with shorting and betting against a company. However, an investor should recognize a few rules before selling short:

- Your reason for shorting should always be better than your reason for buying.
- Only short stocks on which you have some special home-turf knowledge.
- Don't short just because a stock looks overpriced. Overpriced stocks can still go up. Find a catalyst that will push the price of the stock down.
- Get a confirmation, an additional reason, before shorting.

• Short stocks that are breaking down on the charts, especially when competitors are also breaking down.

• Don't short stocks that have large short positions. While these may be the most overpriced, they also have the biggest risk. Short sellers eventually have to cover (buy). If a stock has a large short position, this buying can create a short squeeze that can send the stock soaring. Few investors will want to absorb this type of punishment.

• If the reason that you shorted is no longer valid, cover at once. Maintaining a short position when the rationale is no longer valid is a good invitation to lose money.

With these caveats in mind, there is no reason that individuals should not have some shorts. But don't use shorts as a way of timing the market. Instead, treat shorting the way you would treat buying. If you think that the price is going to decline, take a chance and short it.

There is also nothing wrong with shorting a stock you had been long, or buying a stock you had been short. This is the logical extension of trading around a core position. Let us say that you have owned a stock for two years and watched it double. The company comes out with news that disturbs you. You are convinced it will drop. You decide to sell. But if you really believe that the stock will drop, you could go one step further and short additional shares.

Some of the best "long" investments I have ever made came from stocks I was originally short. When you are short a stock, you are often more conscious of the fundamental and the technical patterns, because you are scared of a short squeeze. In many cases, as I focused on the negatives, I realized that the company was better than I had thought. Not only did I cover my short, but I also went long. Within reason, this is an excellent discipline for most investors.

DIVERSIFY YOUR PORTFOLIO

The subject of guerrilla investing leads to a final question: How diversified should your portfolio be? The answer is not as simple as it might at first appear. Conceptually, it is better to be diversified. The more diversified you are, the less risk you will have. The only problem is that to gain home-turf advantage and defeat the professionals, most individuals will have to stick with what they know. Since most people's knowledge is limited, they will tend to focus on a relatively narrow number of stocks and industries.

The most important factor is risk. **Investors should never put themselves in a position in which the success or failure of one stock or group can change their standard of living.** It is not the purpose of this book to serve as a guide to financial planning. Nevertheless, before investing, you should take a hard look at your assets and liabilities, your standard of living, and your long-term obligations. As a rule, the closer you are to retirement and the more obligations you have, the greater your level of diversification should be. If you are young, have a good job and few obligations, you can be less diversified and take more risks. Above all, never put yourself in a position that jeopardizes your home or your long-term well-being.

You should also look at all of your liquid assets, including those in your retirement plan. If your retirement plan is in the stock of your employer, the remainder of your portfolio should be more diversified. If it is in a mutual fund, the remainder of your portfolio can be less diversified.

Even if you have a large amount of liquid assets and own mutual funds, you should still diversify your stock holdings. In this case, the reason for diversification is not financial, it is psychological. If you concentrate your portfolio in a limited number of stocks, your risk increases dramatically.

Even if a decline in these stocks will not impact your standard of living, it will impact the way that you invest. If your portfolio is crushed, you will be gun-shy about making your next investment.

How can you diversify while sticking with companies in which you have home-turf advantage? There are a number of ways you can achieve this seemingly contradictory goal:

> 1. Don't let any one position become so large that its performance controls your portfolio.

2. If you like a particular industry or group, buy a selection of companies within it so that the performance of one stock will not have as great an impact on your returns.

3. Look for a second industry with different fundamentals for balance. If your largest group of holdings comes from your profession, develop a second group of holdings from your experience as a consumer.

4. Find a few stocks outside these industries in which you can acquire home-turf knowledge.

5. Use mutual funds to buy stocks in fields that you do not understand. If you are buying mostly small-cap growth stocks, buy mutual funds that focus on large-cap stocks, real estate, utilities, or foreign stocks. Small holdings in a number of mutual funds outside of your core strength can offer diversification.

6. Finally, make sure that your retirement plan is invested differently from your portfolio. If you have major investments in equities, put some of your pension fund in bonds, even if the short-term return is lower. If you are buying small-cap stocks, put some of your retirement plan in a more conservative, large-cap fund. If your pension plan is in your company's stock, put a larger percentage of your assets in mutual funds.

You must walk a fine line to invest in what you know and remain diversified. For most investors, the best solution is to focus on what you know and let professionals make investments for you in other areas.

DON'T PLAY HEAD GAMES WITH YOURSELF

In trying to outperform the market, the biggest pitfall for most investors is playing head games with themselves. The stock market is an intensely competitive game, and in playing competitive games, nothing can do in a person faster than the head. Once you begin to second-guess yourself or have emotional reactions to the stocks you own, you are dead.

Your head can cause you serious trouble at two critical times: when you are losing big or when you are winning big. When you are losing big, you tend to question all of your decisions or even panic. When you are winning big, you begin to think you are invincible. In either case, you open yourself up to the possibility of making major errors.

Always heed the following key rules in order to avoid being trapped in your own head games:

DON'T WORRY IF YOU MISS A STOCK

As you look at recommendations that people have made in the past, you tend to focus on the successful stocks you failed to buy. This is a critical mistake. There are tens of thousands of stocks, but you will only own a few at a time. For better or worse, you will miss most stocks.

Sometimes you will miss a stock because you do not understand the company's business or because it does not fit your investing style. In these cases, missing the stock is for the best, no matter how well it performs. You would never have been comfortable with it.

People are always telling me how they missed Microsoft, Intel, Wal-Mart, or Home Depot. But the reality is that value investors would have dumped these stocks after their first move up even if they had found them, while momentum investors would have dumped them the first time they broke down. Unless you are the rarest of long-term investors, it is unlikely that you would have held any of these stocks for their ten- or twenty-year move up. Looking back on a great stock that you could have bought will never help you.

Sometimes you will miss a stock because you are too busy. A friend may have told you about a great stock, but you were involved in a problem at work or with your children's education. By the time you had a chance to focus on the stock, it had already moved up 20 percent. Sorry! Missing stocks is a fact of life. It happens every day, even to professionals. If you start thinking about what could have been, you will be crippled as an investor.

Sometimes you will know that you should buy a particular stock, but for one reason or another you delay making an investment. If this stock is a winner, it will really hurt. You knew to make the investment but could not pull the trigger. Whatever the reason, the worst thing an investor can say is "I should have bought."

If you missed a stock you were monitoring because it did not fit your investing style, dump it off your list. If you missed it because you were too busy, put it at the bottom of your list and look at it again in a few months. Don't chase it now. If you do, you will be buying on emotion. If you missed it because you could not pull the trigger, try to figure out why you did not act. You will probably have another chance if you don't psych yourself out.

TOO EARLY OR TOO LATE? DON'T SECOND-GUESS YOUR SELL DATE

While many investors will rue missed opportunities to buy, almost all will second-guess themselves on when they sell. Because stocks are always in motion, investors will almost always sell too early or too late. Even if you are the consummate technical investor, you will not be able to perfectly pick the top. No matter how much you may have made, if the stock goes up after you sold, you will say to yourself, *I should have held on a little longer.* If it went down before you sold, you will curse yourself for not selling earlier.

Second-guessing yourself on an action you have already taken is a waste of time and energy. When you took action, you did so based on the best information you had at that moment. In almost all cases, your decision will not be perfect. Don't be a Monday-morning quarterback. You cannot go back and replay the trade.

Instead of second-guessing yourself, review the process you went through in deciding to sell. See if you can learn anything. If you stuck to your investing style and sold for reasons you thought were appropriate at the time, you are in good shape, no matter what the stock did afterward. There is no way to predict the future, so the fact that some unexpected event transpired after you sold should not cause you to question your reason for selling. If you sold for reasons that conflicted with your investing style or if you sold on emotion, make a note of why you took action so that you can avoid it the next time.

Don't Beat Yourself Up Over a Bad Investment

All investors make bad investments. A bad investment is a stock that not only goes down, but goes down because your analysis was wrong. You bought it because you thought the new product line would be a success, and it was a dud, or you bought it because you thought that the company would get taken over, and instead it went out and made a foolish acquisition of its own. A bad investment can also be one in which you saw the sign to sell but could not pull the trigger.

Bad investments make investors feel stupid. I can tell you the name of virtually every really bad investment I have ever made. I am not talking about the stocks that went down 5 or 10 percent, I am talking about the real bombs. And I can remember every stock that I round-tripped. (I bought the stock at $10, planned to sell it at $40, but held on when it only got to $36, and rode it back to $10.) I can close my eyes and see the ticker symbols. And if I did try to forget them, one of my customers would be more than pleased to remind me, *"You're the one that put me into. . . ."*

There is no way to feel good about losing money, but you should never beat yourself up over a bad investment. Instead, review your analysis. If you can see how you went wrong, perhaps you will avoid the same mistake the next time. If you cannot see how you went wrong, take the stock off your list. If you do not know why you got blindsided the first time, you will never know when you are about to get blindsided again.

Don't Wait for the Market to Undo Your Mistakes

The hardest mistakes to live with are those you knew to avoid. You saw a stock break down on the charts or the earnings come in less than plan, and you knew to sell. But you waited, in the hope that the stock would get back to your original purchase price so you could get out whole. Unless you have an investing style that gives you a good reason for believing the stock will rebound, do not wait for the market to undo your mistakes. It will rarely happen. If you made a mistake, accept it, and go on to the next stock.

Don't Keep Stocks You Hate

When investors make big mistakes, they often begin to hate the stocks in which they have either lost money or given back money that they had previously made. Yet ironically, many investors tend to hang on to stocks they hate and sell stocks they love. It is as if they feel they must do penance for making the mistake.

When stocks go down, people often say, *"I hate that stock. As soon as it gets back to the price I paid, I am going to dump it."* They must have some subconscious idea that if the stock returns to its purchase price, the mistake will be erased. This is no way to invest. While you should not sell on emotion, neither should you hold on to stocks you hate. If you really hate a stock, you will never be able to make a rational decision about it. It is like a bad marriage, except with stocks the divorce laws are simple. Life is tough enough without having your money invested in a stock that you hate.

Don't Panic If Your Style or Group Is Out of Favor

Because the stock market runs in cycles, there will be times when your style or group is out of favor. You may like small-cap companies in the Rust Belt, but the fashion of the day may favor technology companies. Unless you have an extreme style, such as buying only micro-cap stocks, most cycles will be relatively short. The worst thing you can do when your group is underperforming is panic. Most people panic just before their group is ready to turn.

If your group or style is underperforming, review your analysis. Often the fundamentals turn out to be different from what you had thought. If your strategy was to buy Internet stocks and they all began to crack because of increasing competition, reappraise the opportunities. Other times, macroeconomic issues can change the outlook for an entire industry. If OPEC doubles its production, you would want to reappraise your view of oil stocks. But these types of changes are almost always easy to see and react to.

In most cases, investors panic when their style is underperforming even though nothing is happening in the news. It is often easier to deal with a company that has reported disappointing earnings than with a company that produces good results but is ignored by the market. You look at the fundamentals and can't understand why the rest of the market does not appreciate the company or the industry. *"The market is dumb,"* you curse to yourself. Finally, after months of watching, you give up and decide to switch from Rust Belt stocks to technology stocks. Of course, within a very short period of time, the technology stocks plunge and the Rust Belt stocks start to outperform, but by then you will have switched your strategy and lost on both sides.

The moral is simple. It is fine to review your analysis. It is even fine to modify your investing style, but you should never panic. If you panic, you are lost. As long as your investing style continues to make sense, stick to what you know. If you know about the Rust Belt, you have a chance of winning when you buy companies based in it. If you jump to technology stocks, you are likely to get creamed.

DON'T TRY TO HIT HOME RUNS IF YOU ARE UNDERPERFORMING

If you are well behind the market, do not try to hit home runs. Getting the big hit on an investment is difficult, and mostly it is a matter of luck. If you press and start trying to catch up to the market quickly, by buying options or making other risky investments, you are likely to compound your mistakes and get even further behind.

DON'T THINK YOU ARE SMART JUST BECAUSE YOUR STOCKS ARE OUTPERFORMING

While panicking when stocks are underperforming is bad, thinking that you are a genius when your group or style is outperforming can be worse.

For months, you watched as other stocks in the market moved. Then, your stocks caught fire. Suddenly you are outperforming the market. Your stocks are atop the "new high" list. You start thinking the game is easy and you are smart. You are in deep trouble.

Like a stopped clock, which is right twice a day, all investors have times when their stocks outperform. One of your companies might get taken over, or your industry might come into favor. You may be outperforming the market, but you are no smarter than you were a few months ago when you were underperforming. The risk is that you may begin to think you are invincible and you may start making foolish decisions.

Groups and styles will come and go, but the minute you believe you can always win, you will become more aggressive and start taking unnecessary risks. You may have figured something out and you may be able to outperform the market, but people often get suckered in when they mistake the rotation of the market for their own brilliance. If a guerrilla force was advancing on a battlefield and saw no sign of the enemy, would the general think that the enemy had fled and the war was over? If he did, he would be in for a rude awakening when the counterattack came.

During the late 1960s, I had great success investing in stocks. I did not know much about investing, but I bought stocks of companies that I liked and sold them when it looked like something was going wrong. Then, I started to work at Harvard Business School. All my friends were professors or doctoral students at Harvard. When one of them gave me an idea, I bought it. If it went down, I decided that we were right and the market was wrong. After all, who should know more than a member of the faculty at Harvard? Of course, just because they had business cards that said "Harvard" did not make them right. I got killed thinking that I was smarter than the market. It is a mistake I will try never to make again.

The guerrilla can always win a small battle, but if the guerrilla takes the experience of that battle and decides that it can now defeat the enemy head-on, the guerrilla is in deep trouble. The same is true for an individual. When you are doing well, be thankful and stay humble. Go back to basics and take a long-term view. Look at periods in which you outperformed and periods in which you underperformed. Look for warning signals. Try to figure out what could go wrong. Remember, you are still an individual competing against professionals. Don't think that you are now the investing equivalent of a superpower who can take on the world.

Beating the professionals in the stock market is never easy, but it will become much harder if you let your emotions get the better of you. The best investors are those who remain cool and stick to their investing style. It is often difficult to remain cool, especially if you are losing, but it is essential that you do so. If you are not doing well, take a step back and look at your strategy and your style. Learn from your mistakes, but do not let them haunt you. If you are winning, keep it in perspective. You may be smart, or it may just be your turn to outperform. The day you think you have figured out how to win is the day that you will begin to lose.

GUERRILLA INVESTING REVISITED

Investing in the stock market is like fighting a war. The person on the other side of the trade is your enemy and only one of the two of you will win. If you are to defeat your enemy, you must have better information and be able to act on it more quickly. Unfortunately, if you are an individual investor, the odds are against you. For the most part, your enemy is a professional investor who has more resources, experience, and knowledge than you do. If you attempt to attack such an investor head-on, you will be defeated.

The only way to defeat an opponent who is better armed is to follow the strategy that we call guerrilla investing. You must adopt the mind-set of the general of a guerrilla force that is in combat with a modern mechanized army. You must:

- Know yourself and know your enemy.
- Avoid attacking the enemy's strength.
- Fight on your own turf by investing in things that you understand.
- Find niches your enemy misses, primarily by investing in small or underfollowed stocks.
- Adopt a buy-and-hold strategy, nullifying your enemy's advantages in trading.
- Use your enemy's strength against it, focusing on its inability to change directions rapidly and capitalizing on its need for short term performance, and
- Bet against the consensus. If your enemy is united in one direction, go in the other. The consensus will always be wrong.

In order to win, you must arm yourself with fundamental and technical weapons:

> • Use the analysts' work as a base, and then try to find where the consensus is wrong.
> • Use common sense and your own direct experience.
> • Look at the company's financial statements. Watch especially for unexpected changes in the numbers. See if the growth rate and the price/earnings multiple are consistent.
> • Use charts as an early warning system. Watch for break-outs and tops. The professionals always show clear signs when they are getting ready to move in one direction or another.
> • Look for connections between suppliers and customers and between companies in the same industry. Stocks of related companies often follow similar patterns.
> • Use the tools of the Internet to nullify the advantages of the professionals.
> • Don't get suckered in by what the analysts say. Read between the lines. See if a buy is really a buy, or it is just an attempt to keep an investment-banking client happy.
> • Remember that the market rarely overreacts.
> • Watch for pitfalls and opportunities, especially when insiders are buying or selling or companies are shuffling information.

Once you have a battle plan and the information needed to implement it, you are ready to attack. But before you do so:

> • Find your own investment style that fits within the strategy of guerrilla investing.
> • Don't chase the movements of the market. Stick with a style that works for you.
> • Before you commit your resources to any stock, get to know the company. Understand why you are buying the

> stock and when you plan to sell it.
> • Make ownership an active process. Constantly reevaluate your positions, and watch for signs that something is going wrong.
> • Don't fall in love with your stocks. Like soldiers in a war, they sometimes get killed. You should not fall with them.
> • Don't play head games with yourself. Keep cool and stick to your style. If you do, you will almost always win in the long run.

Use the Internet, both for information and for online investing. Whether you are an active trader or a long-term investor, the Internet provides a quantity and quality of information that rivals what is available to professionals. For the first time, individuals can now receive information with the same timeliness and detail as the professional can. The democratization of information will continue to have a dramatic, long-term impact on the workings of the stock market, and most of the impact will benefit the individual investor.

Finally, and most importantly, never underestimate the power of your enemy. Remember that your enemy is the well-trained army. You are the guerrilla force. You cannot overpower your enemy or win in head-to-head combat. You must approach with great respect. Capitalize on the opportunities you find, but do not overreach. Above all else, remember the dictum of Sun Tzu, as he stated in *The Art of War*, "Know yourself. Know your enemy. In one hundred battles, there will be one hundred victories."